Blurring Intelligence Crime

Willem Bart de Lint

Blurring Intelligence Crime

A Critical Forensics

Springer

Willem Bart de Lint
Finders University
Adelaide, SA, Australia

ISBN 978-981-16-0351-8 ISBN 978-981-16-0352-5 (eBook)
https://doi.org/10.1007/978-981-16-0352-5

This Springer imprint is published by the registered company Springer Nature Singapore Pte Ltd.
The registered company address is: 152 Beach Road, #21-01/04 Gateway East, Singapore 189721, Singapore

Dedication

Since there may be no more books, I will have to triple up on the dedication. Bobae, thank you for your belief in me. It means more than can be expressed here. I know that I am somewhere far short of your image of me, but your belief has kept me on this journey. In contrast, you are actually as well as figuratively as near perfect as a mortal being has a right to be. I am grateful for everything we have shared and I hope and believe that for you the best is yet to come. Elias, perhaps one day you will read this, and if you do know that as it was written I wished only to offer you something more of myself. I hope that you will truly know that the journey is more important than the result. Between the lines is the hope and faith that we may spend some time together. Johannes, here is another thing to be read from me; not biography or history, but somewhat of a chip off the old block, I don't mind saying, after all these years, however misshapen. I learned scepticism around the dinner table; not an unlucky orientation to a world that in all its beauty would be even more glorious were it not for the all-too-human persistence of our basest beliefs and convictions.

Acknowledgements

This book was written in Adelaide from March to October 2020, during which time I benefitted from and am grateful for a teaching break and a research grant from the College of Business, Government and Law at Flinders University. I wish to thank Bobae Kim, whose faith, wisdom and effortless smarts have been an inspiration and saving grace. Bobae's graphic design skills also contributed greatly to making the figures more professional. I wish also to thank Sirpa Virta, whose insights contributed to the last two chapters, particularly with respect to the interpretation of hybrid threat and the political framing of security. Thanks to Gerry Redmond for the support he offered me during the tumultuous and trying year of 2020. Thanks finally to my copy editor, Julia Farrell, for her flexible and all-too-necessary editing interventions that have made the manuscript a little more acceptable to people who are not familiar with the arcane archive of criminology and security. One or two lines of text in Chapters 3, 7 and 8 have been taken from the following journals, gratefully acknowledged.

Globalizations: de Lint, W. (2020). Criminology 9/11. 17(7), 1157–1177, for a partial paragraph each in Chapter 3 and 7; *The Windsor Yearbook of Access to Justice*: de Lint, W. (2008). Intelligent security. 26(2), 195–240), for partial paragraphs in Chapter 8; *American Behavioural Scientist*: de Lint, W. and S. Virta and J. Deukmedjian (2007). Simulating control: a shift in policing. 50(12), 1631–1647, for some lines in Chapter 8.

Contents

Chapter 1
Introduction: Blur and a Critical Forensics of Intelligence Crime

The secret of a great success for which you are at a loss to account is a crime that has never been found out, because it was properly executed.

Honoré de Balzac

Introduction

The shooting of a political or cultural leader, the blowing up of a ship or the hijacking of an airplane may be an act of terrorism, a hate crime or an act of war. What we think we see as we gape in awe at a spectacular, watershed event is dependent on its documentation and review. The outrage attracts and reviles, its attribution is the result of diffuse transactions and invites almost instantaneous commentary. But its fixing is also the measure of government authority, with cultural and political leaders stipulating its genus and offering the *most* correct framing and context. In the meantime, government agents arrive on site, establish a crime scene, authorise an investigation, ponder the evidence and in the result do more than hope that as a legacy the event matches up with the advance of ongoing or emergent social and political imperatives. Experts and authorities of all stripe will be resistant to the multiple significations and uncertain outcome of a truly open investigation and examination. Justice, overburdened with the weight of the event's significance, may succumb to a clamouring insistence: '"our" antagonists cannot be allowed to finesse fair play and get away with murder.'

There are two irreconcilable reviews of events that attend what we will explore as apex and intelligence crime: their attribution more or less as great crimes, and their criminogenesis. In this regard, it will be necessary to note framing or standpoint. The review or attitude toward an event as a crime draws on a standpoint of relative privilege, whether acknowledged or otherwise. This is a privilege of access to information and to a record of how data is produced, reproduced, altered, forged or simply leaves gaps. History is a series of significant events or transactions that have attracted interests and forces in their execution and review. These interests and forces are like

W. B. de Lint, *Blurring Intelligence Crime*,
https://doi.org/10.1007/978-981-16-0352-5_1

storm surges; the look of the shoreline is dependent on atmospheric conditions and water temperature, and once in a while there is a shift of wind and current direction, and the shoreline is radically changed. United States history is a sequence of great victories under the rule of law, as per the writing of many schoolbook texts. Alternatively, it is a rap sheet (Zinn, 1995) featuring theft, pillage and slavery as forms of organised crime are legitimated by an emergent nation-state (Tilly, 1985). Being in a position to overdetermine the review of the event, victors are also in a position to 'rub out' all virtue in the vanquished; they may define up their own actions and define down the actions of those they have displaced. Supreme Court Justice Robert Jackson wished that it were not so that in the aftermath of great conflict 'justice belongs to the victor'. In his opening address at the Nuremburg Trials, he observed: 'Civilization asks whether law is so laggard as to be utterly helpless to deal with crimes of this magnitude by criminals of this order of importance' (Jackson, 1992: 171). The question is apt, and a positive answer will seem to depend on naivete and blind faith. Following great crimes, there is a purging of records and a whitewashing of social and political identity, particularly the subaltern repository of the counter-narrative representing the subordinated view of events, written from under the rubble by history's huddled losers.

In exploring this subject, this book adopts four interrelated neologisms: 'critical forensics', 'apex crime', 'intelligence crime' and 'intelligence blur'. These concepts augment one another. An analysis of critical forensics is best carried out using examples of intelligence crime. Examples of apex crime over-involve intelligence,[1] either normatively or in deviation, depending on your love of the spook. The record of crime involving intelligence transactions is deliberately blurred or papered over, reflecting a type of politicisation that operates through intelligence actors and agencies. In what follows we are concerned with types of events that may implicate anyone able to command the levers of influence of the security apparatus of the nation-state in criminal wrongdoing, from 'patriotic' rogue actor (e.g. Oliver North) to canny careerist (e.g. Henry Kissinger).

In this introduction we will set out some of the themes and concepts that will be further developed in Chaps. 2 and 3. One of these themes is the problem of establishing certainty about criminal events. We are able only to skim the surface—and we will be doing a lot of that!—sufficient to point out that if knowledge about crime is not so certain as it may popularly appear to be, knowledge about political crime and intelligence crime is that much more indefinite. Another theme concerns the standpoint of review. The term 'critical' is used to denote the evaluation of crime and a perspective on the interaction of institutional knowledges.

The Uncertainty of Crime

How do we know crime? Unless we are victims, offenders or eyewitnesses (and even then), we only know it through a discourse, representing a restrictive organisation of ideas. We also know it through methods of capture that record official information (police reports, court reports, victim surveys, emergency department records) by reference to measures of value (records of account, efficacy standards of evidence, registers of experts, chain of custody certification). Together the embedding of a way of thinking about problems and the laboratory or mechanism of discovery may be referred to as 'inscription devices' (Latour & Woolgar, 2013). We know crime through the announcements of legislators, officials and opinion or demand group leaders in mainstream news media, and from the reports of scientific or research institutions. Knowledge is developed at 'centres of calculation' and will generate 'traces of encounters and observations, which can then be mobilised and combined' (Schaffer, 2007: 90). Because none of us are immunized against beliefs that inform a cognitive framing on which we more or less depend to make sense of the world (Jensen et al., 2020), the knowledge is more or less the outcome of relating selected facts to cultural and political preferences, Through this process of allocating categories of conduct according to discursively differentiated or privileged space, our understanding of crime *loops*, or confirms preferences regarding how to see it.

Nelken (1994: 366) has suggested that there is 'artificiality [in] all definitions of crime'. In this regard, there are two important considerations. One concerns the ontology or nature of crime: How does it look? How does it behave? And how might we experience it from a presumptive standpoint? Following Durkheim and Weber, it is mostly understood that we are socialised according to an index of moral outrage that in turn derives from and reasserts a social order—hence its loopy-ness. The effort here is predicated on the view that as social beings we depend upon much that must be taken for granted regarding conduct in conditions of 'high modernity' (Giddens, 1991: 10–34). Individually and collectively we act with reference to the demarcation of criminality and in doing so to produce a discourse of common understanding about the most threatening transactions of and against the social and political order.

As Black (1983) and others (Ewick & Silbey, 1992) have noted, the experience of law, like the experience of crime, is dependent on sometimes irruptive or shocking disenchantment, disempowerment and social (and political) alienation. In most criminology, crime is understood from the standpoint of the presumptive liberal democratic middle class. There is also a presumption of whiteness, or that the default identity or subject identifies with a community that has settled its biggest differences and buried its historical injustices. Hillyard and Toombs (2017: 288), among others, have noted that the predominant gaze, even among the disadvantaged (Young, 1991), looks toward street crime rather than the many depredations committed by corporate and state actors. At the same time, much of criminology is based on a concept of crime that may fragment or become too indeterminant when it is problematised beyond the attachment to criminal law, as in zemiology (Hillyard & Toombs, 2017), peacemaking (Pepinsky, 2013) and constitutive criminology (Henry & Milovanovic, 1991).

We can also perceive crime through its epistemology. In doing so, we ask: what are the conditions, sources or authorities that provide us with our knowledge of crime? One way to address this question is by thinking about its absences, or its architecture as an edifice that is built to mimic prejudice or bias in understanding society or ourselves in the world. In this regard, criminologists have looked at the dark figure, defined as 'occurrences that by some criteria are called crime yet that are not registered in the statistics of whatever agency was the source of the data being used' (Biderman & Reiss, 1967: 2). As recounted by de Castelbajac (2014: 930–932), the metaphor may be traced back to a doctoral dissertation (Oba, 1908), to work by German criminologists who were keen to try to quantify missing figures for various offences, and then to Grünhut (1951) and Mannheim (1965), who queried the 'dark number' in British criminal statistics.

The dark figure is one of the most 'basic criminological notions' (Stevens, 2007: 77); it provides a strong discursive means of indicating a condition or state that then points to a process by which the literally and figuratively dark is transitioned or 'cleared'. As Young (1988: 171, 178 emphasis added) observes,

> a major flaw in establishment criminology has always been its tendency to view the criminal statistics as objective data. That is, as indices of behaviour independent of human evaluation, or as data based on a consensual scale .... The dark figure of crime is not merely a quantitative lacking in official statistics, but is *qualitatively structured*.

Accordingly, 'voodoo criminology' is the attempt to extrapolate a fixed proportion from detected crime to all crime (Young, 2004; Stevens 2007: 82). de Castelbajac (2014: 931) refers to the musings of prominent criminologists, notably Radzinowicz, who for years fixed the mass of crime that is actually committed, made official and punished at no more than about 15% (Radzinowicz, 1964: 917).

That said, it is nonetheless instructive to gauge the depth of the interrogation across criminal categories and the varied extent of over-estimation across crime groups. The raw material of criminology is the base or strata of objective empirical data that may be refined according to the many representations of the disciplinary knowledge.[2] 'Crime'[3] is an artefact of the interface between an event and institutional procedures and processes. From a post-critical point of view, it is not just criminal statistics but also the attempt to quantify the dark figure that reflects the false belief that it is possible to factor out the mechanism of capture. Indeed, if criminal statistics are distorted by how official crime is shown, the dark figure is misshapen by the instruments used to fix it as certain. It is notable that as incidents move up the hierarchy of criminal justice subsystems (that is, from the lower to the higher courts) they are reviewed by a widening field of institutional actors. To put it another way, more subjective measures (like victimisation studies) give way to more objective measures (like national crime reports). But this is not to discount that high level agencies may sometimes face immense political pressure to confirm findings that do not meet objective standards, because sometimes, as we shall see, they do. In this regard there may be a(n unhappy?) synchrony between positive discovery and deconstructionism; if the issue is viewed deeply enough through either lens, there appears to be no underlying stratum of firm bedrock 'beneath' the discursive production of crime facts. In this way, crime is subject to the Heisenberg or uncertainty principle.

In public policy terms, reference to the known unknown of criminal events is made to enlist public resources, particularly law enforcement, in an effort to move the waterline. This waterline may be raised but is often lowered so that more crime is visible to law enforcement and, ultimately, made 'available' to be cleared by prosecution—a phenomenon known as criminalisation. As per Stevens (2007), drug crime offending or drug-related 'volume' crimes are the over-estimated crimes on which police spend most of their time.[4] This is a function of structure, hegemony and institution (Stevens, 2007). Both global and national counts of crimes like terrorism (acts with and without prior law enforcement awareness) and stopped attempts (still defined by law as acts of terrorism) provide the fodder for counter-terrorism action by governments. Consequently, how these counts signify is of great importance to the various vested actors, from politicians to human rights organisations. The more powerful actors will primarily work with the presumptive significations of settled discursive structuration. These actors will, for instance, define terrorism as falling between an act of domestic crime and a declaration of war. More importantly, they will *see* terrorism in the subaltern and exogenous; not as 'we' but as 'they'.

Critical Forensics: On Making Crime Certain

The selection of investigatory evidence is to a large extent a decision of police investigators and the director of public prosecutions or other government authorities. However, to minimise bias, reduce the improper influence of interested parties and maximise true positive results, the collection, preservation and/or analysis is handed to forensics specialists whose work is more or less quarantined and evaluated with reference to the scientific method, subject to blinded procedures and double blind review, and generally follows professional or craft standards.

Much of the miscarriage of justice literature features scandals that involve the 'capture' or instrumentalisation of labs or forensic specialists by police and prosecution interests, and such scandals have been witnessed in most advanced liberal democracies (Sangha et al., 2010). Many of the crime podcasts feature the investigation of 'everyday' or 'street crime' that feature corruption and careerism (see, for example, Giannelli, 2007; McMunigal, 2007). Miscarriages of justice have also been subject to government inquests or commissions of inquiry (see, for example, Goudge, 2008; Kaufman, 1998). These accounts are mostly prescriptive and provide some critical institutional analysis, according to which it would be expected that expertise will depart from principles of best practice where there is an absence of adequate meta-science and oversight and where forensic science's human and capital resources are dependent on productive relations with the prosecution.

At the intersection of the application of scientific methods and processes in solving crimes and political interest in case outcomes lies the concept of 'critical forensics'. Critical forensics refers to inquiries into the institutional conditions that influence the application of scientific methods of collection, preservation and analysis of investigatory evidence for court. It examines the conditions under which disciplinary, organisational or political interests intrude upon, influence and challenge expert jurisdiction and craft principles. Currently, there is no body of work under the label of critical forensics, although there is much research and practice that has developed standards of excellence in this area, in particular the National Academy of Science (NAS) report, titled *Strengthening Forensic Science in the United States* (NRC, 2009); and the President's Council of Advisors on Science and Technology report, titled *Forensic Science in the Criminal Courts: Ensuring scientific validity of feature-comparison methods* (PCAST, 2016). While there are books and articles that speak to the interface of politics and forensics and develop critiques of the systemic conditions, the lack of a critical focus has been noted as potentially impoverishing to the discipline by observers (see, for example, Koppl & Cowan, 2010).

Although context bias and the independence of and accreditation requirements for forensic specialists have all been subject to academic scrutiny, the proneness, institutionally, of forensics labs and specialists to the influence of possibly more powerful and longstanding political actor networks has not been as well studied. Yet their vulnerability in this regard is obvious and requires much vigilance by the courts, media, non-government organisations (NGOs) and others if it is to be documented and redressed.[5] Best practice in crime scene investigation is a focus of significant scholarly and practitioner interest. However, critical forensics represents a gap in the forensics and critical criminology literatures. The novelty of what follows is that it reviews that nexus of political interest and forensic documentation or epistemology in order to provide insight into the intelligence artefact of crime.

From Political Crime to Intelligence Crime

Scholars have problematised the crimes of the powerful (Rothe & Kauzlarich, 2016), corporate and state crime (Jamieson & McEvoy, 2005; Kramer et al., 2002), political criminality (Turk, 1982), white collar crime (Sutherland, 1945) and, more recently, state crimes against democracy (SCAD) (deHaven-Smith & Witt, 2009).[6] However, mainstream criminology is dominated by state-centred attributions of crime such that some of the most egregious and wilful harms remain under-investigated (Michalowski, 2016).

Minor (1975: 390) defines political crime as 'violations of law which are motivated by political intent'. He adds that the elements of such crime include:

> (1) the desire to influence existing public policy or power relations between groups through the commission of the crime, and (2) the predominance of concern for group or societal welfare over considerations of personal gain. This includes so-called 'common' crimes under the above conditions. (Minor, 1975: 391)

A violation of law is determined by government authorities and if authorities are reluctant to make such findings against actors who may be acting in the interests of government, Minor's definition may exclude pro-establishment actors. If we follow Turk (1984: 120) and the perspective of structural conflict theory, political crime is 'whatever is recognized or anticipated by the authorities to be resistance threatening the established structure of differential resources and opportunities'. Turk (1982) is interested in the process of 'political criminalization' as a contributor to political crime, and in particular covert and legally doubtful activities aimed at monitoring, containing and disrupting acts of resistance to the established order. He draws a distinction between political crime and common crime or social deviance. In this vein, Minor (1975: 393, emphasis added) helpfully defines political justice as 'the *discriminatory application of the machinery of criminal justice* to the disadvantage of specific individuals or groups because they are perceived as threatening to the power of the established regime'. When 'agents of justice violate the law in the administration of political justice, they are guilty of political crime' (Minor, 1975: 393).

Clinard and Quinney (1973: 154) argue that, as a distinct category, political crime must include crimes both *for* and *against* government. Anyone committing political crime, whether an opponent or a public official, is a political criminal.[7] Crime against government is intended to change agencies, agents or logics of distribution, whereas crime by government is criminal violation by agents of government that might include criminal *means* such as violations of civil liberties, violations of higher (international) laws and illegalities committed in support of the state. In this regard, the social or moral order is separated from the political order, and the criminal is distinguished from the political. Following this, we might say, with Ingraham (1979), that a political crime is an act that is aimed at violating or defrauding political authority or the legal means of changing it.

This takes us to a consideration of the development of modern democratic governments founded, discursively at least, on the primacy of the rule of law. That consideration can be brief where liberal democracies may be distinguished from authoritarian states as legal subjects. That is to say, in sites where state and government agents acting for the perceived structural interests of the state or government are routinely prosecuted for malfeasance, one may infer that *something*—and it may be the rule of law ideal—is frequently being engaged (see, for example, Transparency International, 2020). Confidence that this is the case will depend on how access to legal procedures is differentially available to actors enmeshed within the established structure of resources and opportunities and how and to what extent such legal procedures maintain that structure (of inequitable access to resources and opportunities).

Several commentators, including Cohen (2001) and Robertson (2002), have observed the growth in international human rights discourse through, notably, international courts, and the complementary rise in the number of investigations of human rights crime by political leaders. As Hogg (2007: 89) argues, the recognition of extra-territorial, extra-national arbiters of crime has developed as conflicts within states and aggression against states from non-state actors have proliferated at the same time that governments and particularly 'weak states' are being overwhelmed by illicit transnational enterprises including the drugs and people smuggling trade. This has created a power relation between state and non-state actors that is the obverse of what inspired criminologists in the 1970s and 1980s to assert that: 'where the state is too weak to be dangerous, non-state actors become too strong' (Cooper [2004] in Hogg, 2007).

Here we can perhaps make an improvement on Turk's conceptualisation. Jihad terrorism is recognised by authorities as neither a straightforward crime nor an act of war. The reason for this is that there is also no recognition by the authorities that the phenomenon represents a grievance by a constituency that may be granted standing to challenge the established political order. If such recognition were to occur, it would invite negotiations on the underlying conflict over interests. This lack of recognition represents an avoidance of the terms of political crime, given that it would by definition include the control agents in that criminality (as per Black, 2004).

If political crime is defined in terms of resistance to the 'structure of differential resources and opportunities', the means and methods of meeting that resistance will also often be understood as political crime. The war on terrorism is stoked and inflamed arguably more from within than from without by authorities who are dependent on the controlled production of 'unease' (Bigo, 2002) or 'the strategy of tension' (Clement & Scalia, 2020), and on the logic and persuasive power of the underlying war interest. If meeting political crime depends on the selective apportioning of rights (that is, by not enabling 'political criminals'), then it can be assumed that security trumps procedure. More than this, to know when to pull the trump card depends on intelligence about the threat. Intelligence whispers to the sovereign regarding the proximity of threat and vital interests. This is to turn inside out the normative sleeve into which the war on terrorism may fit. In the post-normative order, it is the clean division between friend and enemy that is the most precious commodity to be preserved.[8]

Intelligence crime overlaps with political crime, but not completely. There are three dimensions of political crime: *actor identification* with a successor/retrenchment government or political order; a political *object* or target (a meaningful symbol or strategic target, including political, religious, class and ethnic icons, against which to act); and an illegal or legality-stretching *means* in an expressive act (use of violence, denial of human rights). Except for the reference to the presumptive standpoint, the above is almost identical to most definitions of terrorism (cf. Schmid & Jongman, 2008: 1–38).

Intelligence crime has these features and more. Intelligence identifies with the beating heart of the nation-state and special interests in the maintenance of sovereign vitality or national security. In this, intelligence performs at the liminal of succession or retrenchment; it is concerned with enabling or preventing the advancement of actors into positions where they may impact on an existing order as determined by a certain reading of national interest. Targets are connected to what is referred to as national security imperatives or interests. With respect to means, intelligence crime employs legality-stretching devices or measures, deemed necessity to carry out actions against strategic targets—means that many observers have found to be historically consistent despite some ebbs and flows (see, for example, Blum, 2003).

In seeking to harness or depend on sovereign discretion assets or agents are identified with the sovereign (in its vitality as we shall explore) and this provides unique features of cover that makes intelligence criminality difficult to discover, prosecute or review. This is because the means may be covered by presidential directives or other governmental permissions so that they are not illegal although they are otherwise *criminal*. In this, they depend on the normalisation of intelligence means across an *interested* application criminal justice in what we are calling the intelligence blur.

Apex: Political Crime as Spectacle

What is the relation between crimes that are of interest to the most politically empowered and our understanding of those events as criminal events? What is a great crime—in particular, an apex crime—and how do we select it from among all the possible candidates?

Events are designated as significant via descriptive tropes. If crime depends upon governmental recognition and institutional knowledge, as discussed above and in Chap. 3, the review of crime events must pay heed to discourse production—inclusive of references to known unknowns. Accordingly, privileged actors are more or less successful in designating a measure of the outrageousness of an event as well as specific features or dangers and the terms for review.

Apex crime is a watershed event in which the state or government names itself or the national interest as the victim and one of its primary opponents as the likely offender, thus providing a government narrative that is mediated through official sources. It is a class of political crime (such as targeted or terrorist homicide) that involves powerful state or corporate actors in an ordered ambiguity of commission or omission through their deep state networks (Scott, 1996). The designation of victim and perpetrator, investigation, cover-up, legal prosecution and exceptional measures is all familiar content featured in the communication of potential watershed events. Apex crime is a political crime of great social and political importance and may originate within or outside intelligence and the political order. If political actors are in a position to overdetermine a review of crime and if access to high crime is like high policing (Brodeur, 1983)—dependent on access to compartmented information on national security threats—then, in accord with politicisation, only a select group of national security actors are in a position to understand the criminogenesis of a particular apex crime.

A narrative of societal and political justice requires a clear demarcation between offender and victim. This serves to consolidate a consensus or majoritarian order through the public denunciation and penalisation of the ideological and material offender. Because much rides on the outcome of the criminal or legal case, the government's interest in the development of apex and other potentially intelligence crime cases is subject to enormous political pressure. This is the prosaic explanation and the indicator of crimes that are apparently political, but of which the processing by the criminal justice system is often irregular. Departures from best practice forensics and fact-finding will be viewed by a necessarily sceptical public (in liberal democracies at least) as evidence against the official narrative, producing weakened political and societal disorder.

Whatever the real progeny, in an apex crime the government, through its authorities, nominates itself as victim and one or more of its ideological opponents as purposeful perpetrator. The nomination of victim, perpetrator and implicit purpose, made by the government leader or designate, forms a 'government' or 'official narrative'. This narrative, in which there is enormous political investment, is mooted soon after the event and in advance of the criminal investigation. It therefore sets up a *confirmation bias* around evidence discovery, as it determines what is sensible to search and examine. At the same time, however, the sensitivity of the national security discourse and associated statutory obligations and the media's proneness to influence by national security actors compels support of the official narrative. Due to the substantial political interest in the forensic outcomes of apex crime investigation, deviations from or novel applications of best practice forensics are hypothesised to occur with regularity where the government deems an event to have national security implications and applications.

A Critical Forensics of Intelligence Crime

In this book the forensics record of intelligence crime is evaluated with the aim of providing a clearer understanding of where that record has departed from best practice in criminal investigation and forensics, in terms of reference, conventions, methods, measures, principles and protocols. The book explores the intersection between crime, forensics, politics and intelligence and considers the distortions of authority concerning knowledge and discovery. The approach is critical institutional. The analysis is concerned to explore the relation between crime and standpoint and authority and information, such that crime's connection to forensics, politics and intelligence may be reviewed from a position of relative scepticism. As shall be explored, institutions of justice and of police, security and intelligence are reviewable in terms of the framing and ordering that pertains to their activities. This comprises the main point of contention, the breakwater against which 'the actual' (Bhaskar, 2013) is churned into foam or noise.

There is no claim of objectivity with respect to the alternative capture of 'the actual' presented here. Although an effort is made to minimise the use of apparently non-objective assertions, the standpoint is one that may take on what might be described as prejudicial assumptions regarding the behaviour of institutions and individuals striving to master the rules of achievement within them, particularly the conduct of careerist 'apex predators'—those who are capable of negotiating the normative, bureaucratic and logistical or transactional requirements of complex organisations. Whether that motive is simple careerism or fear of reprisal, contrary to the vast commentary on intelligence that assigns either noble or blundering but innocent intent to 'national security' actors, the sceptical assumption here is that the power-knowledge structure of such organisations over-predicts the planning and execution of harmfully immoral projects.

These observations are connected by more than one thread. One of these concerns how we know crime or crime events and who it is that does the knowing and under what circumstances or contexts. In this connection lies the question of the dark figure of crime and also the darker figure of the illicit actions of the sovereign or state actors, or actors that work under the provisional auspices of the crown or executive. This might be referred to as the *endarkenment* of crime and disorder.

Events that shock the social and political order are reviewed in one regard as belonging to a genus. We come at events or are quickly provided with ideological assumptions or an opinion of what belongs in their frame. We shall be referring to this as an ordering principle. According to an alignment between our belief in a just world (Lerner & Miller, 1978) and the perceived necessity of ordering the world (Buzan, 1999: 8), in everyday and national security, we will either view these events as confirming the necessity of the activities of social and political authorities and the political style of those authorities, or with suspicion. If the latter, security and intelligence may be less the servant of sovereign vitality than its master.

With this in mind it is not possible in this book to make claims regarding the quantity of intelligence and apex crime across time or place. This is of interest, but it would involve the measurement of the relative corruption within standard and benchmark forensic or criminal discovery practices and developing a measure of the relative politicisation and prioritisation of an event that involves a significant criminal act. As per the previous discussion, this is too difficult to quantify. Doing so would require the discovery of some controls or constants across time and place but this has been an enigma for criminology and for the study of corruption as well, as there is no index that can measure 'real levels of corruption in all its manifestations' (Transparency International, 2020).[9]

This will be frustrating for some readers as it is quite appropriate to ask what is necessary and sufficient for the attribution of an event as an apex or intelligence crime. If this cannot be answered, how can we really know these crimes? There is no convenient answer to this question. Where a determinative or definitive identification of the underlying phenomenon depends on data or information subject to redaction and destruction, we are left with claim rather than disprovable hypothesis and without the capacity to capture sufficient objective data. In the meantime, there is at least a strong implicit, if not a 'consensus', presumption of the influence of political opinion on crime and intelligence. It occludes crime discovery and recovery and is functional to the necessary maintenance of extant political authority and legitimacy.

Gill (1994: 9–35), drawing on Ransom (1980), divides information or literature on security intelligence into six categories. The first is '*insider*' *accounts*—which are the more or less authorised accounts from usually senior agency actors, who are '*usually reliable sources*', by which he refers to some of the same people that Wilford (2009) discusses as the 'cross-appointed' journalists who drive the preferred narrative of the agencies. The second category is *critical accounts*, which are the whistle-blower accounts or more or less unauthorized exposes of intelligence agency wrongdoing. The third is *academic writings*, which are usually historical in nature but also comprise all of the work of political scientists and others who draw almost exclusively from the published archives and from the last category of material. The fourth category includes *official reports*, referring to the copious body of 'accountability' documents that is generated by the agencies through Inspectors General, oversight hearing transcripts and inquiries, and royal commissions, among others. As Sageman (2014: 570) summarises 'regarding knowledge of terrorism, academic investigation is constrained to popular search engines or secondary sources that stem from news reports', which in turn represent 'politically motivated government leaks and government claims about "'terrorists"—often made for political reasons.'

Critical and political criminology depends upon the critical review of official records and authorities but also on an alternative standpoint from which to develop a counter-narrative. In what follows, the proposed standpoint is somewhat provisional, but assumes that intelligence and security agendas are exploitative of inchoate events. For this reason, the knowledge foundation in this book derives from a critical evaluation of the official record by authorities and a review of additional information provided by whistle-blowers and investigative journalism.

Bigger crimes involve organisational resources and identifying such crimes depends upon knowing the networked organisations. This involves not only the question of who is doing the knowing, but also establishing what is preferred in terms of outcomes. As noted above, in this book a distinction is drawn to determine the relative politicisation of events, as it is expected that some events will be subject to greater politicisation than others. A sociology of institutional knowledge involves paying due regard to the relatively autonomous interests of organisational and institutional actors who are dependent on a relationship with authorities representing or able to claim the will of the sovereign or crown. In intelligence, careerism depends upon access to exclusive and transactable information. The more exclusive, the higher will be the clearance and the more power will accrue to the agent or asset; the more transactable the information, or the more impactful on a target or resource valuable for political change, the more valuable to the organisation will be that actor or asset. Careerists close to or at the centre of sovereign decision-making exploit events to align with their commitment to the ordering principle (security necessity). In the meantime, the capacity to distinguish friend from foe or criminal from victim is at stake. Here, the overture to security and particularly national security and of the interests of those privileged to protect the vitality of the sovereign may be finessed in a world of tradecraft in a context of geopolitical interests.

Against this background, as we will narrate, there is a depoliticising or justice restorative urge. Just as there are strong forces and interests seeking to appropriate resources and recast that appropriation in a retrospective ordering of necessity, so too is there a countervailing force that seeks just distributions or a restoration of the modern ideal that justice is blind. Confidence in a rules-based order is a necessity of civilised interaction and even those who directly benefit from outrageous predations must be covert or very innovative in their careerism—in the Mertonian adaptation—to accomplish the blinding of justice. Nuremburg and other war crimes tribunals as well as truth and reconciliation events and some political revolutions are expressions of that other great urge: to maintain social order under some version of the rule of law.

Working Hypothesis and Bias

In the framing of experience and knowledge imposed by institutional boundaries, we confront the nature of the crime scene and forensics. As we will explore, forensics, inclusive of crime scene investigation, is in one respect a highly objective undertaking, one subject to scrutiny from within and without institutional boundaries. A crime scene is somewhat porous, insofar as it can be viewed and reviewed. On the other hand, investigators, officials, authorities and experts recover and discover artefacts from the site or from other sources and build an account of an event under the seal of the crown, or at least representatives of the state. Once this is done, over 95% of cases will result in the disposition of a guilty plea (Auerhahn, 2012: 95).

In one respect there is no alternative crime scene. Where information has not been tested according to the rules, any claim this can rise to a standard of alternative evidence will be weak because it is based on an evaluation that does not meet the standards of criminalistics or forensics. In the miscarriage of justice literature, victory is represented by winning a new trial using new evidence or retesting old evidence. In discussing the case study crimes in this book, the analyses are only suggestive, they do not report on the examination of new evidence or retest old evidence. They are analysed based on what is generally known about them in the public domain, and we look for hints as to where that knowledge seems to be most threadbare.

This analysis comes with limitations. There are many important procedural, technical, professional and accountability requirements that, in principle and rhetoric, but also in most cases in practice or fact, provide some measurable certainty for claims made in court about facts regarding a crime. When an argument is presented for court there is an opportunity for cross-examination, so that each point or evidence in fact can be examined and subjected to scrutiny. The reader is not in the same position as a barrister and cannot demand access to discovery documentation or call experts to challenge their authenticity. The items of evidence presented in what follows do not have to pass through the filter of the lab or the court and many of them would not pass muster if they did. While it is possible to criticise the objectivity of the court in permitting certain evidence, there can be no strong claim of objectivity on the part of a single author presenting arguments about the evidence of items he has mostly not seen, many of which are not subject to strict selection, expert testing and cross-examination. With these significant caveats noted, in this account, I will select and review apex and intelligence crime and its critical forensics.[10]

As described in Chap. 3, intelligence crimes, inclusive of apex crimes, are a difficult subject. They are not the regular object of much criminological interest and analysis. This is because criminology depends on authoritative sources and in matters of crime such sources often take the form of opinions from government or other actors in the field. Secondly, just as academic freedom in principle has suffered post 9/11 (Carvalho & Downing, 2010; Doumani, 2005), academic exploration of the counter-narrative of intelligence crimes is dangerous to careers.[11] For instance, there is little published work in academic criminology (de Lint, 2020) or political science (Hughes, 2020; van der Pijl, 2019) that provides a strongly sceptical account of the official 9/11 narrative. Thus, the available scholarly record is presumably distorted by institutional constraints on authority (Keller, 2011; de Lint, 2020).

Critical criminology engages in a *deconstruction* of crime and of the criminological enterprise as an artefact of discursive properties (both material and symbolic), which seek to impose a preferred ordering (such as capitalist or neoliberal). To recall Matza (1974), radical criminology in particular is the counter-point to the separation of crime from the conduct and theory of the state. From a critical perspective, and as explained in subsequent chapters, critical criminologists do not depend entirely on the views of legal practitioners or government authorities in the attribution of the 'offence-like incident' (Ashworth, 1994).

While critical criminology queries the labels and processes that produce criminal categories, it does not necessarily originate from an oppositional ordering. Critical criminologists have long bemoaned the setting of crime parameters as more or less a function of (political or corporate) power. The more the crime matters to the politically powerful, the more the influence of the politically powerful will be evident in the attribution of the crime. This is merely another way of stating that actors in the criminal justice process are only independent in theory, and that, as actors in the administration of police, prosecution and courts who draw on scientific expertise, they seek to negotiate between the entreaties of their superiors and consumers and the strict requirements of craft knowledge. As critical criminologists also often point out, how victim and perpetrator, investigation and cover-up, and legal prosecution and exceptional measures are distinguished is subject to knowledge configuration and discourse production.

In order to simplify our analysis or give it some distinctive form, we divide this examination—the critical forensics of intelligence crime—into three stages of inquiry. These represent the interplay of *actors* (government authority, narrator and reviewer) on *artefacts* (event, scene and information identification). These are represented in sequential couplets, but there is interplay between each set of linked artefacts and actors are 'restless' within the stages of inquiry. For instance, and as we shall explore, there may be a crime event according to government authorities, but the event is often presented to us concurrently with a narrative that is affixed to it by actors more or less capable of so doing.

The first stage of our examination considers a hybrid of event and authority. At one level we are asking in relation to an event: 'What is this?' and 'What genus of event has occurred?' For the most part, where big events occur within settled jurisdictions they are embraced or confined by the extant authorities according to scripts (law and custom) that are in place to make a preliminary determination of what is at play and to restore the order that the event has unsettled. In most events in settled jurisdictions, any significant challenge to the interpretation of the event or to the configuration of authorities or the meting out of actor responsibilities is not too contentious. However, not everyone may agree with the designation or 'fixing' of the event and the related authority. Watershed or apex events are loaded with a firm narrative authority that will invite resistance and support in counter-authorities.

The second (somewhat) sequential stage covers the scene and the (investigatory) narrative. Investigation of the scene involves a stock-take of the materials or artefacts that may be gathered as associated with the event according to a working hypothesis or investigatory narrative. This is meant to be done in accordance with the attribution imposed by the relevant authorities, which governs how those materials or artefacts are to be collected and secured. Processing the scene is thus carried out according to a narrative, but there may be conflicting explanations proffered to account for the behaviour or relation of artefacts (such as information, materials and witness accounts). Investigators will work in line with a working hypothesis that informs what is to be collected for further examination, and this produces contextual and confirmation bias.

The third stage considers (suspect) identification and review. This encompasses the confirmation of the identity of crime scene elements and alleged suspects by testing samples according to expert forensic techniques. In this exercise, the review involves an account of the subjugation of the scientific, objective or independent processes of forensic identification to disciplinary evaluation, and to other interests or authorities. Regarding the primary review, confidence in the identification of suspects is achieved where forensic labs are independent of police or prosecution services, where they and the forensic investigators are accredited by a suitable body, where the process can be subject to further independent examination and the results made available to interested parties (the defence in particular), and where the expert testimony is reviewed for claims beyond scope (Du, 2017: 143; Koppl & Cowan, 2010; Giannelli, 2007: 492). Regarding the secondary review, judicial authorities, executive government authorities and third-party actors including academics—in this book we concentrate on national security and intelligence—compete with other cultural or media authorities to offer findings regarding the suspect identification exercise.

Outline of the Book

The next two chapters will further define and set the terms of the analysis. In Chap. 2, there is an exploration of key forensics issues and dilemmas as scientists strive to provide a reliable service that is not corrupted by cosiness with investigators and prosecutors. In Chap. 3, the concept of intelligence crime is elaborated, in particular as intelligence actor crime is an instantiation of sovereign exceptionalism and, for our purposes, an anti-forensics.

Drawing on the concepts and terms presented in the Introduction and Chaps. 2 and 3, in Chap. 4 we examine 9/11 as an apex crime. We explore 9/11 in terms of its authority, its narration or stipulation in the crime scenes and in its review or in the confirmation of its initial construction. We follow this with two chapters on intelligence crime with Chap. 5 concerned with the discovery of crimes by 'us' and Chap. 6 concerned with the discovery of crimes by 'them'. Using case studies, we investigate the crimes in terms of their constitution as *pre-emptively occluded conduct* (transactional) or as *retrospectively occluded conduct* (blur). Chapter 7 presents an analysis of the dimensions of intelligence blurring. Like criminal justice, the craft of intelligence involves the finessing of its independence from political influence and its service to sovereign demands.

In sum, in this book the crimes selected include criminal elements (motive and means), involve significant social and political actors and repercussions, and intelligence actors and agencies in their commission or re-interpretation. The selection is based on a prima facie consistency with conceptualised elements. The book relies upon a case study analysis (using whistle-blower and investigative journalist reports[12]) of intelligence crimes of omission or commission to document the departures from forensics/crime scene investigation best practice. The cases were selected based on whether they met the prima facie definition of an intelligence crime of omission or commission. The information on the cases is drawn from investigator reports, whistle-blower accounts and investigative journalism, and the cases are reviewed against the main criteria for investigation and forensic review. A review or analysis of intelligence crime forensics, by case study, is useful in capturing any patterns of departure from the craft requirements of principle and method. The hypothesis presented herein is that the rush to confirm a prescribed narrative produces tests, analyses and findings that tend to be incomplete, innovative or unrepeatable. For crimes for which 'intelligence crime forensics' are required, practitioners and professional bodies must be alert to the pressures leading to, and hazards of, departure from standard procedures at these sites.

The working hypothesis is that intelligence crime is over-represented in the dark figure of criminality or the known unknown of criminological interest. In applying the logic of a critical forensics to intelligence crime and raising the profile of this genus of crime, it is hoped that this book will encourage greater scepticism about self-serving government accounts of both significant and quotidian or routine conduct.

Notes

1. By intelligence we mean state activity that is dependent on confidential sources and methods performed by agents or officers of the state to produce information or by covert action to support sovereign security (see, for example, Warner, 2020).
2. 'Social democratic' positivist criminologists (Young, 1988: 159), including Radzinowicz, Sparks, and Biderman and Reiss, appear to believe that 'crime' is a constant between the darkness of the uncounted or recorded and the visibility of the recorded phenomenon. After the critical turn, some criminologists began to question these presumed solidities.
3. Following the need to find authority for crime within and beyond the state, some criminologists have sought to use the term 'zemiology' (Hillyard et al., 2004).
4. In being a known unknown, the dark figure has a volume that may be over- or under-estimated. Many criminologists make the claim that it is often over-estimated for the purposes of informing social policy (Stevens, 2007: 78).
5. Networked Knowledge (http://www.netk.net.au/), led by Bob Moles in Adelaide, Australia, is an excellent example of a dedicated website that

provides updates on court challenges and legal changes on miscarriages of justice.

6. Kramer and Michalowski's (2006) model of state-corporate crime incorporates the institutional environment, the organisational level and the interactional to follow relationships across states and corporations. Kramer and Michalowski follow the motivations, opportunities and controls that support or constrain actors in crime perpetration and discovery. Rothe and Mullins (2009) add the international level to the institutional state/structural environment level.
7. However, persons in office who abuse their position for personal gain lack the requisite motivation (politicality or societal welfare, however misconstrued) and are therefore excluded.
8. The preferred means of remedy is (state) terrorism via asymmetrical interventions including drone assassinations, counter-insurgency operations, and in general low-intensity warfare against arguably civilian targets by and for the security-intelligence-dispositive or established structure. In this reading, the choice to use intentional violence does little to distinguish what is done by those who wish to usurp the ordering principle and establish a competing social and political order from those who wish to preserve the established order. We see expressive, explosive and intentional violence in elective 'shock and awe' campaigns by military actors on one side or by non-state belligerents on the other. They are distinguished in the style of the legitimation discourses they adopt, so that the former enjoys recourse to justifications of the use of traditional weapons and structures of a modernised, ritualised violence, while the latter is left to produce a narrative around exploiting the non-traditional weapons and structures of insurgency. And, of course, there is no greater abrogation of the Kantian directive than a dirty war. With respect to instrumentalisation, the key is to determine the extent to which people are used for ends against their objective (ontological security) interests. Crucial here is the notion of transparent, reciprocal governance relations between individual citizens and state authorities. Warfighting involves non-transparent, non-reciprocal relations. And the greater the level of secrecy, the more frequent will be both the licit and illicit use of persons against their objective interests. The relation between crime and power or cultural and economic stratification is of longstanding interest to jurists and criminologists but more widely to philosophers, sociologists, humanists and others interested in justice.
9. Efforts to quantify the dark figure of crime are stymied by the inability to capture the real beyond the actual and empirical, as Bhaskar (2013) has problematised.
10. Here it is important to note that there are more than two competing discourses. Investigative journalism also has rules and procedures and a view and review of an archives, authorities and inscription devices. It would not be possible to review forensics critically without drawing upon investigative reporting. In this regard, there is much now written on how the reporting of apex crimes divides people according to scepticism of government. That is to say, where readers or writers doubt the veracity of the claims by media regarding the Kennedy

assassination, they are branded as conspiracy theorists (see Conclusion in this text).

11. For example, Hughes's (2020) publication in an international relations journal on the lack of IR critique of 9/11 was followed by calls for his termination from the School of Social and Political Science, Lincoln University (personal correspondence).
12. It is known that even critical criminology and leftist journalism (such as *Counterpunch, Znet, The Grey Zone* and the *Intercept*) are allergic to investigations where the 'conspiracy theory' slander has been so effective in discrediting official big crime narratives. *The Guardian, Washington Post* and other establishment news outlets deploy the simplistic generalist conspiracy framing (see Conclusion in this text) to discredit scepticism where the government and particularly national security agencies are involved or are suspected of involvement in a crime in which their role is not fully disclosed.

References

Ashworth, A. (1994). *The criminal process: An evaluative study*. Oxford: Clarendon.

Auerhahn, K. (2012). 'Social control of the self' and pleading guilty in criminal court. *International Review of Sociology, 22*(1), 95–122.

Bassiouni, M. (1990). Effective national and international action against organized crime and terrorist criminal activities. *Emory International Law Review, 4*(1), 9–42.

Bhaskar, R. (2013). *A realist theory of science*. Routledge.

Biderman, A., & Reiss, A. (1967). On exploring the dark figure of crime. *Annals of the American Academy of Political and Social Science, 374,* 1–15.

Bigo, D. (2002). Security and immigration: toward a critique of the governmentality of unease. *Alternatives*. Special Issue, *27*, 63–92.

Black, D. (1983, February). Crime as social control. *American Sociological Review*, 34–45.

Black, D. (2004). Terrorism as social control. In M. Deflem (Ed.), *Terrorism and counterterrorism: Criminological perspectives*. Amsterdam: Elsevier.

Blum, W. (2003). *Killing hope: US and CIA interventions since WWII*. London: Zed Books.

Brodeur, J. P. (1983). High policing and low policing: Remarks about the policing of political activities. *Social Problems, 30*(5), 507–520.

Buzan, B. (1999). Change and insecurity reconsidered. *Contemporary Security Policy, 20*(3), 1–17.

Carvalho, E., & Downing, D. (Eds.). (2010). *Academic freedom in the post-9/11 era*. Springer.

Clement, M., & Scalia, V. (2020). The strategy of tension: understanding state labelling processes and double–binds. *Critical Criminology*, online first.

Clinard, M. B., & Quinney, R. (1973). Corporate criminal behavior. In M. B. Clinard & R. Quinney (Eds.), *Criminal behavior systems: A typology reviewed*. New York: Holt, Rinehart & Winston.

Cohen, S. (2001). *States of denial: Knowing about atrocities and suffering*. New York: Wiley.

de Castelbajac, M. (2014). Brooding over the dark figure of crime: The home office and the Cambridge Institute of Criminology in the run-up to the British Crime Survey. *British Journal of Criminology, 54*(5), 928–945.

de Lint, W. (2020). Criminology 9/11. *Globalizations, 17*(7), 1157–1177.

deHaven-Smith, L., & Witt, M. T. (2009). Preventing state crimes against democracy. *Administration & Society, 41*(5), 527–550.

Doumani, B. (2005). Academic freedom post-9/11. *ISIM Review, 15,* 22–23.

Du, M. (2017). Analysis of errors in forensic science. *Journal of Forensic Science and Medicine, 2017*(3), 139–143.

Ewick, P., & Silbey, S. S. (1992). Narrating social structure: Stories of resistance to legal authority. *American Journal of Sociology, 108*, 1328–1372.

Giannelli, P. C. (2007). Wrongful convictions and forensic science: The need to regulate crime labs. *North Carolina Law Review, 86*(1), 163–236.

Giddens, A. (1991). *Modernity and self identity: Self and society in the late modern age*. Stanford: Stanford University Press.

Gill, P. (1994). *Policing politics: Security intelligence and the liberal democratic state*. London: Frank Cass.

Goudge, S. T. (2008). *Inquiry into pediatric forensic pathology in Ontario*. Toronto, ON: Ontario Ministry of the Attorney General.

Grünhut, M. (1951). Statistics in criminology. *Journal of the Royal Statistical Society,* Series A (General), *114*(2), 139–162.

Henry, S., & Milovanovic, D. (1991). Constitutive criminology: The maturation of critical theory. *Criminology, 29*(2), 293–316.

Hillyard, P., Pantazis, C., Toombs, S., & Gordon, D. (2004). *Beyond criminology: Taking harm seriously*. London: Pluto Press.

Hillyard, P., & Toombs, S. (2017). Social harm and zemiology. In A. Liebling, C. Maruna, & L. McAra (Eds.), *Oxford handbook of criminology* (pp. 284–305).

Hogg, R. (2007). Criminology, crime and politics before and after 9/11. *Australian & New Zealand Journal of Criminology, 40*(1), 83–105.

Hughes, D. (2020). 9/11 truth and the silence of the IR discipline. *Alternatives, 45*(2), 55–82.

Ingraham, B. L. (1979). *Political crime in Europe: A comparative study of France, Germany, and England*. Berkeley: University of California Press.

Jackson, J. R. (1992). Opening Statement at Nuremburg Trials, reprinted in Telford Taylor. *The Anatomy of the Nuremburg Trials: A personal memoir*. New York: Alfred A. Knopf.

Jamieson, R., & McEvoy, K. (2005). State crime by proxy and juridical othering. *British Journal of Criminology, 45*(4), 504–527.

Jensen, M. A., Seate, A., & James, P. A. (2020). Radicalization to violence: A pathway approach to studying extremism. *Terrorism and Political Violence, 32*(5), 1067–1090.

Kaufman, F. (1998). *Commission on proceedings involving Guy Paul Morin*. Toronto: Ministry of the Attorney General. www.attorneygeneral.jus.gov.on.ca.

Keller, R. (2011). The sociology of knowledge approach to discourse. *Human Studies, 34*, 43–65.

Koppl, R., & Cowan, E. J. (2010). A battle of forensic experts is not a race to the bottom. *Review of Political Economy, 22*(2), 235–262.

Kramer, R. C., Michalowski, R. J., & Kauzlarich, D. (2002). The origins and development of the concept and theory of state-corporate crime. *Crime & Delinquency, 48*(2), 263–282.

Latour, B., & Woolgar, S. (2013). *Laboratory life: The construction of scientific facts*. Princeton University Press.

Lerner, M. J., & Miller, D. T. (1978). Just world research and the attribution process: Looking back and ahead. *Psychological Bulletin, 85*(5), 1030–1045.

Mannheim, H. (1965). *Comparative criminology: A textbook* (Vol. 1). US: Taylor & Francis.

Matza, D. (1974). *Becoming deviant*. Transaction Publishers.

McBarnet, D. J. (1978). *The police and the state: Arrest, legality and the law*. Aldershot: Croom Helm.

McMunigal, K. C. (2007). Prosecutors and corrupt science. *Hofstra Law Review, 36*(2), 437–450.

Michalowski, R. J. (2016). What is crime? *Critical Criminology, 24*(2), 181–199.

Michalowski, R. J., & Kramer, R. C. (2006). *State-corporate crime: Wrongdoing at the intersection of business and government*. Rutgers University Press.

Minor, W. W. (1975). Political crime, political justice, political prisoners. *Criminology, 12*(4), 385–398.

National Research Council. (2009). *Strengthening forensic science in the United States: A path forward*. Washington, DC: The National Academies Press. https://doi.org/10.17226/12589.
Nelken, D. (Ed.). (1994). *White-collar crime*. Aldershot: Dartmouth.
Oba, S. (1908). *Unverbesserliche Verbrecher und ihre Behandlung*. R. Noske.
Pepinsky, H. (2013). Peacemaking criminology. *Critical Criminology, 21*(3), 319–339.
President's Council of Advisors on Science and Technology. (2016). *Forensic science in criminal courts: Ensuring scientific validity of feature-comparison methods*. Washington, DC: Executive Office of the President's Council of Advisors on Science and Technology.
Radzinowicz, L. (1964). The criminal in society (Peter Le Neve Foster Lecture). *Journal of the Royal Society of Arts, 112,* 916–929.
Ransom, H. H. (1980). Being intelligent about secret intelligence agencies. *American Political Science Review, 24*(1), 141–142.
Robertson, G. (2002). *Crimes against humanity* (2nd ed.). London: Penguin.
Rothe, D., & Kauzlarich, D. (2016). *Crimes of the powerful: An introduction*. Routledge.
Rothe, D. L., & Mullins, C. W. (2009). Toward a criminology of international criminal law: An integrated theory of international criminal violations. *International Journal of Comparative and Applied Criminal Justice, 33*(1), 97–118.
Sageman, M. (2014). The stagnation in terrorism research. *Terrorism and Political Violence, 26*(4), 565–580.
Sangha, B., Moles, R. N., & Roach, K. (2010). *Forensic investigations and miscarriages of justice: The rhetoric meets the reality*. Toronto, ON: Irwin Law.
Schaffer, S. (2007). "On Seeing Me Write": Inscription devices in the South Seas. *Representations, 97*(1), 90–122.
Schmid, A., & Jongman, A. (2008). *Political terrorism*. New Brunswick: Transaction Publishers.
Scott, P. D. (1996). *Deep politics and the death of JFK*. California: University of California Press.
Stevens, A. (2007). When two dark figures collide: Evidence and discourse on drug-related crime. *Critical Social Policy, 27*(1), 77–99.
Sutherland, E. H. (1945). Is 'white collar crime' crime? *American Sociological Review, 10*(2), 132–139.
Tilly, C. (1985). War making and state making as organized crime. In T. Skocpol, P. Evans, & D. Rueschemeyer (Eds.), *Bringing the state back*. New York: Cambridge.
Transparency International. (2020). Corruptions perceptions index. Transparency.org. https://www.transparency.org/en/cpi#.
Turk, A. (1984). Political crime. In R. Meier (Ed.), *Major forms of crime*. Beverly Hills, CA: Sage.
Turk, A. T. (1982). *Political criminality: The defiance and defense of authority*. Beverly Hills: Sage.
Van der Pijl, K. (2019). *Academic corruption, the Israel lobby, and 9/11, or, why I have resigned from my emeritus status at the University of Sussex*. http://keesvanderpijl.nl/wp-content/uploads/2019/05/Academic_Corruption_the_Israel_Lobby_and.pdf.
Warner, M. (2020). Wanted: A definition of intelligence. In C. Andrews, R. Aldrich, & W. Wark (Eds.), *Secret intelligence: A reader* (pp. 4–12). New York: Routledge.
Wilford, H. (2009). *The mighty Wurlitzer: How the CIA played America*. Boston: Harvard University Press.
Young, J. (1991). Left realism and the priorities of crime control. In K. Stenson & D. Cowell (Eds.), *The politics of crime control* (pp. 146–160). London: Sage.
Young, J. (2004). Voodoo criminology and the numbers game. In J. Ferrell, K. Hayward, W. Morrison, & M. Presdee (Eds.), *Cultural criminology unleashed*. London: Glass House Press.
Young, L. (1988). Radical criminology in Britain: The emergence of a competing paradigm. *British Journal of Criminology, 28,* 159.
Zinn, H. (1995). *A people's history of the United States, 1492—Present*. New York: Harper Perennial.

Chapter 2
Forensic Certainties

> The first forensic DNA case, which occurred in England in 1986, involved a false confession.
>
> Giannelli (2001: 489)

Introduction

The eminent forensic scientist Paul L. Kirk once stated, 'physical evidence cannot be wrong, it cannot perjure itself, it cannot be wholly absent. Only human failure to find it, study and understand it, can diminish its value' (1953: 4). Referring to that human element, law professor Jessica Gabel Cino (2017: 2) observes that forensic science is currently still deficient in the rigours and standards, as well as the quality controls and procedures, that are normally found in science. Justice Antonin Scalia referred to an NAS report (NAS, 2009), *Strengthening Forensic Science in the United States*, in writing the decision for the majority in a 5-to-4 decision in *Melendez-Diaz v. Massachusetts*, with the assertion that 'forensic evidence is not uniquely immune from the risk of manipulation'.[1]

Forensics is the application of scientific disciplinary practices (such as toxicology, odontology, physical anthropology) to the development of an expert evaluation that is intended to support a finding by a court. It also incorporates the subdivisions of criminalistics and crime scene investigation, with which the term is often used interchangeably. That being said, criminalistics is defined more narrowly as directed at the 'recognition, individualization and evaluation of physical evidence by application of the physical and natural sciences to law-science matters' (DeForest et al., 1983: 45). Crime scene investigation involves the temporary expropriation of a site by authorities as it is deemed to possess evidence of a crime, restricting the access to and handling of discovered evidence according to the use of techniques and protocols by authorised personnel.

The purpose of this brief overview is to permit us to identify the expectations of conduct in this work and departures from form. It would be ideal if it were possible

W. B. de Lint, *Blurring Intelligence Crime*,
https://doi.org/10.1007/978-981-16-0352-5_2

to conduct a thorough review of these deviations here, but this is beyond the scope of this study, and the tools needed for such an exercise require further development (see NAS, 2009; PCAST, 2016; Evett et al., 2017). Here we only have space to offer a cursory summary of some important dimensions of the field, in anticipation of the review of the cases of crime we explore in subsequent chapters. We outline the sequence or stages of the crime discovery and recovery process undertaken by authorities in establishing dominion over and classification of the event, the exploitation of the crime scene according to a working hypothesis or narrative, and the stipulation or confirmation of identities by authorised bodies or experts.

Criminal investigations involve the discovery and recovery of evidence in support of an account of a criminal act and the identification of a method and a means and motive (*actus reus* and *mens rea*) with an offender. Forensics is the application of scientific methods to problems of law. Forensic science constitutes a means of testing and reporting on evidence that has probative meaning with respect to the exclusion or inclusion of individuals or items in relation to a crime. It is comprised of principles and applications. We can review the necessary features of these two requirements (discovery and recovery) against good practice. It is the departure from routine practice and good practice that is of interest in the critical review of cases in this book. In all cases of miscarriage of justice such departures from form can be expected. Wherever there has been a failure to apply requisite expertise, there is a strong indication that the integrity of the process has been diminished under pressure. And whether this has occurred by design or accident is, of course, crucially important.

Thematically, this book represents an examination of the problem of certainty with respect to criminality and criminal events. Most of what we review herein pertains to the broad problem of situating and developing techniques and practices that, through the application of scientific principles, will secure forensics as a more robust disciplinary practice. The focus of this quest for greater certainty (and reliability) is not a critique of disciplinary entrepreneurs or relative professionalisation. Instead, we are concerned to identify the everyday expectations governing forensic science and to compare them against what occurs in the cases we consider later, particularly highlighting how politicisation competes with *uncertainty* when forensic scientists and investigators are collecting and analysing evidence. If the political authorities are invested in the outcome of a high-profile case, the independence of forensics means that the findings offered may be *too* certain. If they wish only to have the identity of the suspect confirmed, lapses or departures from protocol are not anathema but instead provide the opportunity for the authorities to exploit the situation to meet objectives.

Discipline (or Truth Claim) Dominion

Fuchs and Ward (1994: 506) observe that people can process 'limited complexities and deal with limited uncertainty'. In the meantime, and perhaps consequently, all institutions are built on disciplinary knowledges (Foucault, 1972) within which actors must ultimately '*decide on and assume something*' so that they will be able to 'get on with their work' (Fuchs & Ward, 1994: 506, emphasis added). This act of disciplinary closure is taken out of necessity, and it will 'conceal these assumptions as blind spots … Even if they are critical and deconstructionist, organizations must, for example, assume that the distinction critical/mainstream is a good and productive one and bury this assumption in self-evident latencies'. Forensics has been far from critical and deconstructionist. It is a discipline that emerged from innovations in criminalistics to bring epistemic and expert authority to bear on cases. Notable in the development of forensics is the work of French criminalist Edmond Locard, who conceptualised the exchange principle (that the perpetrator of a crime will bring something to and take something from a crime scene), and his American student Paul Kirk, as well as Austrian Hans Gross (1911), who is credited with introducing the application of scientific principles and methods in crime discovery.

Forensics may be distinguished from criminalistics and crime scene investigation (in this book we will regularly use forensics as shorthand for both of these subfields). Emerging historically from these and other sources, from the crime lab and the strictures of testifying, exhibiting and summarising in court as expert witness, forensics is a discipline that possesses at least one of the required features of a reasonably robust discipline: quite strong consensus regarding its basic canon or authorities (Fuchs & Ward, 1994)—or truth claims dominion. Nonetheless, it has growing pains, as we shall see.

The first and foremost consideration is the relative autonomy or dominion of the discipline. We say 'relative autonomy' because, as per the analysis of Fuchs and Ward (1994), some disciplines enjoy a base of 'self-evident assumptions' that are less contested than others, both from within and without. Law, for example, is relatively strong in its institution or power-knowledge (Fuchs & Ward, 1994; Smart, 1990). It is attached to a societal necessity and has developed a set of foundational works setting out its boundedness and functional relations, established principles and methods. It also enjoys quite wide autonomy (discretion or sovereignty) and regenerates its own essential learning canon and performs authoritative evaluations of its own social and political vitality and indispensability. With regard to forensic science, in 2009, the NAS National Research Council report (NAS, 2009) took the pulse, and its assessment was heard loudly across the world's forensics community (Butler, 2015: 4). The report found deficiencies in forensics' foundational research and the means used to test validity and reliability (or institutionalised research culture) (NAS, 2009: 29), in the standardisation of reporting, and in accreditation and certification tied to a code of ethics (NAS, 2009: 21, 25, 26). Among its 12 recommendations, the report called for the creation of a National Institute of Forensic Science, mandated accreditation for crime laboratories, the certification of all forensic professionals under a code of ethics, regular quality assurance, and more research on human observer bias and procedures to reduce bias and error. Interestingly, a subsequent major government report on forensics in the US, by the President's Council of Advisors on Science and Technology (PCAST, 2016: 1), which was struck to consider whether there were 'additional steps that could usefully be taken on the scientific side to strengthen the forensic-science disciplines and ensure the validity of forensic evidence used in the Nation's legal system,' recommended that forensic science should be governed *outside the profession* because, by implication, it has not yet reached a threshold status supportive of self-governance. However, given that this report has been criticised by esteemed forensic scientists for mistaking some fundamental principles of forensic application, the take-away may be that there is some contest regarding the discipline's self-evident assumptions.

Nonetheless, a strong argument exists in support of a forensics truth claims dominion, because forensic scientists, for the most part, do meet the task to provide expert findings when following a set of established principles and approaches. As observed in a review article by leaders in the field (Evett et al., 2017), (on whom we rely for the following), forensic science has depended on inference, specifically on a 'logical, probabilistic approach to the assessment of the probative value of scientific observations' (Evett et al., 2017: 17). Evidence is considered within a 'framework of circumstances,' which may require that the scientist is able to present evidence in light of the 'circumstances relevant to the assessment'. It is also considered in terms of the probative value of observations, which requires that two propositions are assessed or that the forensic scientist considers the respective probability of the propositions (17). In addition, there is the match paradigm and the identification paradigm. *Matching* requires the scientist to make a judgement that the *reference sample* (an item from a known origin such as the suspect) and the *questioned sample* (an item recovered from a disputed origin recovered most often from the crime site or individual) possess characteristic qualities 'within the range of what would be expected' if they both had the same origin or source (18). As Evett et al. note (2017), a match does not confirm the same source and is evidentially neutral or suggests a probability without evidential weight. It is with individualisation or *identification* that the scientist is permitted to state that the probability of the match is such that it is 'reasonable to conclude that the two items came from the same source' (19). In addition, it is for the jury to take into account all of the non-scientific information which may be at play,[2] but Evett et al. (2017: 19) observe that forensic scientists must report on evidence and be free to exercise judgment. They note that in assessing the relevance of survey data to a case in which there is some reference material, the relevance of the survey data needs to be evaluated by someone and the forensic scientist is the most likely candidate.

At the same time, Evett et al. (2017: 19) note that there are misconceptions about what the labs and scientists can offer the courts or the public because even peak industry reports get some fundamentals wrong. These authors observe, for instance, that the 'prosecutor's fallacy' or 'transposed conditional' is an error that the PCAST has committed. As Evett et al. (2017) describe it, assessing the probability that a questioned sample came from a given source is not a task that the forensic scientist should offer to undertake.

> The probability of the truth of a proposition is for the jury not the scientist ... The scientist addresses the probability of the outcome of the comparison if the object were the source of the impression: this probability forms the numerator of the likelihood ratio. Just as important, of course, is the probability of the outcome of the comparison if some other object were the source of the impression. (19)

Equality of Arms

Adversarial justice depends on an equality of arms. A basic tenet of justice relating to the right to counsel, the principle of equality of arms (Silver, 1990) requires that procedural conditions be similarly provided to all parties at trial and sentencing. The concept is found under Article 6 of the *European Convention of Human Rights* and in Article 14 of the *International Covenant on Civil and Political Rights*, and is at the very core of fairness in a criminal trial and equal opportunity to procedural justice in an adversarial or democratic legal system. It involves both substantive and procedural equality and may be evaluated according to the relative capacity of each side to present the strongest possible case. The United Nations Human Rights Committee, in its General Comment 32, maintained that 'the right to equality before the courts and tribunals also ensures equality of arms. This means that the same procedural rights are to be provided to all the parties'.[3] Deviation from the requirement is allowed only where 'based on law' and 'justified on objective and reasonable grounds', and where it does not involve 'actual disadvantage or other unfairness to the defendant'.[4] Included guarantees arising from the principle are the right to: a trial in the presence of the defendant, to defend against charges, to have access to legal counsel, to receive free legal assistance and to examine or have witnesses examined. In the US, in the leading case concerning federal rules of evidence, *Daubert v. Merrell Dow Pharmaceuticals, Inc*, Judge Blackman ruled that the court must engage in a 'flexible' inquiry whose 'overarching subject is the scientific validity – and thus the evidentiary relevance and reliability – of the principles that underlie a proposed submission'.[5]

Outside the Innocence Project, a US organisation that seeks to correct justice system errors retrospectively and does not select cases based on the accused's financial resources, most serious cases of homicide in which forensic resources are used do not remotely match the equality of arms ideal. This claim is supported by some famous exceptions to the rule. When OJ Simpson was charged with double murder in 1995, his lawyer put together a 'dream team' of some of the most prominent legal and forensic experts in the country for his successful defence. Likewise if the famous Dr Shepherd criminal case were tried today, 'few defendants could afford such experts. The DNA expert, who provided free services in the Sheppard case, told a journalist that he would have charged $150,000 in an ordinary case' (Giannelli, 2001: 497).

The differential ability to harness forensic expertise represents an *inequality of arms* between the defence and the prosecution (Koppl & Cowan, 2010). It is accepted that in most criminal cases there will be no equality. Instead, it is presumed that police and prosecutors have a winnable case before they appear before the judge, and that therefore the vast majority of cases will be resolved with a guilty plea of some kind. This is only to say, with McBarnett (1978), that due process is *for* crime control for most people in front of the court, or that the balance is skewed towards efficiency.

Truth from Adversity

A further problem is that the means to produce legal truth may misrepresent the scientific findings. Regarding the science, one of the chief issues is the fitness between adversarial and scientific truth discovery and the dominant paradigm of truth that is held to apply. The adversarial system has been criticised as less desirable than the inquisitorial system in meeting the interests of the truly innocent accused (Steffen, 1988). Steffen (1988: 800) maintains that

> storm clouds linger over the role of truth in the criminal justice system and the capacity of the adversarial process to promote effectively the search for truth as a trial objective. A major point of demarcation between man and animal is the singular ability of man to rationalize. Perhaps it is a tribute to that unique human faculty that we have perpetuated the myth that the calculated distillate of our adversary system is truth.

Fact discovery in the adversarial system depends on the observance of procedural propriety in the service of which lawyering is a craft that finesses the ability to best the opposition, a resource that costs. Given the high error rate in forensic techniques, there is much interpretive play in evaluating some forensic materials and traces, thus offering room for finessing or lawyering in the 'play' of the court (Ewick & Silbey, 1992). As per Koppl and Sacks (2013), the system of adversarial justice creates rewards or 'incentives', and these will result in convictions (or acquittals) that are false. Forensic science analyses come into play in legal proceedings generally only where an exclusion was not obtained and exculpatory evidence is more prone to being

> filtered out before court proceedings. Inculpatory evidence is entered into evidence by the government in legal proceedings. So it is expected that most scientific evidence entered into a court proceeding by the prosecution supports its position. (Budowle et al., 2009: 799)[6]

In the meantime, outcomes at trial are dependent on testimonies and exhibits or documents entered into evidence. Expert witnesses may give evidence in respect of their observations. The forensic scientist is called upon to provide a documentary account of the evidentiary value of their observations of case-relevant materials, processes and examinations for examination-in-chief and cross-examination. In brief, the court requires unbiased and objective evidence and experts, and knowledge based on a high standard of reliability and validity that is open and available for review or retesting and is provided under the accepted view that alternative opinions contrary to expert evidence findings must be honestly held. He or she must not assume the role of an advocate, should state the facts or assumptions underpinning an opinion, should provide the documents on which the opinion is based and should offer opinions on the basis of proper research within the scope of the expertise proffered (Sangha et al., 2010: 28–29).

In their examination of forensic investigations, Sangha et al. (2010) refer to the normative requirement as 'the rhetoric'. This is distinguished from 'the reality' of practice. The NAS report (2009) found in general that inadequate empirical support is provided for the claims made by forensic witnesses, particularly where witnesses aver that there is no error rate in their latent fingerprint identification (Mnookin et al., 2011: 735). An investigation by the Federal Bureau of Investigation (FBI) found scientifically flawed and inaccurate testimony, and testimony beyond the competence of FBI examiners (Kelly & Wearne 1998; OIG, 2006). Highly regarded experts in the field (Mnookin et al., 2011: 736) agree that there is insufficient knowledge regarding the 'capabilities and limitations of any particular pattern discipline' and an inferior evidence base permitting the validation of techniques (Saks & Faigman, 2008). Judge and Mnookin et al. (2011) assert that the 'numerous assertions made both in routine practice and in court are neither backed up by sufficient empirical data or research, nor are the kinds of claims that can be justified or validated simply by reference to longstanding experience' (735–736). According to Koppl and Cowan (2010: 240), 'the current epistemic monopoly in forensic science discourages transparency'.

It is not possible to quantify the extent of deviation from the rhetoric, let alone the experience of good practice. Provided here is support for our major claim that if the legal ideal is dependent on and captured by the metaphor of sunshine or light, that ethic is occluded more pronouncedly where the heat is able to blur processes and procedure or where political or sovereign interests wished to be held at bay are able to penetrate decisively into the crime scene, lab and court.

The Institutional Setting and the Organisational Condition—Or Whose Event Is This?

There are two points of departure where we are concerned with understanding the interplay between forensics and intelligence crime. In the first instance, an event takes place and there is an open question regarding its dominion. 'Whose event is this?' may be the question posed of and by government authorities, and sometimes also private stakeholders.

Moynihan's case study research identified fluidity and ambiguity in shared incident command authority. Commenting on the Oklahoma and Pentagon bombings, he found that 'crucial questions of who was in charge and how authority was transferred were a source of contention and negotiation between members' (2009: 906). In both these cases, command authority was quickly seized by locally based incident commanders, who acknowledged that the assertion was necessary to avoid the authority being usurped by federal agency (906). At the same time, incident commanders at both sites had to share authority with the FBI, who was in charge of the crime scene investigation but deferred search and rescue (906). Moynihan found that even where there is an incident command structure, home organisation loyalty produces a dispersion of authority and actors will assert some autonomy to the extent that orders from the incident commander may not be carried out.

Moynihan observes that trust between agency actors, including that developed through previous informal relationships or social capital is crucial to *deconfliction* (908). For instance, in Oklahoma City a 'crucial meeting' was held between the mayor, fire chief, police and a senior FBI agent who were all regular golfing partners. At the Pentagon, office workers were permitted to return to the building to clear national security matters. The crime scene was 'juggled' with other tasks involving national security actors and interests and its control negotiated by actors who drew on trust relationships developed through prior working relationships (909). Moynihan found that clear demarcation of authority is insufficient for effective network coordination, which requires the trust fostered through positive working relationships (912). In sum, event dominion may be slippery, with trust needed to fill the gaps in clear demarcations as mandates may appear to belong to municipal, state or federal police, or even to a private corporate body. It may be added that at the top of the hierarchy are the intelligence services, which have a superior mandate to the site in cases where there may be a national security interest.

The second point of departure relates to the industrial reward structure available to the organisational actors. There is a continuum between individual actor corruption (bad apple), occupational level corruption (rotten barrel, context bias) and sector or institutional level 'capture' or compromise (systemic, institutional or paradigm bias). At the lowest level, of the individual, there is negligence, fraud and breaches of code. In many organisations and institutions, forensic services included, it is often most convenient to rely on the belief that errors are produced by bad or improperly trained people who are indifferent to the moral good (Koppl & Cowan, 2010: 237). For example, in the UK, the West Midlands Serious Crime Squad was disbanded after courts found that officers of the squad were involved in the torture and intimidation of suspects in the 1970s and 1980s (Sangha et al., 2010: 12). In Los Angeles, the Ramparts Division was similarly a pocket of deviance within the Los Angeles Police Department (LAPD) (Koppl & Sacks, 2013: 129). In South Australia, forensic pathologist, Dr. Colin Manock conducted autopsies to determine cause of death in hundreds of cases, including three baby deaths between October 1992 and August 1993, but did so in many cases including these baby deaths claiming facts that were found not to be supported by obvious evidence, as per a coronial inquiry that was struck to review them (Moles, 2004: ch. 10). Despite that it has been established that that Dr. Manock performed autopsies for purposes of determining cause of death without his possessing the required credentials, South Australia has continued to resist acting on the full implication of this finding. As the gross errors of the individual were wrongly permitted to continue, those who did not step into provide system correction were also then providing the bad practice with a institutional insulation (see Moles, 2004). In general, there is a preference to de-institutionalise poor performance by proffering a rotten apple or rotten pocket explanation, or a view that locates the basis of the problem in individual actor or small group misapplication or malfeasance.[7]

Scientists, prosecutors and police investigators operate within organisations in which scarce rewards depend on evaluations within an organisational system that values predictable productivities according to system preferences. Here, we may look for an explanation for errors in the way organisations work. Professional autonomy and common principles or assumptions are two markers of disciplinary strength, but the dependency of labs and scientists on police and prosecutors is the ordinary organisational context (Koppl & Cowan, 2010). Familiar working networks involve crime scene investigators, detectives and forensic scientists in support of an outcome that minimises resistance. Generally, actors in any organisational system recognise that forcing the political fulcrum or the normative political centre into restiveness is like labouring against centrifugal forces. To take action or produce findings that are inconsistent with 'usual suspect' identities may be perceived as failing to properly contextualise one's occupational or professional standards, and casts the professional as overtly idealistic or ideological (counter-ideological), occupying a generally unenviable 'whistle-blower' position. In principle, an expert should be acting 'in the cause of justice'[8]; but some experts perceive that a lucrative pathway exists to maximise their influence and status in consultative roles through which the reward is greater where novel applications may be finessed. This second point is well-rehearsed in the major reports and inquiries on forensic science (see, for example, DOJ IG, 1998; OIG, 2006; NAS, 2009; PCAST, 2016; Goudge, 2008; Kaufman, 1998).

Political crimes, it is reasonable to propose, should be notable for deviations in investigatory and prosecutorial regularity and figure prominently among cases of miscarriages of justice. It does appear to be the case that most miscarriages occur within dirty pockets or in the prosecution of political crime. In their account of the 'British experience' of forensic miscarriages of justice, Sangha et al. (2010: 197–211) found that four out of the nine miscarriage cases involved political actors (in this case, the Irish Republican Army [IRA]) and two of the remaining five involved a deviant police pocket (the West Midlands Police). In the case of the so-called 'Birmingham 6', 21 people were killed and 162 people were injured when two bombs exploded at public houses in Birmingham. Six people who were on their way to the funeral of a man killed in a previous bombing mishap were arrested and then all signed confessions which they subsequently wished to retract on the argument that the confessions were obtained after beatings by the police. Lord Denning denied the Court of Appeal application in this case on the grounds that allowing it would be to countenance the view that the police may be guilty of perjury, violence and threats to the accused and that the obtained confessions were involuntary, and further that such a finding would be 'appalling' to the extent that 'sensible' people would say that the process 'cannot go further'.[9] However, Chris Mullen published *Error of Judgment: the Birmingham Bombings in 1986*, and the Home Secretary referred the case to the Court of Appeal in 1987, were the six accused successfully argued their case based on fresh evidence that the confessions may have been unsound and that they were subjected to police violence, as well as on expert opinion that the evidence of explosive residues found on their hands was based on an unreliable inference. Specifically, the tests carried out by the Home Office forensic scientist Dr Skuse to determine the presence of nitro-glycerine from swabs taken from the hands and belongings of the accused led to conclusions that were 'demonstrably wrong judged by the state of forensic science in 1974'.[10] Several other convictions of people prosecuted for IRA bombings were also ruled unsafe on appeal (Guilford 4, Maguire 7, Judith Ward), leading to a review in part intended to identify and correct 'errors in human judgment that still slip through the criminal justice system' (Royal Commission on Criminal Justice, 1991; Sangha et al., 2010: 197–202).

In the US, political cases such as those involving the Black Panthers and other COINTELPRO and MINARET targets and post-911 terrorism suspects betray a similar pattern of police and prosecutorial abuse. Under the FBI (and Directors William Session (1987–1993) and Louis Freeh (1993–2001), high-profile cases, including the Oklahoma City bombing, the 1993 World Trade Center bombing, and the Ruby Ridge and Waco standoffs, have seen federal agents and the FBI crime lab engage in bad or illegal practices. Veteran FBI crime lab chemist (explosive residue analyst) and special agent Frederic Whitehurst complained to his FBI superiors that sloppy lab work between 1990 and 1995 and in some case altered conclusions was proffered to help the government's case (Thomas & Mills, 1995).

In the trial of Walter Moodie for the mail bombing of Judge Robert Vance, the specialists were not qualified to testify on the subject of explosives residue and, according to Whitehurst, the conclusions offered were akin to fabricating evidence. In the Ruby Ridge case, the Justice Department task force said that if such a performance was '*typical of high profile homicide cases involving the death of a federal law enforcement officer and two citizens (Vicki and Sammy Weaver), we wonder about the response to matters of less importance*' (quoted in Thomas & Mills, 1995, emphasis added). In another high-profile case, the Madrid bombing that occurred on 11 March 2004 on the commuter trains of Madrid and killed 191 people, the FBI supported a conviction based on fingerprint evidence of Brandon Mayfield. Yet Spanish investigators found the actual bomber and an FBI Office of the Inspector General report then ruled that the FBI forensic laboratories and fingerprint protocol and examination were less foolproof than previously thought (Stacey & Unit, 2005; OIG, 2006).

This is in the *context* in which the vast majority (if not totality, as below) of its *everyday* or *routine* cases are found to be sound. The FBI reviewed lab work in more than 250 cases in the mid-1990s and reported that over a million examinations a year were conducted and that it is constantly subject to

> extraordinarily vigorous challenges in court. ... To date the FBI has found no evidence of tampering, evidence fabrication, or failure to report exculpatory evidence ... Any finding of such misconduct will result in tough and swift action by the FBI. (Thomas & Mills, 1995)

It follows that securitisation is to constitutional authority what politicisation is to organisational authority. Refinements in forensics will come to naught if what is available for investigatory recovery and forensic exploitation are only the remnants after site securitisation (that is, where the evidence left for forensics is only that deemed not to be threatening to national security).

Crime Scene Recovery and Narrative Bias

There are basic processes involved in the collection of forensic evidence that begin with the establishment of a crime scene. A crime scene is an array of materials that, as per Locard, may retain traces of exposure to a criminal actor's interaction with it. It is a requirement of police and prosecutorial services to identify suspects where criminal offences have occurred. What is required is the preservation and protection of physical and chemical traces as potential forensic evidence and the exploitation of materials in the support of the criminal prosecution.

This includes, as discussed above, the crime scene's identification as such. Failure to designate or recognise a crime scene is perhaps the first oversight of crime scene investigation and forensics, a problem often related to the issues around establishing investigatory command authority and control discussed above. A crime scene may not be recognised. It is an act of expert discretion that is not always recorded or attributed to a specific actor. In addition, the forensic attribution is not always resourced. Consequently, there may not be adequate accountability for the failure to properly make that timely designation. The failure to dedicate adequate, expert and sufficiently authorised professionals to a scene and thus to draw from it what it possesses while it is still ripe for crime discovery and recovery accounts for much or most of what goes awry in criminal investigation.

Establishing Investigatory Command Authority and Securing Crime Scene Control

It is the responsibility of police and prosecutors to claim or identify a crime and jurisdiction and to establish authority over any sites or property involved in the perpetration of the crime. Investigators are also required to ensure that information to be used for criminal prosecutions is permissibly obtained. Where crime is not claimed or is misidentified and the authority over crime sites is incomplete or ambiguous, there will be an opportunity for inculpatory and exculpatory evidence to be excluded, to vanish or to be tampered with. The onset of the custody chain is with the assertion of the crime and the jurisdiction over named sites and items of investigatory interest. To make this point more clear, acting to designate a place or event as a certain kind of thing is a requisite of propriety in the rhetoric of justice, law and police and forensic professionalism (Sangha et al., 2010: 5), but it is also more or less an artefact of the power relation across authorities.

Establishing who will take control over a crime scene or command a criminal investigation is not always straightforward. Where a possible crime involves the mandates of a variety of government or non-government authorities, there is a need to rule either formally or informally on dominion and institute a chain of command. In the event, where crime scenes are nominated within the mandate by multiple authorities, competing organisational views or perspectives will be produced through a 'mixture of network and hierarchy', in which command authority must be negotiated and is contentious and dependent on trust relations (Moynihan, 2009: 296), but where the boundaries demarcating who is in and out of the network remain 'hard to define' (905). As noted by Moynihan (2009: 895), a clear hierarchy of authority is essential to ensure that the requirements of criminal discovery and forensic recovery are adequately fulfilled. In the US, a management structure called

Incident System Command (ICS) has been introduced to establish the management structure to support deconfliction where events require the involvement of multiple agencies that receive federal funds (297). This system has been credited with helping to implement a standard framework and common lexicon for participating agencies and thus overcoming interagency conflicts (905).

Criminal investigators must seek to interview witnesses as soon as possible, but in the meantime the prosecution must ensure that suspects are interviewed properly with respect to the rules of evidence and constitutional protections. Hearsay and coerced confessions are normally not permitted as evidence because the circumstances in which the statements were given are not adequately reviewable with respect to any oppression, coercion or promised goods that may have attended their obtainment (Ashworth, 1994: 93, 105–109). Where police informants 'create' a crime (Mueller & Stewart, 2015) and thus also a criminal act by a targeted person by introducing materials later to be used in evidence, the technique is largely permissible, so long as law enforcement actors are not 'over-involved' (Ashworth, 1994: 93–96; Colquitt, 2004). Courts in the US, the UK, Canada and Australia have permitted the practice such that a defence of entrapment is unlikely to deter police or protect the accused from unfavourable outcomes stemming from the practice of covert evidence production (Colquitt, 2004).

The Innocence Project offers a window into the misuse or abuse of evidence retrieval in police interviews and forensic techniques and evidence. Overall, between one-fifth and one-quarter of its 377 cases[11] of wrongful conviction were the result, in part, of a false admission or confession (according to data from the Innocence Project, 2020; Narchet et al., 2011; Drizin & Leo, 2004). In addition, invalid or faulty forensic science was a contributing factor in two-thirds of the first 200 exonerees (Saks & Koehler, 2005) and in the convictions of more than half of all DNA exonerees (Innocence Project, 2020). It has also been found that the forensic science judgments in 300 DNA exonerations were based on inadequate or fabricated testing and analysis on conclusions not adequately supported by the data (to the point of misconduct in some cases) (Garrett, 2011). As observed by Koppl and Sacks (2013: 132), false felony convictions may be pegged at probably at least 3.3%.

As per our previous discussion, that percentage can reasonably be expected to rise in cases involving national security or *high-value* political suspects. There is a great deal of pressure on police to resolve such cases quickly, in order to remove the pressure applied by stakeholders including media, demand groups and legislators. As a consequence, political crime has frequently involved police oppressive conduct or wrongdoing and/or the concoction or falsification of evidence and the non-disclosure by prosecution and/or forensic scientists (Ashworth, 1994: 13).

Exploiting the Crime Scene: Retrieving, Processing and Preserving Relevant Information, Materials or Evidence

A 'critical stage in the forensic process' (Julian et al., 2012: 26), crime scene processing recognises that a geographical place is the likely site of a contributing act of criminal occurrence.[12] It involves securing the scene and preserving it in an uncontaminated form to enable the collection and sampling of evidence by the most appropriate practitioners or expert actors. As provided in the work of Lee et al. (2001), investigators are instructed to follow protocols or methods; and crime scene investigation requires linking (processing, reconstructing and reporting) with reference to consilience in the observance of the constituent elements (scene securing, surveying and definition, documenting, interviewing, examining, photographing, and sketching).

Responders are more or less capacitated to, or constrained by, professional ethics; an 'accurate and fair criminal justice outcome can only occur if the scene is processed effectively and professionally' (Julian et al., 2012: 25). The conduct of criminal investigation is set out in various legislation, policy and codes of practice and case law and encompasses the protection of rights and the duties of investigators. As outlined regarding mistakes or errors below, departures from these professional standards or ethics may be accounted for with reference to the everyday or routine constraints imposed by administrative resources or pressures and with regard to mistaken beliefs or superseding priorities.

Preliminary Review of Materials and Working Hypotheses

Wagner-Pacifici (2010: 1356) argues that the attempt to bind events within material and rhetorical boundaries is the objective or mandate of institutional discourses. The co-dependence of power and knowledge instructs us that recognition of a thing is dependent on experience and authority, or the persuasions of power. This is in accord with the sociology of knowledge approach to discourse (SKAD), which posits that an interpretive frame that is provided in an authoritative discourse offers a handle on an event. This 'makes it possible to understand what a phenomenon is all about' (Keller, 2011: 57); in the lab, in the terminology used and in the conventions followed there is a nomenclature that guides or structures the review of phenomena.[13] It is necessary, even if problematic, that actors and agencies use a working hypothesis based on a preliminary review of materials. It is familiar practice within scientific discovery that a hypothesis is needed that informs the discovery of evidence and structures a logical pathway to a finding.

At the same time, it is during the preliminary review of a case or site that a potentially broad array of hypotheses may be mooted or considered for further investigation. The quick production and dissemination by officials of a working hypothesis concerning a crime scene binds events and avoids their innate 'restlessness' (Wagner-Pacifici, 2010). It is also the case that once investigatory resources are spent in the pursuit of a working hypothesis, as more actors and resources have been committed to an outcome, there is a strategic inertia and organisational bias supportive of that working hypothesis (Hodgkinson & Wright, 2002). In a typical homicide, investigators may arrive on scene at a location known to police as involved in the drug trade and quickly adopt the working hypothesis that the homicide is related to drug trade activity. This sets up a *confirmation bias* for evidence discovery, which indicates what is sensible to search for, collect or examine in support of that hypothesis. If the hypothesis allows investigators to clear the case relatively effortlessly with reference to the 'usual suspects', organisational efficiencies including careerism will tend to favour this outcome.

There are at least three points to be made concerning the context in which a working hypothesis is linked to confirmation bias and tunnel vision. The 'default' context is the individual level. The skilled detective is a conduit, ready and able to provide uptake of the most objectively relevant information for sorting according to the most logical and likely explanation of events. This is also the romanticised view of criminal investigation. Homicide police are perhaps among the most skilled criminal investigators[14]; and in the ideal, the detective is free to roam where the 'scent' takes him or her, unconstrained by budget, jurisdiction or administrative interference. The second context is administrative or organisational. Accordingly, the discretionary locus is somewhere in the upper third of an organisation's ranks, which stipulates the templates, schedules, protocols and efficiencies or scripts according to which cases are to be quickly resolved. As observed above, the working hypothesis may derive in the context of organisational and administrative preferences for efficiency. In most organisations collective experience is sorted into types and these provide the templates against which the live case may be matched. There may be an effort to parachute in investigators from elsewhere and to provide them with parameters for evidence collection, including around who to interview and what trace or pattern evidence to look for. Lastly, the disciplinary or discursive power of a working hypothesis may derive from an exogenous origin. Thus, it may derive from a 'higher level' of the organisation or from outside the organisation. There can exist particular reasons why a working explanation has derived from outside the routine domain of investigators. For example, there may be a perceived conflict of interest; or prior relationships between suspects and an investigatory team may produce unsound prosecutions. In addition, the crime may be thought to involve actors connected to investigations and investigators from other agencies (such as the FBI or DEA).

Where an investigation is exogenous in the sense described above, it may be 'political', at least from the point of view of working investigators. In one sense this means that external constraints can be brought to bear on the selection or identification of investigatory targets and the formulation of motives and suspects. In the cases of wrongful conviction discussed above, and in the examples suggestive of the same provided below, investigators may want to task themselves with discovering evidence within the constraints of the preferred hypothesis. According to Reason (1990: 173), in a complex system there are frontline operators and there are also actors who manage or administer systems, so that errors are 'active' when performed by the former and 'latent' when performed by those removed in time and space from immediate involvement. For example, occupational trust relationships in policing can easily push first responders to follow the advice of senior officers instead of making decisions based on 'book learning' (de Lint, 1998; Julian, 2005). Where there is clear opposition between the 'pure' requirements of crime scene investigatory practices or professionalism and the interests of external parties, it is necessary first to document the nature of the departure from form and then to provide a logical basis for future departures from form. This is not to say that there is a hard distinction between political and non-political crimes in this regard. Rather, there is a continuum of influence on the actor networks of criminal investigation in which exogenous pressures will be greatest where powerful external actors and interests are clear and more or less unified on objectives.

There is a growing body of scholarship on how national security or security intelligence actors or agencies are in conflict with criminal justice over the jurisdiction of evidence deriving from events that normally requires a transparent record of the transmission of information into evidence (Roach, 2010; de Lint & Kassa, 2017). When this occurs, the justice ideal mandates that there ought to be something akin to full disclosure, equality of arms, the presumption of innocence and the right to challenge evidence in front of one's peers. However, from the intelligence point of view, criminal justice processing is a form of backwashing. When intelligence has cultivated (gardened or ripened) an illicit actor network and cannot draw more from it, it may turn some of the targets over to criminal justice actors for prosecution. There been much written about the movement of intelligence into evidence for this purpose (see, for example, Mueller & Stewart, 2011; Aaronson, 2011; Zedner, 2007; Monaghan & Walby, 2012). In 'compromise', courts and prosecution have been keen to bend to the claims of national security actors and accept that an agency summary may pass for disclosure, that the prosecution cannot jeopardise intelligence assets or introduce security vulnerabilities, and that in cases of terrorism, the emergent legal regime (terrorism legislation, judges rules, interpretation of precedent) will enable the presumption of innocence to rather firmly disappear (de Lint & Kassa, 2017). In this regard, as noted by Roach (2010: 65), counter-terrorism is 'a secretive intelligence-driven process' that is 'utterly incompatible with … the presumption of innocence and proof of guilt'.

When a case instead develops within the jurisdiction of the attorney-general as a potential crime in which the involvement of intelligence actors or assets and is *discovered*, there is little that can be found in the academic literature concerning how actor and institution authority is negotiated or brokered. Our expectation or hypothesis is therefore that when a criminal prosecution finds its way into the claimed domain of security intelligence, intelligence actors and agencies will generally be able to rebuff whatever authority (and criminality) claims are not consistent with their interests or those of their elite or apex representatives. Consequently, we expect to see a blurring of authorities inclusive of asserting a criminal designation or criminal event where intelligence actors or assets may be involved.

Measures of Identity and Review

As has been described above, the designation of an event by authorities prefigures the review of its investigation. This is to say nothing more than that governments do not wish to be surprised by events, since efficiency is perceived to equate with a timely—that is, immediate or anticipatory—response. There is thus an order that may appear on the surface as an action-reaction, and this is true in routine cases and ordinary events. But surprising events are perceived to require policy adjustments, and in actuality government does ready the response and is vigilant for potentially disruptive events (including natural disasters or pandemics or political assassinations) and in its preparations for a remedy. In this respect, the event is not so much followed by but anticipates a narrative according to which there will be a review of the response. As mentioned above, a narrative follows a policy that anticipates a certain type of event.

Particularly concerning the policy requirement to pre-configure a covering government narrative there will be a conflict with criminal justice in the resolution of big events. Government preparation on broad measures of government efficacy runs counter to the uncertain origin of the event (crime) that may be longstanding in criminal justice. In liberal democracies, criminal prosecution follows an adversarial process in which individual liberty is restricted or denied only where there is sufficient certainty that this may be justified by way of a criminal process based on a finding of fact, a finding that cannot be made by executive authorities. The integrity of fact-finding in the criminal justice system is ensured through the separation of witnesses and the independence of experts so that they are not subject to cross-contamination or tainted by coercive or compelling influence. Scientific methods and processes, including blinding or blinded evaluation, support the independence of facts and insulate them from influence by the values of potentially interested actors before those facts come to bear as evidence in the adversarial court.

At the pinpoint of establishing with strong certainty the criminality of particular persons there is the intersection of the interests of the prosecution and the defence and an accounting of errors, missteps or bad faith in the obtainment of evidence. As we have observed, the integrity of the process depends on the relative equality of forces at this intersection. Much of the criminal procedure involves the (sedimented) resolutions of rights-efficiency contests, victories of fairness and the avoidance of systemically bad outcomes. As we shall see, although we have a record of measures of false positives, forensic fact-finding is still not quarantined from partisan prosecutorial interests. This means that errors are more likely to be inculpatory; but, also of importance, it leaves open sufficient ambiguity so that the sovereign interest in a certain outcome is not comprehensively shut out. The relative intimacy between forensic labs and prosecutors and law enforcement is an obvious site.

Errors and Bias

As neatly summarised by Du (2017: 143), errors fall into two types (false positive and false negative) and three categories, namely, random, gross and systemic. These will each affect the reliability of expert testimony. First, there is the random error, described as an error other than a systematic error (Suzuki et al., 2016: 791) that has sources in 'nondeterministic counterfactuals, sampling variability, a mechanism that generates exposure events and measurement variability' (Suzuki et al., 2016: 791). According to Du (2017: 143), random errors may be minimised by replications or contact tests. Gross errors 'are mainly caused by operators' and are 'due to the negligence of measurements caused by undue human errors' such as recording an erroneous number (Du, 2017: 141). Some gross errors are 'errors against standard', which occur when the forensic scientist is not able to follow or smudges the standards. These may be reduced or nearly eliminated. The 'broadest' category of error is the systematic error, which represents a corruption of the context or scientific independence of the agency, lab or lead personnel. Under systemic error, the means of grounding results in code practices is 'systematically' perverted. This will undermine all the results obtained from methods or equipment, with a tending towards the prosecution, leading to inaccurate results.

Du (2017: 141) observes that systemic and random errors can be tolerated up to a certain level, and that standard is set through peer review, publications and maximum error rates. He notes that the confidence level of error rate is usually necessarily very small to meet scientific requirements, usually between 1 and 5%, or where 95% is generally the acceptable confidence coefficient found 'sufficient for supporting the trier to establish the truth' (142). Du also states that there is 'a strong relationship between the hypothesis test and the error rate' and that it is consequently 'very rare for a scientist to reject a hypothesis without stating the level of confidence at which it was rejected' (141).

Across these classes of errors are the two types of errors—false positives and false negatives. A false negative error refers to the mistaken rejection of a true proposition and a false positive error refers to the mistaken affirmation of a false proposition. In criminal justice processes, from crime identification to suspect matching, there is an opportunity to falsely affirm or falsely disconfirm. However, there is wide variation in the tolerance for permitting the non-prosecution of crime and illegalities across crime types. The Innocence Project case study research has demonstrated that false positive cases are overwhelmingly those involving indigent street criminal accused. As critical criminologists point out, 'crimes of the powerful', particularly where they involve powerful state or corporate actors in pursuit of a tacit government objective, are more susceptible to false negative prosecutorial error. As we observed above, where the first order claiming of the event is by intelligence actors (securitisation), the facts of the crime may be archived or disposed of according to national security preferences.

Context Bias or Context Effects

Koppl and Cowan (2010: 247) make the observation that forensic science is 'a complex tightly-coupled system' within which 'organisations, processes, technologies and incentive systems mediate conflict between individuals (suspects, police, scientists, expert witnesses, lawyers, judges and jurors).' According to these authors, the system produces 'structure-based errors'. Research has found that investigators seek to develop an account of an event that is influenced by cognitive, systematic or context bias (Dovidio et al., 1997; Greenwald & Banaji, 1995). The reasons for this have been tested and retested in various studies, beginning with Milgram and Zimbardo's research on obedience (Zimbardo et al., 2000; Haslam & Reicher, 2012). It is known by anecdote but also from empirical evidence that the context (world-view, class, ethnicity, professional discipline) will influence investigator preferences regarding outcomes (Dror & Cole, 2010; Dror & Hampikian, 2011; Jost et al., 2009). Once an account of an event has been uttered by a respected authority, the investigative actor will be prejudiced to find in favour of it.

Context bias is defined as decision-making that is influenced by knowledge of information that is not relevant or in excess of what is required for the analytical task (Page et al., 2011). Kassin et al. (2013) note that the forensic confirmation bias is possible because of the elasticity of the evidence, where even the 'gold standard' of DNA testing may be subject to some context biasing influence. Forensic confirmation bias (Kassin et al., 2013: 45) denotes 'the class of effects through which an individual's pre-existing beliefs, expectations, motives, and situational context influence the collection, perception, and interpretation of evidence during the course of a criminal case'. The interactions between law enforcement and forensics in practice produce many avenues for context effects. In this regard, and as noted above, the NAS has recommended the removal of public forensic laboratories from the administrative control of law enforcement and prosecutors.[15]

Confirmation Bias, Corroboration Inflation and Tunnel Vision

An operating or working hypothesis is a necessary expedient but also a stimulus that may have derived from a judgment. Once an outcome is preferred, there is a growing interest to maintain support for it so that subsequent examinations will seek to confirm the original hypothesis. This is a fertile environment for the gestation of 'tunnel vision', encouraging a fixation on one particular person of interest (Findlay & Scott, 2006), and the collection and analysis of inculpatory evidence while exculpatory evidence is overlooked or discounted (Haber & Haber, 2013: 65). As noted by Haber and Haber (2013: 65), where 'confirmation bias' is at play, the 'outcome of an investigation is biased by the initial evidence and/or belief; [and] further investigation seeks to confirm the initial belief and ignores or discounts contrary evidence'. It is present where 'an individual's pre-existing beliefs, expectations, motives, and situational context influence the collection, perception, and interpretation of evidence during the course of a criminal case' (65).

As Kassin observes, confessions will also bias subsequent forensic judgments in what is referred to as 'corroboration inflation' (Kassin, 2012). This may occur where a polygraph is set up to be biased towards failing when other forensic judgments have already been made against the offender. As discussed by Kassin et al. (2013) pre-judgment expectations are an infuence throughout the criminal justice process from interrogation through to eyewitnesses, jurors and judges (citing Kassin et al., 2003; Narchet et al., 2011; Charman et al., 2009; Lange et al., 2011; Halverson et al., 1997; Hasel & Kassin, 2009; Dror & Cole, 2010; Dror & Hampikian, 2011). Providing some direction to forensic investigation is necessary, as observed earlier. However, appraisals by experts may be contaminated by these pre-judgment expectations (Kassin et al., 2003; Kukucka & Kassin, 2014; Budowle et al., 2009; Stoel et al., 2014; Page et al., 2012). Altogether, as summarised by Jost et al. (2009: 41, 42), 'the field of social psychology has not seriously doubted the existence of implicit stereotyping and prejudice since at least the early 1990s, if not earlier … [and] the existence of implicit bias is beyond reasonable doubt'. The NAS found serious flaws in the contextual conditions that were productive of cognitive bias (NAS, 2009: 24). According to the NAS (2009), poor forensic science was the most common cause of/factor in the corroboration of mistaken eyewitness identification and false confession, a finding also made in a study of Innocence Project cases conducted by Kassin et al. (2012). In much study of forensic confirmation bias in the forensic sciences, it is concluded that they are plagued with contextual bias (Kassin et al., 2013; Jost et al., 2009).

All categories of errors may be reduced where context effects are designed out of the system. This might be accomplished if institutional structure was permissive. It would involve a system of limiting expertise recognition by the courts on the basis of specific disciplinary accreditation. It would also require a means to certify lab operations as equally available to and independent from each party of the adversarial process (Du, 2017: 143). In any event, the lab and its expertise should be made available to the defence, as per Koppl and Cowan (2010). In addition, court testimony from forensic examiners could be monitored and reported on for areas of deficiency.[16] Context bias is reduced where there is adequate equality of arms to support independent examination of evidence and cross-examination of evidence and expert testimony (Giannelli, 2001: 492). The current situation in most jurisdictions is that, apart from accreditation and expert certification, most of the steps outlined above have not been incorporated into standard practice.

Where security intelligence actors have a significant voice, the diagnosis and prognosis may well be worse. Accordingly, what recedes is a relatively open initial diagnostics as well as curiosity, transparency, consistent observance and the application of standard practice. What is expected to pertain is secrecy and confidentiality, inconsistent application of or departure from good practice and a relatively closed diagnostics absent of curiosity.

Discussion and Implications for This Study

With regard to the components of crime scene investigation and forensic practice there are principles or rhetoric and there is practice that departs from those principles in ways that have been more or less predicted in work on the miscarriage of justice and corruption. The standard explanation for this is that the introduction of political or special interest into the craft or expert domain in the absence of strong oversight and accountability leads to the vast majority of these lapses from form. Our hypothesis is that this explanation is sufficient for the vast majority of cases but may be inadequate where national security actors exercise sovereign discretion.

In Koppl and Cowan's (2010: 238) analysis, forensic science organisations may be understood in terms of a persuasion game model. In this, they posit a suboptimal decision-making environment where 'the jury as a naïve decision-maker and the crime lab is a sophisticated monopoly supplier of information having an interest in the naïve party's decision'. Koppl and Cowan argue that 'biased forensic science as introduced by the forensic expert witness may induce bias in the decision-making of credulous jurors. Here, the forensic expert witness frames the evidence and anchors the evidence so as to tell a story, either explicitly or implicitly for the prosecution' (Koppl & Cowan, 2010: 238). They argue that the supplier chain is a monopoly (of police—forensic laboratory—forensic expert—prosecutor) that serves a 'naïve buyer (either an unsophisticated judge or jury)'. Under these conditions,

> a *full information decision will not generally emerge.* The current organization of forensic science creates a persuasion game in which the single source supplier of information is biased and sophisticated and the receiver of information is naïve. Under these circumstances, the information cannot be 'strongly opposed' since the only supplier of the forensic science results resides in the biased monopoly supplier of information. There may be an interested party who would like to challenge the evidence, namely the defense counsel. But the current structure typically leaves the defense without the knowledge and resources needed to launch a challenge. The result is a less than full information decision which may lead to errors. (Koppl & Cowan, 2010: 238, emphasis added)

We are concerned with more than visibility here; we are concerned with heat. We know that public interest will put heat on criminal investigators, prosecutors and elected officials and that this is understood by the term politicisation; but it is particularly the interests that may oppose routine practices that are of most importance to this examination. Within those, the special interests that may seek to deploy criminal enterprises for political purpose are our focus. We seek to carry out a reasonably robust comparison between the best practice and a seriously flawed application of standard crime scene and forensic discovery protocols so that we may assess some range or level of departure in our selected cases. In sum, we would like to measure such departure as an indication, at least, of the presence of relative heat or politicisation.

If authorities have a differential influence on the direction of investigations and if investigations, once initiated, will tend to confirm prior investigatory conclusions, this effect may be expected to be strongest where those authorities are relatively powerful and unified in their interest in a particular outcome and where investigators are aware of those preferred outcomes. In a study based on interviews with forensic examiners (Charlton et al., 2010), it was found that the interest in closure, a definitive result or in solving crimes and catching criminals was most pronounced in serious and high-profile cases. The interviewees also expressed a strong desire to avoid a false positive. Given that most investigators will hold a 'just world' belief regarding the behaviour of their organisation and of political actors within the international system, it is not surprising that careerism within organisations aligns with the wish to avoid coming into conflict with the views of the political leadership (Ruhe, 1991). These imposed expectations of investigators effect basic perceptions and behaviour, often without awareness of their own desire or wish to support beliefs held by leadership (as per Simon's (1957: 198) 'bounded rationality').

In the following chapters we will review by the case study method apex and intelligence crimes to note the departures from form and practice. The analysis is carried out to test the standard and alternative hypotheses regarding the likely reasons for such departures. That is to say, we expect these cases to confirm the existence of politicisation that detracts from regular practice, but that the politicisation appears to be evaded through information control or *intelligent (sovereign) discretion.*

It would be useful to know a lot about rates of errors across type of case and organisational and institutional context, however, according to Gross (2013), this is largely an 'unknowable figure.' Exoneration findings permit the evaluation of cases known to have involved errors, and several studies have examined the distribution of errors or misconduct in such cases (Dror & Charlton, 2006: 604). The best means of identifying such data—the Innocence Project in the US and the Criminal Cases Review Commission in England—is not all that fit for this purpose. According to the National Registry of Exonerations, reviews resulted in 2616 exonerations (including 1020 homicide exonerations) between 1989 and April 20, 2020 (law.umich.edu). The best we have at present is, as observed above, a gross guestimate of between 1 and 5% of serious violent offences that come to a mistaken or wrong finding.

In general, we would like to know the conditions under which a departure from form is formally or unofficially acknowledged where there is an exoneration or where cases are withdrawn. Obviously, there will be innovations in principles or discoveries of applications or techniques, but these also represent an attempt to push the current boundaries.

> Just when a scientific principle or discovery crosses the line between the experimental and demonstrable stages is difficult to define. Somewhere in this twilight zone the evidential force of the principle must be recognized, and while courts will go a long way in admitting expert testimony deduced from a well-recognized scientific principle or discovery, the thing from which the deduction is made must be sufficiently established to have gained general acceptance in the particular field in which it belongs. (*Frye v. United States*. 293 F. 1013 (D.C. Cir. 1923))

Our hypothesis is that where the crime involves transactional political interests there will be more departures from standard, technique or principle. These will include failures in designating a site, in authorising properly vetted routine authorities, in securing and recovering trace or material evidence, in applying techniques, and in

Stage Action	Artefact	Competencies	Faults
Authorize (establish)	Event	Event authority claimed Establish CS dominion and security Follow prosecutorial requisites	Crime unclaimed or incorrect CS transgressed Prosecution requirements breached
Narrate (stipulate)	Scene	Collect and preserve evidence Examine, identify and test evidence	Mis- or un-identified CS and contents Failure to collect or identify Evidence not tested or examined
Review (confirm)	Report	Demonstrate technique Limit conclusion	Inappropriate or misapplied Summary beyond scope

Fig. 2.1 Forensics steps, measures and errors

interpreting and summarising or reporting the results. Such cases will also be more likely to involve the application of novel practices, techniques or interpretations.

Broadly, we can classify these departures from good or adequate practice. As we have observed above, this may be done with reference to the necessary stages and artefacts as well as competencies and faults. In all of this, some departures are more catastrophic or potentially so than others. If a crime scene is not identified or secured under proper authority, then there is no recovery of information inculpatory or exculpatory. Depending on the nature of the crime, there may not ever be a capacity to revisit the site or collect evidence (see Fig. 2.1).

Conclusion

Our argument is based on analysis of the governance or control of certainties with respect to criminal investigations and forensic reporting. The take-away from this brief and selective overview is that there are some robust systems and measures of forensics and the discipline is also developing techniques of standardisation, accreditation and a body of research and culture. At the level of governance, there is a relative autonomy or independence from law enforcement and prosecution influence or bias that is finding its way toward a disciplinary dominion.[17] Improvement requires that more attention be given to the conditions required for certain outcomes, particularly through good governance, accreditation, the development of common principles and measures, and lab and scientist independence from law enforcement and prosecutor administration.

Our argument is not that there is a lack of professionalism, expertise or commitment. Rather, the point of critical forensics is that the main institutional conflict will emerge from the quest for certainty in systems, measures and procedures. The craft requirement to follow scientific means and protocols will nevertheless remain relatively accommodating of an open-ended institutional context and contrary interests in predetermined outcomes. Yet, the normative and institutional requirements may be in a permanent misalignment. In this regard, Ericson's observation is instructive : 'High standards of due process, evidence, proof, and culpability, criminal law creates a great deal of *uncertainty* in the capacity of the criminal justice system (2007: 25, emphasis added).'

That is to say, the scientist wishes to account for all types of uncertainties with their instruments and measures. This is seen in the development of measures of bias and means of reducing systemic, random and gross errors as well as false positives and false negatives. For the prosecutor working in the context of multiple subsystems (forensics, policing, prosecution and the court), the drive for efficiency may open up enough ambiguity so that external influencers can drive the direction of discretion. In the meantime, the inequality of arms may undermine the principle of the defendant's right to answer in court in front of a jury and gain useful access to the forensic lab. Beyond this, if the matter is of special concern to the sovereign, there will be an interest to conserve the right to make attributions concerning the event. This may involve pre-emptory assertions supporting a preferred narrative and a stipulation of the parameters of review; it may displace regular authorities, require novel interpretations of data and the withholding from public view of sufficient information to test all the relevant evidence.

At the same time that actors accept that there is an ideal practice or rhetorical sweet spot of justice and liberal democracy, they also understand their need to align their work within the everyday administrative and occupational environment of their practice. Political socialisation is a process of coming to know when decisions are consistent with the dominant ordering, or when actions will meet with the least resistance. Consequently, the vast majority of actors will avoid generating findings that do not accord with the worldview of political leadership. If so, they will experience the *less political* option (one that meets with less political resistance) the exploration and testing of findings that derive from a concordance with that worldview. Again, this is in line with the presumption that institutional actors operate according to a belief in a just world and view deviations from standard practice as mere aberrations.

Notes

1. *Melendex-Diaz v. Massachusetts* (No.07-591) 69 Mass. App. 1114, 870 N. E. 2d 676, reversed and remanded.
2. Expert evidence is not to stand in for a final determination of the evidence or the judgment of judge or jury (Sangha et al., 2010: 36). According to Justice Goudge, the court must ensure that evidence complies with the scientific method and thus seek to make findings not simply 'experienced based' but 'evidence based'. According to leading case law in *Daubert v. Merrell Dew Pharmaceuticals Inc.*, true or reliable expertise derives from testable principles, is subject to peer review and provides a known error rate (Moles, 2004). Even so, in *R v. Trochym* ([2007] 1. SCR 239), the Supreme Court of Canada maintained that tests that may pass a clinical standard may not be at a standard of reliability sufficient for a criminal trial.
3. Human Rights Committee, General Comment No. 32, Article 14: Right to equality before courts and tribunals and to a fair trial, U.N. Doc. CCPR/C/GC/32 (2007). University of Minnesota, Human Rights Library

4. General Comment 32, para. 13; Report of the United Nations High Commissioner for Human Rights on the protection of human rights and fundamental freedoms while countering terrorism (A/HRC/22/26), para. 36; Communication No. 1347/2005, Dudko v. Australia, para. 7.4.
5. *Daubert v. Merrell Dow Pharmaceuticals* (509 U.S. 579 (1995) at 94–95).
6. According to Budowle et al. (2009), this should not be misconstrued as forensic scientist bias.
7. However, the ethical codes of forensics have been criticised for vagueness and lack of effect where mistakes or fraudulent practices may not be discovered or even discoverable (Koppl & Cowan, 2010: 240).
8. *R. v. War* 1993 Cr App. R.1 [Ward].
9. *McIlkilleny v. Chief Constable of the West Midlands Police* (1982) 1 Q.B. 283 at 323.
10. *McIlkilleny v. Chief Constable of the West Midlands Police* (1982) 1 Q.B. 283 at 323.
11. This is a rolling number as cases are continuously developed.
12. There may be multiple crime scenes, in which case there is usually one designated as primary (Lee et al., 2001).
13. In addition, there is discourse production or the material foundation of the utterance production that includes the 'interaction between the social actors and the speaker positions' inclusive of institutional and organisational arrangements like media arenas and scientific venues (60).
14. The skill set of, say, forensic engineers, is somewhat different. They may possess knowledge of legal requirements and processes and excellent communication skills and technical expertise, including knowledge of design; but a person who is highly knowledgeable about design is not necessarily a good forensic expert because what is required for an analysis of design failure is 'detective skills' (Brady, 2012: 2).
15. According to the NAS (2009), poor forensic science was the most common cause of corroboration of mistaken eyewitness identification and false confession, which is a finding also made in a study of Innocence Project cases conducted by Kassin et al. (2012).
16. There are several mechanisms by which the means of discovering, sampling and testing evidence is separated from other components of a prosecution. In blinding or blinded evaluation, the assumption is that since actors further down the line will seek the path of least resistance to a preferred outcome, it is necessary to protect officials along the pathway from being coerced or enticed to discover or interpret evidence in keeping with that preference. The integrity of fact-finding in the criminal justice system is ensured through the separation of witnesses and independence of experts so that they are not subject to cross-fertilisation and not tainted by compelling influence.
17. In an overview of the requisites of criminalistics, crime scene investigation and forensics, generally the major reports (NRC, 2009; PCAST, 2016) develop good practice guidelines.

References

Aaronson, T. (2011, September–October). The best terrorists money can buy. *Mother Jones*. https://www.motherjones.com/politics/2011/07/fbi-terrorist-sting-targets/.

Ashworth, A. (1994). *The criminal process: An evaluative study*. Oxford: Clarendon.

Brady, S. P. (2012). Role of the forensic process in investigating structural failure. *Journal of Performance of Constructed Facilities, 26*(1), 2–6.

Budowle, B., Bottrell, M. C., Bunch, S. G., Fram, R., Harrison, D., Meagher, S., et al. (2009). A perspective on errors, bias, and interpretation in the forensic sciences and direction for continuing advancement. *Journal of Forensic Sciences, 54*(4), 798–809.

Butler, J. M. (2015). US initiatives to strengthen forensic science & international standards in forensic DNA. *Forensic Science International: Genetics, 18*, 4–20.

Charlton, D., Fraser-Mackenzie, P. A., & Dror, I. E. (2010). Emotional experiences and motivating factors associated with fingerprint analysis. *Journal of Forensic Sciences, 55*(2), 385–393.

Charman, S. D., Gregory, A. H., & Carlucci, M. (2009). Exploring the diagnostic utility of facial composites: Beliefs of guilt can bias perceived similarity between composite and suspect. *Journal of Experimental Psychology: Applied, 15*(1), 76–90.

Cino, J. (2017). Bad science begets bad convictions: The need for postconviction relief in the wake of discredited forensics. *University of Denver Criminal Law Review, 7*, 1–46.

Colquitt, J. A. (2004). Rethinking entrapment. *American Criminal Law Review, 41*(4), 1389–1438.

de Lint, W. (1998). Regulating autonomy: Police discretion as a problem for training. *Canadian Journal of Criminology, 40*(3), 277–304.

de Lint, W., & Kassa, W. (2017). On being bent for security: Barristers in terrorism prosecutions in Australia. *Journal of Law and Society, 44*(2), 169–199.

DeForest, P., Petraeo, N., & Koblinsky, L. (1983). Chemistry and the challenge of crime. In S. Gerber (Ed.), *Chemistry and crime* (pp. 45–63). Washington, DC: American Chemical Society.

Dovidio, J. F., Kawakami, K., Johnson, C., Johnson, B., & Howard, A. (1997). On the nature of prejudice: Automatic and controlled processes. *Journal of Experimental Social Psychology, 33*, 510–540.

Drizin, S. A., & Leo, R. A. (2004). The problem of false confessions in the post-DNA world. *North Carolina Law Review, 82*, 891–1007.

Dror, I. E., & Charlton, D. (2006). Why experts make errors. *Journal of Forensic Identification, 56*(4), 600–616.

Dror, I. E., & Cole, S. A. (2010). The vision in blind justice: Expert perception, judgment, and visual cognition in forensic pattern recognition. *Psychonomic Bulletin & Review, 17*, 161–167.

Dror, I. E., & Hampikian, G. (2011). Subjectivity and bias in forensic DNA mixture interpretation. *Science & Justice, 51*, 204–208.

Du, M. (2017). Analysis of errors in forensic science. *Journal of Forensic Science and Medicine, 3*, 139–143.

Ericson, R. V. (2007). *Crime in an insecure world*. Cambridge: Polity.

Evett, I. W., Berger, C. E. H., Buckleton, J. S., Champod, C., & Jackson, G. (2017). Finding the way forward for forensic science in the US: A commentary on the PCAST report. *Forensic Science International, 278*, 16–23.

Ewick, P., & Silbey, S. S. (1992). Narrating social structure: Stories of resistance to legal authority. *American Journal of Sociology, 108*(6), 1328–1372.

Findley, K. A., & Scott, M. S. (2006). The multiple dimensions of tunnel vision in criminal cases. *Wisconsin Law Review, 2*, 291–397.

Foucault, M. (1972). The discourse on language. In *The archaeology of knowledge*. New York: Pantheon.

Fuchs, S., & Ward, S. (1994). What is deconstruction and where and when does it take place? *American Sociological Review, 59*, 481.

Garrett, B. (2011). *Convicting the innocent*. Harvard University Press.

Giannelli, P. C. (2001). Scientific evidence in the Sam Sheppard case. *Cleveland State Law Review, 49*(3), 487–498.

Goudge, S. T. (2008). *Inquiry into pediatric forensic pathology in Ontario*. Toronto, ON: Ontario Ministry of the Attorney General.

Greenwald, A. G., & Banaji, M. R. (1995). Implicit social cognition: Attitudes, self-esteem, and stereotypes. *Psychological Review, 102*(1), 4.

Gross, H. (1911). *Criminal psychology: A manual for judges, practitioners, and students* (Vol. 2). Little, Brown.

Gross, S. R. (2013). How many false convictions are there? How many exonerations are there? In C. R. Huff & M. Killias (Eds.), *Wrongful convictions and miscarriages of justice: Causes and remedies in North American and European criminal justice systems* (pp. 45–59). New York, NY: Routledge.

Haber, R. N., & Haber, L. (2013). The culture of science: Bias and forensic evidence. *Journal of Applied Research in Memory and Cognition, 2*(1), 65–67. https://doi.org/10.1016/j.jarmac.2013.01.005.

Halverson, A. M., Hallahan, M., Hart, A. J., & Rosenthal, R. (1997). Reducing the biasing effects of judges' nonverbal behavior with simplified jury instruction. *Journal of Applied Psychology, 82*(4), 590–598.

Hasel, L. E., & Kassin, S. M. (2009). On the presumption of evidentiary independence: Can confessions corrupt eyewitness identifications? *Psychological Science, 20*(1), 122–126.

Haslam, S. A., & Reicher, S. D. (2012). Contesting the 'nature' of conformity: What Milgram and Zimbardo's studies really show. *PLoS Biology, 10*(11), e1001426. https://doi.org/10.1371/journal.pbio.1001426.

Hodgkinson, G. P., & Wright, G. (2002). Confronting strategic inertia in a top management team: Learning from failure. *Organization Studies, 23*(6), 949–977.

Innocence Project. (2020). DNA exonerations in the United States. Retrieved 20 April 2020. https://www.innocenceproject.org/dna-exonerations-in-the-united-states/.

Jost, J. T., Rudman, L. A., Blair, I. V., Carney, D. R., Dasgupta, N., Glaser, J., et al. (2009). The existence of implicit bias is beyond reasonable doubt: A refutation of ideological and methodological objections and executive summary of ten studies that no manager should ignore. *Research in Organizational Behavior, 29*, 39–69.

Julian, R. (2005). *National Institute for Forensic Science: Partnership projects 2002–2004*. Final Report for the National Institute of Forensic Science, Tasmanian Institute of Law Enforcement Studies, University of Tasmania, Hobart.

Julian, R., Kelty, S., & Robertson, J. (2012). 'Get it right the first time': Critical issues at the crime scene. *Current Issues in Criminal Justice, 24*(1), 25–37.

Kassin, S. (2012). Why confessions trump innocence. *American Psychologist, 67*, 430–445.

Kassin, S. M., Bogart, D., & Kerner, J. (2012). Confessions that corrupt: Evidence from the DNA exoneration case files. *Psychological Science, 23*(1), 41–45.

Kassin, S. M., Dror, I. E., & Kukucka, J. (2013). The forensic confirmation bias: Problems, perspectives, and proposed solutions. *Journal of Applied Research in Memory and Cognition, 2*(1), 42–52.

Kassin, S. M., Goldstein, C. C., & Savitsky, K. (2003). Behavioral confirmation in the interrogation room: On the dangers of presuming guilt. *Law and Human Behavior, 27*(2), 187–203.

Kaufman, F. (1998). *Commission on proceedings involving Guy Paul Morin*. Toronto: Ministry of the Attorney General. www.attorneygeneral.jus.gov.on.ca.

Keller, R. (2011). The sociology of knowledge approach to discourse. *Human Studies, 34*, 43–65.

Kelly, J. F., & Wearne, P. (1998). *Tainting evidence: Inside the scandals at the FBI crime lab*. New York: Free Press.

Kirk, P. T. (1953). *Criminal investigation*. New York: Interscience Publishers.

Koppl, R., & Cowan, E. J. (2010). A battle of forensic experts is not a race to the bottom. *Review of Political Economy, 22*(2), 235–262.

Koppl, R., & Sacks, M. (2013). The criminal justice system creates incentives for false convictions. *Criminal Justice Ethics, 32*(2), 126–162.

Kukucka, J., & Kassin, S. M. (2014). Do confessions taint perceptions of handwriting evidence? An empirical test of the forensic confirmation bias. *Law and Human Behavior, 38*(3), 256.

Lange, N. D., Thomas, R. P., Dana, J., & Dawes, R. M. (2011). Contextual biases in the interpretation of auditory evidence. *Law and Human Behavior, 35*(3), 178–187.

Lee, H. C., Palmbach, T., & Miller, M. T. (2001). *Henry Lee's crime scene handbook*. Academic Press.

McBarnet, D. J. (1978). *The police and the state: Arrest, legality and the law*. Aldershot: Croom Helm.

Mnookin, J. L., Cole, S. A., Dror, I. E., Fisher, B. A., Houk, M. M., Inman, K., et al. (2011). The need for a research culture in the forensic sciences. *UCLA Law Review, 58*(3), 725–780.

Moles, R. N. (2004). *A state of injustice*. Melbourne: Lothian.

Monaghan, J., & Walby, K. (2012). Making up 'terror identities': Security intelligence, Canada's Integrated Threat Assessment Centre and social movement suppression. *Policing and Society, 22*(2), 133–151.

Moynihan, P. (2009). The network governance response of crisis response. *Journal of Public Administration and Theory, 19*, 895–915.

Mueller, J., & Stewart, M. G. (2011). *Terror, security, and money: Balancing the risks, benefits, and costs of homeland security*. New York: Oxford University Press.

Mueller, J., & Stewart, M. G. (2015). *Chasing ghosts: The policing of terrorism*. New York: Oxford.

Narchet, F. M., Meissner, C. A., & Russano, M. B. (2011). Modeling the influence of investigator bias on the elicitation of true and false confessions. *Law and Human Behavior, 35*(6), 452–465.

National Academy of Sciences. (2009). *Strengthening forensic science in the United States: A path forward*. Washington, DC: National Academies Press.

Office of the Inspector General (OIG). (2006). *A review of the FBI's handling of the Brandon Mayfield case*. Office of the Inspector General, Oversight & Review Division, US Department of Justice.

Page, M., Taylor, J., & Blenkin, M. (2011). Uniqueness in the forensic identification sciences: Fact or fiction? *Forensic Science International, 206*(1–3), 12–18.

Page, M., Taylor, J., & Blenkin, M. (2012). Context effects and observer bias: Implications for forensic odontology. *Journal Forensic Science, 57*, 108–112.

President's Council of Advisors on Science and Technology. (2016). *Report to the president: Forensic science in criminal courts—ensuring scientific validity of feature-comparison methods*. Washington, DC. https://obamawhitehouse.archives.gov/sites/default/files/microsites/ostp/PCAST/pcast_forensic_science_report_final.pdf.

Reason, J. (1990). *Human error*. Cambridge: Cambridge University Press.

Roach, K. (2010). The eroding distinction between intelligence and evidence. In N. McGarrity, A. Lynch, & G. Williams (Eds.), *Terrorism in counter-terrorism and beyond* (pp. 48–68). Abingdon and New York: Routledge.

Royal Commission on Justice (Runciman Commission). (1991). Royal Commission on Criminal Justice (Runciman Commission): Records. The National Archives. Government of England.

Ruhe, J. A. (1991). Value importance for success: A longitudinal study. *SAM Advanced Management Journal, 56*(1), 10.

Saks, M. J., & Faigman, D. L. (2008). Failed forensics: How forensic science lost its way and how it might yet find it. *Annual Review of Law and Social Science, 4*, 149–171.

Saks, M. J., & Koehler, J. J. (2005). The coming paradigm shift in forensic identification science. *Science, 309*(5736), 892–895.

Sangha, B., Moles, R. N., & Roach, K. (2010). *Forensic investigations and miscarriages of justice: The rhetoric meets the reality*. Toronto, ON: Irwin Law.

Silver, J. S. (1990). Equality of arms and the adversarial process: A new constitutional right. *Wisconsin Law Review, 4*, 1007–1042.

Simon, H. A. (1957). *Models of man*. New York: John Wiley.

Smart C. (1990), Law's power, the sexed body, and feminist discourse. *Journal of Law & Society, 17*, 194–210.

Stacey, R. B., & Unit, T. (2005). Report on the erroneous fingerprint individualization in the Madrid train bombing case. *Historian, 404,* 294–2647.

Steffen, T. L. (1988). Truth as second fiddle: Re-evaluating the place of truth in the adversarial trial ensemble. *Utah Law Review, 1988*(4), 799–846.

Stoel, R. D., Dror, I. E., & Miller, L. S. (2014). Bias among forensic document examiners: Still a need for procedural changes. *Australian Journal of Forensic Sciences, 46,* 91–97. https://doi.org/10.1080/00450618.2013.797026.

Suzuki, E., Tsuda, T., Mitsuhashi, T., Mansournia, M. A., & Yamamoto, E. (2016). Errors in causal inference: An organizational schema for systematic error and random error. *Annals of Epidemiology, 26*(11), 788–793.

Thomas, P., & Mills, M. (1995, September 14). FBI crime laboratory being probed. *The Washington Post.*

US Department of Justice Office of the Inspector General. (1998). *The FBI laboratory: An investigation into laboratory practices of alleged misconduct in explosives related and other cases (April 1997).* Diane Publishing.

Wagner-Pacifici, R. (2010). Theorizing the restlessness of events. *American Journal of Sociology, 115*(5), 1351–1386. https://doi.org/10.1086/651299.

Zedner, L. (2007). Pre-crime and post-criminology? *Theoretical Criminology, 11*(2), 261–281.

Zimbardo, P. G., Maslach, C., & Haney, C. (2000). Reflections on the Stanford prison experiment: Genesis, transformations, consequences. In *Obedience to authority: Current perspectives on the Milgram paradigm* (pp. 193–237). Erlbaum.

Chapter 3
Anti-forensics: Intelligence Crime and Blur

> The form and functions of a forensic science service provider are determined by interactions between: the legal system under which it operates; the law enforcement agency or agencies which it services; the policies of the government of the country concerned; the historical legacy of the evolution of services in that country.
>
> Bedford (2011: 147)

Introduction

In the chalk outline of a body there is an image suggestive of a homicide crime scene where we might find trace elements identifying the perpetrator. Also implied is the agency or actor that has used the chalk to mark the spot. A place is appropriated as a crime scene by an authority that takes carriage and secures the site so that it may be subjected to evaluation and any material in it may be removed for analysis or examined in situ. However, before law enforcement and crime scene investigators arrive on the scene and draw that chalk outline and take dominion, other actors must not have overlooked their own interest in that work; they are vested to take from it what they believe does not belong to the dominion of law and justice. These actors may 'belong to intelligence' or to the maintenance of the vitality of the sovereign. Accordingly, we may be concerned about the possibility that, in some exceptional cases of crime and disorder, an intrusion of the sovereign in the form of politicisation will occur by way of intelligence.

The relation between the 'craft' of intelligence (Dulles, 2006) and the spirit of justice is one of opposites in many features of comparison (see Roach, 2010: 52–53). This includes the dimensions of visibility and publicity, and verification and challenge, as well as methods and means of truth discovery. Consequently, where a confirmation bias is anathema to the requirements of true crime discovery, the 'best truth' (Berkowitz & Goodman, 2000) in intelligence is already directed by policy. Where an adversarial process requires a relative equality of arms, it is a duplicity of arms through the negation of a fair contest that animates intelligence. Where justice must be seen to be done, intelligence work must be done without being seen.

W. B. de Lint, *Blurring Intelligence Crime*,
https://doi.org/10.1007/978-981-16-0352-5_3

In this analysis we will make vivid the typification of intelligence in contrast to criminal justice forensics. We are concerned in this chapter with intelligence that has furtive transactional force, and this will produce a conceptualisation that may be a bit too idealised for some readers. The focus of our inquiry is an investigation of the justice–intelligence intersection and crime, so we are stripping intelligence down to this element of the furtive transactional capacity, or as already *normatively* illicit. In this respect, where breaches of legality are perceived in the *miscarriage* of law terrain, breaches of this 'normative intelligence' are not *deviations* but expressions of sovereign dominion. In the meantime, the relative autonomy of intelligence, like that of forensics, is most available where the outcome has no or very little political consequence.

In this chapter, we continue (from the introductory chapter) our analysis of some key factors or dimensions of crime, intelligence, politics and justice to suggest that there is a relative inevitability in the outcomes of the cases analysed in the subsequent chapters. The approach taken here is critical institutional. It depends upon an understanding of intelligence as a power-knowledge that builds on the refinement of procedures and more or less coercive processes and rules for exclusion with respect to what may be known or made familiar, reasonable or utterable as knowledge or authority. On the basis of this approach we posit that criminal justice, through rule of law legality, brings uncertainties to bear that are anathema to the sovereign. The sovereign seeks to maintain or expand its capacity to identify events according to its own discretionary review of needs and threats. Some space of functional ordering operates between the institutional domains of law and sovereignty. We then provide a conceptualisation of intelligence crime and position intelligence crimes as particularly hostile to ordering by criminal justice and forensic devices.

Critical Institutional Review

Foucault (1980) uses the concept '*le dispositif de securité*' to refer to an apparatus or assemblage of security. The concept incorporates power-knowledge, or disciplinary or institutional authority, and the means of effecting the prohibition of alternative or subordinate narratives. It also implies the preservation of the vitality or urgency of a discourse (of security) in respect of a subject population—a strategic imperative. The term permits us to reflect on the power of institutions, and the relative heft of the security-intelligence dispositive in particular.

In preparation for our analysis of crimes involving political actors and interests, it is necessary to understand how our knowledge of high crime events is dependent on information that is embedded in distinct institutional discourses. It might be useful to assert that there are three institutional domains, pivoting on the terms of justice, order and sovereignty. These domains are taken as power-knowledge brokers. They may be contrasted according to differing mandates and standards. They may also produce an order of priority such that sometimes a version of justice eclipses order and sovereignty, or sovereignty bands with a version of order to eclipse justice. The principal purpose of this exercise is to provide some conceptual space for an analysis of intelligence crime and intelligence crime cases.

Justice or Rule of Law Legality

The rule of law is stipulated in general principles that denote that laws fail when they do not possess sufficient generality, promulgation, clarity, constancy and congruence between what officials do in practice and the terms under which they declare to rule, or where they create contradictions, require the impossible or are retroactive (Fuller, 1964).

Legality also denotes the operation of a system of review or meta-laws by which the interpretation of rules or practices is tested. This may be through a constitution or a bill of rights, for example. Principles of legality are, as Waldon observes, means of 'keeping legal systems in good shape' (Waldron, 2008).

Rule of law legality or justice gains meaning in contrast to the requirement for order and order maintenance, as per Packer (1968), McBarnet (1978) Skolnick (2011) and others. Under a *liberal doctrine* of political organisation there is a presumptive adversarial arrangement in which individual freedom also contests and restrains collective state authority. In mind of Locke, Basaran (2010: 20) notes that the foundation of liberal rule is the claim to protect individual liberties. She continues:

> the dichotomy created between liberal and illiberal rule is central to our way of thinking about security liberties and the infringement of liberties. ... This division has contributed to the depiction of illiberal rule as the opposite of liberal rule and shaped a number of assumptions on the characteristics of illiberal rule, most important of which is the rule of law.... Law appears as the opposite of exception. (20–21)

Blackstone's concept of ratio and equality of arms are interrelated dimensions of rule of law legality. We have discussed equality of arms previously.[1] Some version of Blackstone's ratio underpins 'beyond reasonable doubt' and is the standard of proof used in criminal trials in most Anglo-American jurisdictions (Shapiro, 1991). It is a bedrock principle of due process (Newman, 1993) that, according to some analysts, demonstrates the relative respect for liberal freedoms (and thus classic liberal values) within a political system. As indicated by the quantification of the measure, it sets the bar high against false positive prosecutions (Arkes & Mellers, 2002; DeKay, 1996).

Order and Ordering

There are many ways of drilling down into the essential features of law enforcement, domestic security and the everyday administration of crime control. Packer

(1968) problematised law enforcement in terms of efficiency, but liberalised law enforcement is also a response to disorder in accordance with modern rationality (Weber, 1994). According to Buzan (1999: 8), an ordering principle is a meta-frame or set of assumptions by which to evaluate threats or decide what to do about them. This is communicated through policy frames (Lau & Schlesinger, 2005) that provide structure and limits to otherwise far-ranging imaginings of things. It is a posture or 'direction' regarding the way societies need to prioritise matters of strategic concern (Clemens, 2007: 649). The concept relates a big idea to particular urgent concerns, and imposes a set of values on the immediate phenomenon; it is an *åsiktskorridoren* (in Swedish, the 'opinion corridor', representing the relatively narrow range of views that may be entertained by respectable people).

In liberal democratic ordering, the individual is conceived of as more or less deprived of liberties and state authority as more or less constrained in achieving that deprivation (Donzelot, 2008). Executive power is triggered by manifest threats to the social or normative order, and the response should not be arbitrary, but restricted by public accountability according to established and emergent mores. The constraints of law and rule are embodied in the routines and the slippage of organisations from standards as they attempt to meet efficiencies and 'real world' conditions of practical efficiencies.

In negotiating order, the efficient professional is able to provide a product at a rate determined by competition. *Recipe legality* is the regular brokering of the 'price' between abstract principles and organisational necessity. Practitioners establish the tariff that is acceptable organisationally given the ordering context as above and reference to justice (Ericson & Baranek, 1982). That is to say, order is informed by the social and political context in which courts manifest, as buildings, people, lawyers and judges who draw on common views or prejudices about lived experience, everyday reality or the 'real world' (Ewick & Silbey, 1992).

Law enforcement and security are centred around the problem of functional efficiencies, and as such also around the maintenance of a law and security doctrine based on an ordering principle. The worldview of the law enforcer and security actor is that there is a presumption that 'society must be defended', inclusive in which is the binary ideas of inside/outside, home/away, friend/enemy and good/bad. It may be added that there is a habitus, an identity more or less besieged from without (and, for security intelligence, from within) by malign forces that seek ultimately to storm the castle and install a successor sovereign.

Sovereignty: Vitality and Deep Discretion

Sovereignty must be maintained or restored in its vitality. Sovereign vitality refers to the locus of discretion within and across states (Schmitt, 1985: 5). We may begin with Gill's observation that inside the executive there is what he refers to as the 'secret state', defined in terms of the metaphor of Gore-Tex fabric, which does to sweat and heat what the secret state does to light and information (1994: 80). Gill notes that there are countering techniques that the secret state applies in order to protect its operations and insulate itself against the 'rain' of public inquiry.

Gill includes the US National Security Council (NSC) in the secret state but did not go further to consider the black operations of the intelligence sector that are made deliberately deniable.[2] Nor does he consider how intelligence networks across nation-states may be exploited or finessed. Within nation-states, a vital sovereign power is able to exercise dominion sufficient to rebuff unwanted incursions from parliament (Schmitt, 1988) or judicial authority or lesser factions within the executive.[3] With respect to external relations, vitality for hegemons like the US means countenancing no others to rise to equal strength (Mearsheimer & Alterman, 2001).

In much of the current literature, criminal justice and (national) security actions are *blended* or 'fused' in a retreat from the separation between domestic law enforcement and security intelligence or political policing (Brodeur, 1983; Bigo, 2006). It is said that, post 9/11, the blending of a domestic criminology of the self and a foreign policy of the other has broken the hard binary of Packer's due process/crime control distinction (Zedner, 2003: 24). The friend/enemy opposition that distinguishes crime-fighting and warfighting across internal and external domains is thus blurred or made continuous. According to Finer (2002: 4), it is mistaken to view the military control of civilian affairs as an aberration; it is more accurate to recognise the relative visibility or expedience of overt intervention: 'the military often works on government from behind the scenes … and the modes of military intervention are as often latent or indirect as they are overt or direct'. In securitisation, the claim of exception proves the rule of law: it is a temporary suspension of the visibilities and checks against authoritarian practice, and thus maintains the purity and superiority of law at the same time that it evacuates a space for the freedom of so-called existential security decisions to be quickly made, sometimes even as 'counter-law' (Ericson 2007). This follows Neocleous's (2000: 22) observation that modern liberalism 'is bound inextricably in the project of security' and Dean's comment that liberalism is a *technique of security*, a strategy of governance in which security is *deployed* as liberty (2002: 31).[4]

In the perspective that is mooted by Foucault and others above, the triumvirate of order, law and sovereign vitality is connected by security practices, protocols and discourses through the dispositive. When there is a claimed political crime, a deep challenge to the ideological order, what must be done to defend society is well-established: the sovereign must be sufficiently vital to act in support of the integrity of the political, economic and social union. When the impact of crimes or events is deemed critical to the political authorities of the day, they are also viewed as too important to be offered up to the ambiguity and pluralism of the liberal democratic ideal form, where outcomes may not be in keeping with the established political interests. The intervention must remain under the highest available discretional cover; the closer the matter is to the perceived beating heart of the sovereign, the greater will be the defensiveness of security and police actors and the firmer will be the enlistment of other branches of government in a unified (and, in the extreme, unitary) protection of sovereign vitality.

The law enforcement and security intelligence habitus is thus one more or less identified in the attitude of defence of the order and the ordering principle—more or less zealous and paranoid, in possession of a siege mentality. Political and social values depend upon the sovereign, so it is the sovereign or the beating heart of the monarch that must be supported and nourished. The zealousness of the defence may become an organisational or occupational pathology or simplification, depending on the standpoint from which it is analysed. Former US State Department Coordinator for Counterterrorism Cofer Black's famous 'The gloves come off' quote is an evocative reference to the attitude of defence. Such a statement made explicitly by actors close to the power centre projects a justification for actions against 'the usual suspects' during an ongoing or imminent siege. It was uttered in the context of worldwide support for the US following 9/11, encapsulated in the famous headline in *Le Monde*: 'We are all Americans' (Colombani, 2001).

But how do we see—or fail to see—the underpinnings of sovereignty? What is our standpoint? What restricts the knowledge of security threats? We need to understand the function of security intelligence and how our perception is fed to us from an archive that is only visible in part. We may have an open society in other ways, but in matters of conflict and security, many in congress or parliament and almost all outside the range of light coming back from the core of the state will be supporting the government blindly, just as we would in an authoritarian state. For our purposes, we wish to highlight that intelligence also acts before the law (Kafka, 1988) and sometimes also in anticipation of the vitality of the sovereign for an order that may by pre-emptive or restorative, depending on decisions that may also not be visible (see Fig. 3.1).

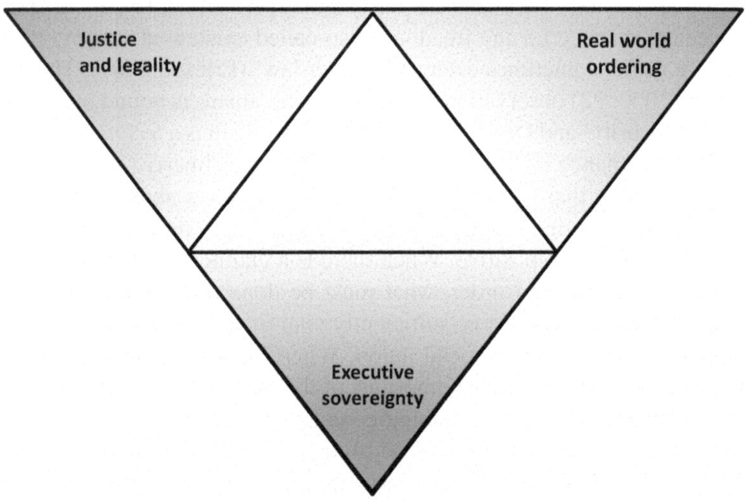

Fig. 3.1 Domains of Order and Discretion

A Criminology of Intelligence Crime

Like political sociology, political criminology is concerned with the structures and forces by which social and political institutions may be observed. For criminology, as we suggested earlier, a political crime is an act that challenges the political authority or order. More narrowly, it is also concerned, as per O'Brien and Littler (2015: 4), with 'exposing the political contexts, agencies and strategies that drive forward contemporary criminal justice and security agendas'. Security agendas are distinguished from domestic crime agendas in significant ways that involve the layering of the political across the normative in a process known as politicisation.

We have noted that crime is best understood as concerned with violations of the social or moral order. We add here that political crime is distinguished from common crime or social deviance, in that it is seen as an emergent violation against the political order. The state wishes to have a double dominion of political crime; as concerns how and when the normative property and presumption of state action is triggered, particularly as states, as Foucault (1988: 152) notes, are interested in citizens to the extent that they may be of use or pose a threat. It also wishes to align the political and social good with the defence of political order in its preferred interpretation. Consequently, illegalities stem from security intelligence on the *ideological* platform that legitimates and sets up the dominion of a sovereign authority and divides the international system into us and them.

Accordingly, the crimes of intelligence actors and assets are by definition ideological crimes; like terrorism and hate crime they are acts expressing a bias against actors that are deemed to represent or possess a demeaned (or subaltern) value. Indeed, viewed from outside the privileged propaganda frame, they appear as straightforward bias crimes; they vilify individuals or groups and deploy terror as a weapon to discipline whole populations. Only some of these acts are the object of crime scene investigations or forensic evidence discovery and recovery. For instance, forensic anthropologists have identified remains and documented evidence of international human rights violations from the bodies of thousands of Bosnians in a mass gravesite in Srebrenica, Bosnia (Jugo, 2017). Extremely infrequently, this has led to the prosecution of some responsible local state actors (Hughes, 2001).

Black (2004: 10, 16) suggests that terrorism is a form of unilateral self-help and a rare type of social control. The events of 9/11 were an attack 'by alien warriors crossing national boundaries in search of justice' (16). In particular, 9/11 represented a conflict between 'the American way of life itself', the 'sensual nature of its popular culture' and the 'heathen character of the American people' (15) against which the terrorists had a grievance. It was also an attack on American authorities who exercise the social control *of that social control*.[5] Therein lies the rub of evaluation based on evidence from events that have an incomplete or corrupted forensic case history. In this regard, even political crime is widely and abruptly analysed only *after* the subordination (or distortion) of subaltern representations (including class and identity). Black's position appears to take the vantage point of cultural superiority despite that his concept of self-help is intended to offer rhetorical respite from the normative load of 'crime'.

Intelligence

Intelligence is a tactic used in the establishment and maintenance of exclusive categories of security exclusion, be they territorial, national or proprietary. Unlike pure violence, the exclusionary tactic of intelligence manipulates the processes of information control, conceptualised by Wilsnack (1980) as including: espionage, or the obtaining of information against the will of targets; secrecy, or the keeping of information from others who may be able to deploy it in their interests; persuasion, or the dissemination of information to coerce consent; and evaluation, or the maximisation of the exploitability of obtained information. The control of information is, according to Iacobucci (2008), 'the fundamental principle of intelligence services and intelligence investigations'.

It is both exclusivity and transactability that define good intelligence. Intelligence is good if it is scarce or arcane and provides something that may be transacted to coerce or compel a course of action (Berkowitz & Goodman, 2000).[6] There is much that may be used to compel or coerce that is not gathered or analysed covertly, so is not intelligence. Actionable intelligence is information that has passed through the intelligence cycle where it is recoded as exclusive or archived. The validity of intelligence in the exploitation of knowledge exclusivities,[7] unlike legal knowledge, does not require an attendant record of the coercion used to achieve it (Roach, 2010: 52).

Involvement in the building of the knowledge and the discipline—and to some extent, the craft—of intelligence is restricted. Authorship or data entry and data combination are rigorously controlled and restricted through tight compartmentalisation, which is also part of the mode of inscription in the intelligence enterprise. Access will be vetted according to citizenship, loyalty, associations and memberships, among other characteristics, and through restricted commissions or privileged access (classification clearance) to the knowledge pool. External review is restricted and the intelligence canon is assured or validated by hierarchical filtering (cf. Brodeur & Dupont, 2006) through security clearances, fellowship or trust networks and the like (de Lint et al., 2007) that feature cross-referencing or vouching of privileged sources and methods that already flow from political limiters (such as political party affiliation, club or organisation membership and loyalty measures). Like the policing function, intelligence is relatively independent of government, including political leadership. It is driven by the building criteria (Foucault, 1972—see Chap. 7), or the power of vast archives and the control of a dispositive or parapolitical assemblage of sources and methods.[8]

Following the above discussion, we may essentialise security intelligence as the development and refinement of a parapolitics or secret political power, which exploits uncommon and arcane information and analysis in potential transactions ordered for a politics of antagonism or related to the weaknesses and strengths of political friends or foes. This activity continuously reinscribes (or redetermines) the life of politics according to the superordinate or exclusive identity while also contemplating the liminal, or the breaking and remaking of boundaries.[9] Both internally and externally, the primary policy question is where and against whom the cut of politics is to be made. The necessary hard distinction or value is likely to be found where power intersects with knowledge in 'centres of calculation' (Latour &Woolgar, 2013).

Intelligence Crime

Intelligence crimes may be divided into two categories, referred to here as Type 1 and Type 2. In Type 1 crimes, the act or actor is identified internally by intelligence agency officials as committing a breach and investigated and processed either internally (for example, by Inspector-Generals) or externally by justice officials (such as Attorney-Generals) for actions. This type of crime includes actions of espionage or illegal actions not commissioned by or in accordance with the implicit or explicit directions of an agency or agency representatives, and which therefore may place the agency in a position of compromise or disrepute. They may be carried out by intelligence actors or assets and, in rare instances, by journalists. These crimes that are carried out by intelligence or security intelligence assets are not the focus of this examination, as they have been very adequately covered elsewhere.

We are concerned with the Type 2 category: criminally harmful intelligence crimes that are carried out by intelligence agencies or authorised intelligence agency actors or assets under the implicit (whether plausibly or implausibly denied) or explicit consent of the agencies and their institutional advocates. They may include transactive[10] acts of commission (predatory acts that produce obvious harm to targets (victims)). They may also involve crimes of omission, in which the intelligence asset or actor provides more or less indirect cover or resources to the asset but is not involved directly in the commission of the act. It may also involve information operations employed as a means of covering the act or deterring or quashing an investigation, including with respect to its genesis with an intelligence service or services (see Fig. 3.2).

In Type 2 crime the event is considered extra-judicial—that is to say, not subject to the remedy of the criminal courts and/or an open-ended investigation and forensic review of the evidence. Consequently, it is expected that intelligence crimes will

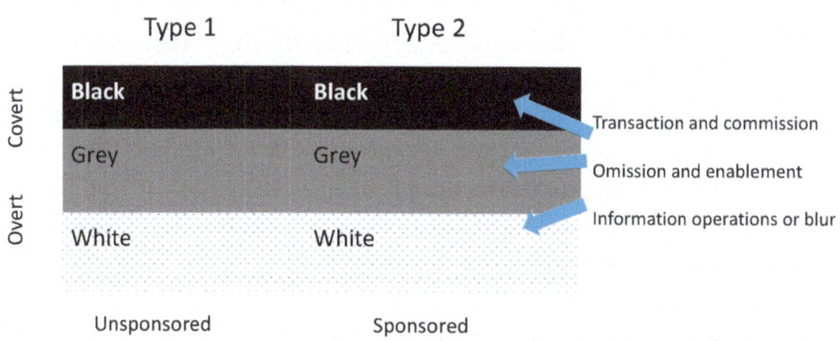

Fig. 3.2 Types of Intelligence Crime by Sponsorship and Acknowledgement

rarely be investigated as such; and, if investigated, they will not be prosecuted; and, if prosecuted, they will rarely lead to a conviction of the agency actor as responsible. Actors working for intelligence agencies who commit crimes that are not sponsored by those agencies may receive preferential treatment from criminal justice actors, as long as they are in good standing with those agencies. Where an action is normally carried out in compliance with mission goals, or where there is no animus against the organisational or agency goals or actors, the crime will not be deemed to warrant a national security scandal that would arise from the publicity of justice processing.

Like the intelligence operations with which they are connected, these intelligence crimes are divided according to their compliance with the often implicit position of the sovereign, their departure from reviewable sponsorship, their level of cover and compartmentalisation, and the degree to which their connection to executive or sovereign sponsors can be denied. They may be crimes that are committed by assets or actors in compliance with executive or presidential orders, including those that fall within the black and grey zones of (deniable) activity. They can thus be categorised as (more or less) sponsored and protected, unsponsored and protected, sponsored but unprotected and unsponsored and unprotected.

One feature of a Type 2 intelligence crime is its mandate from the 'King's arms'. Following the arguments above regarding the dependency of security on the norm-setting antecedent of sovereignty (Tilly, 1985), executive actions undertaken at the behest of the sovereign cannot be criminal. The Crown cannot be rogue any more than it may be charged with committing regicide. The primary mandate is the protection of the Crown or sovereign, offensively, as per the motto of Mossad, 'by way of deception'. This sets up the moral compass of the enterprise. The agencies are protected by layers of bureaucratic legalese to operate under the relatively deniable discretion of the sovereign or Crown.

In this regard, the security assemblage or dispositive is largely unseen. Intelligence crime involves the manipulation of dark criminal networks in the service of state agendas. As we shall see in the exploration of several cases, the clandestine operations (grey and black) of secret intelligence are highly compartmented into units or operations that build credentials based on 'ownership' and control over the most transactive criminal enterprises. That is to say, the more pernicious and capable is the intelligence unit in coercing the criminal enterprise to effect an ideological goal (a political coup, an assassination or a terrorist event that shifts public opinion or policy) without being seen to do so, the more esteemed will be that unit for nurturing (gardening) that capability to fruition.

A third feature of Type 2 intelligence crime is the information operations and the cover provided to limit/prevent the review of such operations. This enlists the institutions of liberal democracy 'freedoms' in the elaboration of the dark power of information operations (we will be using the term 'blur'). In relation to western intelligence agencies and activities, there is a functional fluidity between parliamentary, executive and judicial authorities. By fluidity is meant here their capacity to annex the authority of one of these institutional domains to evade accountability to each of the others (Lustgarten & Leigh, 1994). Thus, parliamentary oversight and control is circumvented to preserve executive and national security capacity, and judicial authority is tripped up with reference to parliamentary accountabilities (as when laws are passed denying judicial scrutiny of intelligence agencies) (Gill, 1994; Lustgarten & Leigh, 1994).

This means that under a 'security of freedom' discourse, Type 2 intelligence crimes are almost unique in respect of their 'illegalities'. Intelligence agencies are enabled by the power of law. They operate through the finessing of legal instruments (for instance, Ericson's [2007] 'counter-law') so that activities that are criminal when undertaken by other actors are ambiguously proscribed when undertaken by intelligence actors (thus the requirement that criminality is defined in terms of deliberate violations of human rights). For instance, in its use of renditions to Egypt and Uzbekistan, the Central Intelligence Agency (CIA) was exploiting its security relations to create a gulag archipelago and did so on the basis of copious legal findings (Yoo, 2002; Bybee, 2002). On the other hand, CIA clandestine operations have also been found to be blatantly criminal, as in the Iran-Contra affair, which involved the CIA in the cocaine trade (Weiner, 2008; Scott & Marshall, 1998). As per the second feature, in liberal democracies this mandate is finessed with regard to other functionalities.

We take to heart, as outlined above, the import of power-knowledge, and particularly the information filter in security intelligence.[11] Our analysis is consistent with a review of the behaviour of crime control. Our object (intelligence crime) is exposed by the behaviour of the authorities in enacting crime control; how they *come to make* designations *or fail to launch* properly constituted investigations. With Type 2 intelligence crimes we define acts that are meant to offer an exemplary challenge to the political status quo in a higher category of terrorism (apex crimes) and/or crimes that operate more or less under the unacknowledged covert cover of the sovereign (intelligence crimes).

Both are deeply political. If politicisation is the pull of well-connected establishment influence on the professional expert actions and choices against the grain of craft knowledge or the practice of criminal justice actors from above or across institutional mandates, apex events and intelligence crime is a furtive and criminal intrusion into resource allocations or policy choices chosen by the constitutional or statutory instruments of government. The source of the influence often cannot be clearly or definitively identified, but it can be hypothesised, if not confirmed, based on the anomalous character of the Petri dish of review. In this, there is more than a little truth that in confirming a high-level political crime it is necessary to investigate the actions of those seeking to hold actors to account; the tell-tale is the cover-up.

In addition to qualitative features, it is appropriate to refer briefly to scale or quantity. It is arguable that Type 2 intelligence crime—that is to say, actors or assets empowered or enabled by intelligence agencies—is among the most prolific and deadly types of crime in recent modern history. CIA assets were used to support Yoweri Museveni, whom it called a 'peacemaker', in the build-up to the Rwandan genocide of 1994, which killed 800,000 people (Epstein, 2017). The CIA was 'intimately involved in equipping and training Guatemalan security forces that murdered thousands of civilians' beginning in 1966, including setting up a safe house that was used for exchanges between the forces and US contacts (Farah, 2002). The agency provided target lists and weapons for a plan that resulted in the killing of

Chilean Army General René Schneider and guided Chile into the military coup of 1973 that led to the deaths of over 40,000 (CBC, 2018). In the meantime, the CIA also helped establish Operation Condor, a banding together of South American military juntas, in which South American intelligence agencies were networked into an assassination and disappearance program under US guidance (Huggins, 1998). In Argentina, unknown covert classified support and the 'broad blessing of the CIA' supported the 'dirty war' and the killing and disappearance of 30,000 people (Hall, 2019). In 1967, 'the blond ghost', Theodor Shackley Jr., masterminded the CIA's Phoenix Operation so that it 'succeeded in assassinating 10,000 civilians in South Vietnam' (Drosnin, 1975; Hancock & Wexler, 2014; Valentine, 2014). Perhaps the biggest of dozens of examples (see Blum, 2003) is the work of Henry Kissinger (Hitchens, 2012), Marshall Green and others in the CIA to turn Indonesia from its neutral stance, beginning in 1965, by fomenting a military rebellion against President Sukarno (Prados, 2006).[12] What followed on the day when General Suharto took control was the shutting down of the media, the criminalisation of the PKI and a purge of the instruments of socialism and unionism (the SOBSI) and every socialist and communist in the country, something that came to be known as 'Jakarta'—a codeword for US-backed mass killing (Bevins, 2020). The CIA assisted in the development of the plan by sending Suharto's men the lists of targets. The scale of the killing may never be known but could be over one million, and as it was occurring a cheerleading western media cast the murderous rampage as a reaction to a prior atrocity that never in fact took place (Bevins, 2020; CBC, 2018). The above examples are the tip of the iceberg.

To the objection that far too many furtive transactions are being deemed intelligence crime it is instructive to recall that crime is meaningful only where there is a reference to intent (through the depoliticised criminal justice lens inclusive of negligent or reckless disregard for human life). In most, if not all, of the cases above, the principal perpetrators or enablers of the transgressive actions were well aware that they were trafficking in a 'dirty' business in the service of an ideological 'mastery.' Despite countless tomes in the terrorism literature to the contrary, in these state-backed actions 'shock and awe' terrorism *is* the delivery mechanism; so much so that the argument is made that the more instantly shocking and disgraceful the action, the more completely defeated is the will of the opposition and thus the more effective is the action (see quote of Benjamin Netanyahu introducing Chap. 5).

The preferred worldview of most denizens of democracy is that the heart of the state reflects its plurality and thus intelligence crimes will be a minimal, unavoidable aberration. However, it is contended here that this view presumes the ideal of classic liberal democracy that is already smudged out of existence by the object in question (intelligence, the political) (Mouffe, 2006; Bruff, 2014). These are crimes of disproportion, qualitatively in their deep and explicit disregard for human rights and life and quantitatively on the scale of their victimisation.

Apex Crime

In this work, we are exploring crimes of omission and commission in interaction sponsored by intelligence actors and assets. In respect of this, the present analysis includes spectacular acts of provocative terrorism, referred to as 'apex crime'. It is proposed that such crime is defined in terms of the boldness of the event, the importance of its object, the singularity of the narrative and the consensus of review.

First, there is a challenging, authority-questioning *event*. Its ontology or phenomenology involves the shock and awe of violent spectacle—a signal event with far-reaching reverberations. It is a bold and belligerent provocation that is intended to signal the first volley in an act of war. It leaves in its wake the open question of its genesis and the nature of the conflict to which it belongs.

Second, its object is a treasured symbol or an active agency in the political, cultural or constitutional order of the target entity. The object is a high-value target because it possesses these political, cultural and also strategic values. In summarising these first two factors, there is an event of spectacular violence that poses a question for authorities.

Third, the event is stipulated or framed by authorities through a *narrative* or knowledge configuration. As Clemens (2007), Wagner-Pacifici (2010) and Frankenberg (2005) suggest, the immediate interpretation of a paradigm event by well-positioned political authorities will overdetermine its significance.[13] This framing, in which there is enormous investment as a matter of the exception in the security of government (Schmitt, 1985), is mooted soon after the event in advance of any criminal investigation.[14] It involves a quickly produced 'government discourse' or 'official narrative.' Consistent with terrorism and political crime, this narrative involves the nomination of the victim (the state), the perpetrator (the state's ideological opponent) and the implicit purpose behind the event (a successor ideology). It also sets up the parameters of the official review of the event to confirm the already-named sequence of causation and significance.

The pressure to recover and discover in line with the official narrative is such that much possibly relevant evidence will not be gathered and tested; that those doing the gathering and testing do not do so to the highest standards; and that the gathering, selection, testing and analysis of the evidence will be limited in scope or terms of reference (that is, according to a confirmation bias) even where there ought to be several lines of inquiry. Nonetheless, it is by reference to the deviation from standard practices and protocols in the selection, mandate, protection and interpretation of evidence from the crime scene (and in the behaviour of experts that contribute to any forensic record or lack thereof, particularly in unusual or innovative interpretations that appear to seek accord with the government/official narrative) that state actor culpability in a signal or watershed crime may be hypothesised and tested.

The fourth factor defining these events is the *review* of the crime or event, dependent on government accounts, which more or less confirms the government narrative.[15] This is established on a national security footing and is subject to irregular processes of discovery and review. Because the event may function to change or preserve a preferred order or government posture, there is much at stake in its interpretation, so the official narrative performs to produce a context bias that politicises the review process. This sets up a confirmation bias for evidence discovery, indicating what may be sensible to search for, examine and test.

Each of these four factors is necessary. That is to say, an apex crime by definition requires that the event (inclusive of its resolution) is spectacular, putting on notice that it has launched an attack on a strategic or cultural asset of major cultural and political significance. In significant crimes involving ideologically sensitive resources, the government authority is under pressure to quickly categorise the event (perhaps as a kind of crime or war) and suggest a perpetrator. This is because, as Wagner-Pacifici (2010: 1356) argues, where events in material and rhetorical boundaries will be incomplete and subject to their innate 'restlessness,' this is the very condition that governments must tamp down on as they are evaluated for decisiveness. The narrative proffered is one in which the state, nation, society, culture or political values are named as the vulnerable commodity, target and victim. The government also broadcasts one or more of its ideological opponents as the purposeful perpetrator. This nomination of victim, perpetrator and implicit purpose establishes the victimology. The hasty publication of a narrative sets up a *confirmation bias* for evidence discovery, indicating what is sensible to search for and examine.

Due to the substantial political interest in the investigations and forensic outcomes of apex crime, deviations from or novel applications of best practice forensics are hypothesised to occur with regularity where the government has deemed an event to possess national security implications and applications. They are prone to be dismissed as irrelevant to the outcome of the investigation. In support of the dominant narrative the forensic record may have serious weaknesses, but the expert authority to challenge these weaknesses is also enfeebled by limited access to original materials, methods, records and testimonies upon which to apply fresh analysis according to alternative theories or hypotheses. The ability to publicly disseminate raw data, tests and analysis comes up against the national security and secrecy claims of the executive branch, whose agents and actors may act to quarantine evidence, tests and results, and may even destroy trace evidence before it can be analysed.

To relate these factors to the previous chapter, and as will be examined in the following chapter, we are exploring an event framed by an authority, a scene in which a narrative is stipulated, and a review that is constrained by official reporting.

Confirmation Bias: Too Important to Be Uncertain

The reconciliation of the sovereign to a liberal democratic political order is achieved by applying the assumptions, methods and means of the law or legality, particularly in its universality, transparency and publicity, and common application. Roach (2010: 52–53) observes important differences between evidence and intelligence: publicity versus secrecy; cross-examination versus summary and uncontested intelligence; disclosure of exculpatory methods and material versus privileged means and methods; external evaluation of evidence by jury or judge on burden of proof vs. internal checks by cleared individuals on internal standards; expertise established versus expertise assumed; and rules of evidence supporting a probative measure versus no external measure of presumptively reliable internal attributions of reliability.

As we have seen, in the conduct of what passes for the actions of the sovereign, a rule of law legality would require that a review must be distinguished, separate and unconflicted. Where criminal action is taken by intelligence on behalf of the sovereign it cannot be the case that there is no common ground or interest between reviewer and reviewed. Both courts and legislators are generally averse to close scrutiny of national security (Lustgarten & Leigh, 1994) precisely because it is often in play that means and methods, including agents and assets, will be exposed and with that the conduct of the sovereign is subject to exposure and uncertain dominion. According to Schmitt (1988) and several others (Agamben, 1998; Agamben & Emcke, 2001; Foucault, 2003), the following lesson is to be taken from this: to so expose the vital organs or spirit of the sovereign is to lay bare the vitality of the nation-state, which, according to the longstanding realist doctrine, is to invite its extinguishing by existential enemies, both outside and inside the nation-state.

The point that law or legalisation is not an antidote to arbitrariness or the reach of exceptionalism has often been made (Agamben, 1998; Bauman, 2000). It is not so much legality, but the relationship with visibility (cf. Garland, 2012) that best describes what might be called the blurring of law values by security intelligence values. Legal practices, as is well known, may be securitised, militarised or intelligencised. This means that the operation of cornerstone principles (transparency, the right to confront one's accusers, equality of arms, disclosure, etc.) is restricted so greatly as to leave only the imprimatur of legal propriety.[16] The manipulation of political visibility through the stewarding, shepherding and criminalising of information possession defers to longstanding legal traditions and institutions, even as these are denuded. But the claim that the law thus achieved is constitutionally 'empty' can also be countered as a view that is weakly nostalgic or reverent about modernism.[17] On the contrary, it is 'strong constitutionalism' together with economic vitality and national security that binds the courts to a significant role. The authority of jurists is relatively weak, but the expert knowledge of legal professionals is harnessed for the stewarding of 'strong' government, and is willingly given. It is already 'intelligencised' in the substitution of security for legalised intelligence norms, including the protection of sources and methods, and of court judgments for executive discretionary authority or intelligence summaries (questions explored further with illustrations in Chap. 7).

This situation is not overcome by the wish that it were not so, or the claim that it is marginal to everyday reality. As we shall explore in subsequent chapters, references to intelligence crime are now regular stories in the mainstream media. These are presented according to the conventions of accuracy or fact-checking where information operations are at play in a nexus between mainstream media outlets and intelligence interests. Currently, as we shall explore, there is a division or rift running down from the executive *into and through* the deep politics or intelligence bureaucracy of the national security state. In the event that there is no firm bipartisan consensus, a deep division runs through the state and there is no unified official narrative, so that covert activities risk exposure *as* crimes. Thus are the limits set on the exposure of intelligence crime—crime that is more or less excused from criminal or forensic discovery or recovery.

Transaction and Blur

Having established some background concerning criminal justice, political interest and intelligence and the interconnections between them, including suggesting why it is valuable to carve out understanding of this discovered species of crime, it may be useful now to indicate how we will be restricting the use of the concept of intelligence crime, particularly concerning transactional actions that are given cover by authorities.

To know intelligence crime it is necessary to foreground the interests and actors normally left in the shadows or marginalised by criminology and sociology. Rather than postulating with much of that literature that these interests and actors have a limited capacity to transact illegal activities in a domain of copious legal restrictions, bureaucracies and oversight agencies, our working hypothesis is that they are provided with the tools sufficient to overcome the restrictive encumbrance and indeed that capable careerists possess more than a marginal capacity to do so. Security intelligence actors that have positioned themselves closest to what we refer to as the sovereign vitality of the nation-state are able to exploit the competing authorities of government and the complex configuration of bureaucracies and oversight. They stand in for the necessary capacity of the sovereign to assert the exception, a capacity that is immersive of the moment and consistent with the absolute requirement for freedom of the sovereign function, averse to the uncertainties posed by retrospective reconciliation to *non-exceptional* government norms or form (see Fig. 3.3).

In this role, there is no doubt a continuum of deniable action. The intelligence sponsor is usually keen to keep the action unacknowledged and unseen (as a covert action). It is true that secret wars cannot easily be denied and not for very long (Cormac & Aldrich, 2018: 482). On the other hand, secret assassinations are often intended to remain unseen, unacknowledged and unavailable to forensic investigation. As Cormac and Aldrich (2018: 482) observe, in the US, Executive Order 12333 and its successor[18] cover 'special activities' that 'are planned and executed so that the role of the United States Government is not apparent or acknowledged publicly'. Moreover, there are two more instruments of secretive covert action, under Special Access Programs (SAP) and Alternative to Compensatory Control Measures (ACCMs), that do not have the requirement of congressional notice on the claim that the Supreme Court must be satisfied that it falls under the president's authority, especially in wartime—and the US is in a state of permanent war (Bacevich, 2010)—to classify and control matters bearing on national security. SAP includes a category of waived programs that permit the agency head to restrict reporting to the Gang of

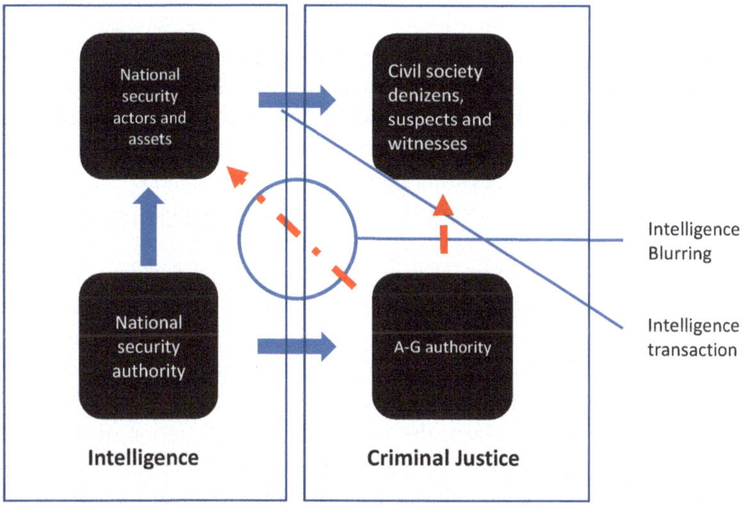

Fig. 3.3 Transactional intelligence crime and blur

Eight. Hundreds of ACCMs that have been effected since 9/11 are strictly compartmentalised, do not require formal approval of agency heads and require no reporting to Congress; and some are known to have covered illegalities (Kibbe, 2020: 318–319).

In addition, already by 2008 there was a US$50 billion private security intelligence market in the US serviced by 100 companies, ranging from behemoth Lockheed Martin to SpectTal, a private company that employs personnel with top-secret clearances who have performed intelligence missions in Afghanistan and Iraq (Shorrock, 2008: 12). Currently, companies including Dynology, the Analysis Corporation and the Global Strategies Group are in a position to exploit their relationships with senior personnel from intelligence, including Paul Brennan who may be able to waive conflict of interest (Ambinder, 2009).

Intelligence crime involves the exploitation of third parties, including corporate and private intelligence and information operations services, arms and drug traders, guerrilla units, mercenaries, terrorist organisations and outlawed political organisations. Intelligence incorporates state actors as assets that are entrusted to act in a covert capacity to provide information and to carry out insurgencies or counter-insurgency repressions. As observed by Scott (1996: 8), this activity mimics the behaviour of undercover policing operations against the trade in narcotics and other illicit organised activities:

> in practice these efforts at control lead to the use of criminal informants; and this practice, continued over a long period of time, turns informants into double agents with status within the police as well as the mob. The protection of informants and their crimes encourages favours, payoffs, and eventually systemic corruption. The phenomenon of 'organized crime' arises: entire criminal structures that come to be tolerated by the police because of their usefulness in informing on lesser criminals.

This is the ambiguous space in which the vitality of the sovereign is maintained and its means to disrupt political networks is nurtured. Following Scott (1996), it is the 'deep state' locus in which a 'covert extra-legal structure of state bureaucracy' (Ahmed, 2012: 18) feeds on covert transactions. In the continuous refinement of intelligence methods in the context of the Schmittian imperative, there is a drive to support actors and assets by providing them with resources and cover in operations that are built up over time to compromise high-level financial, political and even cultural targets.

Cormac and Aldrich (2018) maintain that there are many more such 'special activities' that are *implausibly* deniable than is commonly understood. Relevant here is the inadequate oversight of the expansion of military and intelligence plans and budgets, and the lack of accountability around the funding of such (Lindorff, 2018). The question of what remains unseen and unacknowledged cannot be answered without such an accounting. Given the nature of 'special' action, it would not be possible to make an estimation of what is hidden within and outside the archives or available to select congressional intelligence committee notification or need to know (Kibbe, 2020: 318). To relate this back to our discussion of the dark figure of crime, the dark figure of intelligence crime has an added blurring of black ink that renders the extent of intelligence crime difficult to quantify.

Blur: Anti-forensics or Wrongdoing Erased

Most of our understanding of crime and criminology is dependent upon the foundation of modernism and the emancipatory capacity of law. The suspicious view is that the powerful exploit law to maintain the emancipation of the powerless, but this is a marginal standpoint, most active in the more subaltern places of criminological thought, practice and policy. The sceptical view that the attribution or finding of criminality is relatively dependent on political interest is also somewhat marginal, although quite active in human rights texts. Following Popper (2006) and Hofstadter (2012), the idea that prominent persons who by their stature and knowledge pose a threat to powerful people may be terminated at the behest of rogue actors instrumentalised by a dark portion of the state is deemed 'conspiratorial' in most of social science.

Forensics is concerned with how scientific principles and methods may assist in recovering the traces of crimes and most of criminology is preoccupied with the crimes of relatively powerless persons. We are concerned to highlight the intelligence blur evident across the range of intelligence crime operation and control and the exploitation of the dark archive in information operations is a necessary instrument in the commission of intelligence crime. Here, again, against the liberal 'prejudice' that the arena of intelligence in liberal democracies is by and large open for external review, we draw from political criminology in arguing that the realist construction of sovereign vitality and the competing or prior value of sovereign decisionism or exception need to be considered as more than an inconvenient quibble. In these events at least, the intelligence blur effects a diminishment of the relative values of 'absolute' rule of law legality.[19]

On this point it is necessary to acknowledge that smart criminals involved in organised crime also attempt to cover their tracks or pre-empt the criminal and forensic investigation. There is a continuum of expert know-how between organised or illicit criminal networks and intelligence crime actors. Indeed, through this interplay each side has refined its methods. If we build the analysis by drawing on Tilly's (1985) observations, it is no surprise that there is much overlap between the two sides as the cultivation of illicit networks implicates the sovereign in the continuation of illicit state crime. The difference is in the expectation of protection and cover for actions, not only by the executive but also by the other branches of government, who also ultimately take the hard choice proffered that 'society must be defended'.

The nexus between law enforcement and security intelligence is the liminal space between a domesticated order governed by modern legality and an 'international system' in which 'the strong do what they can and the weak suffer what they must' (Thucydides, 1996: 5.89), finds fertile ground. It also marks the relation between the preservation of the established order in the identity of the middle-class sensibility and the adaptive transmogrification of the political heartland through the absorption of cosmopolitanism and cultural or ethnic diversity. In the meantime, the sovereign's capacity to maintain the realm of modern liberal democratic institutions and beliefs is threatened so this also must be defended.

Conclusion

Against the claims of observers of security intelligence agencies and actors that most contentious hidden information is merely embarrassing to government or is simply over-inclusive in seeking not to reveal asset identities or methods, the *prejudicial* critical institutional assumption here is that the dark space of national security is a fertile domain for criminal predations. It is a matter of historical and verifiable fact that governments wilfully engage in campaigns of disinformation across domestic security and foreign policy and do so by establishing a domain of activity that protects decision-makers and punishes whistle-blowers.[20] The maintenance of that domain depends in part on the framing of security and national security, in particular the regular or episodic countering of the 'public law' requirement of the liberal democratic constitutional state.

There is an assumption that big intelligence crimes may be hidden, sometimes even in plain sight. In addition, there is a dismissal of the dark archive as containing mostly embarrassing material evidencing what is already well-known. There is a popular compulsion not to believe that the authorities may be harmful or malign. Even where there is also a great deal of scepticism about and distrust of government, there is a desire to see the problem as an aberration and to sweep up the bad apples or even rotten barrels and return to a status quo ante. This is complex because it involves the urge to believe (contrary to the evidence discussed above) in a just world in which 'your side' is genuinely involved in the pursuit of the good, and the occasional mistake or some bad apple should not be used to claim otherwise. As is known based on authority studies (Blass, 1999) and research into cognitive bias, witnesses to events will push their experience along in the wheelbarrow of comfortable belief (Lerner & Miller, 1978). Prosecutors largely fail to prosecute police and, in contrast to their treatment of other accused, are conflicted by ongoing organisational and institutional attachments so that grand juries very rarely hear sufficient inculpatory evidence (Levine, 2015, 2016: 745).

We must understand intelligence crime as political crime which exploits the authority and legitimacy of the sovereign nation-state. In its capacity to fold into an archive of its own design, intelligence crime remains unseen or, if seen, unrecognised as belonging with the sovereign capacity. This indicates that this crime is always already a measure of political power and capacity, and the solidarity behind the political union, a matter to which we will return in subsequent discussion. Since the approval of the public must be maintained in liberal democracies (Dahl, 1971), governments are highly reliant on public relations or information operations, as intermediaries through which the agency of the message is obscured.

According to some observers, liberal democracies have been whittling away at the justice ideal to install a new normal. Security policies build up the dispositive as an affordance (Michael & Still, 1992) to support the state's preferred view of political constituency. The authoritarian neoliberal order is achieved by jump-starts, particularly as policy-makers respond to signal events (Bruff, 2014; de Lint, 2020). The dispositive fosters political identity by postponing, containing or inviting the collapse of biopolitics into a 'zone of indistinction'.[21] This involves a reinvigorated vitality of the sovereign (or the executive security prerogative) that is praised by 'establishment' liberals and conservatives. This presses down on the body of justice and overdetermines the criminal justice outcome. It is as if, as some have said (Schmitt, 1988; Ericson, 2007), liberal democracy is too weak, particularly in respect of criminal justice. It suffices to rely on the assertions of the sovereign according to a probabilistic calculus based on summaries of underlying raw and analysed intelligence. As Ahmad and Monaghan (2020) have observed,

> the 'war on terror' has transitioned from exceptional legality and a focus on wars abroad into a dissipated but broadening field of security governance. With the threshold of probability, the state is required to marshal evidence based on events, likelihoods, and concrete proof of criminal activities.

This is not to suggest that this is always or mostly effective. Public scepticism about government is also such that alternative sources and authorities are rising in popularity. Opinion polls provide evidence that a large segment of the voting public does not find government credible on many important policy questions (Robinson et al., 2013; Hetherington, 2005). Today there is much angst among corporate media opinion-makers and government policy-makers over the rise of 'false news', particularly as social and alternative media provide conduits for versions of events that are hostile to both official narratives and scientific opinion (Flintham et al., 2018).

Given the wide disconnect between what Marxists would call the system contradictions in the normative environments of intelligence and those of criminal justice, it is unsurprising that there is a great deal of hand-wringing concerning how to manage the optics of trust under such conditions of institutional collision and contradiction.

This chapter has developed the concept of intelligence crime and intelligence blur, by which we refer to the eclipsing of legal and political authority by security intelligence. While the exclusionary cut lies at the heart of the modern liberal state order (Lazar, 2006), intelligence offers a negative productive power or a purposeful negation of life into history. Thus, a dispositive or 'security apparatus' produces an intelligence-based anti-politics in which cloaked knowledge justifies, penetrates and, at strategic moments, overturns popular and nation-state sovereignty.

Notes

1. Blackstone's concept of ratio comes from his policy discussions, and stipulates that 'it is better that ten guilty persons escape than that one innocent suffer' (Blackstone, 1809). Benjamin Franklin suggested the sceptical Republican emphasis of US jurisprudence by making the task of government more challenging: 'it is better that 100 guilty Persons should escape than that one innocent Person should suffer' (Franklin, 1970).
2. For instance, the NSC, through documents including NSC 10/2, ordered the CIA to carry out clandestine operations, but in such a manner that, if discovered, the US Government would be in a position to deny its role in the operation. Fletcher Prouty describes how, as a member of what he referred to as the 'secret team' and as a briefing officer for the CIA at the Department of Defense, he was in a privileged position to have pivotal network access via almost daily contact with the President, the Chairman of the Joint Chiefs of Staff and the Secretary of Defense. This allowed him to develop operations that were provided by innuendo, or that permitted unstated directives in secret, deniable operations from the centre of power (Prouty, 2011).
3. See, for instance, the discussion of Dick Cheney's actions in Scott (2007) and Suskind (2006) and the discussion of the weakness of parliamentary democracy in Schmitt (1988).
4. Neocleous (2007) notes that Locke's work was crucial for the liberalisation of the absolutist doctrine. The sovereign function is the production of security, for which the main criterion is necessity rather than the rule of law. This places the priority of the rule of law in the realm of security. Since the key role of the state is the protection of property rights, the function of the sovereign is to secure those rights, and liberty is bound up in the project of security.
5. In fact, an apparent minority of those named as the 9/11 terrorists demonstrated these beliefs in their actions prior to the attack.
6. Please note that intelligence is being simplified in the present analysis. It is most frequently understood to consist of a division between operations and analysis between technology, culture, consumers and the intelligence cycle. For a good overview see Berkowitz and Goodman (2000).

7. For Agamben (1998), it is the necessary exceptional or sovereign practice of cutting the sacred in the act of discovering bare life, a cut the methodology or sources and methods of which cannot be exposed without undermining the strength or power of the sovereign. For Mouffe (2006), this is a cut that continuously produces a new antagonism from agonism.
8. The visibility of intelligence production oscillates according to the discretionary cut (through sovereignty) of an executive authority (Stehr & Adolf, 2018).
9. In discussion about law, too, we have a story of its 'beleaguered foundation' (Fitzpatrick, 2002: 242), in myths or in the objectification of pre-existent or emergent values and interests. The founding of law in original or foundational acts of violence is a story about the establishment of a sovereign who is then too dynamic or active to be incorporated into law's ambit. As pointed out in Brighenti (2006: 106) the maintenance of legitimate and illegitimate spheres of commercial activity (in drugs or in support of politics) is a legacy of the beleaguered foundation.
10. The term 'transactive information' denotes latent political capability or information weaponisation, as the revelation of such information will produce a kinetic impact on a valued relation in support of the interests of the consumer.
11. By intelligence we mean state activity that is dependent on confidential sources and methods performed by agents or officers of the state to produce information or by covert action to support sovereign security (see, for example, Warner, 2020: 10).
12. During the Gerakan 30 September Movement, soldiers were sent out to kidnap some of their army commanders accused of plotting a right-wing coup, a ploy that offered cover for General Suharto to take control of Jakarta, and from there the country. The military, possibly with the aid of RAND Corporation consultant Guy Pauker, cooked up a story that the Communist Party of Indonesia (PKI) had taken the alleged leaders of the right-wing coup back to the Halim Air Force Base, where naked dancing women mutilated and tortured the generals (Bevins, 2020). This ruse was used to support the counter-revolution that is still celebrated today
13. When an event is nominated as an open challenge to the ordering principle (Buzan, 1999) or the status quo ante of social and political norms, security pivots on the ambiguous (de Lint & Virta, 2004). As we know from long experience (Blum, 2003), this presents an opportunity to cajole support for a refreshed faith in government authorities, allowing them to restore or expand the reach of empire and the space of exception (Schmitt, 1988).
14. As per Keller (2011), an act's ontology, phenomenology and transactability (or nature, knowledge and implicit purpose) are quickly stipulated or fixed by a government leader or designate according to an 'establishment' or 'official' narrative of the crime event.
15. In a secondary review of the event, experts and the media confirm somewhat tautologically the official narrative. The sensitivity of the national security discourse in addition to its statutory obligations, and the media's proneness

to influence from information operations by national security actors, urges support for the official narrative. In line with this, resources and authorities that are dependent on those terms of reference are directed to actors and agencies that may be more likely to align with the narrative and away from hypotheses that would lead to alternative lines of inquiry. As a crime with watershed political stakes or high political significance, a signal crime requires the mediation of events through the device of national security instruments of information control. Primary information or hard data may be subject to national security exceptions on public law information control (such as secrecy or confidentiality restrictions). The mainstream media, and particularly high-placed media sources, provides the official narrative with supportive information transmission to internal and external audiences. Academic and industry authorities rely on official pronouncements and verifiable 'facts' that derive from government disclosures. The result is that one conspiracy (the official narrative) is reviewed as truth and other narratives are branded as conspiracy. Consequently, a critical or radical forensics of apex crime is left bereft of the requisite authorities.

16. As is also well-known, the history of adversarial law may be characterised in terms of the severance of physical coercion from disclosure and bargaining (cf. Langbein, 1978; Green, 1997). That history has aligned with the development of the modern legal subject, in particular its reliance on the putative contest between equals. However, the development above is not simply the return of the inquisition. The practices of the inquisition occurred in the Middle Ages whereas 'combined effects' interrogation is being sutured to the extant institutions of the modern liberal nation-state.
17. Intelligence bureaucracies have finessed the monopoly on 'national security' to further the advantages accruing from the opacity of their files and the inviolability of their sources and methods. The nature of these monopolies and advantages also push the core of intelligence work in the direction of collection rather than analysis, and within this, towards covert action rather than passive surveillance (cf. Gill, 1994; Johnson, 1989; Marchetti et al., 1974; Wise & Ross, 1967; Richelson & Ball, 1985). As a consequence, sophisticated intelligence has become temporally and structurally aggressive, used for intervention prior to an undesired event occurring. Information or communications networks may accordingly be corrected, in the disciplinary sense, before they are fully operational. The finest intelligence work becomes secret action carried out pre-emptively. Secret information that can serve public policy without being available to public scrutiny is the special product of intelligence agencies. When political security information has leaked out and is no longer rarefied, the operation of the institutions of liberal governance (legislatures, media, judiciary, etc.) are invited to apply a retroactive seal of approval.
18. Executive Order 12333–United States intelligence activities, 4 December 1981, https://www.archives.gov/federal-register/codification/executive-order/12333.html(accessible on 18 March 2018); S. Rep. No. 102–85 (1991), p. 43.
19. Please note, this paragraph is reproduced from de Lint (2008) courtesy of Windsor Yearbook Access to Justice.

20. Recent examples include domestic US counter-intelligence across the FBI, NSA and CIA (Churchill & Vander Wall, 1990), Vietnam (Ellsberg, 2003) and the recent regime change wars in Iraq (Robinson, 2017), Afghanistan (Whitlock, 2019) and Syria (McKinney, 2012).
21. According to Agamben's reading (1998), this is because behind nation-state politics is a sovereign power that continuously achieves the transmogrification of sacred life into bare life. It is this politicisation of bare life, or the rendering of the exception as the rule and the margin as the centre, that characterises the realist political order.

References

Agamben, G. (1998/1995). *Homo sacer: Sovereign power and bare life* (D. Heller-Roazen, Trans.). Stanford, CA: Stanford University Press.

Agamben, G., & Emcke, C. (2001). Security and terror. *Theory and Event, 5*(4), 1–2.

Ahmed, N. M. (2012). Capitalism, covert action and state-terrorism: Toward a political economy of the dual state. In E. Wilson (Ed.), *The dual state: Parapolitics, Carl Schmitt and the national security complex*. Ashgate.

Ahmad, F., & Monaghan, J. (2020). From probabilities to possibilities: Terrorism peace bonds, pre-emptive security, and modulations of criminal law. *Crime Law Soc Change*

Ambinder, M. (2009, December 30). White House grants ethics waiver to John Brennan. *The Atlantic*. https://www.theatlantic.com/business/archive/2009/12/white-house-grants-ethics-waiver-to-john-brennan/32798/.

Arkes, H. R., & Mellers, B. A. (2002). Do juries meet our expectations? *Law and Human Behavior, 26*, 625–663.

Bacevich, A. J. (2010). *Washington rules: America's path to permanent war*. Metropolitan Books.

Basaran, T. (2010). *Security, law and borders: At the limits of liberties*. Routledge.

Bauman, Z. (2000). *Modernity and the holocaust*. New York: Cornell University Press.

Bedford, K. (2011). Forensic science service provider models: Is there a 'best' option? *Australian Journal of Forensic Sciences, 43*(2–3), 147–156.

Berkowitz, B. D., & Goodman, A. E. (2000). *Best truth: Intelligence in the information age*. Yale University Press.

Bevins, V. (2020). *The Jakarta method: Washington's anticommunist crusade and the mass murder program that shaped our world*. Public Affairs.

Brighenti, A. (2006). Dogville, or, the dirty birth of law. *Thesis Eleven, 87*(1), 96–111.

Bigo, D. (2006). Internal and external aspects of security. *European Security, 15*(4), 385–404.

Black, D. (2004). Terrorism as social control. In M. Deflem (Ed.), *Terrorism and counterterrorism: Criminological perspectives*. Amsterdam: Elsevier.

Blackstone, W. (1809). *Commentaries on the laws of England: In four books* (Vol. 1). A. Strahan.

Blass, T. (1999). The Milgram paradigm after 35 years: Some things we now know about obedience to authority. *Journal of Applied Social Psychology, 29*(5), 955–978.

Blum, W. (2003). *Killing hope: US and CIA interventions since WWII*. London: Zed Books.

Brodeur, J.-P. (1983). High policing and low policing: Remarks about the policing of political activities. *Social Problems, 30*(5), 507–520.

Brodeur, J. P., & Dupont, B. (2006). Knowledge workers or 'knowledge' workers? *Policing & Society, 16*(1), 7–26.

Bybee, J. S. (2002). Memorandum for Albert R. Gonzales, Counsel to the President Re: Standards of conduct for interrogation under 18 U.S.C. §§ 2340–2340A. http://dspace.wrlc.org/doc/bitstream/2041/70967/00355_020801_004display.pdf.

Bruff, I. (2014). The rise of authoritarian neoliberalism. *Rethinking Marxism, 26*(1), 113–129.

Buzan, B. (1999). Change and insecurity reconsidered. *Contemporary Security Policy, 20*(3), 1–17.

CBC News. (2018, April 18). Indonesia discusses massacres that killed 500,000. CBC News. https://www.bbc.com/news/world-asia-36076069.

Churchill, W., & Vander Wall, J. (1990). *The COINTELPRO papers*. Boston: South End.

Clemens, E. S. (2007). Toward a historicized sociology: Theorizing events, processes, and emergence. *Annual Review of Sociology, 33*, 527–549.

Colombani, J.-M. (2001, September 12).We are all Americans. *Le Monde*, Paris, France.

Cormac, R., & Aldrich, R. J. (2018). Grey is the new black: Covert action and implausible deniability. *International Affairs, 94*(3), 477–494. https://doi.org/10.1093/ia/iiy067.

Dahl, R. A. (1971). *Polyarchy: Participation and opposition* (Vol. 54). Yale University Press.

Dean, M. (2002). Liberal government and authoritarianism. *Economy and Society, 31*(1), 37–61.

de Lint, W. (2008). Intelligent security. *The Windsor Yearbook of Access to Justice, 26*(2), 195–240.

de Lint, W. (2020). Criminology 9/11. *Globalizations, 17*(7), 1157–1177.

de Lint, W., O'Connor, D., & Cotter, R. (2007). Controlling the flow: Security, exclusivity, and criminal intelligence in Ontario. *International Journal of the Sociology of Law, 35*(1), 41–58.

de Lint, W., & Virta, S. (2004). Security in ambiguity: Towards a radical security politics. *Theoretical Criminology, 8*(4), 495–519.

DeKay, M. (1996). The difference between Blackstone-like error ratios and probabilistic standards of proof. *Law & Social Inquiry, 21*, 95–132.

Drosnin, M. (1975, August 22). Phoenix: The CIAs biggest assassination program. *New York Times*. https://www.google.com/url?sa = t&rct = j&q = &esrc = s&source = web&cd = &cad = rja&uact = 8&ved = 2ahUKEwj7yJjE47fsAhXWzzgGHVGbCwcQFjAAegQIAhAC&url = https%3A%2F%2Fwww.cia.gov%2Flibrary%2Freadingroom%2Fdocs%2FCIA-RDP90-01208R000100190002-1.pdf&usg=AOvVaw0mTg0QQlKeHp9LVeqEz3mL.

Donzelot, J. (2008). Michel Foucault and liberal intelligence. *Economy and Society, 37*(11), 15–34.

Dulles, A. (2006). *The craft of intelligence: America's legendary spy master on the fundamentals of intelligence gathering for a free world*. New York: Rowman & Littlefield.

Ellsberg, D. (2003). *Secrets: A memoir of Vietnam and the Pentagon Papers*. Penguin.

Ericson, R. V. (2007). *Crime in an insecure world*. Cambridge: Polity.

Epstein, H. (2017, September 12). The violence that shocked the world in 1994 did not come from nowhere: While the CIA looked on, its allies in the Ugandan government helped to spread terror and fuel ethnic hatred. *The Guardian*.

Ericson, R. V., & Baranek, P. M. (1982). *The ordering of justice: A study of accused persons as dependents in the criminal process*. Toronto: University of Toronto Press.

Ewick, P., & Silbey, S. S. (1992). Narrating social structure: Stories of resistance to legal authority. *American Journal of Sociology*, 1328–1372.

Farah, D. (2002, February 17). Al Qaeda's road paved with gold. *Washington Post*.

Fitzpatrick, P. (2002). 'No higher duty': Mabo and the failure of legal foundation. *Law and Critique, 13*(3), 233–252.

Finer, S. E. (2002). *The man on horseback: The role of the military in politics*. Transaction Publishers.

Flintham, M., Karner, C., Bachour, K., Creswick, H., Gupta, N., & Moran, S. (2018, April). Falling for fake news: Investigating the consumption of news via social media. In *Proceedings of the 2018 CHI Conference on Human Factors in Computing Systems* (pp. 1–10).

Foucault, M. (1972). The discourse on language. In *The archaeology of knowledge*. New York: Pantheon.

Foucault, M. (1980). 'The confession of the flesh' interview. In Colin Gordon (Ed.), *Power/knowledge: Selected interviews and other writings* (pp. 194–228). New York: Vintage.

Foucault, M. (1988). The political technology of individuals. In L. M. Martin, H. Gutman, & P. H. Hutton (Eds.), *Technologies of the self* (pp. 145–162). University of Massachusetts Press.

Foucault, M. (2003). *'Society must be defended': Lectures at the Collège de France, 1975–1976* (Vol. 1). Macmillan.

Fuller, L. L. (1964). *The morality of law*. Yale University Press.

Franklin, B. Works 293. (1970). Letter from Benjamin Franklin to Benjamin Vaughan (14 March 1785).

Frankenberg, R. (2005). A bridge over troubled waters, or what a difference a day makes: From the drama of production to the production of drama. *Social Analysis, 49*(3), 166–184.

Garland, D. (2012). *The culture of control: Crime and social order in contemporary society*. University of Chicago Press.

Gill, P. (1994). *Policing politics: Security intelligence and the liberal democratic state*. Routledge.

Green, A. (1997). How the criminal justice system knows. *Social and Legal Studies, 6*(1), 5–22.

Hall, K. (2019, April 12). Declassified documents show CIA knew Latin juntas killed dissidents abroad. *McClatchy Newspapers*.

Hancock, L., & Wexler, S. (2014). *Shadow warfare: The history of America's undeclared wars*. Counterpoint.

Hetherington, M. J. (2005). *Why trust matters: Declining political trust and the demise of American liberalism*. Princeton University Press.

Hitchens, C. (2012). *The trial of Henry Kissinger*. Atlantic Books.

Hofstadter, R. (2012). *The paranoid style in American politics*. Vintage.

Huggins, M. K. (1998). *Political policing: The United States and Latin America*. Durham, NC: Duke University Press.

Hughes, S. C. (2001). *The involvement of the forensic anthropologist in human rights issues* (Master's thesis). University of Tennessee. https://trace.tennessee.edu/utk_gradthes/4136.

Iacobucci, F., The Honourable Frank. (2008). *The Internal Inquiry into the Actions of Canadian Officials in Relation to Abdullah Almalki, Ahmad Abou-Elmaati and Muayyed Nureddin*. Ottawa: Queen's Printer.

Johnson, L. K. (1989). *America's secret power: The CIA in a democratic society*. Oxford University Press on Demand.

Jugo, A. (2017). Artefacts and personal effects from mass graves in Bosnia and Herzegovina. *Les Cahiers Sirice, 2*, 21–40.

Kafka, F. (1988). Before the law. In Nahum N. Glatzer (Ed.), *The collected short stories*. London: Penguin.

Keller, R. (2011). The sociology of knowledge approach to discourse. *Human Studies, 34*, 43–65.

Kibbe, J. D. (2020). Covert action and the Pentagon. In C. Andrews, R. Aldrich, & W. Wark (Eds.), *Secret intelligence: A reader* (pp. 512–526). New York: Routledge.

Langbein, J. H. (1978). Torture and plea bargaining. *University of Chicago Law Review, 46*(1, Fall), 3–22.

Latour, B., & Woolgar, S. (2013). *Laboratory life: The construction of scientific facts*. Princeton University Press.

Lau, R. R., & Schlesinger, M. (2005). Policy frames, metaphorical reasoning, and support for public policies. *Political Psychology, 26*(1), 77–114.

Lazar, N. C. (2006). Must exceptionalism prove the rule? An angle on emergency government in the history of political thought. *Politics and Society, 34*(2), 245–275.

Lerner, M. J., & Miller, D. T. (1978). Just world research and the attribution process: Looking back and ahead. *Psychological Bulletin, 85*(5), 1030–1045.

Levine, K. (2015). How we prosecute the police. *Georgia Law Journal, 104*, 745–776.

Levine, K. (2016). Who shouldn't prosecute the police. *Iowa Law Review, 101*(4), 1447–1496.

Lindorff, D. (2018, November 27). How US military spending keeps rising as the Pentagon flunks its audit. *The Nation*. https://www.thenation.com/article/archive/pentagon-audit-budget-fraud/.

Lustgarten, L., & Leigh, I. (1994). *National security and parliamentary democracy*. Oxford: Clarendon.

Marchetti, V., Marks, J. D., & Wulf, M. L. (1974). *The CIA and the cult of intelligence*. New York: Knopf.

McBarnet, D. J. (1978). *The police and the state: Arrest, legality and the law*. Aldershot: Croom Helm.

McKinney, C. (2012). *The illegal war on Libya*. SCB Distributor.

Mearsheimer, J. J., & Alterman, G. (2001). *The tragedy of great power politics*. WW Norton & Company.

Michael, M., & Still, A. (1992). A resource for resistance: Power-knowledge and affordance. *Theory and Society, 21*(6), 869–888.

Mouffe, C. (2006). *On the political*. Verso.

Newman, J. O. (1993). Beyond reasonable doubt. *New York University Law Review, 68*(5), 979–1002.

Neocleous, M. (2000). Against security. *Radical Philosophy, 1*(100), 7–15.

Neocleous, M. (2007). Security, liberty and the myth of balance: Towards a critique of security politics. *Contemporary Political Theory, 6*(2), 131–149.

O'Brien, M., & Littler, M. (2015). Introduction: On political criminology. *The Journal of Political Criminology, 1*(1), 1–6.

Packer, H. (1968). *The limits of the criminal sanction*. Stanford University Press.

Popper, K. (2006). The conspiracy theory of society. In D. Coady (Ed.), *Conspiracy theories: The philosophical debates*. London: Ashgate.

Prados, J. (2006). *Safe for democracy: The secret wars of the CIA*. Ivan R. Dee.

Prouty, L. F. (2011). *The secret team: The CIA and its allies in control of the United States and the world*. Skyhorse Publishing.

Richelson, J. T., & Ball, D. (1985). *The ties that bind: Intelligence cooperation between the UKUSA countries—The United Kingdom, the United States of America, Canada, Australia and New Zealand*. Allen & Unwin.

Roach, K. (2010). The eroding distinction between intelligence and evidence in terrorism investigation. In N. McGarrity, A. Lynch, & G. Williams (Eds.), *Counterterrorism and beyond* (pp. 48–68). Abington: Routledge.

Robinson, P. (2017). Learning from the Chilcot Report: Propaganda, deception and the 'war on terror'. *International Journal of Contemporary Iraqi Studies, 11*(1–2), 47–73.

Robinson, S. E., Liu, X., Stoutenborough, J. W., & Vedlitz, A. (2013). Explaining popular trust in the Department of Homeland Security. *Journal of Public Administration Research and Theory, 23*(3), 713–733. https://doi.org/10.1093/jopart/mus025.

Suskind, R. (2006). *One percent doctrine: Deep inside America's pursuit of its enemies since 9/11*. Simon & Schuster.

Schmitt, C. (1985). *Political theology* (G. Schwab, Trans.). Chicago: University of Chicago Press.

Schmitt, C. (1988). *The crisis of parliamentary democracy*. Cambridge, MA: MIT Press.

Scott, P. D. (1996). *Deep politics and the death of JFK*. California: University of California Press.

Scott, P. D. (2007). *9/11 Commission deception, Cheney's actions on 9/11, and why he should testify under oath*. http://www.peterdalescott.net.

Scott, P. D., & Marshall, J. (1998). *Cocaine politics: Drugs, armies, and the CIA in Central America*. University of California Press.

Shapiro, B. J. (1991). *'Beyond reasonable doubt' and 'probable cause': Historical perspectives on the Anglo-American law of evidence*. University of California Press.

Shorrock, T. (2008). *Spies for hire: The secret world of intelligence outsourcing*. New York: Simon & Schuster.

Skolnick, J. H. (2011). *Justice without trial: Law enforcement in democratic society*. Quid Pro Books.

Stehr, N., & Adolf, M. T. (2018). Knowledge/power/resistance. *Society, 55*(2), 193–198.

Thucydides. (1996). *The landmark Thucydides: A comprehensive guide to the Peloponnesian War*, Ed. Robert B. Strassler. New York: Free Press.

Tilly, C. (1985). War making and state making as organized crime. In T. Skocpol, P. Evans, & D. Rueschemeyer (Eds.), *Bringing the state back in*. New York: Cambridge.

Valentine, D. (2014). *The Phoenix Program: America's use of terror in Vietnam* (Vol. 5). Open Road Media.

Wagner-Pacifici, R. (2010). Theorizing the restlessness of events. *American Journal of Sociology, 115*(5), 1351–1386. https://doi.org/10.1086/651299.

Waldron, J. (2008). Positivism and legality: Hart's equivocal response to Fuller. *New York University Law Review, 83*(4), 1135–1169.

Warner, M. (2020). Wanted a definition of intelligence. In C. Andrews, R. Aldrich, & W. Wark (Eds.), *Secret intelligence: A reader* (pp. 4–12). New York: Routledge.

Weber, M. (1994). The profession and vocation of politics. *Weber: Political Writings, 309*, 313–315.

Weiner, T. (2008). *Legacy of ashes: The history of the CIA*. New York: Anchor Books.

Wilsnack, R. W. (1980). Information control: A conceptual framework for sociological analysis. *Urban Life, 8*(4), 467–499.

Wise, D., & Ross, T. B. (1967). *The espionage establishment*. New York: Random House.

Whitlock, D. (2019, December 9). At war with the truth: The Afghanistan papers. *Washington Post*. https://www.washingtonpost.com/graphics/2019/investigations/afghanistan-papers/documents-database/.

Yoo, J. C. (2002, August 1). Response to Alberto Gonzales' request for views on legality of interrogation techniques. United States Department of Justice, Office of the Legal Counsel. http://www.gwu.edu/~nsarchiv/NSAEBB/NSAEBB127/020801.pdf.

Zedner, Z. (2003). The concept of security: An agenda for comparative analysis. *Social & Legal Studies, 23,* 153.

Chapter 4
The Events of September 11, 2001: Apex Crime

> Let us never tolerate outrageous conspiracy theories concerning the attacks of September the 11th.
>
> G. W. Bush

Introduction

To borrow from the von Clausewitz aphorism, crime is politics by other means.

Terrorist crimes are meant to be outrageous and shocking. They are conceived to jar the receiver by way of an abrupt style of message delivery. Where effective, they are a tsunami that sweeps across the political and social landscape. As observed earlier, just as 'low' street crime may be shocking and push the pause button on the social, 'high' political crime is likewise alarming and resonates across the whole social and political body, asking of the sovereign and the polity: what is your response?

As described in Chap. 3, we conceive of apex crime as expressing political urgency or sovereign vitality where there is a highly expressive and violent attack involving a precious cultural or political resource. The event is realised in the authority over it, the narrative of the crime and the identity (or political influence) of review. These acts are too big to be framed by uncertainty. In their volatile expression they challenge the sovereign in its core ambiguity as a security definer, which is then revivified in its swift reaction. They are distinguished according to the binary division of the nation-state and its enemies. As such, the government framing of the event, inclusive of the meaning of the morality play that it has mooted, will be defended as if in a war to the death with existential forces.

In evaluating a watershed event through critical forensics as apex crime, we are concerned to discover how it measures up against the standard practices of the crime claim and crime scene investigation, as well as to adherence with prosecutorial integrity. In addition, we ask: how does it stack up in terms of the application of forensic techniques and the use of forensic expertise and conclusions?

W. B. de Lint, *Blurring Intelligence Crime*,
https://doi.org/10.1007/978-981-16-0352-5_4

As noted in Chap. 2, we are concerned less with deviations attributed to rogue actors than with irregularities arising from proper procedures and crime discovery. An alternative or critical forensic account observes lapses or oversights and failures or possible errors in evidentiary protocols but can only be indicative of alternative perpetrators. These failures or departures can be found in three broad fields: criminal process, the crime scene investigation and forensic applications.

In this analysis, we explore 9/11.

Event and Authority: 'We Have Some Planes'

An event like 9/11 will be experienced as an extreme normative tsunami. At one level, in response to such a shocking act of violence we ask, 'What is this?' and 'How can we classify this event by a genus?' Yet before clarity or consistency can be achieved through an account or representation of the event, there is a moment of cacophony, noise blending with signal in shaking voices and shocking images.

The first stage of this examination considers the binary of event and authority. An event that involves a bold or spectacular transgression against an ideologically significant target may shake institutions and structures to their foundations (Sewell, 2005: 100). Such events are more or less 'extreme' (Javorsek Ii & Schwitz, 2014: 642), 'irruptive' (Hess & Martin, 2006; Sewell Jr, 1996) or consistent with 'strategic surprise' (Levite, 1987); and may be meant to challenge an order and authority.

As we shall see, authorities will normally be in some disarray in the wake of such events, which jolt and dislodge. For the most part, where big events occur within established jurisdictions they are embraced or confined by the authorities according to scripts (law and custom) that are in place to make a preliminary determination of what is at play and to restore the order that the event has unsettled.

It is in questioning the role or righteousness of that authority that the event opens up ambiguity, but that uncertainty is also an elixir to sovereign vitality. In this respect, extreme, surprising or irruptive events may be welcomed by the sovereign. It is as if, without sufficient prodding, the sovereign may become too complacent. In the immediate wake of the kinetic act—and even during it—the uncertain vacillation of authority is corrected and reviewed by reference to routines of procedure and in line with legislation and policy already drafted and awaiting a favourable political wind. The event asks the question of sovereign security and the answer may either alter or preserve the ordering principle, a set of assumptions, posture or direction regarding the way the nation (and nations aligned with it) needs to address and prioritise matters of strategic concern (Buzan, 1999: 8; Clemens, 2007: 649).

In the case of most events occurring in established jurisdictions, the interpretation of the event and the configuration of authorities or the allocation of actor responsibilities is not too contentious and generally meets with overwhelming consensus. However, not everyone may agree with the designation or 'fixing' of the event and therefore its framing and jurisdiction. Watershed or apex events are loaded with a firm narrative authority that will invite both resistance and support from counter-authorities. There is nothing remarkable about this. All governments have plans to address contingencies or emergencies and take into account public opinion when determining the preferred casting of otherwise uncertain phenomena.

As a crime, a big event or apex crime asks questions of authorities. Such crimes bring into relief the means of the liberal democratic state as a justified authority, assuming that is where they occur. The separation between politics, the designation of crime by institutions and the relative constitutional powers of the judiciary and the executive may either be challenged or maintained. In the ideal, these bodies will limit cross-contamination, to use the forensic metaphor, so that they may respond to their mandates without pressure from adjacent, encroaching authorities or from other public or market bodies. As a crime, the event is meant to be matched up to the requisite features of criminal processing according to the requirements of evidence and proof and prosecutorial conduct. To determine causes the response to the event includes an investigation to gather concrete proof, and to identify perpetrators in accordance with reviewable procedures and results.

In practice, much crime is more or less vigorously prosecuted based on the pressures or interests that are brought to bear on the case. Many low-level crimes in impoverished communities are not cleared or resolved because political pressure or demand group interest is insufficient to capture the necessary government resources. Where a missing person or homicide involves a wealthy or well-connected individual, relatively more resources are devoted to its resolution, with the reputation of law enforcement and prosecutors seen to be at stake. In situations of political conflict such as 'the Troubles' in Northern Ireland and the UK during the 1980s, the October Crisis in Canada in 1970, and the antiwar and race riots in the US during the late 1960s and early 1970s, national authorities, emergency measures or war measures are enacted, permitting extensive curfews, detentions and military patrols. As we know, authorities claim jurisdictions and in enacting that claim are more often than not effective, but especially when there is no strong opposition to such claims-making.

More importantly, and to return to the point, where an event produces an open investigation that probes sovereign authority it will be reflexively avoided. Any genuinely external exploration of an event that encompasses the dominion of extant sovereign authority or that may challenge the mettle of sovereign decision-making or national security state interests, as we observed in the previous chapter, is more or less off-limits; it may be extinguished on national security grounds for the uncertainty that it unleashes on the political order. Consequently, we may expect to see some dramatic departures from measures aimed at preventing context bias in cases of political crime in general and high echelon or apex political crime in particular.

Claiming the Crime: Not just a Crime, but an Act of War

The attack that occurred on 11 September 2001 (9/11) was almost immediately framed as an act of war *and* a crime across borders. There was extraordinary solidarity between President George W Bush and government spokespersons, both within the

US and internationally, in support of the state's claims-making directly following the event, despite the counter-factual evidence on display (Landau et al. 2004; Bush, 2001):

> Our war on terror begins with Al Qaeda, but it does not end there. It will not end until every terrorist group of global reach has been found, stopped and defeated. … Our response involves far more than instant retaliation and isolated strikes. Americans should not expect one battle, but a lengthy campaign unlike any other we have ever seen. It may include dramatic strikes visible on TV and covert operations secret even in success. (Bush, 2001)

On 12 September, the North Atlantic Treaty Organization (NATO) declared that Article 5 of the NATO agreement was satisfied, so that NATO jurisdiction was engaged and each NATO ally was committed to providing assistance against 'these acts of barbarism'.[1] On 14 September, President Bush signed into law Proclamation 7463, asserting the existence of a national emergency since 11 September 2001, and invoking sections of the *National Emergencies Act*.[2] Proclamation 7463 has since been extended annually, with Trump doing so in September 2019. In the strikes' immediate aftermath, the New York State Legislature met in an emergency session in secret and passed the strongest anti-terrorism law in the country.[3]

As a consequence of its ambiguous construction as both crime and act of war involving transnational parties, 9/11 would be exploited to produce novel interpretations, or exceptions to both national and international criminal and other legislation and authorities (Slaughter, 2009; Ralph, 2009). One consequence among many was the setting aside of legal protections, including habeas corpus (Bybee & Yoo, 2002; Yoo, 2002). Where adversarial criminal procedure requires a nominal reference to equality of arms, the right to see and challenge evidence and other legal rights, the ambiguous and complex construction of the 9/11 crime claim produced transgressions and breaches normally inconsistent with natural justice.

Establishing Event Authority or Control

The first requirement for a criminal investigation is the claiming of the 'offence-like incident' (Ashworth, 1994: 4). It must be defined as criminal and require a remedy available through criminal law. Criminal investigations must be authorised, but who has command and control of an investigation and under what conditions are two important questions the answers to which inform understanding of the nature of the outcome and the critical evaluation of cases. The 9/11 Commission commissioners and investigators expended a good deal of effort trying to establish the chain of command authority directly following what the Commission referred to as the 'attack on the United States' (Kean & Hamilton, 2004). Some existing authorities were the 1995 *Presidential Decision Directive (PDD) 39: US Policy on Counterterrorism* and a 1997 annex that provided scope to the Federal Response Plan to include acts of terrorism. In January 2001, the FBI and Federal Emergency Management Agency (FEMA) issued a United States Government Interagency Domestic

Terrorism Concept of Operations Plan, affirming FEMA's lead role in consequence management and the FBI's role in crisis management.[4]

On the day of the event, at the top level of government, there appeared to be ambiguity concerning who was in charge (Tapper, 2001). While G.W. Bush was transiting from a Florida school back to Washington, Vice-President Dick Cheney claimed that he was acting as Commander-in-Chief: 'I was in a position to see all the stuff coming in, receive reports and then make decisions in terms of acting with it' (in Scott, 2007: 1). He did so from the Presidential Emergency Operations Center, or PEOC, located under the White House. It was also from that location that Secretary of Transportation Norman Mineta received Cheney's approval at 9.45 am to instruct the Federal Aviation Administration (FAA) to land all planes at the nearest airport (Balz & Woodward, 2002). Mineta later testified that Cheney was already present and in charge when he arrived at the PEOC 'at about 9:20 am' (9/11 Commission 2003: 220). The Commission did not pursue the inconsistency of Cheney's claim that he did not arrive at the PEOC until 9:58 am against Mineta's much more plausible assertion that Cheney was in charge at 9:15 (Scott, 2007: 3). Observing contradictions between the statements of Cheney, Richard Clarke, Mineta and the 9/11 Commission, Scott (2007: 11) concludes that the Continuity of Government (COG) plan must have been in place. COG, established in Executive Order 12656, protects the executive function during emergencies and permits the setting aside of constitutional and statutory requirements.[5] Cheney made reference to COG when a threat to the President was sent to the PEOC, saying that it 'reinforced the notion here ... that the government has been targeted and that we need to be extra careful about making certain we protected the *continuity of government*, secured the president, secured the presidency' (White House, Office of VC, 2001, emphasis added).

Establishing the Crime Scene Dominion

If there was ambiguity (was there a COG plan in place?) at the highest level, there was also some uncertainty regarding the crime scene dominion at the various crash sites. 9/11 has been referred to as 'the largest crime scene in history' and the FBI's 'PENTTBOMB' became the Bureau's biggest and most complex investigation, involving 7000 agents (Smith, 2002: 192). The FBI gained control of the Somerset County and Ground Zero crash site and shared control of the Pentagon crash site. It also immediately began collecting evidence across the country including at Logan and Dulles airports where the planes departed and at the flight schools in Florida and elsewhere where the hijackers may have visited (Fainaru & Grimaldi, 2001).

At Ground Zero, the situation was dynamic. Office of Emergency Management (OEM) Director Richard Sheirer was apparently in charge, aided by Mike Burton, Executive Deputy Commissioner of the New York City Department of Design and Construction (DDC). The New York Office of the Chief Medical Examiner (OCME) was assisted by the New York Police Department (NYPD), the Port Authority of New York (PAPD), the Fire Department of the City of New York (FDNY) and the

Disaster Mortuary Operation Response Team (DMORT), among other agencies or persons (Mackinnon & Mundorff, 2006: 487).[6] The OEM was told to make itself functional within the Emergency Operations Centre (EOC).[7] The EOC was moved temporarily to the Police Academy Library and then to Pier 92 (Wachtendorf, 2004), but before that there was a command post in the lobby of the North Tower, where Fire Chief Joseph Pfeifer reported that Sheirer had gathered with 'other high level people in government' (Pfeifer, 2001). The Commission asked Sheirer what steps the OEM was taking to address that the Port Authority, Fire Department and Police Department were left to work without coordination, but 'no rationale for Sheirer's prolonged lobby stay, no information conveyed to commanders, and no steps to coordinate the response were ever discovered' (Barrett & Collins, 2006: 34).[8]

Fire Captain Kevin Culley stated, concerning senior OEM officials' whereabouts: 'I don't know what they were doing. It was Sheirer's decision to go there on his own. The command center would normally be the focus of a major event and that would be where I would expect the director to be' (in Barrett & Collins, 2006: 32). John Farmer, 9/11 Commission staff member, said of Sheirer:

> We [the 9/11 Commission] tried to get a sense of what Sheirer was really doing. We tried to figure it out from the videos. We couldn't tell. Everybody from OEM was with him, virtually the whole chain of command. Some of them should have been at the command center. (in Barrett & Collins, 2006: 31)[9]

Ryan (2010: 46) observes that OEM Deputy Director Richard Rotanz was provided with information by a Secret Service agent who was with him at WTC-7 that a third plane was en route to New York. Acting on information from an unidentified representative of the New York City Department of Buildings, members of the OEM were also told that there was confidence that that 'building's stability was compromised' and in danger of 'near imminent collapse'. Fire Chief Joseph Pfeifer noticed that

> Right before the South Tower collapsed, I noticed a lot of people just left the lobby, and I heard we had a crew of all different people, high-level people in government, everybody was gone, almost like they had information that we didn't have. (in Ryan, 2010: 47)

After WTC1 and WTC2 collapsed, Ground Zero became a 16-acre field of debris. It was some 1.8 million tons and was very deep (down to 22 m), and at one place 22 m high. According to Barry Mawn, Director of New York's FBI office, in New York police and the FBI completed a grid search of streets 'looking for clues' near the site of the WTC (Mawn, 2001). The designation of the crime scene and the banning of photographers from Ground Zero were implemented two weeks after the event, on 25 September (Coletti, 2001).

The EOC applied coding categories to allocate operational divisions. Codes included 'debris management', 'remains identification', 'remains recovery', 'site and facility security' and 'credentialling.' The system did not discriminate between access to 'hot' or dangerous and 'cold' or relatively inert zones of the secured sites. Another coding category was 'forensics', which designated the debris that was to be brought to the Fresh Kills Landfill at Staten Island (Wachtendorf, 2004).

Credentialling was the process of identifying which personnel were authorised to access secured locations and the issuing of documentation to prove such authorisation as well as communications regarding valid credentials. According to the House Committee on Science (US Congress, 2002):

> Early confusion over who was in charge of the [WTC collapse] site and the lack of authority of investigators to impound pieces of steel for examination before they were recycled led to the loss of important pieces of evidence that were destroyed early during the search and rescue effort. ... Some of the critical pieces of steel – including the suspension trusses from the top of the towers and the internal support columns – were gone before the first BPAT [Building Performance Assessment Team] team member ever reached the site.

As pointed out by Ryan (2010: 52) and Wachtendorf (2004), various agencies and individuals were being credentialled to have access. This included agencies that may have had the means to collect evidence of explosives, some of which may also have had a conflict of interest with respect to that evidence. Ryan observes that Lieutenant Colonel Blitch of Special Operations Command (SOCOM) and the Science Applications International Corporation (SAIC), one of the largest suppliers of non-governmental investigators to the National Institute of Standards and Technology (NIST), 'had the means and opportunity to neutralize any unwanted explosives that might have been buried in the pile at Ground Zero. And his employer had done research on the laser ignition of nanothermites' (Ryan, 2010: 52).

Authority over the crime scene at the Pentagon involved both civil and military jurisdiction. The Commonwealth of Virginia had authority for crimes within its borders, but a crime by foreign terrorists would trigger national emergency authorisation (by the US Attorney General and the FBI). In addition, the Pentagon under the Department of Defense had authority over its own personnel and materiel. As a result, the Departments of Justice and Defense both assumed jurisdiction (Goldberg et al., 2007: 178). As per the Federal Response Plan, the Department of Justice was authorised as the lead federal agency under which operational responsibility, including law enforcement and 'command operations', went to the FBI. FEMA had an Incident Response Team (IRT) which was responsible to the mayor's special adviser Richard Schwartz. Its units joined the search from the afternoon of 11 September for 10 days (Goldberg et al., 2007: 97).

Arlington County Fire Department (ACFD) Assistant Chief James Schwartz became the person to exercise command and control, including over the Incident Command System (ICS). The AFCD was in control of the Pentagon site for 10 days. On 11 September, under Special Agent Christopher Coombs (followed by Robert Blecksmith and Arthur Eberhart), the FBI *operated* from on-scene at the Incident Command Post in South Parking. However, the FBI was not *in command* until 21 September, after the ACFD relinquished its command (Goldberg et al., 2007: 73). The FBI then passed control back to the Pentagon on 26 September (Goldberg et al., 2007: 127).

The Pentagon had its own police, the Defense Protective Service (DPS), a force of 250 that worked with the Secret Service and the CIA (Goldberg et al., 2007: 157) and was responsible for protecting the building and the people inside it. In the minutes after the building was hit, there were as many as 30 additional law enforcement and military units that came to the site to offer assistance in search and rescue, collecting evidence and safeguarding the building and materials, and maintaining a perimeter control (Goldberg et al., 2007: 178). It was DPS officers that were first on scene and fire trucks arrived in just five minutes. After the second plane hit the WTC, DPS Chief John Jester directed the DPS Communications Director Michael Nesbitt to reassure others that the Pentagon remained secure and that Terrorist Threat Condition could stay on 'normal', indicating no present threat of terrorist activity (Goldberg et al., 2007: 178–179). Virginia State Troopers were also on scene almost immediately to assist with the rescue. The DPS and the Pentagon's Building Management Office took responsibility for evacuating about 20,000 personnel from the building.

In the meantime, the FBI established a Joint Operations Center (JOC) at Fort Myer, commanded by Special Agent in Charge Timothy Bereznay and opened from 12 September, to which 26 government organisations sent representatives (Goldberg et al., 2007: 146). The FBI had many resources nearby, with the Washington Field Office at Judiciary Square and the Strategic Information Operations Center at its headquarters on Pennsylvania Avenue. However, the Bureau was delayed in being able to bring the equipment it needed to the site due to the traffic chaos around the Pentagon, but was not given permission to use helicopters to bring it in (Creed & Newman, 2008: 177–179). The FBI was to 'handle crisis management and consequence management responsibilities'. At the same time, the Army Operations Center (AOC) in the Pentagon itself also remained functioning throughout the first day.

The DPS liaised with the FBI and Secretary of Defense Donald Rumsfeld, among others. It was claimed that in the first hour after the attack, 'the improvised teams of emergency medical responders worked exceptionally well… "There wasn't any, 'Wait a minute. We're the Army and so we're in charge here'"' (interview quoted in Goldberg et al., 2007: 140). Still, the personnel authorised to be at the crime site, including the sensitive impact zone within the Pentagon, numbered 4000 (Goldberg et al., 2007: 171). Three people were arrested by the DPS a day after the attack disguised as firefighters, who were deemed to be thrill-seekers (Goldberg et al., 2007: 170).

The jurisdiction question was resolved with reference to an investigatory bias. As described by Navy Captain Glenn Wagner, Director of the Armed Forces Institute of Pathology (AFIP), which carried out forensic identification in consultation with the FBI:

> 'So jurisdiction became a very important aspect since it clearly was an act of terrorism and the FBI was running the operation. The FBI and the US Attorney General really wanted to keep this on the federal side and were relieved to get confirmation that the Pentagon was [an] exclusive[ly] federal jurisdiction and that there wouldn't have to be any more state involvement than was absolutely necessary in the search and recovery. At that particular point the AFIP in the mobilization of our resources and the mobilization of DoD [Department of Defense] resources became a priority.' (in Goldberg et al., 2007: 178)

The FBI conducted interviews with eyewitnesses to confirm on site that a 'commercial airliner' had hit the building (Goldberg et al., 2007: 158). The FBI also collected photographic evidence with the assistance of combat photographers, identified and walked grid zones and conducted line sweeps beginning on the west-side lawn. It also identified, tagged and removed bagged items relating to the plane or possible victims and took custody of items it deemed to be evidence that had been brought to North Parking. The National Medical Response Team (NMRT) also arrived on site 'within hours' to do testing for toxic substances, poisons, and chemical, biological or radiological residues (Goldberg et al., 2007: 159–160).

United Airlines Flight 93 smashed into a field above a reclaimed coalmine near Somerset Airport, Pennsylvania, with tremendous force, producing a fireball and a smoke plume of debris. The FBI took control of the crime scene at the site of the crash and 150 of its agents came to be involved in the investigation and recovery of evidence. They cordoned off a 3-mile-wide area around the crash to accommodate the debris field. A half-ton piece of one of UA93's engines was discovered far away from the crash site.[10] Apart from the engine pieces, smaller pieces were found up to 8 miles from the site. One of the black boxes was recovered at a depth of 25 feet under the ground. Before security was established at the crash site, many members of the public were one site, some of whom were seen 'stuffing objects down their shirts' (Thompson, 2017: 6–7).

The National Transportation Safety Board (NTSB) was not asked to conduct formal investigations of the four crashes that occurred on 9/11 and was not invited to lead an investigation into the cause of the crash of Flight 93 (Lappe & Marshall, 2004: 40–41). The NTSB has the mandate and sole jurisdiction to investigate crashes of passenger jets, unless it is declared a crime scene by the US Attorney General. Consequently, it 'did not determine the probable cause' of any of the four crashes. At Ground Zero, the crashes were designated as 'criminal acts' and therefore the FBI was made 'lead investigatory agency'. At the Pentagon and Somerset County, Pennsylvania, the crash investigations were not carried out by the NTSB because a Memorandum of Understanding (MOU) between the Department of Defense and the FAA recommended the use of the Armed Forces DNA Identification Laboratory (AFDIL) and this body performed the DNA identification of the crash victims at both sites (Smith, 2002: 194).

Following Prosecutorial Requirements

As observed previously, to properly establish a prosecution, authorities must maintain the integrity of evidence, protect the rights of witnesses and the accused, and provide full disclosure to the defence of evidence that may be exculpatory, including that pertaining to an alternative suspect or suspects. They must also be free of conflicts of interest that may compromise the investigation, prosecution or forensic evaluation.[11]

Regarding habeas corpus, hundreds of South Asian and Muslim immigrants were rounded up by the FBI as 'persons of interest' under NY Penal Law ss 490.00.[12] They were held without bond, hearing or charges for weeks or months (most at the Metropolitan Correctional Center [MCC]), where some were beaten. They were denied rights to phone or speak with an attorney and some were held in lock-down for 23 h a day in cells lit for 24 h a day, and shackled when escorted. Not one of them was ever charged in connection with the attacks of 9/11, but some were deported, most often on technical grounds (Lieberman, 2011; Accurso, 2020).

Also arrested and detained under immigration charges and/or the national security provisions as 'of special interest to the government' were 'at least 60 Israeli Jews', including five who were caught filming the WTC on the day (Mintz, 2001; Melman, 2001) and two additional Israelis who were apprehended in connection with a 'considerable criminal venture associated with Urban Moving Systems'.[13] The five who were allegedly filming were caught on the day and one was found with US$4700 in his sock (ABC News, 2006). They were transferred to the FBI's Criminal Division and Foreign Counterterrorism Division, responsible for espionage cases, and held at the Metropolitan Detention Centre in Brooklyn for two months. They were polygraphed (as much as seven times) (ABC News, 2006) and the results were said to be 'indicative of deception' regarding their 'responses to relevant questions relating to the issue of intelligence affiliation' (IRMEP, 2013). The FBI also searched Urban Moving's offices and removed documents and hard drives and questioned the owner. The government declined to present evidence of their links to the terrorism conspiracy, and they were released on bond and then permitted to leave the country. The FBI concluded that they were conducting 'unilateral espionage' for Mossad, and that their employer, Urban Moving Systems, was a front organisation (Perelman, 2002). On their return home to Israel, one of them spoke on television and said: 'Our purpose was to document the event' (ABC News, 2002; Stein, 2014; Shea, 2004).

By December of 2004, the US Justice Department was publicly declaring torture as abhorrent. But in mid-March 2002, the CIA developed a list of 10 'enhanced interrogation techniques', after obtaining a secret legal opinion (Bybee, 2002; Bybee & Yoo, 2002).[14] The new legal opinion on 'combined effects' provided language to allow the CIA to continue to employ the harshest interrogation techniques it has ever used (Ross & Esposito, 2005). CIA official John Kiriakou claimed that CIA interrogators were receiving very specific directions on which harsh interrogation technique to use from the Deputy Director of Operations at CIA headquarters, giving individual approvals for an 'intention shake' followed by an 'open-handed belly slap', for example (Esposito & Ross, 2007). Changes to the executive orders, including those 'governing torture or interrogation, were also covered by the administration's legal position that a president can "waive" or "modify" a published executive order without any public notice – simply by not following it' (Feingold, 2008).[15]

Regarding the rights of accused or petitioners for remedy against breaches of habeas corpus, the situation on 11 September 2001, was described retrospectively in *Zayn Al Abidin Muhammad Husayn v. Robert Gates* as follows (emphasis added):

> The Supreme Court held in Boumediene y. Bush. 128 S. Ct. 2229 (2008), that the Constitution guarantees military detainees at Guantanamo Bay an opportunity to contest their detention in federal habeas corpus proceedings. At the same time, the Court recognized that inquiry by civilian courts into military detention operations during a time of ongoing conflict would entail a host of serious difficulties that do not arise in ordinary domestic civil litigation – for example, the potential for the litigation to interfere with ongoing military and national

> security operations, the risks inherent in providing military captives access to sensitive information, and the challenges of evaluating evidence and information obtained in military or intelligence operations on foreign soil. The Court recognized that it was simply incongruous to expect that detainee habeas corpus litigation could proceed under the open-ended procedures that operate in everyday domestic civil litigation, or even the narrower procedures that federal courts employ in typical statutory habeas corpus actions. The Court took it as given that courts hearing habeas corpus challenges would craft procedures appropriate *to the wartime military context.*

In the meantime, 9/11 was exploited to blur the standard 'beyond reasonable doubt'. Vice-President Dick Cheney advocated for the use of the CIA's 'enhanced interrogation techniques' against persons captured in relation to 9/11 based on a view of uncertainty that came to be known by some as the 'one percent doctrine' (Suskind, 2006). As illustrated in Suskind (2006), with regard to alleged terrorist threats to the US, this doctrine means that a 1% chance of intent should be treated as if 100% certain. However, 25% of CIA detainees who were subject to torture were later proven to be innocent. Many tortured detainees accepted plea deals to escape indefinite or lengthy detention (such as David Hicks [Human Rights First, 2007]). Cheney commented on the 25% margin by stating: 'I'm more concerned with bad guys who got out and released than I am with a few that in fact were innocent ... I have no problem as long as we achieve our objective. ... I'd do it again in a minute' (in Bankoff, 2014).[16] It so happens that in laboratory research 95% is a generally accepted standard, referred to as a confidence coefficient. This pertains to statistical procedures that generate interval estimates (Du, 2017: 142). As summarised by Du (2017: 142), 'False-positive errors, rather than negative errors, should be the priority control in forensic science. In criminal proceedings ... adoption of an expert testimony with positive errors is more likely to lead to innocent people being judged as guilty.'

The lack of prosecutions of alleged 9/11 conspirators is attached to a long and sordid sidebar related to the exceptional measures the US undertook to carve out 9/11 as a hybrid between war and crime. By 2021, there would be only one person convicted in a US court in connection to 9/11. In April 2005, Zacarias Moussaoui pleaded guilty to six charges related to his participation in the 9/11 conspiracy (but not the 9/11 crimes, as no evidence linking him was presented),[17] and was sentenced to life in prison a few weeks later. Osama bin Laden was never charged, the US declining to negotiate with the Taliban over his extradition to the US, seeking instead to launch Operation Enduring Freedom (the war in Afghanistan) (Benini & Moulton, 2004) and then Operation Geronimo (the assassination of bin Laden) (Hasian, 2012). Khalid Sheikh Mohammed, Ramzi bin al-Shibh, Mustafa Ahmad al-Hawsawi, Ali abd al-Aziz Ali and Walid Bin Attash are all facing trial by military court at Guantanamo Bay, after Congress refused to permit their trial in the District of New York (Smith, 2019). The UN Special Rapporteur on Torture Nils Melzer reported in May 2019 that Julian Assange has been subjected to psychological torture. This fact would perhaps be amusing for Khalid Sheikh Mohammed and his fellow Guantanamo detainees, the former having been subjected to waterboarding 183 times. We are perhaps nearing the final stage of a process that began with the sweeping up of alleged 9/11 conspirators in CIA operations and then their secret rendition across a gulag of black sites. It is arguable that the US has been avoiding placing a challengeable record of 9/11 evidence before the court, and the use of 'enhanced interrogation' prior to plea deals or signed confessions would obviously, and arguably deliberately, challenge principles of legality and rules of evidence (see, for example, Scheppele, 2005).

The court and members of the public seeking to assert due process reasonably seek a strong level of confidence in representations of evidence, which is dependent on the accuracy and precision of the hypothesis test and an understanding of the difference between forensic procedures and laboratory operation. If beyond reasonable doubt is the threshold requirement, it is important that inaccuracies in determining the threshold be cautiously enumerated, so that if there is a strong chance of a false positive that trace evidence of gunshot residue has been found on a suspect, that would, of course, be necessary information to apply.

A criminal trial can provide authorities with an opportunity to prove their version of an event. In the case of an echelon political or apex crime, the separation of military and civilian jurisdiction will be difficult if not impossible, as will be the disaggregation of justice from insertions of intelligence standards or values. In the case of 9/11, the identification of a clear-cut crime is unlikely to eventuate from the investigation of the event. The fact that the suspects, having been subjected to years of isolation and torture, may be found guilty under a military authority 20 years after the event will not dampen scepticism regarding how US authority anticipated and reacted to this event.

Scene and Narrative

> In thanking and praising the workers, Deputy Secretary Wolfowitz declared that 'like the mythical Phoenix bird, the building, too, has risen from its ashes to be reborn'. Indeed, from the beginning the reconstruction effort had been named the Phoenix Project.
>
> Goldberg et al. (2007: 203)

Framing is a process of selecting what belongs within and outside discursive boundaries. It is a necessary feature of the capture of events. Official framing is intended to keep 'discord within conventional bounds' (Entman, 2003: 415) or ensure that interpretation is not made too prone to indeterminate and restless ambiguity (Wagner-Pacifici, 2010).[18]

As described in Chap. 2, at least a provisional narrative account is useful even in a complex whodunnit. Most cases depend on making a choice regarding what to select for sampling and analysis, and that choice requires a working hypothesis of what may have occurred, how it took place, where and when it took place, and sometimes also why it may have taken place in the way speculated. In this respect, as defined in Chap. 2, 'tunnel vision' both distorts and illuminates. It illuminates, in that it provides a way forward regarding the potentially infinite measure of things related to a crime event. It distorts, as above, where viable alternative explanations are disallowed or summarily dismissed because they do not fit the official frame.

At noon on 11 September, two hours after the events, Senator Orrin Hatch reported that he had been briefed by the 'highest levels of the FBI and of the intelligence community', who had 'come to the conclusion that this looks like the signature of Osama bin Laden, and that he may be the one behind this' (Hancock, 2001).

Identifying, Collecting and Preserving Evidence

To understand where departures from good practice may be found, it is useful, as Julian et al. (2012: 25) note, to conceptualise crime scene management. Crime scene identification and exploitation depends on the setting, constituting or mandating of authorities, which in turn depends on a preliminary view of the nature or definition of the event by knowledgeable investigators. As these requirements are interdependent, it is this conundrum between authorisations and identifying and collecting evidence that is behind some major oversights or broken investigatory pathways. The establishment of the crime is coincident with the stipulation of crime scene boundaries and securing its contents, so there is much fluidity in the competencies or measures of adequate performance that pertain.

Almost immediately after the events of 9/11, the OCME was tasked with recovering tissue and bone for victim identification (Smith, 2002: 192). In total, 1.2 million tons was brought to Fresh Kills Landfill to be sifted for human remains under OCME authority. The task, 'identification of victims', appeared to be the primary or perhaps sole objective (Shaler, 2005). Debris from Ground Zero began to arrive on the night of 12 September. At the site, there were around 100 NYPD officers, 20–30 FBI agents and some DOS as well as agents from other state, federal and NGO agencies (Wachtendorf, 2004: 82).

At the Pentagon, the 'largest concentration of body parts' was found near the 'punch-out' hole at C Ring, the deepest point of penetration. All remains went to a temporary morgue in North Parking and then were sent to Dover Port Mortuary for final identification by the AFIP in consultation with the FBI (Goldberg et al., 2007: 177–178). This was done under continuous custody, with FBI agents accompanying the remains after they were labelled (from 13 September) and then transported by the state police to Dover Port. At Dover Port, there were 400 personnel, including military personnel under the Armed Forces Medical Examiner (AFME), forensic anthropologists from the Smithsonian Institution and the FBI, autopsy assistants from the AFIP and the National Naval Medical Center, and dental investigators also sourced from the AFIP. These were all under the control of site commander and AFIP Director, Navy Captain Glenn Wagner, who reported to the Army's Surgeon General (Goldberg et al., 2007: 180).

The remains at the Pentagon site included 183 victims and the 5 hijackers. Based on interviews with Wagner and others, Goldberg et al. (2007) found that two witnesses were present when handling personal effects including handbags and wallets. Autopsies were also performed 'where possible' on some of the bodies to help determine cause of death and to enable the issuance of a death certificate. Where autopsy reports were produced, they were made available to the victims' families (Goldberg et al., 2007: 181–182). Many (65) of the victims were identified by dental investigation and many others through DNA evidence, although nuclear DNA was not available due to fire degradation and mitochondrial DNA required additional genealogical research. Most victims at the Pentagon were confirmed to have died from blunt force injuries and most of the remainder died from asphyxiation, with some others undetermined. Two navy, two army and one aircraft victim remained unidentified. Further, the individual identities of the bodies deemed to be those of the hijackers could not be determined as no reference DNA or dental records were available. These remains were given over to FBI custody (Goldberg et al., 2007: 182–183).

At Ground Zero, the focus was not on a homicide investigation but on the recovery of victims and disposal of the debris. Glanz and Lipton (2001) reported that Mayor Rudy Giuliani displaced New York City's Department of Sanitation and created the DDC under Michael Burton, who oversaw the 'most aggressive possible schedule of demolition and debris removal'. Burton considered a forensic examination of evidence to be unnecessary: '"We know why they fell," he said. "Because they flew two planes into the towers"' (in Glanz & Lipton, 2001). Matthew G. Monahan, a spokesman for the city's DDC, said, '"The city considered it reasonable to have recovered structural steel recycled"' (in Glanz & Lipton, 2001). As per Manning (2002), in an editorial in *Fire Engineering*:

> Such destruction of evidence shows the astounding ignorance of government officials to the value of a thorough, scientific investigation of the largest fire-induced collapse in world history. I have combed through our national standard for fire investigation, NFPA 921, but nowhere in it does one find an exemption allowing for the destruction of evidence for buildings over 10 stories tall.

In a departure from protocol, the crash site of UA93 was not searched and recorded in 60-square-foot grids, as per the preference of Coroner Wallace Miller and forensic anthropologist Dennis Dirkmaat, due to an overrule by the FBI (Longman, 2002: 262). The FBI argued that this would be too time-consuming, and instead divided the site into five large sectors. Doing more, the FBI said, would serve 'no real investigatory purpose' as 'there was no mystery to solve about the crash. Everybody knew what happened to the plane'.

As per the OCME, 'the primary purpose of the investigation' at the Fresh Kills Landfill site 'was to identify the victims rather than, as is more traditionally the case, first establishing the cause and manner of death. For the World Trade Center disaster, *neither the cause nor the manner was in question*, with the vast majority of victims signed out as "blunt force trauma, homicide"' (Mackinnon & Mundorff, 2006: 488, emphasis added). The identification procedure was via an assembly line and it pursued remains to 'every fragment larger than a thumbnail' for DNA testing.

> From the very beginning, officials at the OCME recognized that the sheer scale and extraordinary severity of the disaster necessitated an innovative approach to the identification process. Chief Medical Examiner Dr. Charles Hirsch decided that the few intact bodies recovered from Ground Zero, together with any victims who subsequently died in the city's hospitals, would not be autopsied. (Mackinnon & Mundorff, 2006: 487)

It was thus decided 'from the very beginning' by officials at the OCME and in particular the Chief Medical Examiner Charles Hirsch that there would be no autopsy of the few intact bodies recovered.

> The transfer of the remains from one specialist team to another was undertaken by individual escorts, who were usually either a Member of Service or a DMORT team member. Each escort remained with a single, assigned case and its paperwork at all times, thereby ensuring continuity and chain of custody. (Mackinnon & Mundorff, 2006: 490)
>
> Other forensic specialists within the multidisciplinary team also faced similar problems during the identification process, as they responded to the unique nature of the disaster by radically adapting their standard disaster victim methodologies. As an anecdotal example, single teeth were found with great regularity embedded in muscle tissue or areas of the body that were anatomically impossible to reconcile (their presence in such areas overwhelmingly demonstrating the force and velocity that caused them to be removed from an individual and subsequently impacted into another). The vast majority of the dental identifications only occurred, however, when the dental arcade – or reasonably sized fragments thereof – were present. Single, isolated teeth rarely resulted in dental identifications but were, instead, identified through DNA analysis. This was unexpected and, as there were a multitude of isolated teeth found that ultimately could not be associated with other remains, unfortunately prolonged the process of final identification and repatriation. (Mackinnon & Mundorff, 2006: 491)

Robert Shaler led the forensic examination by the OCME and identified 1588 of the 2749 victims and three of the Flight 11 and Flight 77 hijackers (Colford, 2005). However, the three hijackers (whom he believes were seated towards the back of the plane) were not matched by name but to a list of 10 nameless profiles provided by the FBI:

> No names, just a K code, which is how the FBI designates 'knowns,' or specimens it knows the origins of. Of course, we had no direct knowledge of how the FBI obtained the terrorists' DNA. (Colford, 2005)

With respect to what caused the buildings to collapse, US Representative Joseph Crowley (D-NY) testified that the loss of important physical evidence 'is borderline criminal'. Glenn Corbett of John Jay College averred that the 'lack of significant amounts of steel for examination will make it difficult, if not impossible, to make a definitive statement as to the cause and chronology of the collapse … [W]e are staffing the BPAT with part-time engineers and scientists on a shoestring budget' (Committee on Science 2002). Even at WTC7, where there were no bodies to recover and no rescue operation, the debris was moved quickly from the scene. When asked why this had occurred, Commission Co-Chairman Lee Hamilton replied, '[Y]ou can't answer every question when you conduct an investigation' (in Solomon, 2006). Anthony Wiener (D-NY) complained that 'This amounts to a crime scene investigation, yet … there wasn't even a weapon found, there weren't even fingerprints taken, and if truth be told there wasn't even a detective assigned to the case until very late in the process … there has been no comprehensive investigation … crucial evidence has been mishandled' (C-Span, 2002).

At the Pentagon, the same decision regarding the recovery of bodies was made. As represented by its historical archive (Goldberg et al., 2007: 122), 'All evidence including human remains had to be removed from the building since, according to FBI Special Agent-in-Charge Arthur Eberhart, otherwise "we would have been there for months and months and months"'. FBI Special Agent Tim O'Connor was in charge of the evidence recovery but was told that it was unnecessary to photograph and document every piece of the plane because 'the smaller fragments don't prove anything'. He was directed to photograph only unique plane parts (Creed & Newman, 2008: 181–183). An NTSB official determined that the recovery of all pieces was not necessary because 'it's clear what happened here. We don't need pieces of the wings and stuff like that. But we do need the black boxes' (Creed and Newman 2008: 351–352).

The recovery and identification of the remains from Flight UA93 was conducted at the Pennsylvania National Guard Armory in Friedens, Pennsylvania. Between 75 and 100 specialists, including pathologists and fingerprint experts, worked there to identify 1500 items that were mostly samples of scorched human tissue remains using dental records and fingerprints, where available. Most of the DNA analysis that was required was carried out at the Armed Forces DNA identification laboratory in Rockville, Maryland. All 40 passengers and flight crew were identified; the four hijackers were also identified from genetic profiles (History Commons, 13 September–19 December 2001).

Despite the condition of the crash site and the lack of sizeable pieces of evidence, several pieces of evidence were recovered that allowed the hijackers to be identified, including a Saudi Arabian ID card, a Youth Hostel Association Card, part of a Florida driver's licence and two passport photos all belonging to Ahmed Almani, a Saudi Arabian passport belonging to Saeed Alghamdi; and a section of Ziad Jarrah's passport (History Commons, 12 September).

At Ground Zero, the 'black boxes' (they are actually bright orange) containing flight data and cockpit voice recordings for American Airlines Flight 11 and United Airlines Flight 175 were officially not found or deemed to be of no forensic value. On 14 September, United Airlines Flight 77's black boxes were found. Although located in the tail of the plane, they were found close to a debris pile near the hole in the C ring wall. These were, according to Goldberg et al. (2007), transferred to the NTSB for analysis. It was determined that 'the voice recorder was too damaged' to provide information, but the data recorder revealed that the plane hit the Pentagon at 460 knots at 9:37:45 (NTSB, National Transportation Safety Board, 2002a: 2). This is much greater than the earlier reported speed (by185 mph) and almost twice the FAA speed limit for aircraft flying below 10,000 feet (Lengel, 2016).

According to a background comment from an NTSB member: '"Off the record, we had the boxes. You'd have to get the official word from the FBI as to where they are, but we worked on them here"' (in Lindorff, 2005). NYFD firefighters Mike Bellone and Nicholas De Masi claimed that they found three of the four boxes and that federal agents took them and asked them not to mention the acquisition. This account is more plausible than the 9/11 Commission finding that the boxes were not recovered because the boxes are able to withstand 2000-degree Fahrenheit temperatures for one hour. As per Shaler (2005), the sifting of debris from Ground Zero was meticulous, aimed as it was at the discovery of the minutest fragments of human remains. The

9/11 Commission also referred to this level of sifting when it noted that a report alleging an incident involving a gun on one of the planes was deemed unreliable because no evidence of the firearm was found at Ground Zero (9/11 Commission T7 2001). NTSB Director of Public Affairs Ted Lopatkiewicz later suggested that the irregularity (of not locating the black boxes at Ground Zero) was a product of the nature of the event: 'It's very unusual not to find a recorder after a crash, although it's also very unusual to have jets flying into buildings' (in Lindorff, 2005). The FBI denies that it has received the boxes.

There were several reports of an electrical disruption just prior to the crash of Flight 93, including from the Mayor of Indian Lake Borough, suggestive of the need to investigate whether hydroelectric interference played a part in disrupting the plane's flight mechanisms (Carlin, 2002). There were also 10 eyewitness reports that one or more jets or planes (several witnesses believe they saw a mid-sized military plane) flew just above treetop level and circled the area before and after UA93's crash. The FBI stated that there was a Fairchild Falcon 20 business jet that was permitted to pass by the crash site, which provided a verbal report of the scene. And two FBI agents later visited witness Susan Mcelwain, and told her that the plane she had seen was a white Learjet (Lappe & Marshall, 2004: 38–40). Based on the comparison of the flight's data recorder against the utterances of hijackers from the cockpit voice recorder (as publicly presented), there is support for the theory that the hijackers crashed the plane because they feared losing control of it.

Recalling our previous observations regarding the exclusion of Mineta's testimony from the 9/11 Commission report, John Farmer (2009: 277), who assisted in its writing, found that the Commission was lied to 'in great detail' regarding the timeline and availability of fighters to shoot down any of the hijacked planes, including whether fighters were in the air to intercept and shoot down UA93.

Examining and Testing Evidence

According to the US House Committee on Science (Committee on Science 2002), most of the steel from the upper floors of the Twin Towers and some of the 'critical pieces' including the 'suspension trusses from the top of the towers and internal support columns' 'were gone before the BPAT team member ever reached the site'. Without the steel or sufficient quantities of it, there would not be an adequate means to test the hypothesis that explosives were used to bring the towers down. In addition, there was no search conducted for explosive initiators, some of which would have survived the destruction. A search for evidence of the presence of explosive instigators and fragments of wire, batteries or switches is mentioned in the Department of Justice training manual (47), but Ryan (2010: 50–51) observes or alleges that the agency that provided the largest contingent of non-governmental investigators to the NIST WTC investigation was the SAIC: 'SAIC technicians raced to Ground Zero within hours to install an ad hoc communications network for first responders and local financial companies' (Ryan, 2010: 53).

The FBI arrived at Dulles International Airport at 12:40 pm to investigate Flight 77[19] (History Commons: Nelson, After 12:40 pm). As the Bureau appeared to do everywhere it went that day, its first step was to seize all security evidence from perimeter and interior CCTV recordings. In this case, the FBI agents took it from the west checkpoint where the five alleged hijackers had passed through in the main terminal. They showed the security supervisor in charge of the checkpoint, Ed Nelson, the segments featuring each of the men and Nelson later reported that he was surprised that the agents were able to identify the suspects from the footage so quickly (Trento & Trento, 2006: 36–37). Nelson reported that the agents 'were not asking about the hijackers – they were focusing on what my screeners might have done wrong'. One FBI supervisor stated that 'The orders came from headquarters through the local Washington-area FBI field offices and the Joint Task Force on Terrorism. The teams of agents were told to "get the screeners to admit they had violated FAA recommended procedures"' (Trento & Trento, 2006: 36). The FBI has not been able to reconcile a report from one airport employee of a confrontation he had with five Middle Eastern men who he suspected were trying to get access to a secure area of the airport between 8 and 8:45 pm on 10 September. However, he was interviewed by the FBI and shown pictures of the hijackers, of whom he was able to recognise two (Nawaf Alhazmi and Marwan Alshehhi) (Trento & Trento, 2006: 43–44).

Setting aside all the evidence of prior warnings of the attack, not long after 10 am on 11 September FBI agents George Piro and Ken Williams were already arriving at a flight school in Phoenix where one of the alleged hijackers of Flight 77, Hani Hanjour, had previously undertaken some training. The agents received a call from a Boston office agent who was already at Logan Airport looking over the passenger manifest from the flight, who told Piro and Williams that they should look into Hanjour, to which Piro replied, '"I'm holding the file in my hands right now"' (in Graff, 2011). Moreover, a customs official later claimed that he was able to determine the names of all 19 hijackers by 11 am (Mintz & Lengel, 2001). Already on 12 September it was being reported that the authorities had identified people in several cities who were 'accomplices' and 'helped plan and execute the attacks,' and that the authorities had biographical details on many of them (Johnson & Risen, 2001).

The investigative journalist Seymour Hersh has quoted a former high-level intelligence official as saying:

> 'Whatever trail was left was left deliberately – for the FBI to chase'. 'This guy sits in a cave in Afghanistan and he's running this operation?' one CIA official asked. 'It's so huge. He couldn't have done it alone.' A senior military officer told me that because of the visas and other documentation needed to infiltrate team members into the United States a major foreign intelligence service might also have been involved. (Hersh, 2001)

Three months before 9/11, Robert Wright wrote: 'The FBI has proven for the past decade it cannot identify and prevent acts of terrorism against the United States and its citizens at home and abroad. Even worse, there is virtually no effort on the part of the FBI's International Terrorism Unit to neutralize known and suspected terrorists residing within the United States' (in C-Span, 2011). Judicial Watch claims that under FBI Director Louis Freeh, 'in case after case throughout the 1990's, the FBI seems to have tailored its investigative efforts to fit somebody's pre-arranged script. The question is, who wrote that script – and why?' (Judicial Watch, 2003).

Even though the 9/11 investigation is decidedly about the role of intelligence, the 9/11 Commission, under its terms of reference and lead investigator Philip Zelikow, built a narrative that it was a lack of imagination and information-sharing that was to blame for a lack of preparedness in defending America, as opposed to the actions of specific individuals or units. For instance, the Commission made much of the idea that the intelligence community lacked the imagination to consider 'planes as weapons' or 'planes into building'. The intelligence community itself knew this to be untrue and in fact, on the day or week of the 9/11 attack, many from the military and intelligence community were participating in a training event that included just that scenario (Ahmed, 2005: 304–313). The intelligence dimension of the investigation was being shaped by witnesses who had handlers to manage their testimony.

Identity and Review

We have distinguished between three stages of apex or intelligence crime examination. There is toing and froing as the uncertainties of the crime and event are negotiated by investigators and officials. In this regard, in the immediate wake or fallout of the event is a crystalline 'deer-in-the-headlights' moment – when we ask 'what *is* this?' – as explored in Chap. 3, in which both the social and political are fused in a saturated uncertainty. As critical security scholars have amply demonstrated (see, for example, Weaver, 1995), such moments are the red blood cells of securitisation. The haste with which political and cultural authorities act as one to both identify the event and, by naming a perpetrator, push the narrative along a favoured trajectory is also well-known and needs no attribution of sinister motive or pre-planning to be sensible. As observed in Chap. 3, such a response is embedded into the routines and measures of 'good' government.

This uncertainty is mitigated where political and justice authorities 'act as one', and certainty is achieved where the narrative is fixed towards the identification of the suspect. As noted earlier, there are two directions that are offered simultaneously: the investigation gets its terms of reference, the suspect is named and a retrospective review of the event leads up to the certain, consensus-restoring or undisputed end point of that identification. At the same time, the investigation asks, what is the crime? where is the evidence? who has their fingerprints on the crime?

This brings us to the relation of identity and review. The first point to make here is to postulate the synergy between the terms of reference, review and identification. If politicisation has force or power and the political authority comprising the political (as per Mouffe, 2006) is not bifurcated or divided—and intelligence crimes and apex events do test this—then it is expected that actors representing the interests of significant political interests will enter the crime scene and seek to claim dominion. From the point of view of police and forensics, interested political intervention (that is to say, where actors are shaping discovery of materials where they operate with context bias) is anathema; it contaminates the site and prevents its sterilisation. Such intrusion pulls the narrative threads in favour of the preferred outcome or review. In this regard, Philip Zelikow of the 9/11 Commission has been credited with effectively vetoing the pursuit of alternative lines of inquiry outside the narrow lanes of the hijackers and their helpers within al-Qaeda (Griffin, 2005). As summarised by Kean, Hamilton and Rhodes (2007), the Commission was constituted and structured through its terms of reference to protect Republicans, Democrats and the White House from information that could be deemed to be partisan in its damage. In this and other respects, it was an instrument of whitewash from the top.

Summary Beyond Scope

NIST was appointed to provide reports on WTC1, WTC2 (NIST, 2005) and WTC7 (Sunder et al., 2008; McAllister et al., 2008) and, as summarised in Banovic et al. (2007: 29), it 'neither found nor invoked any extraordinary events beyond the terrorist attack that damaged the structure and removed insulation'. NIST consequently concluded that the fires caused the collapse—representing the first and only time that fire has been found to cause the complete collapse of a steel-framed building. It therefore supported other authorities' account of the cause of death for all killed at the site as the planes crashing into the towers.

On the other hand, Richard Gage's Architects and Engineers are among many demand groups that have developed resources that cast doubt on the NIST conclusions and have called for a reinvestigation (ae911truth.org). NIST acknowledges that the buildings were more than sufficiently robust to withstand the impact of the planes. They attribute much to the absence or inferiority of cladding and the temperatures of the fires. The weakening of the steel from the jet fuel, which burned off in 10 min, 90% of it on the outside of the towers, is key to NIST's hypothesis. But it is difficult to find support for the theory that the temperatures could have been raised high enough to weaken the steel sufficiently to produce the cascading effect of buckling of the truss members, the sagging floors pulling column connections inward, the increased axial loads, the pull-in forces from the sagging floors, the loss of lateral support from the failure of truss seat connections, and then, finally, the weakening of the core columns, among other purported failures (Jones, 2006). Indeed, this complex series of events, which would not have been visible to the eye (which saw the core column support fail first), appears to be necessary because what the eye sees (symmetrical and synchronous collapse of the building) was ruled out of scope by NIST and its terms of reference.

NIST therefore did not explore evidence that the steel reached temperatures that were too hot to account for. Most of the 100,000 tons of steel and 90,000 tons of concrete per WTC1 and WTC2 building was ejected laterally (the steel at 115 kph). The concrete was pulverised into 30% of the 13-cm blanket of dust across a 3-square-mile area in Lower Manhattan and was, with much of the steel (98% of which was found outside the perimeter in a 200-metre radius), unavailable above the building's footprint to produce the mass necessary for buckling, pulling, weakening sequence), which in any case does not accommodate a rate of 66% of freefall (or freefall in the WTC7) collapse (Brookman, 2010; Jones et al., 2008a: Harrit et al., 2009). With respect to WTC7, FEMA has concluded that fire-induced collapse had a low probability of occurrence (Gilsanz et al., 2002). NIST (Sunder et al., 2008; McAllister et al., 2008) places the burden of the complete, progressive and symmetrical collapse of WTC7 on the failure of a single column (column 79) and suggests that a blast-induced demolition scenario was not seriously considered because 'controlled demolition usually prepares most, if not all, interior columns with explosive charges, not just one column' (McAllister et al., 2008: 614–615). However, this is clearly confirmation bias. As Brookman (2010: 3) points out, NIST also made the argument that one weakened column was enough to do the trick, without seeking the evidence for the controlled demolition hypothesis (see also Jones et al., 2008b). In the case of WTC7, NIST used a computer simulation that loaded up the assumptions from the resulting collapse parameters and developed an account that contained gaps and contradictions, including a freefall of 2.5 s that it cannot explain.

In the meantime, 118 first responder FDNY members were interviewed and reported hearing or feeling explosions (McQueen, 2006). Video evidence shows liquid molten iron (requiring a temperature of 2800 degrees Fahrenheit—which fire cannot produce). Active thermitic material and molten iron in nano-particles was found in dust samples (Harrit et al., 2009; Larsen, 2009). Engineers Pablo Lopez and Andrew Pontecorv report that in the B2 basement level of WTC1 'the massive core columns of the tower, which are over two feet wide and made of four-inch thick steel plate, appear to have suffered "a compound fracture: the upper sections looked as if they had been kicked, with incalculable fury, about a foot south of the sections they were resting on"' (Glanz & Lipton, 2004: 293). Hazardous material expert Don Carson said that pieces of steel were pulled out of the rubble '"still cherry red … like the charcoal you put on your grill"' (Gittrich, 2001).

> Perhaps the deepest mystery uncovered in the investigation involves extremely thin bits of steel collected … from 7 World Trade Center. … The steel apparently melted away, but no fire in any of the buildings was believed to be hot enough to melt steel outright. … A preliminary analysis at Worcester Polytechnic Institute [WPI] … suggests that sulfur released during the fires – no one knows from where – may have combined with atoms in the steel to form compounds that melt at lower temperatures. (Glanz & Lipton, 2001)

As above, the 9/11 Commission and NIST reports do not mention this evidence and do not investigate the plausible explanation that nano-thermite was used in a controlled demolition.

The torture of the '9/11 suspects' was noted in a box in the 9/11 Commission report and then completely discounted in terms of how it compromised the evidence used. When the Commission was established to investigate the event, it built its famous 'we have some planes' narrative of the crime based on summaries produced from the interrogations of rendered suspects at CIA-operated black sites and at the facility at Guantanamo Bay, and from the false accounts of employees of the NSA, CIA and other agencies. At least four of the people whose interrogation figured in the 9/11 Commission report have claimed that they provided interrogators with information in order to stop being tortured (Kean et al., 2007: 146). Ninety-two videotapes of the interrogations were intentionally destroyed by the CIA on the drafting of a cable by its current director, Gina Haspel (Taddonio, 2018). It is at least a good possibility that Haspel is the 'female expert' and 'key architect of the agency's defense of its detention' and 'enhanced interrogation program' (Cole, 2014).[20] One of the Commission's main sources of information, Abu Zubaydah, who was the first 'high value detainee', was tortured and credited with a long list of key activities and high-level al-Qaeda connections; but it is now known, and even the CIA conceded in 2006, that he was not a member of al-Qaeda and that he has since been delisted by the United Nations Security Council (UNSC) from the Islamic State and al-Qaeda Sanctions List (Church, 2018). The 9/11 Commission was even part of the chain of torture because Commission members forwarded questions to the CIA, 'whose interrogators posed them on the panel's behalf. … An analysis by NBC News found that more than a quarter of the report's footnotes – 441 of some 1,700 – referred to detainees who were subjected to the CIA's "enhanced" interrogation program, including the trio who were waterboarded' (Newsweek, 2009).

Discussion and Analysis

As we have noted earlier, investigators need some direction to recover the impression, biological, digital or documentary residues from/of principal actors, agents and associates and to exploit the potentially available evidence from crime scenes. At the same time, a proper investigation requires steps to mitigate context bias and separate investigators from a confirmatory bias. The following observations may be made.

First, several high-profile leaders publicly accused Osama bin Laden and al-Qaeda of being responsible for the attack. At all three sites the view among the lead investigators was that the crime was a terrorist attack by foreign actors using hijacked passenger planes and that the collection and identification of bodies (and plane parts and black boxes) was the limited investigatory and forensic objective. FBI investigators were on the trail of the hijackers (at Dulles and Logan airports and at the flight school in Phoenix) within a couple of hours of the crashes. When searches were established at Ground Zero, the Pentagon and Somerset County, investigators were told that the priority was the recovery of the bodies and, at the Pentagon, any tell-tale evidence of or on the planes, including the flight path and cockpit voice recorders.

In this, the work at Ground Zero, the Pentagon and Somerset was not conducted with equivalent investigative and forensic objectivity. Although hundreds of bodies were signed out of the Fresh Kills Landfill as 'blunt force trauma, homicide', autopsies were not performed on any of the victims. As discussed above, this was because the OCME stated that the 'cause and manner of death was not in question'. At Dover Port, however, autopsies *were* performed, and this led to the positive identification of all of the hijackers—albeit with no matching identification by name. At Somerset County, the FBI was early and quick to state that the cause of the crash was not in doubt and insisted on the deviation from crash site investigatory practice in at least one respect. There, too, the recovery and identification of bodies was complete, inclusive of the hijackers.

Second, because of this orientation or bias regarding cause of death, evidence that might have supported an alternative conclusion was not collected or, if collected, not subject to analysis. While rule of law legality offers at least an overture to equality of arms, absent from the 9/11 investigation was a nod to the requirement that the alleged accused needed to have exculpatory evidence gathered. For instance, the 9/11 Commission and SEC sought to tie market and trading irregularities to bin Laden and al-Qaeda and if such ties could not be found, to reassess them as inconsequential. Mackinnon and Mundorff (2006) note that there were high-impact injuries on some of the victims at Fresh Kills Landfill, in which bones from some were driven like missiles into other bodies and that many bodies were pulverised. This was partially investigated in terms of its consistency with cases of fire-caused building collapse, but it could have been evaluated as evidence for an alternative cause of death hypothesis. At Ground Zero and each of the other sites, there was no collection of evidence of explosive residues from the site, the steel or the bodies, as far as can be discovered from the reviewed information. As we know, even though the debris from Ground Zero was removed and the steel shipped off to China, material and documentary evidence remained available, but was not analysed. No explosives residue or materiel was sought for examination, and no interviews of witnesses were conducted to either support or reject the conclusion that the buildings were wired with explosives. Yet the FDNY separately made a collection of recorded accounts from first responders of explosions heard prior to the planes hitting the building and also during the collapse (McQueen, 2008). These were not forensically examined for consistency with regard to the timing of the explosions and compared to other forensic data, including seismic data, to support this hypothesis (Kim & Baum, 2002). In each of these cases, potential evidence was not collected, analysed and provided where it was possibly exculpatory concerning the defence against wider conspiracy charges laid against the co-conspirators.

Third, nonetheless summaries beyond the scope of the investigation were produced. The 9/11 Commission lacked the tools under chief investigator Philip Zelikow and its terms of reference to probe the rehearsed statements of agency leaders to unveil the untruths that were uttered (Farmer, 2009: 235–290). It was prevented from interviewing many of the principal actors—especially the whistle-blowers—or heard from them only in part, accompanied by their agency minders. The Commission did not follow up on obvious inconsistencies to discover whether there was a common thread among them, which would normally demand further investigation; yet these inconsistencies are now clearly evident to readers of the 9/11 timeline available at the History Commons (Griffin & Woodworth, 2018; History Commons, 2020).[21] There is an asymmetry whereby the accounts of vetted government agency leaders were taken as empirically authoritative, despite them being known to be false, even by the Commissioners (Farmer, 2009; Kean et al., 2007); whereas the necessarily fragmentary and partial accounts of unofficial voices—including those of whistle-blowers—were reviewed reflexively as improbable and false. The Commission nonetheless attributed the events of the morning of 9/11 to a comprehensive lack of preparedness, inadvertent bureaucratic bungling and a lack of imagination and information-sharing between agencies (Kean & Hamilton, 2004). Since it did not pursue several leads that suggested how dots might have been *disconnected* (Fenton, 2011) and did not address evidentiary inconsistencies that were quite blatant (Farmer, 2009: 235–290), these summary evaluations may be appropriately celebrated for their narrative finesse rather than more generally, and, as per Pillar's (2006: 1022) analysis, for a 'prominence and success that has made it the envy of commissions of inquiry everywhere'.

Fourth, novel applications or techniques were invented to account for anomalous findings. The most inventive one belonged to NIST. NIST had to attempt to account for complete symmetrical collapse at or near freefall in three steel-framed buildings without resort to an explanation that would not involve either planes or jet-fuel-ignited fire in the causative role. The 9/11 Commission had to account for the 'stunning collapse of competence' of the government's response to 9/11 (Farmer, 2009: 290). The FBI, meanwhile, had to support an explanation that circled around how al-Qaeda was a product of and supported by the Pakistani Intelligence Service (ISI), the CIA, Israeli intelligence and the Saudi royal family, each of which then did not apparently wish to know at the agency lead level the national security threat al-Qaeda posed (Clarke, 2008; Wright, 2002). To cover innovations in omission, Zelikow offered that agencies lacked imagination to foresee what, earlier, the FBI had been accused of wishing only to monitor from a distance (Wright, 2002).

The NIST, 9/11 Commission and FEMA reports have been discredited by independent investigators—despite the destruction of evidence. For example, Hulsey et al. (2019) released a report of a four-year study concluding that the 'collapse of the WTC7 was caused not by fire but rather by the near-simultaneous failure of every column in the building'. A six-year inquiry by a 9/11 'Consensus Panel'—structured arguably for bias for the 'defence' in counterpoint to NIST's alleged bias for the prosecution—examined the available evidence of the NIST reports and could not find support for the single-column pull-out collapse theory for WTC7 or the pancake collapse for WTC1 and WTC2 (Griffin & Woodworth, 2018). In November 2018, the US Attorney in Manhattan announced that he would refer the findings of a report by the non-profit Lawyers' Committee for 9/11 Inquiry to a federal Special Grand Jury.[22] That body also filed a lawsuit against the FBI for failing to investigate evidence related to the WTC demolition known to the Bureau in its 2015 review of the 9/11 Commission report.

Conclusion

A few points of summary may be offered. In the investigation of the events that occurred on 11 September 2001 there were substantial deviations from standard prosecutorial standards. There was a suspension of habeas corpus that swept up men on the basis of the profiling of suspects as Middle Eastern. There was a suspension of the illegality of torture that gave authority to the CIA to set up black sites for 'enhanced interrogation' that then provided 'evidence' in support of the conclusion that the event was localised to some al-Qaeda cells. There was ambiguity at the highest reaches of government and at some of the crime scenes regarding command authority. There was a consequent failure to establish a quarantined crime scene.

It would be possible to devote an entire book to an exploration of the investigatory and forensic lapses where a significant plane crash has occurred—and 9/11 involves four such crashes—and note the irregularities in the establishment of authorities, the recovery of evidence and the examination of forensics.[23] The point is that governments will seek to initiate such investigations explicitly to quell ambiguity first in the interpretation of the evidence and then in the outcome. This is not unusual, as all prosecutors are naturally averse to ambiguous interpretations where they can be damaging. The key difference is that where a state agency may be accused of a crime of commission or omission there is a natural justice requirement to remove the conflict of interest. In these cases, a positive finding against a government actor will expose and subject to further public scrutiny a reinforced allegation that the government's narrative of the event is not to be believed and thus the objective of quelling ambiguity has failed.

From a critical point of view, if 9/11 is a crime against the state or by non-state actors seeking to use violence towards an ideological purpose, it is a political or state crime that requires a criminal remedy that complies with and re-enacts the processes of the rule of law. As we now know, post 9/11 there has been a convergence of 'enemy' and 'criminal' in terms like 'enemy non-combatant', 'non-state belligerent', 'enemy non-person' and 'war on terrorism'. This terminology supports a precautionary regime that permits what some have called a reversal of onus in the standard elements of crime in terrorism cases (Roach, 2010; de Lint & Kassa, 2017; Meuller & Stewart, 2016). It has pushed domestic policing and foreign security into a fusion that has railed against the prohibition of domestic psy-ops and the *Posse Comitatus Act* of 1878.[24] The response to 9/11 has included the use of moral suasion on international institutions to harmonise (or Westernise) global criminal policing cooperation (such as via Interpol and Europol) and criminal remedy (as per the International Criminal Court and International Court of Justice) to bring suspected belligerents to account (Deflem, 2010). At back of this, means have run roughshod over international instruments (such as at Geneva and Nuremberg).

The question posed here is whether the case assigning criminal responsibility for those killed on 9/11 has been made in accordance with the standards of criminal investigations and forensic discovery. This question has been asked before and it will surprise some readers to know that the list of persons doubting the official story goes well beyond the famous group of engineers and architects led by Richard Gage. This list also includes many academics, lawyers, first responders and 41 former intelligence officers (Miller, 2009). Concerning this last group, who is better placed to doubt the preferred view of governments?[25] The experience and expertise of the former intelligence officers is impressive, and among these officers are a former director of counter-terrorism (Terrell Arnold), a former deputy coordinator of covert intelligence programs (US state department) (Edward Peck), seven CIA veterans including Raymond McGovern, William Christison, former director of the CIA's regional and political analysis, Melvin Goodman, former division chief of the CIA's office of Soviet Affairs and Robert Baer, considered by Seymour Hersh to be formerly the best on the ground field officer in the Middle East. Baer claims that the evidence points to an inside job, a conclusion supported by the CEO of OSS.net, Robert David Steele. There are also nine former high-ranking FBI agents who have come out publicly in doubt of the official narrative.

The lack of a criminal investigation and the failure of officials to collect, evaluate and analyse evidence stemming from multiple lines of inquiry has led to calls for a properly constituted investigation. It is to be remembered that victims' families wanted a full inquiry into what caused the deaths of office workers, plane passengers and first responders at WT1 and WTC2, the Pentagon and Somerset County, and that two government inquiries (Joint Inquiry of the House and Senate Intelligence Committees into 9/11; Kean & Hamilton, 2004) and a number of technical reports (NIST, 2005; Sunder et al., 2008; McAllister et al., 2008) were undertaken in order to provide answers, but that the criminal cases against the accused 9/11 hijackers have been hampered by prosecutorial irregularities.

Although much was made of the lack of bureaucratic imagination and information-sharing in the 9/11 Commission report, the account requires a deep understanding of how intelligence works both institutionally and bureaucratically and of how its careerists may finesse the affordances through a specialist reading of the national security mandate. The furtive and complex dispositive of security intelligence stands in opposition to the common or public knowledge and liberal democratic values that are still required in criminal discovery. If 9/11 involved the interplay and inter-operation of longstanding terror networks and intelligence agencies in a push-pull of ideology, resources, people and protection or cover, then much of the archive of 9/11 involves compartmentalised, disconnected actor standpoints that are not meant to be seen in their entirety or to be reconciled with the whole event (Fenton, 2011). On the contrary, 9/11 may be an object-lesson in the blurring of criminal investigation by not just political interests, but by intelligence interests.

Notes

1. Statement by the North Atlantic Council. NATO. September 12, 2001. https://www.nato.int/docu/pr/2001/p01-124e.htm.
2. 50 U.S.C. 1601 et seq.; 66 FR 48197; Page: 48197–48199.
3. NY Penal Law ss 490.00 (McKinney-2008 & Supp. 2010).
4. "Terrorism 2000/2001;" 7 (definition quote); DoJ synopsis PDD 39, 1, http://www.ojp.usdoj.gov/odp/docs/pdd39.htm; CONPLAN: United States Government Interagency Domestic Terrorism Concept of Operations Plan, Jan 01 http://www.fbi.gov/publications/conplan/conplan.pdf.
5. Executive Order 12656 of 1988 as: 'any occurrence, including natural disaster, military attack, technological emergency, or other emergency, that seriously degrades or seriously threatens the national security of the United States' (Executive Order 12656 of Nov. 18, 1988, 53 FR 47491, 3 CFR, 1988 Comp., p. 585, http://www.archives.gov/federal-register/codification/executive-order/12656.html).

6. A temporary command post was set up at One Police Plaza where the NYPD command post was also established (together with a firehouse on Houston Street where the OEM mobile command unit bus was located).
7. New York's $13 million EOC was constructed in 1999 on the 23rd floor of WTC7 and outfitted with workstations for up to 68 agencies. It was among the most sophisticated of its type in the world and touted as capable of withstanding winds of 240 kph.
8. Earlier, Zarillo and fire department captain Abd Nahmod met with OEM Deputy Director Richard Rotanz and EMS Division Chief John Peruggia, at which, according to Peruggia:it was brought to my attention, it was believed that the structural damage that was suffered to the towers was quite significant and they were very confident that the building's stability was compromised and they felt that the north tower was in danger of a near imminent collapse' (in MacQueen, 2008).
9. Later in the afternoon, according to Richard Zarrillo, an EMT, OEM warned those in and at the WTC7 'that the buildings are going to collapse; we need to get our people out' (Zarillo, 2001) and the building was abandoned at 5:20 pm prior to the collapse (Wachtendorf, 2004).
10. The FBI does not specify the distance, but notes 'a considerable distance'.
11. Book-length examinations, in addition to shorter pieces, have provided ample evidence that each of these necessary elements of a prosecution was breached in the 9/11 investigations. In a piece by Ryan (2010), the tangled thread of some of the interrelations between the 9/11 Commission investigators and the security, defence and intelligence companies in WTC1, WTC2 and WTC7 is explored. Fenton (2011) and Ahmed (2005) follow other connections between the intelligence community, al-Qaeda and security and weapons and finance companies. In a book on their experience, the Commissioners, Kean and Hamilton stated that government officials 'obstructed justice' when they misled the Commissioners about several key lines of inquiry (Kean et al., 2007). Several books by David Ray Griffin (2004, 2005, 2012a, b) document further oversights and contradictions within the investigations. The 9/11 Commission findings may be contrasted to the History Commons 9/11 timeline to provide the reader with confronting evidence of the contrasting narrative.
12. It was reported that a federal grand jury was convened in White Plains, New York, 'to investigate the 9/11 attacks, which was 'casting a wide net' and able to hear subpoenas; this was evidently discontinued when, in early October, the Justice Department was said to have taken over all 9/11-related prosecutions (Markon, 2001).
13. January 3, 2001 New York Polygraph Unit/A-1, in The Institute for Research: Middle Eastern Policy, 2013. The Israel Lobby Archive. https://www.israellobby.org/urbanmoving/. The same source cites a document from an FBI report to Kansas City, Newark and New York remarking on 'Zoomcopter' kiosks 'manned by Israelis and suddenly abandoned. … After receiving this information, FBI Philadelphia inquired about the kiosks in the local malls and learned

that all had been abandoned in a similar fashion that same day. Further investigation revealed that the same day, toy helicopter kiosks in malls located in Washington, DC, Hickory, North Carolina, Arlington, Texas and in all the malls in the local Philadelphia area had been abandoned within the same two hour period. … It was evident that an extremely well-organized and effective communication system existed between these Israelis nationwide.'

14. As Michael Scheuer (Scheurer, Committee on Foreign Affairs, 2007) (chief of the Bin Laden unit under Clinton and designer and manager of the rendition program) explained in a 17 April hearing before members of the House of Representatives, '[t]here is no operation at the CIA that is conducted without the approval of lawyers. It is the bane of our existence'.
15. Such secret lawmaking puts legislators in the dark about the operability of published executive branch mandates.
16. Researchers have investigated how the qualitative value may translate into a quantity (Dhami, 2008). In this respect, it is interesting to note that surveys of students, the general public and judges may produce slightly different evaluations of that quantity. Students have been found to interpret the standard to fall somewhere near .99 at the most serious offence type (Martin & Schum, 1987); the general public was found to place it less firmly at .92 (Hastie et al., 1983); while surveys of judge opinion placed it somewhat less stringently around or even somewhat below .90 (McCauliff, 1982). It should be cautioned that much of this research is dated, as is the federal court ruling that the quantity should be pegged at a value above .90 (United States v. Fatico, 1978). This summary draws from Dhami (2008: 4).
17. United States of America v. Zacarias Moussaoui—Indictment. Archived 2009-07-15 at the Wayback Machine United States District Court for the Eastern District of Virginia Alexandria Division, United States Department of Justice, December 2001.
18. Wagner-Pacifici (2010: 1356) argues that material and rhetorical boundaries are innately 'restless'. That is to say, the attempt to put the fix on things is ongoing, but things shift as perspectives and assumptions about their properties and manifestations change. Foucault (1972) and others have argued that there is no natural or objective end point to interpreting the meaning of things. As critical legal scholars have also observed, contemporary legal doctrine is the expression of the confluence of vision and practicality, where each of these is suffused with the interests and prejudices of a particular epoch or time (Unger 1982: 121). Consequently, as postmodernists have pointed out, it is in one regard a matter of administrative expedience and in another a matter of ideological or institutional preference that the hunt for meaning or the placement of the boundary ceases at some given point. The necessity to place a fix on the signified preoccupies both the investigation of a crime scene and the stipulation of a narrative concerning the crime event. In much study of discretion it is noted that there is a divide between craft knowledge and book knowledge or between a more 'instinctive' and a more 'rules-based' attitude towards investigation and even in the interface of the habitus and field

relations (Bourdieu, 1990). In studies of justice it is also frequently observed that discretion is a necessary capacity, from police officer to judge and jury, because as much as justice is a quality of mercy, forgiveness or toleration, it requires the setting aside of or constant reframing of rules and procedures, and a repositioning of the actual into the hypothetical (de Lint, 1998). To remove discretion from the practice of justice is in this way to remove animus from habitus or humanity from human systems. Humanity is uttered in discretion.

19. A detailed account of the FBI investigation is well beyond the scope of this chapter. Books by Trento and Trento (2006), Creed and Newman (2008), and Burnett and Giombetti (2006) as well as the 9/11 Commission report and the History Commons 9/11 Timeline provide that more detailed account.
20. Please note that Cole does not speculate on who this CIA agent is, whether Haspel or someone else.
21. The CIA and the ISI helped bin Laden to build the Khost tunnel complex and, alongside Saudi intelligence support, recruited mujaheddin from several primarily Muslim countries (Harding, 2000; de Borchgrave, 2001). An under-cover CIA agent supported a tourist visa for Sheikh Omar Abdul-Rahman, a bin Laden protégé, who set up in an MAK charity front with a branch in Brooklyn known as the Al-Kifah Refugee Center (Friedman, 1993). Senior ISI officials also helped 1993 WTC bomber Ramzi Yousef travel to the US in August 1992, perhaps given that Yousef had been 'developing high level contacts in Pakistani intelligence' (Reeve, 2002: 136–137) with the covert support of the CIA (Labaviere, 1999: 220–221). In April 1995, the FBI was given a handover of computer files from the CIA on Yousef and his network of plotters but some of the data had been erased and the FBI believed that the CIA intentionally erased the files, possibly to maintain the compartments of its own privileged connections to the network (Kocieniewski, 1995). Yousef was also later suspected by Richard Clarke of possible involvement in the Oklahoma City bombing in April 1995: 'Could [Yousef] have been introduced to [accused Oklahoma conspirator Terry] Nichols? We do not know, despite some FBI investigation. We do know that Nichols's bombs did not work before his Philippine stay and were deadly when he returned' (Clarke, 2008: 127). It is claimed that 9/11 was the second-wave resurrection of the Bojinka plot, in which 12 hijacked planes were to fly into prominent US buildings, a fact known but left from an FBI memo that summarises its interrogation of fellow Bojinka plotter Abdul Hakim Murad (Lance, 2011: 280–282; Fainaru & Grimaldi, 2001).
22. The Lawyers' Committee filed the petition to the US Attorney for the Southern District of New York demanding that the US Attorney present to a Special Grand Jury the 'extensive evidence of so-far-unprosecuted federal crimes relating to the destruction of the three World Trade Center Towers on 9/11'.
23. Indeed, there are books and articles that have reviewed the evidence of many significant plane crashes in which there has been significant political interest or a political victim. This includes TWA Flight 800 on 17 July 1996, in the ocean off East Moriches, New York, which was investigated by the FBI and National

Safety Board (NTSB) to rule out eyewitness reports that a missile hit the plane (NTSBa); the crash of a light plane that killed JFK Jr on 16 July 1999 off the coast of Martha's Vineyard, which the NTSB investigated and concluded was caused by pilot error or spatial disorientation (NTSB, 2000b); and the crash of a Beechcraft Twin Air A100 plane that killed Senator Paul Wellstone and seven others on 25 October 2002 in Minnesota during a tight senatorial race against Republican nominee Norm Coleman. Wellstone's death occurred two years after a plane crash killed Missouri Governor Mel Carnahan, who was also in a tight election contest on 16 October 2000. The NTSB investigation of the Beechcraft plane crash found pilot error in the failure to maintain adequate airspeed (NTSB, 2000b; Katz, 2016). The plane crash caused a fire that burned for over seven hours and the victims were identified by dental records.

24. 18 U.S.C. § 1385, original at 20 Stat. 152.
25. It may be argued that intelligence officers within agencies are not very well placed to review intelligence practices because they are bunkered in information silos. That is not the predicament of ex-intelligence officers who may no longer need to adapt their perspective to agency wishes.

References

ABC News. (2002, August 2). *The white van: Were Israelis detained on September 11 spies?* ABCnews.com. http://web.archive.org/web/20020802194310/http://abcnews.go.com/sections/2020/DailyNews/2020_whitevan_020621.html.

ABC News. (2006, January 6). *Were Israelis detained on Sept. 11 spies?* ABC News. https://abcnews.go.com/2020/story?id=123885&page=1.

Accurso, A. (2020, March). Suicide or murder? Jeffrey Epstein's death still drawing attention to bureau inadequacies. *Prison Legal News*. https://www.prisonlegalnews.org/news/2020/mar/4/suicide-or-murder-jeffrey-epsteins-death-still-drawing-attention-bureau-inadequacies/.

Ahmed, N. (2005). *The war on truth: 9/11 disinformation and the anatomy of terrorism*. Northampton: Olive Branch.

Ashworth, A. (1994). *The criminal process: An evaluative study*. Oxford: Clarendon.

Balz, D., & Woodward, B. (2002, January 27). America's chaotic road to war. *Washington Post*. http://www.washingtonpost.com/ac2/wp-dyn/.

Bankoff, C. (2014, December 14). Dick Cheney simply does not care that the CIA tortured innocent people. *New York Magazine*.

Banovic, S. W., Foecke, T., Luecke, W. E., McColskey, J. D., McCowan, C. N., Siewert, T. A., et al. (2007). The role of metallurgy in the NIST investigation of the World Trade Center towers collapse. *Journal of Minerals, Metals and Materials Society, 59*(11), 22–30.

Barrett, W., & Collins, B. (2006). *Grand illusion: The untold story of Rudy Giuliani and 9/11*. New York: Harper.

Benini, A. A., & Moulton, L. H. (2004). Civilian victims in an asymmetrical conflict: Operation enduring freedom, Afghanistan. *Journal of Peace Research, 41*(4), 403–422.

Bollyn, C. (2012). Solving 9-11: The deception that changed the world. http://pvsheridan.com/Solving_911.pdf.

Bourdieu, P. (1990). *The logic of practice*. Stanford University Press.

Brookman, R. H. (2010, March 26). *The NIST analysis: A close look at WTC 7*. AE.org. http://citeseerx.ist.psu.edu/viewdoc/download?doi=10.1.1.397.7142&rep=rep1&type=pdf.

Burnett, D., & Giombetti, A. (2006). *Fighting back: Living beyond ourselves*. Advantage Books.
Bush, President G. W. (2001, September 20). Text: President Bush addresses the nation. *Washington Post*. https://www.washingtonpost.com/wp-srv/nation/specials/attacked/transcripts/bushaddress_092001.html.
Buzan, B. (1999). 'Change and insecurity' reconsidered. *Contemporary Security Policy, 20*(3), 1–17.
Bybee, J. (2002). *Memorandum for Albert R. Gonzales, Counsel to the President Re: Standards of conduct for interrogation under 18 U.S.C. §§ 2340–2340A*. http://dspace.wrlc.org/doc/bitstream/2041/70967/00355_020801_004display.pdf.
Bybee, J., & Yoo, J. (2002, August 1). *Memorandum for John Rizzo Acting General Counsel of the Central Intelligence Agency: Interrogation of al Qaeda operative*. US Department of Justice, Office of Legal Counsel. https://www.washingtonpost.com/wp-srv/nation/pdf/OfficeofLegalCounsel_Aug2Memo_041609.pdf.
C-SPAN video Archived 2011-09-01 at the Wayback Machine, address to the National Press Club on May 30, 2002, with Judicial Watch, via rationalveracity.com.
Carlin, J. (2002, August 13). Unanswered questions: The mystery of Flight 93. *Independent*.
Church, C. (2018, August 1). What politics and the media still get wrong about Abu Zubaydah. *Lawfare*. https://www.lawfareblog.com/what-politics-and-media-still-get-wrong-about-abu-zubaydah.
Clarke, R. A. (2008). *Against all enemies: Inside America's war on terror*. New York: Simon & Schuster.
Clemens, E. S. (2007). Toward a historicized sociology: Theorizing events, processes, and emergence. *Annual Review of Sociology, 33*, 527–549.
Cole, M. (2014, December 18). Bin Laden expert accused of shaping CIA deception on torture program. *NBC News*. https://www.nbcnews.com/news/investigations/bin-laden-expert-accused-shaping-cia-deception-torture-program-n269551.
Coletti, E. (2001, September 25). *City: No more photographs at WTC site*. Associated Press.
Colford, D. (2005, November 12). FBI had DNA samples of 9-11 terrorists before attack. *The New York Daily News*. https://freedom4um.com/cgi-bin/readart.cgi?ArtNum=13219.
Creed, P., & Newman, R. (2008). *Firefight: Inside the battle to save the Pentagon on 9/11*. Ballantine Books.
De Borchgrave, A. (2001, June 14). *United Press International exclusive: Osama bin laden – null and void*. UPI.
de Lint, W. (1998). Regulating autonomy: Police discretion as a problem for training. *Canadian Journal of Criminology, 40*(3), 277–304.
de Lint, W., & Kassa, W. (2017). On being bent for security: Barristers in terrorism prosecutions in Australia. *Journal of Law and Society, 44*(2), 169–199.
Deflem, M. (2010). *The policing of terrorism: Organizational and global perspectives*. Routledge.
Dhami, M. K. (2008). On measuring quantitative interpretations of reasonable doubt. *Journal of Experimental Psychology: Applied, 14*(4), 353–363.
Du, M. (2017). Analysis of errors in forensic science. *Journal of Forensic Science and Medicine, 3*, 139–143.
Entman, R. (2003). Cascading activation: Contesting the White House's frame after 9/11. *Political Communication, 20*, 415–432.
Esposito, R., & Ross, B. (2007, December 10). Coming in from the cold: CIA spy calls waterboarding necessary but torture. ABC News.
Fainaru, S., & Grimaldi, J. (2001, September 23). FBI knew terrorists were using flight schools. *Washington Post*.
Farmer, J. (2009). *The ground truth: The untold story of America under attack on 9/11*. New York: Riverhead.
Feingold, R. (2008, May 8). Government in secret. *Los Angeles Times*. https://www.latimes.com/archives/la-xpm-2008-may-08-oe-feingold8-story.html.
Fenton, K. (2011). *Disconnecting the dots: How 9/11 was allowed to happen*. Trine Day.

Foucault, M. (1972). The discourse on language. In *The Archaeology of Knowledge*. New York: Pantheon.

Friedman, R. (1993, March 30). The CIA and the Sheikh: The agency coddled Omar Abdul-Rahman allowing him to operate in the US – Now this unholy alliance has blown up in our faces. *Village Voice*.

Gilsanz, R., et al., in Corley, G. (2002). *World Trade Center Building performance study: Data, collection, preliminary observations, and recommendations*. New York: Federal Emergency Management Agency Region II. Chapter 5 (5–31).

Gittrich, G. (2001, November 1). Fire may smoulder for months. *New York Daily News*.

Glanz, J., & Lipton, E. (2001, December 25). Experts urge broader inquiry in towers' fall. *New York Times*.

Glanz, J., & Lipton, E. (2004). *The rise and fall of the World Trade Center*. New York Times Books.

Goldberg, A., Papadopoulos, S., Pitney, D., Berlage, N., & Welch, R. (2007). *Pentagon 9/11*. Washington, DC: Historical Office, Office of the Secretary of Defense.

Graff, G.M. (2011). *The threat matrix: inside Robert Mueller's FBI and the war on global terror*. Little, Brown.

Griffin, D. R. (2004). *The new Pearl Harbor*. Northampton, MA: Olive Branch Press.

Griffin, D. R. (2005). *The 9/11 Commission report: Omissions and distortions*. Northampton, MA: Olive Branch Press.

Griffin, D. R. (2012a). *The new Pearl Harbor revisited: 9/11, the cover-up, and the expose*. Interlink Publishing.

Griffin, D. R. (2012b). *9/11 ten years later: When state crimes against democracy succeed*. Interlink Publishing.

Griffin, D. R., & Woodworth, E. (2018). *9/11 unmasked: An international review panel investigation*. Olive Branch Press.

Hancock, J. (2001, September 12). In attack, suspicion turns inevitably to bin Laden. *The Baltimore Sun*. https://www.baltimoresun.com/news/bs-xpm-2001-09-12-0109120193-story.html.

Harding, L. (2000, November 13). Bin Laden: The question facing the next US president. *Guardian*.

Harrit, N. H., Farrer, J., Jones, S. E., Ryan, K. R., Legge, F. M., Farnsworth, D., ... et al. (2009). Active thermitic material discovered in dust from the 9/11 World Trade Center catastrophe. *The Open Chemical Physics Journal, 2*(1), 7–31. https://doi.org/10.2174/1874412500902010007, http://www.bentham-open.org/pages/content.php?TOCPJ/2009/00000002/00000001/7TOCPJ.SGM.

Hasian, M., Jr. (2012). American exceptionalism and the Bin Laden raid. *Third World Quarterly, 33*(10), 1803–1820.

Hastie, R., Penrod, S., & Pennington, N. (1983). *Inside the jury*. Cambridge, MA: Harvard University Press.

Hersh, S. (2001, October 1). What went wrong: The CIA and the failure of American intelligence. *The New Yorker*.

Hess, D., & Martin, B. (2006). Repression, backfire, and the theory of transformative events. *Mobilisation: An International Journal, 11*(2), 249–267. https://ro.uow.edu.au/artspapers/692.

History Commons 2020, September 12, 2001 and shortly after: 9/11 hijackers' effects found at Flight 93 crash site. http://www.historycommons.org/context.jsp?item=a091201shanksvilleeffects#a091201shanksvilleeffects.

History Commons. (2020). September 24, 2001-December 26, 2002: Identity of 9/11 financier constantly changes. http://www.historycommons.org/searchResults.jsp?searchtext=witnesses+9%2F11&events=on&entities=on&articles=on&topics=on&timelines=on&projects=on&titles=on&descriptions=on&dosearch=on&search=Go.

Hulsey, L., Quan, Z., & Xiao, F. (2019). *A structural reevaluation of the collapse of World Trade Center 7*. INE report 18.17 prepared for Architects & Engineers for 9/11 Truth.

Human Rights First. (2007, March 31). Surrealism at Guantanamo. Human Rights First. https://www.humanrightsfirst.org/2007/03/31/march-31-2007-surrealism-at-guantanamo.

Institute for Research: Middle Eastern Policy. (2013). 'Joyous celebration' during 9/11 World Trade Center attack. Institute for Middle East Research. https://www.israellobby.org/urbanmoving/.

Javorsek Ii, D., & Schwitz, J. G. (2014). Probing uncertainty, complexity, and human agency in intelligence. *Intelligence and National Security, 29*(5), 639–653. https://doi.org/10.1080/02684527.2013.834218.

Johnson, D., & Risen, J. (2001, September 13). As FBI tracks hijackers, FBI tie is cited. *New York Times*.

Jones, S. E., Farrer, J., Jenkins, G. S., Legge, F., Gourley, J., Ryan, K., et al. (2008a). Extremely high temperatures during the World Trade Center destruction. *Journal of 911 Studies*, 1–11.

Jones, S. E. Legge, F. M., Ryan, K. R. (2008b). Fourteen points of agreement with official government reports on the World Trade Center destruction. *The Open Civil Engineering Journal, 2*(1). https://doi.org/10.2174/1874149500802010035, http://www.bentham.org/open/tociej/openaccess2.htm.

Jones, S. E. (2006, September). Why indeed did the WTC buildings completely collapse? *Journal of 9/11 Studies*. http://www.journalof911studies.com/volume/200609/WhyIndeedDidtheWorldTradeCenterBuildingsCompletelyCollapse.pdf.

Judicial Watch. (2003). U.S. Supremes rule in favor of JW. Press release. http://www.judicialwatch.org/archive/newsletter/2003/0203b.shtml.

Julian, R., Kelty, S., & Robertson, J. (2012). 'Get it right the first time': Critical issues at the crime scene. *Current Issues in Criminal Justice, 24*(1), 25–37.

Katz, P. (2016, February). The wellstone accident: Even bigger birds can stall and fall. *Plane and Pilot Magazine*. https://www.planeandpilotmag.com/article/the-wellstone-accident/.

Kean, T. H., & Hamilton, L. H. (2004). *The 9/11 report: The national commission on terrorist attacks upon the United States*. St Martin's Paperbacks. http://govinfo.library.unt.edu/911/report/911Report.pdf.

Kean, T. H., Hamilton, L. H., & Rhodes, B. (2007). *Without precedent: The inside story of the 9/11 commission*. New York: Vintage.

Kim, W. Y., & Baum, G. R. (2002). *Seismic observations during September 11, 2001, terrorist attack*. Maryland Geological Survey.

Kocieniewski, D. (1995, April 16). Terrorism evidence destroyed. *Newsday*.

Labaviere, R. (1999). *Dollars for terror: The US and Islam*. New York: Algora.

Lance, P. (2011). *1000 years for revenge: international terrorism and the FBI – The untold story*. New York: Regan Books.

Landau, M. J., Solomon, S., Greenberg, J., Cohen, F., Pyszczynski, T., Arndt, J., et al. (2004). Deliver us from evil: The effects of mortality salience and reminders of 9/11 on support for President George W. Bush. *Personality and Social Psychology Bulletin, 30*(9), 1136–1150.

Lappe, A., & Marshall, S. (2004). *True lies*. New York: Plume.

Larsen, B. R. (2009). Active thermitic material discovered in dust from the 9/11 World Trade Center catastrophe. *The Open Chemical Physics Journal, 2*(1), 7–31.

Lengel, R. (2016, October 14). Aircraft landing speeds explained. *Flying*. https://www.flyingmag.com/aircraft-speed-limits-explained/.

Levite, A. (1987). *Intelligence and strategic surprises*. Columbia University Press.

Lieberman, D. (2011). Infringement on civil liberties after 9/11. *New York Law School Law Review, 56*, 1121–1128.

Lindorff, D. (2005, December 19). 9/11: Missing black boxes in World Trade Center attacks found by firefighters, analyzed by NTSB, concealed by FBI. *Counterpunch*.

Longman, J. (2002). *Among the heroes: United 93 and the passengers and crew who fought back*. New York: HarperCollins.

Mackinnon, G., & Mundorff, A. (2006). The World Trade Centre: September 11, 2001. In T. Thomspon & S. Black (Eds.), *Forensic human identification* (pp. 485–499). CRC Press.

Manning, B. (2002, January). Selling out the investigation. *Fire Engineering*. Editorial.

Markon, J. (2001, October 22). Grand jury probing attacks on September 11 is probing witness ties to hijackers. *Wall Street Journal*.

Martin, A. W., & Schum, D. A. (1987). Quantifying burdens of proof: A likelihood ratio approach. *Jurimetrics, Journal of Law Science and Technology, 27*(4), 383–402.

Mawn, B. (2001, September 18). Ashcroft says more attacks may be planned. CNN. https://edition.cnn.com/2001/US/09/17/inv.investigation.terrorism/index.html.

McAllister, T. P., Gann, R. G., Averill, J. D., Gross, J. L., Grosshandler, W. L., Lawson, J. R., … & Nelson, H. E. (2008). Structural fire response and probable collapse sequence of World Trade Center Building 7 (Vol. 1). Federal Building and Fire Safety Investigation of the World Trade Center Disaster (NIST NCSTAR 1-9). Washington: US Government Printing Office.

McCauliff, C. C. (1982). Burdens of proof: Degrees of belief, quanta of evidence, or constitutional guarantees. *Vanderbilt Law Review, 35*(6), 1293–1336.

McQueen, G. (2006). 118 witnesses: The firefighter's testimony to explosions in the Twin Towers. *Journal of 9/11 Studies*, 2, 1–60.

McQueen, G. (2008, January 11). Waiting for seven: WTC 7 collapse warnings in the FDNY oral histories. *Journal of 9/11 Studies*. http://www.journalof911studies.com/volume/200701/MacQueenWaitingforSeven.pdf.

Melman, Y. (2001, September 17). 5 Israelis detained for puzzling behavior' after WTC tragedy. *Haaretz*. https://www.haaretz.com/1.5396918.

Miller, A. (2009). 41 U.S. counter-terrorism and intelligence agency veterans challenge the official account of 9/11. Voltarie.net.org. https://www.voltairenet.org/article160100.html.

Mintz, J. (2001, November 23). 60 Israelis on tourist visas detained since Sept. 11. *Washington Post*. https://www.washingtonpost.com/archive/politics/2001/11/23/60-israelis-on-tourist-visas-detained-since-sept-11/a918a45b-e406-4b97-b9b8-cab7d0c9de20/.

Mintz, J., & Lengel, A. (2001, September 21). FBI arrests Kuwaiti liquor store clerk. *Washington Post*.

Mouffe, C. (2006). *On the political*. Verso.

Mueller, J., & Stewart, M. (2016). *Chasing ghosts: The policing of terrorism*. Oxford.

National Commission on Terrorist Attacks Upon the United States (2004, May 18). Testimony of the New York City of Emergency Management Richard J Sheirer opening remarks. New York.

National Institute of Standards and Technology. (2005, September). *Final report on the collapse of the World Trade Center towers*. NIST NCSTAR1. Gaithersburg, MD: NIST.

National Transportation Safety Board. (2000a). *In-flight breakup over the Atlantic Ocean Trans World Airlines Flight 800 Boeing 747-131, N93119 near East Moriches, New York July 17, 1996*. National Transportation Safety Board. https://www.ntsb.gov/investigations/AccidentReports/Reports/AAR0003.pdf.

National Transportation Safety Board. (2000b). *Aviation accident final report*. NTSB ID: NYC99MA178.

National Transportation Safety Board. (2002a). *Flight path study: American Airlines Flight 77*. Washington: Office of Research and Engineering.

National Transportation Safety Board. (2002b). *Loss of control and impact with terrain, Aviation Charter, Inc., Raytheon (Beechcraft) King Air A100, N41BE, Eveleth, Minnesota, Oct. 25, 2002*. Aircraft Accident Report. NTSB/AAR-03/03, PB2003-910403, Notation 7602.

Newsweek Staff. (2009, March 13). The 9/11 Commission's blind spot. *Newsweek*. https://www.newsweek.com/911-commissions-blind-spot-76531.

Perelman, M. (2002, March 15). Spy rumours fly on gusts of truth. *The Forward*. https://forward.com/news/national/325698/spy-rumors-fly-on-gusts-of-truth/.

Pillar, P. R. (2006). *Good literature and bad history: The 9/11 commission's tale of strategic intelligence*.

Ralph, J. (2009). The laws of war and the state of the American exception. *Review of International Studies, 35*(3), 631–649.

Reeve, S. (2002). *The New Jackals: Ramzi Yousef, Osama bin Laden, and the future of terrorism*. London: Northeastern.

Report from the Committee on Science, US House of Representatives. (2002, March 6). Learning from 9/11: Understanding the collapse of the World Trade Centre. http://web.archive.org/web/20021128021952/http://commdocs.house.gov/committees/science/hsy77747.000/hsy77747_0.htm.

Roach, K. (2010). The eroding distinction between intelligence and evidence in terrorism investigation. In N. McGarrity, A. Lynch, & G. Williams (Eds.), *Counterterrorism and beyond* (pp. 48–68). Abington: Routledge.

Ross, B., & Esposito, R. (2005, November 18). CIA's harsh interrogation techniques described. *ABC News.*

Ryan, K. J. (2010, November 18). Evidence for informed trading on the attacks of September 11. *Foreign Policy Journal.*

Scheppele, Kim Lane. (2005). Evidence from torture: Dilemmas for international and domestic law. *American Society of International Law Proceedings, 99*, 271–276.

Scheurer, M., Committee on Foreign Affairs. (2007). *Extraordinary rendition in U.S. counterterrorism policy: The impact on transatlantic relations.* Joint Hearing before the Subcommittee on International Organisations, Human Rights, and Oversight and the Subcommittee on Europe of Committee on Foreign Affairs. House of Representatives One Hundred Tenth Congress First Session April 17, Serial No. 110–128. https://fas.org/irp/congress/2007_hr/rendition.pdf.

Scott, P. D. (2007). *9/11 Commission deception, Cheney's actions on 9/11, and why he should testify under oath.* http://www.peterdalescott.net.

Sewell, W. H., Jr. (1996). Historical events as transformations of structures: Inventing revolution at the Bastille. *Theory and Society, 25*(6), 841–881.

Sewell Jr, W. H. (2005). *Logics of history: Social theory and social transformation.* University of Chicago Press.

Shaler, R. (2005). *Who they were: Inside the World Trade Center DNA story – The unprecedented effort to identify the missing.* Simon & Schuster.

Shea, G. (2004, September 15). *Israeli surveillance of the future hijackers and FBI suspects in the September 11 attacks and their failure to give us adequate warning.* Memorandum to National Commission on Terrorist Attacks on the United States and Senate and House Intelligence Committees. http://ariwatch.com/Links/SheaMemorandumIsrael/SheaMemorandumIsrael.htm?fbclid=IwAR0Wj2HzbccSLgwfpenYvr9KiQ4Zujua000UEBaFQmolJBQjFgK1Majp9xM.

Slaughter, A. M. (2009). *A new world order.* New York: Princeton University Press.

Smith, D. (2019, August 31). Trial for five men charged with planning 9/11 to start in 2021, 20 years after attack. *The Guardian.* https://www.theguardian.com/us-news/2019/aug/30/khalid-shaikh-mohammad-9-11-trial-start-date.

Smith, W. (2002). The forensic community's response to 911. *Analytical Chemistry, 74*(7), 190a–195a.

Solomon, E. (2006, August 21). *Interview: Lee Hamilton, truth, lies and conspiracy.* Canadian Broadcasting Corporation.

Stein, J. (2014, May 8). Israel's aggressive spying in the U.S. mostly hushed up. *Newsweek.* https://www.newsweek.com/israels-aggressive-spying-us-mostly-hushed-250278.

Sunder, S. S., et al., National Institute of Standards and Technology. (2008). *NCSTAR 1A: Final report on the collapse of World Trade Center Building 7.* Washington: US Government Printing Office.

Suskind, R. (2006). *One percent doctrine: Deep inside America's pursuit of its enemies since 9/11.* Simon & Schuster.

Taddonio, P. (2018, May 9). *CIA Director nominee supported destruction of torture tapes.* PBS Frontline.

Tapper, J. (2001, September 12). Bush, challenged: Bush's reaction is literally up in the air. *Salon.*

Thompson, J. W. (2017). *From memory to memorial: Shanksville, America and Flight 93.* University Park, PA: Pennsylvania State University Press.

Trento, J., & Trento, S. (2006). *Unsafe at any altitude.* Hanover: Steerforth.

Unger, R. M. (1982). *The critical legal studies movement.* Harvard.

United States Congress, House Committee on Science. (2002). *Learning from 9/11: Understanding the Collapse of the WTC.* Statement from Dr Arnet L. Bement Jr. 107th Congress, 2nd Session.

US Congress. (2003, July 24). *Report of the Joint Inquiry on the Terrorist Attacks of September 11.* House Permanent Select Committee on Intelligence and the Senate Committee on Intelligence 108th Congress. 1st Session. Washington: US Congress.
US. v Moussaoui, US District Court for the Eastern District of Virginia. Prosecution Trial Exhibits Exhibit PA00101-01455a.
Wachtendorf, T. (2004). *Improvising 9/11: Organizational improvisation following the World Trade Center disaster.* Doctoral dissertation, University of Delaware.
Wagner-Pacifici, R. (2010). Theorizing the restlessness of events. *American Journal of Sociology, 115*(5), 1351–1386. https://doi.org/10.1086/651299.
Weaver, O. (1995). Securitisation and desecuritization. In R. D. Lipshutz (Ed.), *On security*. New York: Columbia University Press.
White House, Office of Vice President. (2001). *NY B9 Farmer Misc- WH 1 of 3 Fdr- 11-19-01 Newsweek Interview of Cheney 450. 0/11 Document Archive.* https://www.scribd.com/document/16869695/NY-B9-Farmer-Misc-WH-1-of-3-Fdr-11-19-01-Newsweek-Interview-of-Cheney-450.
World Trade Center Task Force Interview, Chief Joseph Pfeifer. (2001, October 23). https://static01.nyt.com/packages/pdf/nyregion/20050812_WTC_GRAPHIC/9110138.PDF.
Zarillo, R. (2001, October 25). *World Trade Center Task Force Interview.* http://graphics8.nytimes.com/packages/pdf/nyregion/20050812_WTC_GRAPHIC/9110161.PDF.
Wright, R. G. (2002). *Address to the National Press Club on May 30, 2002, with Judicial Watch.* C-SPAN video Archived 2011-09-01 at the Wayback Machine, circa 23:30 of the CSPAN video. www.motherjones.com/politics/2011/08/fbi-terrorist-sting-targets.
Yoo, J. C. (2002, August 1). Response to Alberto Gonzales' request for views on legality of interrogation techniques. United States Department of Justice, Office of the Legal Counsel. http://www.gwu.edu/~nsarchiv/NSAEBB/NSAEBB127/020801.pdf.

Chapter 5
Intelligence Crime 1: Let's Not Be Too Hard on Ourselves

> Epstein is a very hard client to represent without getting blurred….
>
> Charles Fried quoted in Bruch (2019)

> Terrorism follows an inexorable, built-in escalation. To be effective, it must continually horrify and stupefy. Yet once we have become accustomed to a particular level of violence, a new outrage is required to shock our sensibilities. It used to be enough for terrorists to hijack a plane to attract international attention; next it became necessary to kill a few hostages; in the future, more violence will be required.
>
> Benjamin Netanyahu (1986: 218)

Introduction

In this chapter we probe into Type 2 covert sponsored intelligence crimes that are carried out by 'our side', and regarding which there must be, as per our previous discussion, a solicitous forbearance. 'Crime' involves a violation of norms that is affirmed to be serious enough to warrant the strongest disapprobation. We are concerned with violations of norms that are serious enough, all things being equal, to be designated as crime and to warrant criminal prosecution and penalty but which successfully evade the forensic attention of everyday criminal prosecutions. In our usage here, the term 'forensics' refers to the use of scientific methods, including replicable, transparent procedures, to solve crime.

Following on from earlier observations it is necessary to state at the outset that what is presented here is a counter-narrative. As we discussed in Chapter 3, a working hypothesis is a necessary evil of investigation. A rationale for the inclusion and analysis of evidence depends on it. The discussion below supports a viewpoint taken throughout this book with respect to the whodunnit of crimes involving state actors: that an absence of evidence is not evidence of absence.

Two assumptions are made that the reader is asked to consider. The first is that actors close to the centre of a government who also have some capacity to set aside (or modify) bureaucratic or legal prohibitions may do so to support the interests

W. B. de Lint, *Blurring Intelligence Crime*,
https://doi.org/10.1007/978-981-16-0352-5_5

of a faction of the 'national security' apparatus or dispositive.[1] Evidence for this assumption is copious (Blum, 2003; Agee & Wolf, 1978; Thomas, 2007; Prouty, 2011; Bevins, 2020). The US Office of Special Plans (OSP), for example, was created in September 2002 (and existed until June 2003) to convey raw 'cherry picked' intelligence (concerning Saddam Hussein's alleged chemical WMD) to senior Bush administration officials (Wolfowitz, Feith, Rumsfeld and Cheney) who could then intervene in the analysis rather than relying on the equivocal summaries of trained analysts (Hersh, 2003). The CIA Director, George Tenet, did not stand in the way of this 'fixing' of intelligence; indeed, he sat behind Colin Powell, at Powell's request, when he made the pitch to the United Nations regarding Iraq's weapons of mass destruction (Hersh, 2003). The OSP was no doubt modelled on the 40 Committee (Wise, 2005), which Henry Kissinger chaired as President Gerald Ford's Assistant to the President for National Security Affairs, and which consisted of a handful of top officials from intelligence, and military and foreign affairs. This politicisation of intelligence may be understood as belonging to deliberate agency or to its 'perfect failure' (Phythian, 2006).

The second assumption, consistent with our discussion of political criminality earlier (Chapter 3), is that there will be a relative incapacity to provide a remedy for the criminal actions referred to above even where that criminality has been exposed. The US-led 'war on terror' has displaced 37 million people (of which 9.7 million were Iraqis) and led to the deaths in direct war violence of 800,000 people (Watson Institute, 2020). There has been no serious repercussion to those involved in the development or utilisation of the OSP, including its chief protagonists, to support the illegal war. And as we observed earlier and shall be exploring further in the following chapter, the security assemblage (or dispositive) absorbs or conditions expectations; this includes the strident vilification of oppositional voices, like that of Julian Assange, who exposed Iraqi war crimes. Such intelligence whistle-blowers are viewed as deeply threatening to the necessary hegemony and reviewed by corporate media and a politicised judiciary in accord with the denigration proffered by defenders of intelligence impunity (Cook, 2020).

In the meantime, it is obvious that where the crimes *are not* exposed to external pressures there will be negligible chance of a public forensic investigation. As per our thesis, we expect that exposure and remedies will be consistent with the prima facie level of criminality and the destabilisation of a network of actors at or near the centre of sovereign power. Even where there is a public exposure of a secret operation, the opportunity for interested government actors to select and frame the event will go a long way towards protecting (a version of) the national interest to project its ongoing legitimacy. The preferred projection is to paint these exposed operations as mistakes by zealous or rogue actors and not representative of routine operational activities, interests, ethics, etc. Because highly placed government actors are able to persuade judicial authorities in large part by making oblique reference to bigger dangers in the empowering of enemies of the state (as in the case of Johnson to Chief Justice Earl Warren in the lead-up to Warren's appointment), the lack of completeness in the investigation of forensic facts in this domain is accepted and permitted to fall—alongside the lesser domino of equality under the law.

In its selection of enemies (targeting) and opportunistic nurturing of assets (gardening), the attitude of covert operational intelligence may be more or less offensive and aggressive. Omand and Pythian (2018: 30) observe that all prohibitions may be legitimately infringed in the right conditions, noting the possible exception of torture, a 'rare example of a justifiable conviction-driven ethic'. As previously discussed, a critical institutional approach does not long pause on the question of the ethics or morality of this work. As concerns human rights in intelligence, it may be summarised that the constraint placed on practice by ethics is one that an army of intelligence service lawyers work overtime to excise or befuddle. As we have just seen, torture, too, has been justified, as per the Bybee and Yoo memos (2002; Yoo, 2002; Bybee, 2002) even if not permanently. The chief protagonists of 'enhanced interrogation' are rewarded (Goodman, 2019b) while 'quaint' Geneva conventions seem to pass away in the wings as kinetic interventions up the Iraqi body count. Setting a moral 'defeat mechanism' on intelligence, as we averred, is to permit the liberal check on sovereign vitality that has been deemed so fatal (Schmitt, 1988). As also follows from the summary provided in Chapter 3, the normalisation of exception is for the necessary vitality of the sovereign. Concerning that regularity, with this chapter we move from the infrequent spectacular of apex crime to the routine and quotidian of intelligence crime.

From the Spectacular to the Quotidian: Routine Operations, Remarkable 'Mistakes'

What are the common devices of covert operations that may be deployed to achieve the furtive transactional agenda? How does intelligence compel or coerce? At its apex, the power of intelligence is exceptional access to arcane transactive information. Intelligence provides a product to a consumer. Where the apex consumer is the sovereign, it is advised on strategic necessities and preferences. Intelligence offers what is known of the 'enemy's' strength (analysis) and what may be done to reduce or neutralise it (operations).

The spectacular cannot by definition be a regular performance or outbreak from the routine. The sovereign awaits the growth of a threat to a size that will permit it to deploy or redeploy resources, sometimes in a major 'pivot'. The Gulf of Tonkin incident is known to have permitted such a major turn, as did Pearl Harbour, the Kennedy assassination and 9/11. As noted previously, and as documented in the analysis of the 'strategy of tension' (Clement & Scalia, 2020), spectacular acts of terrorism will produce faux clarifications in which a binary us/them ordering may suddenly find widespread popular support. At least for some critical historians and political scientists, such dramatic events may involve a faction of leadership in an act of omission (Levite, 1987; Prouty, 2011; Rusbridger & Nave, 1991). However, most of the time, the countering that is needed is not to 'go massive, sweep it all up, things related and not', as per Rumsfeld's response to 9/11 (Borger, 2006).

Careerism in covert or clandestine intelligence is measured by the latency or *ignition threat* of the illicit enterprise network. This is measured, in turn, by the involvement of operations assets in the most transactive illicit networks. Intelligence assets or agents nurture illicit or criminal networks by attracting or recruiting profiteering corporate and state sponsors and luring licit enterprises and individuals into compromising associations with the illicit or criminal network. This encases the network in a sarcophagus of *protection* in a manner not inconsistent with Tilly's (1985) state gestation analysis; by compromising potential political, administrative or legal overseers the activity may be secured from official scrutiny or by rendering the case as too hot to handle. Accordingly, there is a continuity between the *furtherance* of the transactive capacity in the means of intelligence in cultivating illicit or criminal enterprise networks (such as drugs, terrorism or arms-trading) and the ends of political change in the *deployment* of the network—ignition or 'lighting the fuse'.

If the objective is to obtain transactive information that may be deployed when sufficiently ripened (hence the gardening metaphor), intelligence agencies play a long game. Careerists seek to maximise alignment with the point of harvest so that, as above, they support the relatively autonomous power of the agency by reference to this latency: they may refer to the threat of ignition (or holding back on extinguishing the detonation). In respect of that long game, decisions to minimise compromising agency actors in illegalities by 'shutting it down' or 'mopping it up' may not be easily made. Still, the bigger the operation, the more potentially compromising all actions relating to it will be. If the sticky threads of the web touch elite politicians—as, for instance, in the GW Bush–bin Laden and the HGW Bush–Iran Contra/BCCI connections (Castro, 1992; Beaty & Gwynne, 2004)—then very powerful political interests are engaged to assert immunity and to restrict scrutiny into the built criminal network.

In nurturing organisations like al-Qaeda, the CIA and other intelligence organisations advance towards the long-game ideological goal. There is a large body of work that has investigated the features of state-sponsored, -supported or -nurtured terrorism as an effective means of ideological subversion. There is much documentation and analysis of the covert grey and black operations of the CIA and other intelligence agencies, as referred to previously (Blum, 1986; Weiner, 2008). There is a well-documented track record of CIA involvement in infiltration, discrediting and the covert funding or training of death squads to upend or destroy offside political organisations (Blum, 1986; McCoy, 2003; RFE/RL, 2019). Beginning with the post-World War II Gladio or stay-behind units (Ganser, 2005), this work has involved the proactive use of cut-outs and proxies, the encouragement of terrorist bombings, and, later, the creation of airlines (Air America), banks (BCCI), front companies (Urban Moving Systems), media plants (Operation Mockingbird) and technology innovation companies (InQtel, Promis). For Mossad, the term of reference is represented in its motto: 'by way of deception, thou shalt do war'. Both parts of this sentence ought to be understood separately and in conjunction. To wage war is to deploy permissive violence; to do so deceptively is to employ that violence without producing a record of it beyond what is desired by the agency (Wilsnack, 1980). This, as discussed previously, should not be a controversial description of the practice of the covert operations of the so-called secret intelligence agency, which requires that public inquiry (and also often oversight agency investigation) is prevented from access its recesses (Gill, 1994: 80–82).

This reading of the record is well-known, but it is often, as we noted previously, banished from liberal and even left-leaning analyses of intelligence.[2] There is also very little scholarly work on the use of the honeytrap (see, for example, Mijalkovic, 2014). Glorified in, for instance, Fleming's MI6-based James Bond character, sex-espionage is the cultivation of a trust relationship for the purposes of compromising targets so that their resources may be used to support the agenda of the exploiting agent. The honeytrap will typically be crafted and resourced by the intelligence agency (who needs to gain access to the compromising sex material) but carried out by agents, who are not professional members of the intelligence agency. Videorecordings of sex that is as compromising as possible to the target, particularly sex with drugs or under-age or sado-masochistic behaviour, fits the bill (Mijalkovic, 2014: 15).

The agent may be motivated by ideology or money. Mijalkovic (2014: 6) notes that one of the best-known examples of sex being exploited to discover secrets by a state asset is Mata Hari, a Dutch exotic dancer who was executed in 1917 'for spying for the Germans on orders from French authorities' (Mijalkovic, 2014: 6). The KGB developed specialist courses to improve the skills of sex-espionage, which included the teaching of sex techniques to young women recruited for their vulnerability and looks as 'soldiers of their bodies', and it would film the use of these techniques for detailed analysis to allow for improvement by the agents being recruited for the purpose (Mijalkovic, 2014: 9). MI5 used the Eve Club, an intelligence checkpoint in Belgium, as a sex-espionage unit (Mijalkovic, 2014: 10). Mark Kennedy, a British undercover police officer, infiltrated environmental groups and engaged in long-term sexual relationships with female activists in order to gain their trust (Schlembach, 2018). Mossad, as will not surprise followers of intelligence, is the craft leader in sex espionage work (Mijalkovic, 2014: 8–12).

The crimes of Jeffrey Epstein and the alleged crimes of Ghislaine Maxwell are still being unravelled. Whether an Epstein–Maxwell illicit network implicates and then also involves political elites in its restricted exposure remains for now a matter of speculation, but in considering the case here, we wish only to propose that such a conspiracy is consistent with the everyday operation of clandestine means and methods. An argument has already been made that this type of crime involves intelligence agents and espionage assets doing what they reasonably believe they are supported in and rewarded for doing (Goodman, 2019a; Giraldi, 2019; Howard, 2019). It is well-established that Israel is active in ensuring that the political class of the United States should be persuaded or compelled to support whatever version of national interest Israel may propose (Mearsheimer & Walt, 2007; Giraldi, 2019). This is straightforward IR realism or power politics (Mearsheimer & Alterman, 2001). There should be no doubt that Israel, like the US and Russia, is well-motivated to use deceptive war when efficiencies support the gambit, and that it does so using its own view of proper targeting and gardening of illicit networks on the understanding that the end justifies the means.

In selecting and examining the alleged crimes of Epstein and Maxwell as a possible case of honeytrap or sex-espionage (and 9/11 as involving the enabling and cultivation of intelligence assets first developed during the Cold War), we are taking the analysis beyond what is politely considered *acceptable* in relation to allegations of wrongdoing by 'us'. The same standards do not apply when it comes to crimes by 'them', as Noam Chomsky (2015) has been at pains to point out over the decades. In other words, I am applying the standard that is met when the *Guardian* or *Washington Post* uses unnamed and unaccountable intelligence sources or experts from within the propaganda branch of the state (Cook, 2020). In rhetorical logic there is a very good rule that a poor justification is poor whatever the goal of the persuader. On the other hand, given the excessive dependence of liberal intelligence analysts on strategic leaks and disclosures from the archive (where it is common sense that the national security story that the archive is permitted to tell should not be destabilising), it may also be acceptable to put the thumb on the scales in the other direction (that of scepticism regarding that narrative). This means that this account, too, is merely a plausible reading of some of the available evidence or public information. As per the method proposed, it is in providing an account of the departure from standard investigatory and forensic practices that we see the outline of that political protection; this occurs in national security or intelligence interceptions of criminal procedure, investigative discovery and forensic recovery. This is also what we mean to imply by qualifying forensics with the term 'critical'.

We begin with straightforward facts. In the case of the Rainbow Warrior bombing and the arrest of Raymond Davis we see the prosaic or quotidian operations referred to above, only we see them because they did not live up to the intelligence ideal.

'Oops, Won't Do It Again': *Rainbow Warrior*[3]

On 11 July 1985, the Greenpeace ship *Rainbow Warrior* was rigged with two limpet mines that were detonated 10 minutes apart in Auckland Harbor by two agents of the Direction Générale de la Sécurité Extérieure (DGSE—the French secret service), killing a photographer, Fernando Pereira. The bombing was the culmination of 'Opération Satanique,' a secret mission to counteract Greenpeace anti-nuclear activism that involved 12 spies infiltrating New Zealand under a variety of covers or legends.

One of the spies, lieutenant Christine Hugette Cabon, 33, was instructed by the DGSE to determine the Rainbow Warrior's itinerary and to 'pave the way for other agents to sabotage it' (Meier & Dennett, 2017). She was to charm the information from Greenpeace members and did so with such elan that New Zealand conservationist and friend of Jacques Cousteau, Jean-Marie Vidal, wrote a testimonial to Greenpeace in New Zealand in March 1985 celebrating Frederique Bonlieu's (as she introduced herself) credentials as scientist, sailor and conservationist: 'she shares our beliefs' (King, 1986: 50). Considering her objective, there is a sinister irony in how Cabon used the Greenpeace office to conduct 'research' into how the French might better understand Pacific Islander hostility to French nuclear testing.

From this base of the Auckland Greenpeace offices near Auckland Harbour Cabon proceeded to draw from her hospitable Kiwi hosts (King, 1986: 51). Recalling the brief remarks on the morality of intelligence operations in the previous section, her conduct may be contrasted to the Greenpeace organisational ethic, which in its openness and hospitality made itself agonisingly vulnerable to the foreign interlopers. While engaged in this 'partitioned' reconnaissance for Opération Satanique and living temporarily off the spoils of volunteer donations to Greenpeace, Cabon told a reporter for a local paper, the *Inner City News*:

> Here you are very far from your enemies. In Europe we are very close to them. We need Nuclear weapons to be safe and independent. Trying to find peace with weapons is a very big paradox, but without this defence we risk becoming Finland, which is influenced by Russia. (55)

She refused the photographer permission to take a picture. King's detailed investigation examined how Cabon confused her generous hosts by expressing views that showed little sympathy for environmental values. Once her work was done she surprised her hosts by paying for a farewell party (and providing Beaujolais) and impressed them with many letters from France, which stopped coming just before the bombing (except for one more letter that offered her condolences after the event which read: 'I am with you, with all my heart'). Within a month of the bombing New Zealand police established that she was working for the DGSE (King, 1986: 59–60). As she told reporters who later visited her in France, she was compartmented, or not made aware of the whole operation (Meier & Dennett, 2017).

Eleven more French agents would arrive after Cabon's departure, three by way of a yacht out of New Caledonia, the *Ouvéa*. Such is the detail of knowledge of what these sailors did upon arrival between landfall at Parengarenga in the north of the North Island and their serpentine journey south towards Auckland that King can describe in meticulous detail who spotted and first spoke to the Frenchmen and how their demeanour was apprehended. When they came ashore and asked after petrol and a hotel their manner was sufficiently out of place to trigger a call-out to the local ranger to alert him to their presence (King, 1986: 66–76).

As the *Ouvéa* was arriving in Parengarenga, two more agents, Commander Alain Mafart and Captain Dominique Prieur, arrived at Auckland Airport, disguised as a trading manager and his sociology lecturer wife (King, 1986: 67–70). In a few short weeks, the agents would take the *Ouvéa* to the open sea where it would be scuttled, after the crew was transferred to the French submarine the *Rubis*. It would later be determined by police that on the yacht had been the explosives that were transferred to agents Tonel and Camurier (who carried out the planting of the bombs), and to the Zodiac, the inflatable boat used to approach the *Rainbow Warrior* (144). Ten agents would return safely to France, but Mafart and Prieur would be caught, arrested, tried and convicted in a criminal court.

It happened that the bombs were placed on the hull earlier than planned and as a consequence the tide was too low when the Zodiac needed to be taken out of the water at the prearranged landing place. As a result, there were many sightings of the Zodiac as it tried hastily to find alternative landing in the dark. There were also witnesses as the Yamaha outboard and oxygen tanks were jettisoned in the attempt to disappear the evidence under an overpass. Some cyclists saw this and their eyewitness account tied the outboard through a serial number to a London marine shop address, the name of Eric Andries and the purchase of the Zodiac (King, 1986: 136–138).

Not known by the French agents was that the Auckland Outboard Boating Club had a volunteer group that watched the boats and harbour for suspicious activity. Two of these volunteers were able to relate to police how they watched two men bring the Zodiac ashore and unload its contents into a van, in what the volunteers thought was probably a burglary of one of the boats in the harbour. And although police were too late to catch them red-handed and to find the Zodiac with all of its identifying features removed, they had a registration number for the van. The evidence attaching the boat, the van, the men and the bombing would be overwhelming. Mafart and Prieur were given permission by the DGSE in Paris to take an earlier departure flight but on their last night at the Gold Star Auckland Airport Motel in Mangere they clumsily disposed of some muddy clothes and life raft stickers (King, 1986: 140–144). On the other hand, there is 'nothing known about the shape or size of the bombs used. They destroyed themselves and hence the evidence' (136). The cost of he operation has never been officially provided but calculated to be about US$400,000 (Dobbs, 1985).

There was a contest between authorities to frame this event. The French Government initially denied responsibility, claiming that it did not 'deal with its opponents in such ways' (Dobbs, 1985). It launched a commission of inquiry that concluded that the DGSE was involved only in spying on Greenpeace. The operation was in fact carried out on the orders of Charles Hernu, Minister of Defenc (and thus the François Mitterrand government) by the DGSE (Dobbs, 1985). The French Government wished to rely upon its international status and was so assured in its ability or capacity to avoid the open discovery of its actions in a New Zealand court that it initially labelled the act that it commissioned as 'terrorist'.

The use of the commission of inquiry is noteworthy. The French Government knew the facts at the highest level, and yet it sought publicly to explore the matter by appointing Bernard Tricot, formerly chief of staff to the late General Charles de Gaulle. The Tricot Report, released less than seven weeks after the bombing on 25 August 1985, found no evidence that the DGSE agents had played any part in the crime and were merely observing Greenpeace. It cleared both the French Government and the secret services of responsibility for the sabotage. However, newspapers even in France were already openly sceptical of the government's claims and the French Prime Minister, Laurent Fabius, told media:

> If it were to appear that criminal acts have been committed by French nationals, judicial action will be immediately exercised. ... Our condemnation is not, as has sometimes been rumoured, a condemnation against the poor execution of a questionable project. It is an absolute condemnation against a criminal act. The guilty, whoever they be, have to pay for this crime. (quoted in Andrews, 1991)

By mid-September 1985, a fresh French investigation was ordered. In an about-turn, Fabius told reporters that the truth had been hidden from Tricot and his investigators. At this time, it was admitted that funding for the operation had been authorised by Mitterrand's top military aide, General Jean Saulnier (Dobbs, 1985). New Zealand had been strongly referencing Mitterrand government culpability by referring to the act as a 'criminal attack in breach of the international law of state responsibility committed on New Zealand sovereign territory' (King, 1986). On this account, one of the pieces of evidence was obtained by a French-speaking police constable who reported the following exchange between Mafart and Prieur while in custody awaiting trial: Prieur commented, 'It's a pity somebody has to die, even a child', to which Mafart replied, 'That's the way it has to be' (King, 1986: 147).

Both Mafart and Prieur would spend their detainment on a French military base as per the agreement France had reached with New Zealand following their conviction and sentencing (initially charged with arson but later convicted of manslaughter on a ten-year term). That agreement, brokered by UN Secretary-General Javier Pérez de Cuéllar in June 1986, also awarded New Zealand NZ$13 million in reparations. However, in violation of the agreement the agents were released after serving less than two years, after which they were promoted. Six years later, Swiss authorities arrested one of the *Ouvéa* crew members, Gerald Andries. While Andries was held in Basel on an Interpol warrant issued in the summer of 1985, police and prosecutors prepared the case for extradition with 85 sworn affidavits (Frew, 1991). However, New Zealand yielded to internal and external political pressure and retreated from the case, allowing the last shred of public accountability to be extinguished (Meier & Dennett, 2017).

Analysis

The Lange and Mitterrand governments were ideological opponents on the subject of nuclear power and this produced a conflict between their police and intelligence services as well as their state and diplomatic authorities. This conflict between the two governments, with the French position viewed at best as extraordinarily arrogant by New Zealand while also being dependent on New Zealand's acceptance of French denials of culpability, rendered back-channel diplomatic resolutions unavailable. Second, there was 'red hot' evidence that had been gathered by New Zealand police that made its way into the hands of willing and able judicial authorities and journalists; the Mitterrand denials would be confounded when Prieur and Mafart pleaded guilty to the reduced charge and it became impossible to separate them from the DGSE/Mitterrand government operation, which was subject to the widest and most excruciating public exposure (as evidenced by the *Washington Post* headline 'France says its agents sank ship' in August 1985 [Dobbs, 1985]).

Secondly, we know about the *Rainbow Warrior* bombing in a fine detail that is excruciating not only to the French, but also to those in the Nine Eyes—a signals intelligence alliance that includes both France and New Zealand—whose sins of omission have escaped comment or rebuke. Apparently, the New Zealand intelligence services, including the Government Communication Security Bureau (GCSB) and the Security Intelligence Service (SIS), were not aware of this operation by a friendly nation on New Zealand sovereign land and were permitted to remain tight-lipped regarding what it might have meant for the Nine Eyes relationship. It was the New Zealand Police who uncovered the plot through routine investigative work (and not through intelligence from these security agencies, as far as the public record is concerned). The omission here is inherent to the *transnational* character of intelligence and its crimes, as the transnational alliance responsibilities are often cited to beat back 'host', 'local' or 'national' intelligence agency answerability, oversight and accountability (Hager, 1990; de Lint, 2016).

The effort to reduce the specific threat of Greenpeace to the nuclear program in the pacific was successful inasmuch as the boat was rendered inoperative. Nonetheless, and despite the obvious calculation, cost and planning and the description offered by the arrested agents and by the matter-of-fact description of the operation by Cabon (Meier & Dennett, 2017), the case is considered an aberration, and as inconsistent with the routine work of these agencies. However, it is axiomatic only that the covert activities of intelligence agencies are not meant to be disseminated except to authorised knowers who are expressly forbidden from sharing that information. Indeed, the reporting and recording of criminally illegal activities to oversight agencies or parliamentary or congressional committees and then the public at large is anathema to the operational values of covert intelligence. Normally or routinely oversight committees will seek to avoid inspection but may do so where an action reflects partisan political interests or offends a bipartisan political consensus (Lustgarten & Leigh, 1994).

Lastly, efforts to pre-emptively counter the criminal and forensic investigation of the bombing were sophisticated in planning but failed in application. Mistakes were made concerning the legends, the disposal of the evidence and in anticipation of further high-level protections that might be required considering that the act committed by France was not on the open sea but in a valued resource (Auckland Harbour) of a friendly power. The operation was a strategic failure because the facts were no longer capable of being covered by plausible deniability after a failed attempt first through the public denials of the French authorities and then by the Tricot Report. Ultimately, the reflex French position was untenable in front of the publics of France, New Zealand and the international audience and its ordering norms. In the meantime, the bombing was an intelligence crime. It was an illegal or criminal activity carried out with the full authorisation of the Mitterrand government by agents of the DGSE directly and permanently employed by those authorities.

'Hands Off Our Man'

On 26 January 2011, in Lahore, Pakistan, Raymond Davis shot and killed Faizan Haider and Faheem Shamshad at a red traffic light. A third man, Ibad-ur-Rehman, was run over by an SUV driven by an official from the US consulate, whom Davis had contacted for immediate assistance. Davis was captured after he shot the two motorcyclists 'through his car windshield' and then 'finished one of them off' in 'broad daylight' (Lindorff, 2011). As recounted in Hayat (2020: 56), the event, which occurred in a busy street, became an immediate media sensation that was fuelled by the release of a police interview:

> News anchors were particularly troubled by how Davis had done all this '*din diharay*' (in broad daylight). They commented on his 'relaxed and non-cooperative attitude' during interrogation, referring to video clips from the police investigation where Davis was seen refusing to sign police papers and exasperatedly gesturing with his hands as if 'he was done' (*Express Tribune* 24/7). It was one white man to a whole country—the ratio was excessive. (Hayat, 2020: 56)

Davis's account of what occurred was that he shot the men in self-defence because he was being robbed, but he also said that they were Pakistani spies 'out to kill him' (Hayat, 2020: 56). Eleven days after the killings, Faheem's wife took poison and died just after telling reporters that she feared there would be no justice because Davis would be released under political pressure from the US (Hayat, 2020: 57). On 15 February, US President Barack Obama called for the release of 'our diplomat'. The Obama administration cited the event in suspending high-level talks with Islamabad (Agencies, 2011). Secretary of State Hillary Clinton and Obama made statements that Davis was a US Embassy official and must therefore be governed under diplomatic immunity. However, he was not on a list of 48 officials submitted by the US to the Pakistani Foreign Office and was added to it only a couple of days after the shooting (Lindorff, 2011). From Davis, Pakistani authorities claimed that they found logs of 27 mobile phone calls between the Pakistani Taliban and Laskhar-e-Taiba, a 'terror cell' blamed for the assassination of Benazir Bhutto and the kidnapping and murder of *Wall Street Journal* reporter Daniel Pearl (Arsenault, 2011).

What was Davis's mission and was his act a crime? He was, according to an intelligence source, the 'acting head of CIA in Pakistan' (Crilly, 2011). The *Guardian* (Walsh & MacAskill, 2011) reported that, upon its government's request, US media had agreed not to divulge that Davis was indeed a CIA operative, not a diplomat. It was also claimed at the time of his arrest that he was a covert security officer for the CIA and had previously been a Green Beret and Blackwater/Xe employee. Moreover, there was initial speculation that Davis was identifying targets for predator drone attacks inside Pakistan (Lindorff, 2011).

While the negotiations between the US and Pakistan were ongoing, a prosecution was prepared and on 16 March Davis faced the Lahore High Court. However, the case was suspended and a Shariah court was hastily instituted, which directed that US$2.3 million be paid by the US Government as 'blood money' to secure Davis's release, official pardon and return to the US (Arsenault, 2011). Even this involved defiance of an Exit Control List and the removal of counsel for the victims' families under forced detention during trial (Hayat, 2020: 58). The deal happened prior to the Lahore court being able to provide a ruling on Mr Davis's argument for diplomatic immunity, a negative ruling on which 'could have set a precedent for other countries to deny CIA operatives diplomatic protections.'[4]

Analysis

What was the CIA doing in Pakistan? And what was it doing in Indochina in the 1960s and 1970s? Robert Anderson writes that 'I was Ray Davis' while he worked for the Phoenix Program during the Vietnam War in the 1960s. He was given a State Department ID, told to claim diplomatic immunity if arrested, and helped to carry out 'a systematic assassination' of 60,000 people across Indochina who were 'identified as not loyal to U.S. goals'. Because of his status, no trial for any murder he committed was legal (Anderson, 2011). Davis's official story was at least partially repudiated when the deal brokering his release in Pakistan was reported. The *New York Times* (Galli & Mazzetti, 2011) reported that 'US officials insisted Wednesday the CIA made no pledge to scale back operations in Pakistan or to give the Pakistani intelligence agency a roster of US spies operating in the country—assertions that Pakistani officials disputed'.

As revealed by Wikileaks, in October 2009, the Joint Prioritized Effects List (JPEL), a kill or capture list of targets compiled by the Joint Special Operations Command, was raining down terror on many Pakistanis. As in Vietnam under the Phoenix Program, the metric of success was the number captured or killed. As pointed out by Matthew Hoh, formerly the senior US foreign service officer in Zabul province, the list includes Afghans holding every kind of non-combat function in the Taliban (Porter & Noori, 2011). In Pakistan and Yemen, US drone strikes 'killed as many as 1147 unknown people in failed attempts to kill 41 named individuals' and in Pakistan 874 people were killed in multiple strikes reported to have targeted only 24 men; and 'it took the US six attempts to kill Qari Hussain,' during which 128 people including 13 children were killed (Reprieve, 2014). The CIA also supports Special Operations Forces 'search and seizure' raids in Afghanistan and Pakistan (against whom the US has not declared war). In these, commanders were under pressure to find targets for raids as McCrystal and Petreaus expanded these 'search and seizure' raids (Lindroff, 2011). As Porter and Noori (2011) conclude, there was a ten-fold increase in raids around the time of Davis's capture. The increase in the target list could not have been accomplished without a relaxation of the criteria for including someone on the JPEL.

According to Lindorff (2011), it is possible that Davis's mission was not merely to do reconnaissance on Laskhar-e-Taiba, as per the Pakistani *Express Tribune*, but to 'orchestrate terrorism'. If his mission was in fact to stoke the flames of a terror group and thereby to push the Global War on Terrorism (GWOT) around the global chessboard, in at least a few versions of national security this would not be anathema (Blum, 2003; Bevins, 2020; Thomas, 2007). It is the strong view of offensive realism that 'our' own assets must force the war along to locations or zones where our side wants it to be fought. This means two things: that the war or ordering problem *is identified as a certain type of terrorism* and that acts of terrorism *occur under the control of those agencies countering it* (see, for example, Mueller & Stewart, 2016).

It is most expedient to dismiss this account and its import, just as the case of the *Rainbow Warrior* has also been dismissed, as an aberration; and this is what is done by the scholarly literature and the corporate news media, except in rare background features. It is assumed that the instrumentation of national security, unless otherwise proven, accords with the publicly vetted mandates of government agencies to observe the rule of law. 'We' stay within the parameters of rule, jurisdiction and mission. While it is acknowledged that such missions may require actions that are abhorrent—as per the Doolittle Report (1954) that over 60 years ago forcefully raised the spectre of the 'dirty means' employed by democracies—it is by rote assumed that errant means within a democracy will always remain far removed from errant means without one ('gentlemen don't read each other's mail').[5] The spectacle of top CIA employee Raymond Davis ensnared in the crosshairs of the world's media can only be a *novelty* suggestive of a *rogue* faction or *misunderstood* narrative.

'Belongs to Intelligence'

In the Epstein case, a crime was alleged in March 2005 and investigated by Palm Beach Police. It began after a 14-year-old girl from Royal Palm Beach High School and her parents made a complaint that Epstein molested her at his Palm Beach mansion. The account of the police investigation provided by Palm Beach Police Chief Michael Reiter is that the investigation was immediately launched following the first victim's interview. This was because the witness account was compelling and subsequent interviewing of more victims only added to the urgency. Importantly, he notes that there was great consistency throughout the accounts of the complainants, who mostly did 'not know each other'. At the same time, they "'weren't perfectly aligned': [this] would have been a red flag that the stories were coordinated" (in Fitzpatrick & Schapiro, 2019). The investigation was kept low-key and within a month police found incriminating evidence from 'trash pulls' outside the Epstein mansion: specifically, they retrieved written notes regarding telephone messages for Epstein containing girls' names and telephone numbers, one matching the girl with the time she said she was at his mansion.

At this point, the investigation was, much like the New Zealand police investigation of the *Rainbow Warrior*, unimpeded. There was an allegation that a wealthy 50-year-old was molesting teenage girls, a type of crime detestable to police. However, Reiter knew that Epstein was well-connected. He was concerned that the high-level ties between Epstein and his associates and the Palm Beach and/or Florida legal and political community might derail the investigation before it properly began (*Miami Herald*, 2020; NBC News, 2019).

By May 2006, the Palm Beach Police had found 13 girls and made the case to Palm Beach County State Attorney, Barry Krischer. Six months into the investigation, according to Reiter and the *Palm Beach Post*, the prosecution ran into roadblocks and 'a shift of attitude from the state prosecutors' (Fitzpatrick & Schapiro, 2019). The police were permitted to sign a probable cause affidavit charging Epstein and two assistants with multiple counts of unlawful sex acts with a minor. Reiter and his detectives believed that they were 'sabotaged' by prosecutors as they tried to bring charges against Epstein: their search warrants went unsigned and they were tailed by private investigators hired by Epstein, who also dug through their trash to find discrediting information (Musgrave, Pacenti & Ramadan, 2019). In addition, Epstein's defence counsel appeared to know 'details about the probe before they were made public' (Fitzpatrick & Schapiro, 2019). Epstein's victims were also threatened and followed (Brown, 2018). Nonetheless, police continued the investigation, and in October 2005, one of Epstein's assistants happened to call one of the girls as she was being questioned by the police. Apparently, needing to hasten the investigation, a search warrant was executed on the property on 20 October, but police found that his computers had apparently been recently removed—'and all the wires were left hanging there'—indicating a rushed effort just prior to the police arriving (Fitzpatrick & Schapiro, 2019).

Faced with apparent roadblocks, Reiter sought to provide a case to the FBI for a federal prosecution, based on witness accounts that Epstein's crimes involved the trafficking of underage girls across state lines or in multiple state jurisdictions. The FBI saw a prima facie case and opened a federal investigation in July, and by November 2006 began interviewing witnesses in New Mexico and New York as well as re-interviewing the Florida witnesses. The Bureau provided the evidence for a 53-page indictment listing 36 underage victims (*Miami Herald*, 2020).

There are departures from the standard procedures of robust investigation and forensic recovery and discovery in the Epstein case that rise to the level of anomalousness. First, there was an inexplicable resistance to pursue the case to the extent that is expected for a crime of this magnitude. According to the statement by Chief Reiter, 'Epstein found every loophole' (Fitzpatrick & Schapiro, 2019) and it was in the office of Barry Krischer that the case met firm, and unexplained, resistance—although a prosaic explanation was offered in that the victims were being slandered as prostitutes (Musgrave et al., 2019). Ward (2019) observes that Chief Reiter believed that the 'fix was in' as soon as Epstein lawyer Alan Dershowitz became involved, after which Palm Beach Police experienced pressure from Krischer to downgrade the charges. The Palm Beach State Attorney's office, according to US Attorney in Miami Alexander Acosta, 'was willing to let Epstein walk free. No jail time. Nothing' (in Giraldi, 2019; see also Derysh, 2018).

Second, there was an immunity for co-conspirators clause in the Acosta brokered deal that was also unique, at least in Reiter's years of experience in policing (Derysh, 2018). This may have been what caused prosecutors, when they later arrested Maxwell, to time the offences against her at a relatively early period in her relationship with Epstein (NBC News, 2019).

Third, as is evidenced from the July 2020 indictment of Maxwell for crimes committed prior to the immunity period mooted by the Acosta-brokered agreement, the criminal investigation of Epstein was slow to be launched and extraordinarily protracted from investigation to indictment to plea (in the 2007 charges).

According to the Maxwell indictment, Epstein was engaging in criminal exploitation of girls 'from at least or before 1994' (US (US DC SDNY) v. Ghislaine Maxwell 20CCR 330) but was not investigated for these crimes until March 2005. This was not due to reticence on the part of the Palm Beach Police or particularly its chief,

Reiter, but it does support the view that investigations of well-connected people are slow to gather support and may be stymied (Rothe & Kauzlarich, 2016).

Fourth, it is in the context of the plea deal that the reporting of Epstein's possible status as an intelligence asset first emerged. It was referenced in reporting on Acosta's interview for the position of Secretary of Labor (Ward, 2019). Later, in a press conference held on 9 July 2019, Acosta 'declined to answer' as to 'if he had ever been told that Epstein was an intelligence asset during the handling of the 2008 child sex abuse case against the jet-setting financier' (Dunleavy, 2019). Acosta's reply did not provide a denial:

> So, there has been reporting to that effect. And let me say, there's been reporting to a lot of effects in this case. Not just now but over the years. And again, I would, I would hesitate to take this reporting as fact. (Acosta in Dunleavy, 2019)

Analysis

As observed by Goodman (2019a), if Epstein believed he was an intelligence asset, his lawyers would have needed to explore supporting evidence for the belief that he was being sanctioned in his 'work' for government authorities (such as blackmail material on targeted individuals). His lawyers could then have compelled the government to provide any exculpatory evidence to support his public authority defence, or 'face harsh sanctions'. These could include penalties against prosecutors or dismissal of the charges. As noted by Goodman (2019a), the prosecution and the federal government would seek to avoid this and in this avoidance lies the basis for apparently furtive negotiations for a very unusual plea deal.

Second, the circumstances of Epstein's death are questionable. Higher incidence of deaths in custody relative to deaths of persons not in custody is common in the US. Suicide is the leading cause of death in US jails and prisons and suicide prevention in this context has been called 'a joke' (Accurso, 2020). On the other hand, death in custody is less commonplace where authorities presumably wish to ensure the safety of prisoners of an exceptionally high profile who are known or suspected to possess information about serious crimes. Epstein was a high-value witness in an ongoing investigation (Maxwell, Prince Andrew) who was also recovering from a prison assault and/or attempted suicide.

One key piece of evidence would be the guard logs because these record the movements of inmates and 'all their interactions with other inmates'. But in this case the guards were prosecuted for altering those logs. Another important piece of evidence is the video recordings of the cell block, but these were 'accidentally deleted' by the Bureau of Prisons (Accurso, 2020). Rudolph Giuliani said of Epstein's death at the MCC that he (Giuliani) had been at the facility 'probably 20 times as prosecutor and defense lawyer' and that 'the whole thing is completely incredible to me' (Cretz, 2019). New York Mayor de Blasio called the death 'way too convenient' as Epstein could now not incriminate others (BBC News, 2019). US Attorney General

William Barr was satisfied that the circumstances did not add up to anything more than coincident errors (Reed, 2019).

Third, if Epstein was part of a criminal conspiracy, an unpacking or auditing of the financial supports and resources (the money trail) would be a key part of the investigation. In his New York mansion there were three US passports (Hayes et al., 2019) and it is alleged that there was also an Austrian passport (which is a neutral country and therefore more desirable for evading the need for a visa) (apparently out of date), which begs the question of its acquisition (Giraldi, 2019). Epstein signed a redrafted will two days before his death in custody and appointed Bill Gates's former science adviser as an alternate executor. The will was also witnessed by New York lawyer Gulnora Tali, who 'declined to comment on the circumstances of the meeting' (Hill et al., 2019). The will instructed executors to transfer his assets of almost US$600 million to a trust but did not list the beneficiaries (Hill et al., 2019). Epstein had accounts with Deutsche Bank until late 2018, and before that with JP Morgan Chase (Strasburg & Hong, 2019). Where the money came from is unclear other than from three sources including an illegal 'Ponzi' scheme partnered with Towers Financial Corporation CEO Steven Hoffenberg, which was 'one of the biggest Ponzi schemes in history before the two were caught by the FBI' (Parry & White, 2020). Leslie Wexner, who built a fashion empire called L Brands that includes Victoria's Secret, is the second known source of Epstein's apparently illegal wealth. Wexner, who severed ties with Epstein in 2007, claimed that Epstein misappropriated 'vast sums of money' from him, including US$46 million. The third source of his wealth is real estate. Wexner also gifted Epstein his Upper East Side mansion, alone valued at US$77 million, as well as the commercial airliner dubbed the Lolita Express and a yacht, but the total transfer of wealth from Wexner to Epstein is likely to be greater (Singham, 2019).

After Maxwell was arrested, she was denied bail after apparently not deigning to provide details to support her claims to the court regarding securities and the nature of her finances. The house in which she was arrested belonged to a corporation that, according to her, permitted her free lodgings. She claimed to have no income whatsoever, but had multiple bank accounts in her name, including in Switzerland, some amounting to millions of dollars. A mystery corporation she claimed not to know the name of provided for her privileged lifestyle (Hurtado & Alexander, 2020). These raise questions suggesting a wider network of actors than Maxwell–Epstein, including the well-resourced assets that were providing initial, and apparently in Maxwell's case ongoing, maintenance. Determining the nature of the enterprise, under the assumption that there was, and whether it was self-funded through blackmail or that the sex tapes were exfiltrated to other parties would be essential in any investigation into the two accused.

Lastly, was the third party intelligence and, if so, which agency or agencies? If Epstein 'belonged to intelligence' which agency? As former CIA case officer Philip Giraldi notes, it is not the CIA, but more likely a foreign intelligence agency that would have an interest in compiling dossiers 'on prominent American movers and shakers like Bill Clinton' (Giraldi, 2019). The public authority defence would be relevant if the agency was a US agency, but not if it was a foreign agency. Former National

Security Agency (NSA) analyst and counterintelligence officer John Schindler wrote that:

> It appears that Jeffrey Epstein was involved in intelligence work, of some kind, for someone—and it probably wasn't American intelligence either. The U.S. Intelligence Community is lenient about the private habits of high-value agents or informants, but they won't countenance running sex trafficking rings for minors on American soil, for years. (Schindler, 2019)

Based on an interview with a 'former high-ranking military agent', Ari Ben-Menashe, who worked for Israel's Military Intelligence Directorate from 1977 to 1987 and was acquitted by a US jury that accepted that in 1990 his alleged contravention of the US *Arms Export Control Act* was on behalf of Israel (Hutchinson, 2011), it is claimed by Howard that Epstein worked for Mossad (Howard, 2019). Ben-Menashe, who dealt in arms trading with heads of state and prominent corporations and banks around the world (Hutchinson, 2011), claimed to have been a handler of Ghislaine's father, Robert Maxwell, who introduced Epstein to Mossad handlers before Robert died in 1991. Robert is thought to have done work for Mossad but, according to Thomas (2007: 398), the agency killed him, in or around his yacht, the *Lady Ghislaine*, 'when he threatened to reveal Israel's intelligence secrets' and as he faced impending prosecution for defrauding the *Mirror*'s staff of its pension, the biggest fraud in British history to that time.[6] Robert was given a state funeral in Israel at which 'six serving and former heads of Israeli intelligence listened while Prime Minister Yitzhak Shamir eulogized: "He has done more for Israel than can today be said"' (in Giraldi, 2019).

A friend of the Maxwells, Laura Goldman, believed not only that Robert Maxwell was a Mossad spy but also that Ghislaine carried on his work (Howard, 2019). Giraldi (2019) notes that most of the intelligence agents with whom he has raised the question of the intelligence connection agree that the explanation best fits the sex videorecording and control room setup and the character of Epstein's targets and connections (Robert and Ghislaine Maxwell, Leslie Wexner, Shimon Peres, Ehud Barak and Barry Krischer). Several of his victims say that his homes were wired with cameras and that he kept the footage in a safe. The FBI and New York authorities that raided his Manhattan apartment have refused to confirm that such tapes exist, but reference to 'hundreds of lewd photographs' found in a safe was made in the press conference held on 8 July 2019 (Hayes et al., 2019). Ben-Menashe claimed, 'unequivocally', that Epstein was running a 'classic honey pot operation' (in Howard, 2019). Giraldi (2019) argues that there is 'no other viable explanation for his filming of prominent politicians and celebrities having sex with young girls'.

Giraldi (2019) observes that there would appear to be an Israeli exemption on spying against the US, and that hundreds of Israeli spies known to the FBI have been on US soil (revealed by *Fox News* in 2001) but that 'the justice department will never go after them'. This contention may find support in a scandal that occurred in December 2019, when a story broke that the 'US government' and 'former top US officials' concluded that 'Israel was most likely behind the placement of cell-phone surveillance devices that were found near the White House and other sensitive locations around Washington'. The story continued that, 'unlike most other occasions when flagrant incidents of foreign spying have been discovered on American soil, the Trump administration did not rebuke the Israeli government, and there were no consequences for Israel's behaviour, one of the former officials said' (Lippman, 2019). In a prominent story in *Newsweek* in January 2014, the subject of the 'hushing up' of brazen Israeli spying on the US—even to the point of an agent being found in a vent in Al Gore's bathroom—was picked up around the world (Stein, 2014).

Giraldi (2019) also contends that rank-and-file intelligence officers in the CIA are not fans of Israeli intelligence because it swamps channels with false claims concerning Israel's enemies. These rank-and-file grumblings are within house because at the political level, the producer-consumer nexus of the agency, there is a different orientation. He also observes that the mainstream media and 'the deep state' have been successful in making the Epstein case go away, particularly as an investigation into Israeli interests:

> As a former intelligence officer myself, there is little doubt in my mind that what Epstein did and how he did it was an intelligence operation. … The CIA would have had no interest in compiling dossiers on prominent Americans, but American movers and shakers like Bill Clinton, with his 26 trips on the Lolita Express, former Governor Bill Richardson, or former Senator George Mitchell are precisely the types of 'agents of influence' that the Mossad would seek to coerce or even blackmail into cooperation. Other compelling evidence for a Mossad connection came from Epstein's relationship with Ghislaine Maxwell, who reportedly served as his key procurer of young girls. (Giraldi, 2019)

Steven Hoffenberg revealed that Epstein was boastful that he had Prince Andrew's secrets to sell to Israel's intelligence agency Mossad (New Zeland Herald, 2019; Parry & White, 2020). With Maxwell, Epstein was engineering more involved blackmail plots as an asset of Mossad:

> they created the plan of installing the honeypot cameras and had taken over the house in Manhattan [given to him by his billionaire client Les Wexner] to blackmail the politicians. … He then took over the house in Florida and put in cameras. The cameras were to record rapes, it wasn't just about gathering intelligence, but compromising the politicians. … When he befriended Andrew, he had a deal with the Israelis to gather the intelligence and information from people who Epstein took into his homes and his plane. … I remember Andrew was at many of his events when he took over the house in Manhattan, that was in the early years. … He told me that Ghislaine Maxwell was going to be the breakthrough to bring him into that orbit—to be able to be part of the agency in Israel—and that's what did occur. (Parry & White, 2020)

Tradecraft has regularly involved the compromising of key individuals. However, if Epstein was an asset with multiple foreign intelligence agencies, then there would be the question of reputational damage to domestic intelligence agencies, raising the matter to a national security confidence crisis, as occurred during the fall-out over revelations of intelligence wrongdoing and in the broad sweep of investigations into the intelligence community during the mid-1970s, including the Church Committee hearings (McGarr, 2016).

At least by the end of 2020, the Maxwell–Epstein case remained largely inexplicable. The duo benefitted from a lifestyle that had been funded merely through fraud and blackmail—as per Wexner's account of being defrauded by Epstein—or supported by a third party that would gain from the relationship. Since both have been protected by highly connected individuals and mysterious corporate backers up until recently, it is possible that a compound hypothesis provides the best explanation. The first part of this hypothesis is that the duo was working a honeypot in an illicit network that was managed by intelligence assets or agents.

The second take-away from this story is that the exposure and revelations, including the second prosecution of Epstein, which looked as if it would lead to public revelations and a long prison sentence, and the prosecution of Maxwell, which looked to be ending similarly, may be the consequence of a deep divide in the US intelligence community, a bifurcation of power between two strong factions. As explained previously, while the blackmail of important political or corporate actors through a honeypot may be a variation on everyday covert means, the *revelations* in this case are anathema to the public culture and objectives of US national security. In this regard, it may also be relevant that Israel, in addition to the longstanding resentments among low-level agents noted by Giraldi above, has recently been losing public support even among elite opinion-making and US politicians (Russonello, 2019) and by shifts against it according to some recent US opinion polling (Cortellessa, 2019). The intelligence division would appear to signal that Epstein–Maxwell is a prize for those in the intelligence community wishing to assert push-back or payback. According to this hypothesis, this would occur as a split between a Republican intelligence faction is finessed by a Democrat intelligence faction through strategic leaking, and vice versa. The Gang of Eight would be susceptible where within-party splits would lead to responses based on the view that 'the enemy of my enemy is my friend' regarding such leaking.

Is the activity in which Epstein was involved also an intelligence crime? There are two possibilities. One is that Epstein (with Maxwell or not) acted together but otherwise independently of other actors. If the latter they threatened VIPs with blackmail, but purely for their own aggrandisement. This is partly supported by some published witness statements. The second possibility is that their crimes involve the blackmailing of VIPs for one or more external parties and that government sponsors are already involved in remedying the exposure damage. The lack of a reasonable account or a ready explanation for the vast funds accrued to support Epstein in his enterprise provides for a reasonable suspicion in favour of the second hypothesis.

Conclusion: Necropolitics on Offer?

After the release of Steven Spielberg's movie *Munich*, which covers the events surrounding the murder of 11 Israeli athletes in Munich at the 1972 Olympics including *Operation Bayonet*, which set out to kill all the Palestinians involved, some of the Mossad agents originally involved in this operation reflected at interview on the film. The agents objected to the film's attempt to cast the moral reflections of the agents in opposition to universal values opposing violence and killing, and also the imputed equivalency of the Palestinian 'terrorists' and Mossad agents. On the contrary, said one agent, they had 'no hesitation' in assassinating their targets (in MacAskill & Black, 2006). With regard to the violence, another said: 'We identified completely with our mission after what the terrorists did to our athletes in Munich. I never asked myself, like Avner in the movie, if I was doing the right thing' (in MacAskill & Black, 2006). In this regard, we should bear in mind that Israel has a policy that supports covert state-sponsored assassinations. At the same time, another retired Mossad agent reflected on 'the need to terrorise' the Palestinians:

> We tried not to do things just by shooting a guy in the streets, that's easy—fairly. By putting a bomb in his phone, this was a message that they can be got anywhere, at any time and therefore they have to look out for themselves 24 hours a day. (in MacAskill & Black, 2006)

Likewise, when Kiwi journalists caught up with Cabon in France decades after the bombing of the *Rainbow Warrior*, she 'had nothing to say to the New Zealand public', observing that 'it would have too many implications' (in Meier & Dennett, 2017). She added that 'all military people who serve their countries can find themselves in situations they hadn't wished for' (in Meier & Dennett, 2017). The reporters also interviewed French historian Gerald Arboit, who put the matter bluntly:

> It was a successful operation, mission accomplished. Pereira [the Dutch casualty] was collateral damage, which is not unusual for a DGSE mission. What went wrong was that Prieur and Mafart were arrested. (in Meier & Dennett, 2017)

To put this another way, an intelligence operation is a sovereignty event and the sovereign is who defines the universal. In intelligence, the rogue actor is normalised, even glorified—so long as they act in the service of agency objectives as defined by it. The operation is an expression of the necessary discretion of the sovereign that is revitalised in the exception. In reflecting on this, it is no surprise to find that the universal is threaded through the particular position or interest without compunction or hesitation. An intelligence operation is carried out by agents loyal to the 'crown' or 'presidency', whose role it is to warn, advise and sometimes to devise by means of deception the maintenance or elevation of the relatively superior position. In Wallerstein's (2011) terms, through deception they load the system to exclude an ever-changing periphery in favour of the ever-changing centre.

We have learned from counter-terrorism operations past (Ganser, 2005) and present (Anderson, 2011; Mueller & Stewart, 2016) that they are conceived, monitored and pushed forward as careerists in law enforcement, intelligence and government are 'enlightened' by select exposure to the classified archive. Such operations deploy actionable information to leverage the control of strategic assets. They grow in part by ensnaring and compromising, by developing a transactional capacity even to the point of what has been referred to as the 'strategic surprise' (Levite, 1987). A terrorist event, even the comprehensively momentous 9/11, is therefore rarely so unexpected to echelon intelligence actors, even in its particulars. The instrumentalisation of compromised intelligence actors or assets also belongs in the playbook, with perhaps the most pressing question being whether all of the layers of possible cover will be sufficient should too many uncontestable facts emerge. We chose the *Rainbow*

Warrior as exemplary, in part because it demonstrates what can occur when all of the cover is stripped from the operation. When that occurs, particularly across a division between actors in the intelligence community (or where there is an exploitable consensus within a national security community [as in the case of New Zealand] by criminal justice advocates), there may be an excruciatingly incontrovertible forensic exposure of intelligence actor conduct.

To belong to intelligence is to belong to a social and political order that in many respects depends upon an inversion of the universals of law and morality that animate criminal justice and crime discovery. As earlier observed, to engage in deception and exert maximum pressure on political actors is not to shirk exploitation of available vulnerabilities, an imperative related directly to the avoidance of the weakness of parliamentary democracy (Schmitt, 1988). It also requires the anticipation of crime discovery. There is a known division between the universality principle and the law of exception, so what is needed is the capacity to be willingly subjected to the greater ideological, binary objective that defines the ethos of the operational intelligence actor. In this chapter we have briefly examined less than a handful of cases of intelligence crime in this context. There are many other recent cases that fit the bill.[7]

Sovereign authority does not simply appear out of thin air; it is brokered through conflict. Agamben (1995) describes a process of foundational exclusion that is dynamic and subject to the continuous re-drawing by sovereign exception. He sees the political community as constituted by its power to ban a subject to a place outside its jurisdiction or legal protection (Agamben, 1995). Similarly, Aradau and van Munster (2009) see the origin of law or a legal system in a foundational crime and Wallerstein (2011) argues that the world system is *loaded* so that an ever-changing periphery will be politically excluded sufficiently to serve the needs of an ever-changing centre.

An alternative explanation of the Davis affair, the *Rainbow Warrior* bombing and the Epstein–Maxwell alleged crimes, if these events belong to intelligence, is to view them in terms of a revaluation of life according to the preferences associated with an enabled dark state sovereign. What is a normalised outside the sanctum is necropolitics (Mbembe, 2003). This begins with war, extends to the covert conflict zones that cut across the blurry boundaries between empires and, in the absence of sufficient countervailing institutions, is liberated to feed itself by way of furtive elaborations of its 'death machine'.

Notes

1. The term faction is used because there is evidence that sometimes there are warring factions that are capable of exploiting these means.
2. As we also know, there is little scholarly work that measures up 9/11 against these state crime dimensions (deHaven-Smith & Witt, 2009; Scott, 2014; Hughes, 2020; de Lint, 2020).
3. This account is drawn mostly from Mike King's research as published in his excellent book, *Death of the Rainbow Warrior* (1986).

4. The US refused to say where the money to pay for Davis's release came from. It appears that the 'deal' with the families was brokered by Inter-Services Intelligence, Pakistan's intelligence service. CIA Director Leon Panetta met in a long session with ISI Chief General Schuja Pasha, and Pasha told Panetta that the ISI would agree to a deal freeing Davis and would help broker a 'blood money' payment if the Agency agreed to 'identify all the Raymond Davises working in Pakistan behind our backs'. Panetta is said to have agreed to the deal 'in principal'. In addition to the 'blood money, the *New York Times* reported that 'American officials impressed upon both Pakistani civilian officials and Gen. Ashfaq Parvez Kayani, Pakistan's military chief, that Congress could decide to hold up more than $3 billion in annual aid to Pakistan if Mr. Davis were not freed' (Galli & Mazzetti, 2011).
5. See the reference from Kruh (1988: 65) in Chapter 7.
6. Three pathologists performed post-mortems, with two concluding that he had a heart attack and the third saying that he fell off his yacht and drowned (Verkaik, 2006).
7. For instance, the brutal murder of prominent Saudi dissident and *Washington Post* journalist Jamal Khashoggi on 2 October 2018 at the Saudi Arabian Consulate in Istanbul, in a coordinated assignment by as many as two dozen Saudis attached to the state, which came to light in grisly detail because of leaked video and audio data from Turkish intelligence. Knowledge of this was first denied by Saudi Arabia, but as more details of the assassination were leaked Riyadh admitted the crime, but as unsanctioned by the Crown Prince Mohammed bin Salmon. The Saudis prosecuted at least some of those said to be responsible—a court sentenced five people to death—but then was able to get pardons from Khashoggi's children and have the death sentences commuted.

References

Accurso, A. (2020, March). Suicide or murder? Jeffrey Epstein's death still drawing attention to bureau inadequacies. *Prison Legal News*. https://www.prisonlegalnews.org/news/2020/mar/4/suicide-or-murder-jeffrey-epsteins-death-still-drawing-attention-bureau-inadequacies/.

Agamben, G. (1998/1995). *Homo sacer: Sovereign power and bare life* (D. Heller-Roazen, Trans.). Stanford, CA: Stanford University Press.

Agee, P., & Wolf, L. (Eds.). (1978). *Dirty work: The CIA in Western Europe*. L. Stuart.

Agencies. (2011, February 16). Obama asks Pak to release Raymond Davis. *The Indian Express*. https://indianexpress.com/article/news-archive/print/obama-asks-pak-to-release-diplomat-raymond-davis/.

Anderson, R. (2011, February 28). Same cover, same lies. *Counterpunch*. https://www.counterpunch.org/2011/02/28/same-cover-same-lies/.

Andrews, M. (1991). *The Rainbow affair*. Seafriends: A New Zealand Community Website. Community Development Trust. http://www.seafriends.org.nz/issues/res/rw_mike_andrews.htm.

Aradau, C., & Van Munster, R. (2009). Exceptionalism and the 'war on terror': Criminology meets international relations. *British Journal of Criminology, 49*, 686–701.

Arsenault, C. (2011, March 18). *Spy game: The CIA, Pakistan and blood money*. Aljazeera.com.

BBC News. (2019, August 11). *Jeffrey Epstein: Questions raised over disgraced financier's death.* https://www.bbc.com/news/world-us-canada-49309317.
Beaty, J., & Gwynne, S. (2004). *The outlaw bank: A wild ride into the secret heart of BCCI.* Beard Books.
Bevins, V. (2020). *The Jakarta method: Washington's anticommunist crusade and the mass murder program that shaped our world.* New York: Hachette.
Blum, W. (1986). *The CIA: A forgotten history—US global interventions since World War 2.* Zed Books.
Blum, W. (2003). *Killing hope: US and CIA interventions since WWII.* London: Zed Books.
Borger, J. (2006, February 25). Blogger bares Rumsfeld's post-9/11 orders. *The Guardian.* https://www.theguardian.com/world/2006/feb/24/freedomofinformation.september11.
Brown, J. (2018, November 28). For years, Jeffrey Epstein abused teen girls, police say: A timeline of his case. *Miami Herald.* https://www.miamiherald.com/news/local/article221404845.html.
Bruch, C. (2019, July 29). Alan Derschowitz: Devil's advocate. *New Yorker.*
Bybee, J. S. (2002). *Memorandum for Albert R. Gonzales, counsel to the President Re: Standards of conduct for interrogation under 18 U.S.C. §§ 2340–2340A.* http://dspace.wrlc.org/doc/bitstream/2041/70967/00355_020801_004display.pdf.
Bybee, J., & Yoo, J. (2002, August 1). *Memorandum for John Rizzo Acting General Counsel of the Central Intelligence Agency: Interrogation of al Qaeda operative.* US Department of Justice, Office of Legal Counsel. https://www.washingtonpost.com/wp-srv/nation/pdf/OfficeofLegalCounsel_Aug2Memo_041609.pdf.
Castro, J. (1992, March 9). Spookier than we thought. *Time.*
Chomsky, N. (2015). *Rogue states: The rule of force in world affairs.* Haymarket Books.
Clement, M., & Scalia, V. (2020). The strategy of tension: Understanding state labelling processes and double-binds. *Critical Criminology* (online-first).
Cook, J. (2020, September 24). The US is using the Guardian to justify jailing Assange for life: why is the paper so silent? *Counterpunch.* https://www.counterpunch.org/2020/09/24/the-us-is-using-the-guardian-to-justify-jailing-assange-for-life-why-is-the-paper-so-silent/.
Cortellessa, E. (2019, March 6). New poll: Americans' support for Israel falls to lowest point in a decade. *Times of Israel.* https://www.timesofisrael.com/new-poll-americans-support-for-israel-declines-to-lowest-point-in-a-decade/.
Cretz, C. (2019, August 13). Rudy Giuliani: Jeffrey Epstein death 'completely incredible'. *Fox News.* https://www.foxnews.com/media/rudy-giuliani-jeffrey-epstein-death-new-york.
Crilly, B. (2011, February 22). Raymond Davis was acting head of CIA in Pakistan. *The Telegraph.*
de Lint, W. (2016). La Nuova Zelanda e lo Spionaggio a Sovranita Limitata. *Limes: Revista Italiana di Geopolitica.* Leggi Il Da venerdì 8 luglio.
de Lint, W. (2020). Criminology 9/11. *Globalizations, 17*(7), 1157–1177.
deHaven-Smith, L., & Witt, M. T. (2009). Preventing state crimes against democracy. *Administration & Society, 41*(5), 527–550.
Derysh, I. (2018, July 11). 'Completely wrong': Former prosecutor says Alex Acosta is lying about Epstein plea deal. *Salon.* https://www.salon.com/2019/07/11/completely-wrong-former-prosecutor-says-alex-acosta-is-lying-about-epstein-plea-deal/.
Dobbs, M. (1985, September 23). France says its agents sank ship. *Washington Post.* VOA News. https://www.voanews.com/south-central-asia/hrw-cia-trained-death-squads-behind-afghan-war-crimes.
Doolittle, J. (1954). *The report on the covert activities of the Central Intelligence Agency.* CIA Government Library. https://www.cia.gov/library/readingroom/docs/doolittle_report.pdf.
Dunleavy, J. (2019, July 10). Acosta dodges when asked if Epstein was an 'intelligence asset'. *Washington Examiner.*
Fitzpatrick, S., & Schapiro, R. (2019, September 21). Ex-Florida police chief: Epstein case 'the worst failure of the criminal justice system' in modern times. *NBC News.* https://www.nbcnews.com/news/us-news/ex-florida-police-chief-epstein-case-worst-failure-criminal-justice-n1057226.

Frew, W. (1991, December 17). Extradition underway for third *Rainbow Warrior* agent. *Financial Review*. https://www.afr.com/politics/extradition-under-way-for-third-rainbow-warrior-agent-19911217-k4pam.

Galli, C., & Mazzetti, M. (2011, March 16). Hushed deal frees CIA contractor in Pakistan. *New York Times*. https://www.nytimes.com/2011/03/17/world/asia/17pakistan.html.

Ganser, D. (2005). *NATO's secret armies: Operation Gladio and terrorism in Western Europe*. Routledge.

Giraldi, P. (2019, August 11). Was Jeffrey Epstein a spy for Israel in US? *Islam Times*. https://www.islamtimes.org/en/article/810068/was-jeffrey-epstein-a-spy-for-israel-in-us.

Gill, P. (1994). *Policing Politics: Security intelligence and the democratic state*. London: Frank Cass.

Goodman, L. (2019a, October 4). Jeffrey Epstein 'belonged to intelligence'. *Who. What. Why.*

Goodman, M. (2019b, May 2). The rehabilitation of Gina Haspel by the *New York Times*. *Counterpunch*. https://www.counterpunch.org/2019/05/02/the-rehabilitation-of-gina-haspel-by-the-new-york-times/.

Hager, N. (1990). *Secret power*. Wellington: Craig Potton.

Hayat, M. (2020). Empire's accidents: Law, lies, and sovereignty in the 'war on terror' in Pakistan. *Critique of Anthropology, 40*(1), 49–80.

Hayes, M., Wagner, M., & Hammond, E. (2019, July 8). Jeffrey Epstein charged with running sex trafficking ring. *CNN*. https://edition.cnn.com/us/live-news/jeffrey-epstein-court-07-08-19/h_e3804670684b6c525109fe95fbb94318.

Hersh, S. (2003, May 5). Selective intelligence. *New Yorker*. http://www.newyorker.com/archive/2003/05/12/030512fa_fact.

Hill, J., Katersky, A., & Hutchinson, B. (2019, August 21). Jeffrey Epstein redrafted will 2 days before jail suicide. *ABC News*. https://abcnews.go.com/US/jeffrey-epstein-signed-redrafted-days-jail-suicide/story?id=65072382.

Howard, D. (2019). *Epstein: Dead men tell no tales*. Skyhorse Publishing.

Hughes, D. (2020). 9/11 truth and the silence of the IR discipline. *Alternatives, 45*(2), 55–82.

Hurtado, P., & Alexander, S. (2020, July 17). Mystery of Ghislaine Maxwell's wealth hangs over Jeffrey Epstein sex abuse case. *Time*. https://time.com/5868402/ghislaine-maxwell-net-worth-mystery-epstein-trial/.

Hutchinson, B. (2011, November 11). The unbelievable life of Ari Ben-Menashe. *National Post*.

King, M. (1986). *Death of the Rainbow Warrior*. Auckland, NZ: Penguin Books.

Kruh, L. (1988). Stimson, the black chamber, and the 'gentleman's mail' quote. *Cryptologia, 12*(2), 65–89.

Levite, A. (1987). *Intelligence and strategic surprises*. Columbia University Press.

Lindorff, D. (2011, February 7). Exclusive: the deepening mystery of Raymond Davis and two slain Pakistani motorcyclists. *This Can't Be Happening*. https://thiscantbehappening.net/exclusive-the-deepening-mystery-of-raymond-davis-and-two-slain-pakistani-motorcyclists/.

Lippman, D. (2019, December 9). Israel accused of planting mysterious spy devices near the White House. *Politico*. https://www.politico.com/story/2019/09/12/israel-white-house-spying-devices-1491351.

Lustgarten, L., & Leigh, I. (1994). *National security and parliamentary democracy*. Oxford: Clarendon.

MacAskill, E., & Black, I. (2006, January 27). Munich: Mossad breaks cover. *The Guardian*. https://www.theguardian.com/media/2006/jan/26/bbc.israel.

Mbembe, A. (2003). Necropolitics. *Public Culture, 15*(1), 11–40.

McCoy, A. W. (2003). *The politics of heroin: CIA complicity in the global drug trade, Afghanistan, Southeast Asia, Central America*. Chicago: Chicago Review Press.

McGarr, P. (2016). *Unquiet Americans: The Church Committee, the CIA and the intelligence dimension of US public diplomacy in the 1970s*. Manchester University Press.

Mearsheimer, J. J., & Alterman, G. (2001). *The tragedy of great power politics*. W. W. Norton.

Mearsheimer, J. J., & Walt, S. M. (2007). *The Israel lobby and US foreign policy*. Macmillan.

Meier, C., & Dennett, K. (2017, July 9). Thirty-two years after the *Rainbow Warrior* bombing, unrepentant French spy Christine Cabon is found. *Stuff*. https://www.stuff.co.nz/national/94208355/thirtytwo-years-after-the-rainbow-warrior-bombing-unapologetic-french-spy-christine-cabon-is-found.

Miami Herald. (2020). Perversion of justice: Investigating Epstein. https://www.miamiherald.com/news/local/article238237729.html.

Mijalković, S. (2014). 'Sex-espionage' as a method of intelligence and security agencies. *Bezbednost Beograd, 56*(1), 5–22.

Mueller, J., & Stewart, M. (2016). *Chasing ghosts: The policing of terrorism*. Oxford.

Musgrave, J., Pacenti, J., & Ramadan, L. (2019, November 20). How the Epstein saga could've been ended years ago: To his first prosecutors, victims were prostitutes. *The Palm Beach Post*.

NBC News. (2019, July 9). Watch: Alex Acosta defends Jeffrey Epstein plea deal in 2017, 2018. *NBC News*. https://www.nbcnews.com/video/watch-alex-acosta-defends-jeffrey-epstein-plea-deal-in-2017-2018-hearings-63537221811.

Netanyahu, B. (1986). *Terrorism: How the west can win*. London: Weidenfeld & Nicolson.

New Zealand Herald. (2019, January 25). 'My Super Bowl trophy': Epstein 'boasted' about selling Prince Andrew's 'secrets' to Mossad spy. *New Zealand Herald*. Lifestyle. https://www.nzherald.co.nz/lifestyle/news/article.cfm?c_id=6&objectid=12303369.

Omand, D., & Pythian, M. (2018). *Principled spying: The ethics of secret intelligence*. Washington, DC: Georgetown University Press.

Parry, E., & White, C. (2020, January 24). Spy claims: Jeffrey Epstein 'boasted he was selling Prince Andrew's 'secrets' to a Mossad spy and called him his 'Super Bowl trophy'. *The Sun*. https://www.thesun.co.uk/news/10814102/jeffrey-epstein-boasted-he-was-selling-prince-andrews-secrets-to-a-mossad-spy-and-called-him-his-super-bowl-trophy/.

Phythian, M. (2006). The perfect intelligence failure? US pre-war intelligence on Iraqi weapons of mass destruction. *Politics & Policy, 34*(2), 400–424.

Porter, G., & Noori, S. (2011, March 17). *UN reported only a fraction of civilian deaths from US raids*. Inter Press Service. Archived from the original on 31 March 2011.

Prouty, L. F. (2011). *The secret team: The CIA and its allies in control of the United States and the world*. Skyhorse Publishing.

Reed, K. (2019, November 26). US Attorney General Barr adds to coverup in death of Jeffrey Epstein. *World Socialist Website*. https://www.wsws.org/en/articles/2019/11/26/barr-n26.html.

Reprieve. (2014). US drone strikes kill 28 unknown people for every intended target, new Reprieve report reveals. https://reprieve.org.uk/press/2014_11_25_us_drone_strikes_kill_28_each_target/.

RFE/RL. (2019, October 31). HRW: CIA-trained 'death squads' behind Afghan war crimes.

Rothe, D., & Kauzlarich, D. (2016). *Crimes of the powerful: An introduction*. Routledge.

Rusbridger, J., & Nave, E. (1991). *Betrayal and Pearl Harbour: How Churchill lured Roosevelt into war*. New York: Summit Books.

Russonello, G. (2019, November 1). Criticise Israel: For democratic voters it's now fair game. *New York Times*. https://www.nytimes.com/2019/11/01/us/politics/democrats-israel-polls.html.

Schindler, J. R. (2019, October 7). It sure looks like Jeffrey Epstein was a spy: But whose? *The Observer*.

Schlembach, R. (2018). Undercover policing and the spectre of 'domestic extremism': The covert surveillance of environmental activism in Britain. *Social Movement Studies, 17*(5), 491–506.

Schmitt, C. (1988). *The crisis of parliamentary democracy*. Cambridge, MA: MIT Press.

Scott, P. D. (2014). *The American deep state: Wall Street, big oil, and the attack on US democracy*. Rowman & Littlefield.

Singham, M. (2019, July 25). Following the Jeffrey Epstein money trail. *FreeThought Blogs*. https://freethoughtblogs.com/singham/2019/07/15/following-the-jeffrey-epstein-money-trail/.

Stein, J. (2014, May 8). Israel's aggressive spying in the U.S. mostly hushed up. *Newsweek*. https://www.newsweek.com/israels-aggressive-spying-us-mostly-hushed-250278.

Strasburg, J., & Hong, N. (2019, July 23). Jeffrey Epstein's financial trail goes through Deutsche Bank. *The Wall Street Journal.* https://www.wsj.com/articles/jeffrey-epsteins-financial-trail-goes-through-deutsche-bank-11563911131.
Thomas, G. (2007). *Gideon's spies: The secret history of the Mossad.* Dunne.
Tilly, C. (1985). War making and state making as organized crime. In T. Skocpol, P. Evans, & D. Rueschemeyer (Eds.), *Bringing the state back in.* New York: Cambridge.
Verkaik, R. (2006, March 10). The mystery of Robert Maxwell's death. *The Independent.*
Wallerstein, I. (2011). *The modern world-system I: Capitalist agriculture and the origins of the European world-economy in the sixteenth century.* University of California Press.
Walsh, D., & MacAskill, E. (2011, February 20). American who sparked diplomatic crisis over Lahore shooting was C.I.A. spy. *The Guardian.*
Ward, V. (2019, August 19). Jeffrey Epstein's sick story out for years in plain sight. *Daily Beast.*
Watson Institute. (2020). *Costs of war.* Watson Institute, Brown University. https://watson.brown.edu/costsofwar/.
Weiner, T. (2008). *Legacy of ashes: The history of the CIA.* New York: Anchor Books.
Wilsnack, R. (1980). Information control: A conceptual framework for sociological analysis. *Social Problems, 8*(4), 467–499.
Wise, D. (2005, January 19). The secret committee called 'Forty'. *New York Times.* https://www.nytimes.com/1975/01/19/archives/the-secret-committee-called-40-at-least-in-theory-it-controls-the.html.
Yoo, J. C. (2002, August 1). *Response to Alberto Gonzales' request for views on legality of interrogation techniques.* United States Department of Justice, Office of the Legal Counsel. http://www.gwu.edu/~nsarchiv/NSAEBB/NSAEBB127/020801.pdf.

Cases

US (US DC SDNY) v. Ghislaine Maxwell 20CCR 330.

Chapter 6
Intelligence Crime 2: 'Smear,' or Crimes Committed by 'Them'

'Events, dear boy, events.'
Attributed to former British Prime Minister
Sir Harold Wilson in answer to the question of what can knock a government off course

Introduction

In Chapter 5 we reviewed vignettes featuring alleged intelligence crime committed by us. Through its transactions and exclusivity, intelligence offers ample opportunities to redirect the gaze of investigation from an intelligence asset towards a preferred target. As previously observed, much international relations and security studies scholarship accepts that the interests of states are paramount and that they may trump observance of the rule of law in the international system. Where 'we' are the perpetrators engaged in conflict with 'them', trust replaces public scrutiny of criminal actions, so that it may make sense to say that criminal justice investigation pauses silently at the portal of national security, which is already vetted, cloistered and instructed on the necessary conditions that must attend our hushed defence. If someone 'belongs to intelligence', the necessary house-cleaning carried out must *not* be seen, as per justice, but in contrast to public transparency. This is so as to maintain the integrity of secret defence capabilities and/or the vitality of the sovereign, and under the assumption that at worst there may occasionally be a rotten apple or bad barrel. The collapse or disarray of criminal justice when in competition with security intelligence values is to be expected where the relative heft of the national security–intelligence dispositive is in ascendance. In the result, we expect not to see much of the conflict in the public sphere. This presumptive standpoint cannot be helped; it derives from a necessary belief in 'our' just world moral supremacy (Lerner, 1980), a view that is employed in a range of contexts, from careerism to military procurements. It is entrenched in the proclivities of establishment liberals and conservatives alike, who recognise and support in justice–intelligence the echo of the civil–military relation (Feaver, 1996).

W. B. de Lint, *Blurring Intelligence Crime*,
https://doi.org/10.1007/978-981-16-0352-5_6

This presumptive standpoint appears out of the cold fog when we see a breach. Where criminal justice values have a relative power and advantage and the establishment media play along, we can expect to see the pantomime of intelligence criminality in grisly, excruciating detail. In this regard, a unique historical moment occurred in the mid-1970s in the US. In the context of revolutionary social and political unrest following a decade or more of illegal political surveillance of Americans (Rosenfeld, 2012), an unpopular and in some ways illegal war (Falk, 2015), and an impeachment scandal involving a split deep state (Aberbach & Rockman, 1976), parts of the secret intelligence archive were exposed by a burst breakwater. As a consequence, an excess of the furtive transactions (COINTELPRO, MINARET, CHAOS—see Chapter 7) against political opponents of establishment Democrat and Republican politics (Rosenfeld, 2012) necessitated a hasty re-legitimation in which intelligence was subject to the strictures of public prosecution or inquiry (US Congress, 1976; US House of Representatives, 1979). As we observed in Chapter 5, such stark exposure also greeted agents of *Opération Satanique*, who were yanked in from the cold New Zealand fog and subjected to the hot scrutiny of justice. In that case criminal justice interests got the better of intelligence in part, at least, because both the media and governing authorities were aligned against an ideological opponent of New Zealand's nuclear non-proliferation policy and were (initially, at least) unwilling to quash the story.

Where the attitude faces out toward 'they'—those who may represent geopolitical obstacles to our political and even our cultural hegemony—the normative expectation of intelligence practice and justice scrutiny is reversed. When it comes to 'our'[1] opponents or adversaries (for example, Russia, Iran or China), often vilified as 'rogue states', there is a presumption that their prima facie illegality and criminality should be made subject to a 'rules-based order.' To draw attention to standpoint is to highlight the insidious nature of intelligence and its long tail of subterfuge: 'we' commit such crimes in the exception to preserve the superior political ideology, a view preserved by national security secrecy; while 'they' commit such crimes because it reflects their wickedness at the core. Ours is a regrettable deviation from otherwise exemplary regard for professional ethics and morality; theirs is routine, everyday and projects the moral abyss of their genesis. As we shall explore here and in Chapter 7, most accounts of security intelligence feature this bifurcation of intelligence crime stories, either explicitly or implicitly depending on the source.

In the tension between shaping the future and cleaning up the archives resides much of the brief for state security: is crime or disorder figuratively a dead body killed by the usual suspects according to positive review or capture, or is it a whodunnit with tentacles reaching deep into powerful societal and institutional interests? The answer to this depends on framing (Entman, 2003; Boyd-Barrett, 2019: 12). In this chapter we review several intelligence crimes presumptively committed by 'them'. From a critical institutional standpoint, it is relative discursive power (or power-knowledge) that will largely determine the outcome of the controversy. As we shall see and explore further in Chapter 7, information operations prime the pump so that events appear with a ready narrative and direct the review in the interests of the national security state. We divide the analysis according to the terms previously conceptualised—that is, their event and authority, the scene and narrative, and the review and identity. That said, the focus is on the last of the three couplets.

We consider two events: the shoot-down of Malaysian Airlines Flight MH17 in 2014, and the 2018 assassination by poisoning of Sergei Skripal.[2] We are interested in the first case because it involves a transnational criminal prosecution of an apparent war crime where the elements of apex crime (significant event, near-immediate official narrative, confirmatory bias, politicisation by forensic authorities, and summaries beyond scope of evidence) and the smearing of events by the intelligence apparatus may be present. The second case is an intelligence crime of unknown cause that offers a segue into an analysis of the proliferation of intelligence treatments (information operations) through establishment media and new information outposts that supports a propaganda view of hybrid threat actors.

MH17

On 17 July 2014, Malaysian Airlines Flight MH17, a Boeing 777-200ER, was flying at an altitude of 33,000 feet above the separatist-held territory of eastern Ukraine, when it broke apart and crashed, killing all 298 passengers and crew. Victims were from numerous nations, but the majority (196) were Dutch nationals, followed by 43 Malaysians and 28 Australians.

The next day, former US Secretary of State Hillary Clinton said, 'Putin has gone too far' and called for making 'Russia pay the price' once its culpability had been confirmed (Murray & Agencies, 2014). On the same day, Australian Prime Minister Tony Abbott said that the plane appeared to have been brought down by Russia-backed rebels and that Russia 'will be shunned by the international community unless it accepts some responsibility' for the crash (in Knott, 2014). Then US Secretary of State John Kerry claimed on 12 August 2014, less than four weeks later, that 'we saw the take-off. We saw the hit. We saw the airplane disappear from the radar screens. So there is really no mystery about where it came from and where these weapons have come from' (in Parry, 2016a).

Event and Authorities: Joint Investigatory Team (JIT) Terms of Reference

The UN Security Council (UNSC) met on 21 July and condemned the downing of the plane in Resolution 2166.[3] The event led Australia and the Netherlands to pursue criminal responsibility, rather than a civil aviation investigatory protocol covered by the Chicago Convention.[4] As observed by Williams (2016: 211), although an international criminal justice remedy may provide 'justice to the victims', it was unclear why this approach was sought in this case when previous incidents of planes being shot down (particularly when flying over conflict zones) have 'not been subject to international law'. Nonetheless, in late July, the Netherlands Public Prosecution Services began a criminal investigation and Australia, Belgium, the Netherlands and Ukraine set up a Joint Investigative Team (JIT) to carry it out. Its purpose was to establish the 'facts of the case' and 'the truth of what happened', 'gather criminal evidence for prosecution' and 'identify those responsible' (Government of the Netherlands, 2020). There was also an effort to set up an MH17 Tribunal under the jurisdiction of the International Criminal Court (ICC), since Ukraine has accepted the jurisdiction of the ICC with respect to acts on its territory (Williams, 2016: 212).

As Williams (2016: 213) observes, international and national criminal procedures may be followed in such cases and there is even a possibility of 'internationalising a national criminal process' but each would require proper composition, the protection of interests of fair rights of trial for defendants, and the application of substantive and procedural law and diligence with regard to ensuring the cooperation of involved actors. The ICC avenue would be unlikely to be successful, because to take jurisdiction and find Russia answerable, it would be necessary to determine that the act of shooting down a civilian plane was undertaken with intent and knowledge as part of a plan or policy; that Russia had effective control over the separatists; and that, under Article 8 of the Rome Statute, the war crime of murder was intentional and directed at persons the perpetrator knew to have protected status (such as civilians not engaged in direct hostilities) (Williams, 2016: 214–220).

As a result of an evaluation of the option of criminal prosecution in light of the claims of jurisdiction and the shortcomings of taking the case to the ICC (as well as the ad hoc international tribunal option under the UNSC Chapter VII powers), the Dutch legal system was deemed the most suitable option (Williams, 2016: 231). The Draft Statute to establish an international criminal tribunal for MH17 (the MH17 Tribunal) that was vetoed by Russia provided for the establishment of the JIT and also anticipated and provided for a provision on trials in absentia and for a complementary jurisdiction in the national courts of a UN member state, in this case, the Netherlands. However, as observed by Williams (2016: 223), this removes the rights of the accused if they do not attend court.

Under its mandate to learn about such events and to improve aviation safety, the Dutch Safety Board led the air safety investigation to determine the cause of the crash. It concluded that a Russian-built Buk surface-to-air missile hit the plane from a single warhead from an area controlled by the separatists, from which they had previously shot down Ukrainian military aircraft in the same way. The Dutch Safety Board investigation did not determine whether the act was due to a mistaken identification of the plane or why or who committed the shoot down (Dutch Safety Board, 2015).

The JIT was comprised of officials from five countries (the Netherlands, Belgium, Malaysia, Australia and Ukraine). It was led by the Dutch Public Prosecution Service, as well as police and criminal justice authorities from Australia, Belgium, Malaysia and Ukraine. If Ukraine was to be involved, then the Russian Federation would require equal representation under the principle of equality of arms. Both these nations lack credibility in equal measure based on being parties to the conflict. Russia has a claim to jurisdiction as does Ukraine. In addition, the Netherlands would need to be clear of any possible conflict of interest in terms of its support for any one side of the conflict. When a trial commenced in 2020 based on the Special Tribunal for Lebanon (STL) precedent, it did so without the presence of four of the accused.[5]

On 28 September 2016, the JIT released its report stating that the plane had been downed by an 9M38 series missile launched from a Buk trailer. The trailer, the report stated, was brought from and delivered back to the Russian Federation and launched from a region called Pervomaiskyi, which 'beyond reasonable doubt' was controlled by the pro-independence Donbas militias (Government of the Netherlands, 2020). On 5 July 2017, the JIT determined that the Netherlands would conduct the prosecution of those responsible for downing flight MH17. On 24 May 2018, the JIT announced that a Russian army Buk missile installation brought down the flight; however, the JIT clarified that it was not claiming that the Russian Federation or people from the Russian Federation were involved (Government of the Netherlands, 2020).

In the publishing of a minority report there is an opportunity for the dissenting judges to make plain and clear the reasons for not agreeing to a consensus view. The JIT terms of reference permitted any of the four parties to block the release of its investigatory findings. In the terms of reference, the Ukrainian Government, represented by its intelligence service, the SBU, had a veto power on the release of information to or by the JIT and represented Ukraine to the JIT (Parry, 2016a). Malaysian Prime Minister Mahathir Mohamad questioned the objectivity of the investigations into the downing of the MH17 flight and said that Russia was being made a scapegoat for the tragedy:

> We are very unhappy, because from the very beginning it was a political issue on how to accuse Russia of the wrongdoing. … Even before they examine, they already said Russia. And now they said they have proof. It is very difficult for us to accept that. (in Sipalan, 2019)

It is arguable in sum that the composition of the JIT and the subsequent criminal trial are inconsistent with the requirements of justice to act with neutral arbitration and objectively neutral fact-finding. We note, citing Williams (2016: 211), that an airline downing over a conflict zone is not normally a matter that animates states to demand a criminal prosecution. Understanding such an event without considering the broader context is also to strip it of its political emergence. As suggested by van der Pijl (2018b), Boyd-Barrett (2016) and Parry (2016a), the US has a long-term strategic objective, including the disciplining of Russia and China under a rules-based system in which the US is the most powerful actor. Via its Secretary of State, the US has established a number of priorities for the region which include toughening European Union sanctions on Russia; finding alternatives to Gazprom (the Russian energy company), so that the EU would not be dependent on Russia for gas; and making Europe do more in concert with the US to support its interests in Ukraine. The Director of the European Council on Foreign Relations, Mark Leonard, noted in 2015 that, 'without MH17 it would have been pretty difficult to find sufficient support for the increased sanctions on the Russian economy' (van der Pijl, 2018b). As we discuss later, the alleged poisonings of Skripal and Navalny were cited similarly to support this objective.

Scene and Narrative: Context Bias

Boyd-Barrett (2016: 2) has identified no fewer than 10 Manichean subplots to the Ukrainian crisis, in which the shoot-down is an event. The Kiev regime, alongside its US and EU sponsors and partners, has been 'almost uniformly' supported by the establishment western media (2), led by the *Guardian*, *New York Times* and *Washington Post*. Boyd-Barrett (2016) also observes that there is a 'not dependent' counter-narrative that emanates from the Russian media (2). At the same time, he concludes that one of the Manichean subplots is a lack of context offered by the western establishment media other than that Kiev is still in Moscow's 'icy grip' of 'expansionist ambitions' (4). Another subplot is that the shooting down of the civilian airliner 'was unmistakably and immediately recognizable as the work of ethnic Russian separatists, likely aided and abetted by Russia, possibly deliberate' (5). For Boyd-Barrett, and for us, the 10th subplot is 'sanctions against Russia' (6)—a justice storyline that depends upon Russia's vilification as a rogue actor that will not be restrained by less belligerent measures.

The fact that Kiev allowed civilian planes to fly over a war zone was not considered evidentiary by the JIT but was questioned by the Dutch Safety Board. As to who might benefit most from the *purposeful* downing of a passenger plane (consistent with criminal responsibility), little or no explanation has been offered as to how such an act might serve the Russian Federation. The benefit of a successful *attribution* of Russian Federation responsibility has already been highlighted above (and see also van der Pijl, 2018b). Russian Foreign Ministry spokeswoman Maria Zakharova said that prosecutors concocted evidence to fit a predetermined verdict and that Ukraine was complicit in the downing of the plane. Malaysian Prime Minister Mohamad appeared to shock western media outlets with his statement of non-confidence in the JIT process (Reuters Staff, 2019).

Bias in Evidence Collection

The Dutch Prosecution Service made a decision in June 2019 to hold a trial of three Russians and a Ukrainian in the Netherlands under Dutch law based on the criminal investigation of the JIT. Evidence collection, as we saw in Chapter 2, requires a record of possible contamination, including by its handling by interested or conflicted actors. In the work of the JIT, despite all of the remonstrations to the contrary, much of the evidence was collected by a partisan actor, the Ukrainian security services, or SBU. The SBU was an active participant in the conflict with ethnic Russian rebels and then supplied a selection of phone intercepts and other information to the JIT. The conditions under which the witness statements used in support of the Dutch prosecution's determinations were provided are not known, except to the SBU. As observed by Parry (2016a, b), there are 'troubling gaps' in the information thus presented, consistent with expectations given the partisan interests involved.

In addition, context bias may logically be at play where the Australian and Dutch investigators had shared a field office in Kiev while taking in evidence from the SBU (Parry 2016c).

As suggested by van der Pijl (2020), the situation collects the 'hallmarks of a show trial'. The observations is supported where there is scant vehicle for cross-examination and no exculpatory evidence of witnesses is referred to in the report as also having been collected and reviewed. For instance, there were eyewitnesses who claim to have seen two Ukrainian military jets shadowing MH17 before it exploded (van der Pijl, 2018a: 122–123). It was the Ukrainian SBU that provided the claim, not substantiated by other sources, that the Buk trailer was transported from and back to Russian Federation territory.

Selective bias in the collection and examination of intelligence evidence in this case is likely or plausible. The data from three US satellites that were in orbit over Dombass at the time of the crash was said to be released to the JIT, but for 'security reasons' could not be presented for public scrutiny in the report. The US Government failed to 'share usable data from its own intelligence services' that may have assisted (Parry, 2016a). The Dutch themselves, in an intelligence report released in October 2015, found that only the Ukrainian military had anti-aircraft missiles in eastern Ukraine capable of hitting a plane at 33,000 feet (Parry, 2016a).

Where the Australian Federal Police has been involved in the collection of evidence, it would appear that it has framed this collection squarely within the 'Russia did it' narrative. In a call for witnesses on its website—afp.gov.au—the AFP issued a 'new call for witnesses on who commanded deployment of the missile' (AFP, 2019). The request reads:

> the JIT wants information about those persons who commanded deployment of the BUK. … Recent analysis of information obtained by the JIT reveals Russian influence goes beyond military support of the self-proclaimed Donetsk People's Republic (DPR) in eastern Ukraine. Communications between DPR fighters and Russian officials was used on a daily basis to discuss administrative, financial and military matters. The JIT wants to identify the people involved in these communications. (AFP, 2019)

Contrary or exculpatory evidence finally began to be made public with the commencement of the trial in absentia of the four accused in June 2020. One of the lawyers for the defence, Sabine ten Doesschate, said that the alleged launch site near the village of Pervomaiskyi was not within the zone suggested by the arms-maker Almaz-Antey and the Belgian Military Academy:

> We must conclude that the JIT's calculations may be based on false information and using a method without factual underpinnings. … That can mean that (other) potential launch sites have been rejected because they fell outside the possible launch area as calculated. (Silk, 2020)

In the meantime, the prosecution alleged that the information proffered by Russia that Ukraine owned the Buk missile fired at MH17 'showed clear signs of manipulation' (Silk, 2020).

Not available to either side was follow-up with regard to an alternative avenue of investigation. Parry (2016a) reported that he personally was told by a source who was briefed by US intelligence that CIA's conclusion pointed toward a rogue Ukrainian operation involving a hard-line oligarch with a possible motive of shooting down Russian president Vladimir Putin's official plane returning from South America that day, with similar markings as MH-17.

This is certainly a credible counter-narrative, one suggesting the use of the conflict and the criminal prosecution as a favourable cover for the failure of other crimes of intelligence.

Identities and Review

The official narrative regarding MH17 may be regarded as one in which Bellingcat played no insignificant part in propounding. Founded by Eliot Higgins, Bellingcat refers to itself as an investigative journalism website 'that specialises in fact-checking and open-source intelligence' (Bellingcat, 2020). It has won several awards and prizes for investigative journalism. It receives its funding from the National Endowment for Democracy (NED) and several Dutch NGOs. It has been successful at offering itself as a reliable source or conduit for establishment media in offering support to preferred government or official narratives of major intelligence events. In so doing, it is regularly cited by the BBC, the *Guardian* and other media sources. Despite the accolades, and reminiscent of the White Helmets, Bellingcat's investigatory targets, findings and funding seem to reflect and advance the preferences of Anglo-American intelligence—fand as if from an insider.

In the MH17 case, Higgins wished to dismiss Russia's counterclaims:

To believe that Russia's claims about images of the Buk in Ukraine being faked are true, you would have to believe in a conspiracy, planned months, if not years, in advance, using fake social media posts posted online before MH17 was shot down; carefully crafted videos and photographs being created; fake satellite imagery distributed by Stratfor, Digital Globe, and Google, the involvement of multiple journalists and/or fake witnesses both prior to MH17 being shot down and afterwards; a separatist commander telling Reuters a Buk was transported through Luhansk on July 17, 2014; and multiple audio recordings faked to carefully support the fabricated imagery. (Bellingcat, 2020)

As argued by former CIA analyst Ray McGovern—whose organisation, Intelligence Officers for Sanity, provides a nice counterpoint to Bellingcat—that governments are more than capable of planning operations and faking video or audio evidence has already been proven by actors within the US Government, who admit to having done so. McGovern observes that the shooting down of MH17 should remind Americans of KAL-007, another passenger plane brought down in the vicinity, about which he provided a synopsis.

KAL-007 was shot down on 1 September 1983 when it strayed hundreds of miles off course and into strategically sensitive airspace in Kamchatka and Sakhalin Island. A US spy plane had been in the vicinity hours earlier, so the Soviets were on alert in the area. When a Soviet Sukhoi-15 fighter jet came to intercept, the jet's pilot tipped its wings to signal for the plane to land but failed to receive a response from the passenger plane, whereupon, after several minutes, Soviet ground control ordered the pilot to shoot it down, which it did, killing 269 passengers and crew. McGovern (2014) notes the case because the Soviets admitted to making the mistake, but the Reagan administration wished to maximise the propaganda bonanza and proceeded to falsify the exculpatory evidence from the US electronic intercepts. He quotes Alvin Snyder, then-director of the US Information Agency's television and film division and author of *Warriors of Disinformation* (1995), who wrote in his book that the USIA director 'ordered his top agency aids to devise ways of playing up the story overseas. The objective, quite simply, was to heap as much abuse on the Soviet Union as possible' (in McGovern, 2014). The US media obliged but the campaign went further, and a 'doctored transcript' of the communications intercepts was presented to the UNSC so that, against what the US knew of the evidence, the perception was presented that the Soviet Union 'cold-bloodedly carried out a barbaric act' (in McGovern, 2014). Snyder observed the words of a senior USIA official: 'The moral of the story is that all governments, including our own, lie when it suits their purposes. The key is to lie first' (in McGovern, 2014).

In addition to Bellingcat and the book by van der Pijl (2018a), there is an alternative body of investigatory work that is being compiled (see, for instance, softpanorama.com). Readers are invited to compare and contrast the work of Bellingcat and that of Softpanorama on the subject of MH17. Softpanorama is a web-based repository of stories or threads concerning social and political issues and, according to its own account,

> advocates scepticism as an approach to study both the technical and social phenomenon. The latter is generally about questioning the preconceived attitudes, facts or opinions/beliefs stated as facts, and critical examination of claims that are taken for granted by the corporate MSM. (softpanorama.com)

Important to note here is that the allegation or contention of the politicisation of the investigation, and its concomitant subjection to intelligence or more specifically to information operations, is reflexively dismissed as counter-evidentiary and conspiracist. Even where the terms of reference for an investigation are structured against independence and where evidence is gathered from and assessed by one interested party, the resulting conclusion is still somehow to be reviewed as if it were a depoliticised product.

This agenda is given legs through the work of hybrid actors in what is referred to as hybrid warfare. As we shall explore further below, agencies like Bellingcat, Cambridge Analytica, the Institute for Statecraft (IfS) and the Centre for Hybrid Threats have emerged as conduits between ad hoc agencies like the JIT and information operations. This chain link, questioned by Maté and observed by Snyder above, is obscured when facts are claimed as already proven. The insertions become the reflex, the influence of a hidden hand may not be in evidence, and there is a remarkable obduracy behind the consensus narrative.

Skripal, Douma and the Organisation for the Prohibition of Chemical Weapons (OPCW)

On 4 March 2018, Sergei and Yulia Skripal were found semi-conscious on a public park bench in Salisbury, UK. Sergei Skripal had been an officer of the GRU or Russia's Main Intelligence Directorate and was convicted in 2006 of treason and served time in prison for acting as a double agent before being released in 2010 from a Russian jail in a spy swap with Britain at a Vienna airport. He then worked with MI6 and lived openly in Britain for eight years prior to the poisoning (BBC News, 2018a).[6]

The father and daughter were attended by a female doctor who administered first aid on Yulia, who was found 'vomiting and fitting' (Kingsley and Pérez-Peña, 2018). They were taken to Salisbury District Hospital. The doctor was not affected by the poison but a police officer, Detective Sergeant Nick Bailey, who had been to their house was sent to hospital in serious condition and treated (Mendick, 2018). After three and four weeks of treatment, Yulia and Sergei were no longer critical and on 9 April Yulia was discharged and placed into 'secure' custody (BBC News, 2018b). Investigators said that there was a perfume bottle found in a bin containing sufficient Novichok to kill thousands of people (Corbin, 2018). In the next few weeks, the Skripals' house would be subject to a thorough decontamination and rebuilding by a military team and contractors (Sky News, 2019).

Already on 6 March, two days after the Skripals were found semi-conscious, the investigation was taken over from the Wiltshire Police by the Counter Terrorism Command of the Metropolitan Police, and its head, Assistant Commissioner Mark Rowley appealed for witnesses (BBC News, 2018c). On 9 March, 180 military and security experts and agencies were deployed to assist the investigation, including from the Explosive Ordnance Disposal and Search Group and the Defence Chemical, Biological, Radiological and Nuclear Centre, conveniently located 6 kilometres northeast of Salisbury (BBC News, 2018c). The Skripals' house was being completely encased in a protective sarcophagus and the amount of the poison said to have been recovered was capable of killing thousands. However, it was claimed to have been in a perfume bottle that was picked up on the street and diners at the restaurant the Skripals had attended before going to the park bench were simply told to 'wash possessions' and that the threat to the public was low (BBC News, 2018d).

Event and Authority

On 12 March, British Prime Minister Teresa May stated in parliament that the chemical agent with which the Skripals had been poisoned had been identified as belonging to the Novichok family that was developed in the Soviet Union in the 1980s and that Moscow was likely to be behind the attack (BBC News, 2018e). The initial British position was that either Russia was directly responsible through its agents or that it had permitted the chemical to fall into rogue hands. The May Government delivered what was described by intelligence reporters in the *Guardian* as an ultimatum to Russia to explain which of these possibilities pertained (Asthana et al., 2018). Foreign Minister Boris Johnson met with European counterparts to make the case that too many European countries had been shaken off course by Russian disinformation and that this event should be exploited to assert or reaffirm European and NATO consolidation—and an international response to Russian aggression (Johnson, 2018).[7] The British diplomatic effort paid off, with a joint statement issued on 15 March from France, Germany, the US and the UK asserting that Russia had breached international law with the poisoning, and casting the action as a threat to all. In addition, there was an expulsion of 100 Russian diplomats from over twenty western countries, and in April a G7 statement further solidified the position and added that the poisoning was deemed to be part of a wider Russian destabilisation campaign (UN, 2018). Moscow denied that the attack had been perpetrated by the Russian state.

So powerful was the dominant narrative that Jeremy Corbyn came under sustained attack over his initial response in which he 'failed to condemn the Kremlin directly for carrying out the poisoning,' including from Labour MPs (Stewart, 2018b: Rawnsley, 2018). The French Government spokesperson Benjamin Griveaux said that France would wait until the 'facts were completely true' because it does not do 'fantasy politics. Once the elements are proven, then the time will come for decisions to be made' (Irish et al., 2018). The hesitation was brief (Stone, 2018). The leaders of Germany and the US, Angela Merkel and Donald Trump, assured British Prime Minister Theresa May that they took 'her' views on possible Russian involvement very seriously. Then the US, Britain, Germany and France issued a joint statement blaming Russia on 15 March (Bienkov, 2018).

Intelligence authorities contributed their support to the narrative. On 14 September, the Swiss Federal Intelligence Service claimed that, a few months earlier, two Russian 'spies' had been discovered by a joint Swiss, Dutch and British intelligence team in the Netherlands and had been expelled for an attempted hack into an OPCW-designated laboratory in Spiez, which was tasked by the OPCW with confirming that the samples from Salisbury were Novichok (Schreuer, 2018). Bellingcat also jumped into the affray. It released a picture prominently presented throughout the world's media of two Russians it identified as agents of the GRU that were tracked to Salisbury and close proximity to the Skripals' home address. These agents were subsequently interviewed on Russia Today (RT), where they appeared to be fumbling and incompetent.

If other crimes require the separation between political and judicial authorities, intelligence crimes feature strict compliance to the official narrative and the use of intelligence tools in the stigmatisation of significant leaders who are non-compliant. A brute force effort is required to produce a consensus among the political class that may be led or augmented by the information operations of organisations such as the IfS. In the Skripal affair, the position of both the French Government and the UK leader of the opposition, Jeremy Corbyn, was initially not to make any accusations prior to the forensic case being made; but their public positions were quickly reversed following negative publicity that included a photoshopped depiction of Corbyn by the BBC *Newsnight* wearing a Cossack hat, typically identifying a Russian national (BBC News, 2018f).

Scene and Crime

The *Chemical Weapons Convention* (CWC), signed in 1992, prohibits the development, stockpiling and transfer of chemical weapons by 193 states party members through a verification and compliance regime and represents a major development in the area of multilateral arms control (Mathews, 2002: 53; Borrett et al., 2018). The CWC is implemented through the activities of the OPCW, which has overseen the destruction of the vast majority of the declared stockpiles (96.5% by 2018) (Borrett et al., 2018: 612) and has been recognised by a Nobel Peace Prize for this work (in 2013).

The OPCW has a scientific advisory board and a working group on investigative science and technology in addition to monitoring and inspection capabilities for the chemicals that are contained in the CWC's Annex of Chemicals. Samples collected from sites may be analysed onsite or offsite, after sample splitting at the OPCW laboratory, or at an approved or designated laboratory (DL). Where there are ambiguities arising from the onsite analysis, the protocol is to conduct an 'unambiguous identification using two independent analysis techniques by two independent laboratories (which are blinded from one another)' (Borrett et al., 2018: 612). The OPCW carries out non-routine inspections under 'contingency operations', which in the past have included inspections in Syria, Libya and Iraq, as well as fact-finding missions through its Executive Council (Borrett et al., 2018: 613). Designated biomedical laboratories are subject to proficiency tests to maintain their DL status.

An analysis carried out by chemists at the British Defence Science and Technology Laboratory (DSTL) in Porton Down,[8] located 8 miles from the site of the poisoning, concluded that the Skripals were poisoned from the nerve agent Novichok. DTSL officials perform tests to support police investigations and have told reporters that they keep material 'forensically secure' for a 'proper evidentiary trail' (Corera, 2018). The OPCW, which visited the poisoning sites in Salisbury, stated that the chemical substance found was of 'high purity, persistent and resistant to weather conditions', and it could not determine the amount used (Roul, 2018: 12). The experts at the DSTL were not able to pinpoint the source of the Novichok, and it has since been confirmed that the Novichok group of military-grade nerve agents were widely available. Russia was not given access to the Skripals, and there was no exchange of the allegedly inculpatory evidence. Since the Skripals are Russian citizens, the *Vienna Convention on Consular Relations* asserts obligations to grant consular access within 10 days of a request, even under supervised conditions, that may not have been followed in this case, without repercussion.

In 1997, Jose Bustani was appointed to the position of Director-General of the OPCW by a Conference of the Parties (COP) and then reappointed in 2001. In 2002, the US decided that his resignation was desirable and pressed for his removal, citing claims that Bustani did not act with sufficient fiscal discipline. The US threatened to withhold its share of the OPCW's budget, amounting to 22% or US$60 million (Murphy, 2002: 711). At the time, Bustani was negotiating with the Iraqi Government towards its entry into the OPCW, which would give OPCW inspectors access to whatever Iraq did or did not have with respect to chemical weapons. If the US was keen on the removal of these weapons, such a move should not have been a deterrent to strong US interests. We now know from US Secretary of State Colin Powell that the dossier on Iraqi chemical weapons was false and that the country had destroyed its arsenal, but from the point of view of the US, which had already decided on military action against Iraq (Clarke, 2004), its possession of chemical weapons was something on which to 'fix' intelligence as a national security threat. John Bolton, as US Under-Secretary of State for Arms Control in International Affairs went in person to visit Bustani at the OPCW headquarters in The Hague in March 2002 and told him that 'Cheney wants you out. … You have 24 h to leave the organization, and if you don't comply with this decision by Washington, we have ways to retaliate against you. … We know where your kids live. You have two sons in Washington' (quoted in Hassan, 2018). The encounter was confirmed by the then OPCW Special Assistant to the Director-General, Gordon Vachon (Hassan, 2018). The next month, in April 2002, the COP held a special meeting and voted to terminate Bustani's appointment on immediate effect. Such a move was unprecedented, unlawful according to the International Labour Organization (Hassan, 2018) and contrary to the independence immunities necessary for the OPCW's independent exercise of its functions (Murphy, 2002: 712).

Identities and Review

Sir David Omand (2018)[9] reviewed the Skripal event for the Centre of Excellence for Hybrid Threats (Hybrid CoE). Omand contends that the Russian state committed the act:

> The obvious Russian-ness of the weapon used on the Skripals, a Novichok nerve agent, must have been chosen by the perpetrators precisely so that the attack could be attributed back to the Russian state. In that way the attack could fulfill the twin purposes of intimidating Russian emigres in the UK and deterring any serving Russian official, especially in the secret intelligence world, from assisting the West. (Omand, 2018: 6)

Omand appears to be offering a synopsis of the event consistent and drawn from the kernel of the view presented by British, EU and NATO authorities,[10] while adding that the Russian state and Vladimir Putin is engaged in information warfare and other hybrid threat tactics:

> There was *a hint of intimidation* in President Putin's first public response to the news coverage of the attack in Salisbury. He naturally denied Russia's culpability while carefully *injecting a note of menac*e. 'If it was military grade agent,' he said, 'they would have died on the spot, obviously'. (Omand, 2018: 6 emphasis added)

Omand linked the 'brazen nature of the Russian denials and the spreading of "fake news" stories about the attack' to an attempt 'to try to cause the maximum confusion'. He notes: 'the hybrid threat context is clear, linked directly to [NATO, EU, UK] exasperation and concern over the lawless and reckless behaviour over many years of the Russian state under President Putin' (Omand, 2018: 5). A *Guardian* story took up the theme of Russian psyops, with Heather Stewart (Stewart, 2018a) reporting that 'experts had uncovered an increase of up to 4,000% in the spread of propaganda from Russia-based accounts'.

Omand's argument is curious. On the one hand, Russia is said to have deliberately chosen to place its fingerprints all over the crime. If the NATO–UK version of events is to be believed, Russia sent two agents overseas to Britain as Putin was preparing to contest an election to use the poison on the Skripals because they were on Putin's 'hit list'. British authorities used intelligence sources and supported investigative journalist sources (Bellingcat and the IfS) to claim publicly that Russia used the 'military-grade' nerve agent Novichok to poison former FSB agent and British Secret Service agent Sergei Skripal and his daughter.

At the same time, Russia is accused of trying to spread confusion and to disown the attack, the evidence of which Lavrov has said has been destroyed by British officials (Salam, 2018). One of the Russian scientists who developed Novichok, Loenid Rink, said that 'it's hard to believe that the Russians were involved, given that all those caught up in the incident are still alive. Such outrageous incompetence by the alleged spies would have simply been laughable and unacceptable' (in Osborn, 2018). Also, as per Alan Rodier, Director of the French Centre for Research on Intelligence, the practice of killing a spy who had been party to an inter-service swap would have breached the norms of intelligence tradecraft (Sputnik News, 2018). Another victim later allegedly died from exposure to the agent from picking up a matching perfume vial on the street that had apparently been dumped in the Skripal's trash (Sanchez and dos Santos, 2018). That only made the forensic question more urgent and no more explicable.

Glyn (2018) unpacks the inconsistencies in the official narrative surrounding the Skripal poisoning. He notes that there is a lack of motive for Russia, in particular because the poisoning occurred just prior to Russia hosting a major sporting event and the spy-swap had been long ago effected. In addition, Glyn argues, the use of a poison known to have been manufactured previously by the Soviet Union; the recipe for which had been made available to the public in a book by a military chemist, Vil Mirzayanov; and which was not on the list of banned chemical weapons by the OPCW made for an unlikely choice. Novichok's lethality also made it surprising that it did not kill the Skripals, given the contact they had with the agent.

Omand contends that the 'propagandistic narratives and dirty tricks' are the 'repertoire of Soviet subversive activity' (now Russian) (2018: 6). This begs the question on the genesis of Omand's account. Is it not being proffered from a pulpit of hybrid methods of persuasion or disinformation? Indeed, an alternative account queries the relation of the Skripal case to government-funded false or hybrid truth dissemination that derives from London's IfS and the Integrity Initiative (II). This is detailed in

Seeker (2019), Stevens (2019), and McKeigue et al. (2019), and Blumenthal and Ames (2019) and is based largely on documents hacked by the group Anonymous.

The IfS was founded in 2006 in Scotland but is located at 2 Temple Place, London and is apparently owned by an ex-SAS officer (Seeker, 2019) and directed by Christopher Donnelly, formerly a reserve officer in the British Army Intelligence Corps and previously head of the British Army's Soviet Studies Research Centre at Sandhurst (Stevens, 2019). It is a registered charity (in Scotland) and receives funding from the Foreign Office, the State Department, NATO headquarters and private donations (Seeker, 2019). Under the auspices of the IfS, the II, headed by public relations icon John Rendon, is a 'military-intelligence front operation' comprised of staff who are largely intelligence and public relations specialists (Blumenthal & Ames, 2019). Its information operations campaigns feed reports and studies to promote a 'tougher stance' towards and hype the threat of Russia to democratic institutions in establishment media and social media, especially Twitter (Blumenthal and Ames, 2019). The funding for the II totalled £582,635 in 2017–2018 and £2.6 million in 2018–2019. In 2018–2019, £1.96 million was donated from the Foreign and Commonwealth Office (FCO) and the remainder came from the US State Department, NATO and the American neoconservative Smith Richardson Foundation. Facebook donated £100,000 (Stevens, 2019). According to Stevens (2019) it is 'supported' by senior journalists, including at the *BBC* (Jonathan Marcus), the *Times/Sunday Times* (David Aaronovitch and Dominic Kennedy), the *Guardian* (Natalie Nougayrede and Carole Cadwalladr), the *Financial Times (*Neil Buckley), and the *Economist* (Edward Lucas).

On 11 March, just seven days after the poisonings, the II set out what it called the necessary 'narrative' on the event. It declared, 'Russia has carried out yet another brutal attack, this time with a deadly nerve agent, on someone living in Britain' (Stevens, 2019). According to the trove of leaked documents from the Anonymous collective:

> Just days after the poisoning of the Skripals, the IfS proposed that the Foreign and Commonwealth Office 'study social media activity in respect of the events that took place, how news spread, and evaluate how the incident is being perceived' in various countries. Within days, the II's 'Operation Iris' swung into operation. As well as monitoring media coverage with its own team, it recruited the global investigative solutions firm Harod Associates to analyse social media activity related to the Skripals affair. (Stevens, 2019)

In this account, the media outlets listed above played a key role in presenting the government narrative. According to these documents, the journalists involved included David Aaronovitch and Dominic Kennedy at the *Times*, Natalie Nougayrede and Carole Cadwalladr at the *Guardian*, Edward Lucas at the *Economist*, Neil Buckley at the *Financial Times*, and Jonathan Marcus at the BBC. Security consultant Dan Kaszeta, who was touted as a chemical weapons expert but is actually an expert in crisis response planning (Seeker, 2019), was paid over £2000 to write anti-Russia articles published by the II.

As of 20 March 2020, several scholarly articles had been published citing the Skripal poisoning and some have a Google Scholar record of citations. The articles are in several disciplinary categories including chemistry, arms control, international (diplomatic) relations, security, communications, law and public administration, among others. Some of the themes raised in this scholarly work are consistent with the treatment of intelligence crimes by both the media and academic work. Exemplary here is an article by Animesh Roul in the *Journal on Chemical and Biological Weapons.* In this article, the author provides an account of the Skripal poisoning and the findings of the OPCW and DSTL, and dismisses the veracity of the Russian claim that it abandoned its chemical weapons program in the 1990s and that Novichok was not being made or warehoused in contravention of the ban on chemical weapons treaty. Further, Roul cites as a conspiracy theory Russia's claims to the contrary, and brings in as additional support for the 'Russia did it' hypothesis that Russia was also responsible for the chemical weapons attacks in Syria (Roul, 2018: 11–12). Mark Urban (2018) is cited seven times for his book, *The Skripal Files: The Life and Near Death of a Russian Spy.* As noted by reviewer Luke Harding, despite offering all sorts of intriguing detail concerning the underworld of espionage, Urban does not answer the question of why Russia would use a nerve agent in an amateurish attempt on Skripal's life.

There are a number of articles that take up the hybrid warfare and disinformation theme. Boyd-Barrett (2019: 89) positions Skripal against a 'new phase of long-standing rivalry for hegemony in EurAsia and further afield, pitching four mega-powers into dances of cautious alliance and precipitate disruption'. Caruthers (2019: 1) claims that Russia 'employs a set of non-linear tactics against Western democracies' (hybrid warfare) in which disinformation and propaganda are used in a 'comprehensive' strategy of non-military means. This theme of hybrid threat is also picked up by Kolman (2019) along the same contours of exposition. In a very well-cited article in *Food and Chemical Toxicology*, Nepovimova and Kuca (2018) note the historical emergence of the v-type toxins but point out that the claims of Britain and Russia were not possible to verify at the time of publication. Another exceptionally well-cited article in *ACS Chemical Neuroscience* cites the Skripal assassination attempt as it speaks to the question of how nerve agents work and how to counter them (Costanzi et al., 2018: 875). Most articles make mention of Skripal (assuming the nature and cause of the event) to make a point about other issues—for example, related to dermatology (Lavery & Wolf, 2019), nursing (McGhee et al., 2020) or chemical weapons control (Sanders-Zakre, 2018). As Giddens (1986) has observed, off-hand references to the 'absent totality' do much to instruct an audience as to the uncontested or uncontestable nature of the events so referenced.

OPCW Forensic Credibility: Chemical Weapons Attack, Douma, Syria

On 7 April 2018, reports surfaced of a chemical attack in Douma, a suburb of Damascus. The OPCW announced that it would be sending a fact-finding mission (FFM) to investigate, which it did a few weeks later, visiting one of the sites in Douma and collecting samples. There had been dozens of reports of 'chemical weapons attacks' in Syria, 85 since 2013 on which the OPCW had reported (Arms Control Association, 2020), but this one arrived almost concurrent with the Skripal poisoning. Also, it would be the first occasion when the OPCW would exercise its new authority under its Investigation and Identification Team (IIT) to attribute responsibility (Arms Control Association, 2020).

Scene and Crime

The US, Britain and France launched bombing raids on Syria on 13 April, before any evidence from this latest alleged chemical weapons attack could be gathered and analysed under CWC terms. The next day, France provided an intelligence assessment that concluded that it was 'beyond possible doubt' that the attack took place, and that it was 'carried out against civilians' and as 'part of a wider offensive in the Eastern Ghouta enclave' (Arms Control Association, 2020).

As reflected in the statement above, the event placed the OPCW in the crosshairs. It would either support or fail to support a strong message consistent with intelligence interests and in favour of the US-led geopolitical narrative that would then provide the casus belli for military action against a state deemed to have committed war crimes. As observed by OPCW whistle-blowers (Maté, 2020a) below and noted above with reference to Bolton's visit with Bustani in 2002, the agency had been under long-standing political pressure. The reputations and interests of several of the strongest global actors would be difficult to ignore and provide the impetus for a confirmation bias. The information released on the internal deliberations within the OPCW over drafts (OPCW, 2018) and its Final Report (2019) offers a rare glimpse into the tensions between scientific discovery and integrity, careerism and the fixing of national security intelligence around an official narrative. That careerism should pertain to and influence the findings of this report would not be inconsistent with much research into such agencies (Whitman, 1998).

The OPCW FFM found in its original draft report (OPCW, 2018) that two industrial gas cylinders, one at each of the two locations of the alleged chemical attacks, 'might have been the source ("insufficient evidence to affirm this")' of the 'chlorinated organic derivatives' (the actual chemical/s were not identified) that were detected in the environmental samples. In addition, it found that no nerve agents were detected. The original draft also stated that

> some of the signs and symptoms described by witnesses and noted in photos and video recordings taken by witnesses, of the alleged victims are not consistent with exposure to chlorine-containing choking or blood agents such as chlorine gas, phosgene or cyanogen chloride. Specifically, the rapid onset of heavy buccal and nasal frothing in many victims, as well as the colour of the secretions, is not indicative of intoxication from such chemicals. (OPCW, 2018: 1.11)

In addition, at section 1.12, the report states that

> The large number of decedents in the one location (allegedly 40 to 45), most of whom were seen in videos and photos strewn on the floor of the apartments away from open windows, and within a few meters of an escape to un-poisoned or less toxic air, is at odds with intoxication by chlorine-based choking or blood agents, even at high concentrations. (OPCW, 2018)

At section 1.13, the report states that the FFM team was also unable to account for the relatively moderate damage to the cylinders that were 'allegedly dropped from an unknown height' when compared to the damage to the 'rebar-reinforced concrete roofs'. One cylinder was positioned on a bed, and the FFM notes that specialists in metallurgy and structural engineering might be able to provide an 'authoritative assessment of the team's observations'. The FFM said that the incongruity between the evidence of the alleged witnesses and the exposure video footage 'cannot be rationalized' and that the likely explanations would include that the victims were exposed to another highly toxic chemical (that is, one not detected at the sites alleged to be the source of the exposure) or that the fatalities resulted from 'a non-chemical-related exposure' (OPCW, 2018: 1.13).

The Final Report excluded much of the above, including reference to the implausibility of the undamaged cylinders, and stated:

> The FFM identified the likely source of chlorine as the industrial gas cylinders found by the FFM team on the roofterrace (Locations 2) and in the bedroom (Location 4) during the visits. ... The team has sufficient evidence at this time to determine that chlorine, or another reactive chlorine-containing chemical, was likely released from cylinders.

But did report at 1.6 that

> The analysis results of the selected samples identified no presence of scheduled chemicals or degradation products of organophosphorus scheduled chemicals either in the first twenty environmental samples selected for analysis or in blood plasma samples from alleged casualties.

In addition, it excluded reference to the inability to enter a nearby warehouse 'and facility' that was suspected of producing chemical weapons, simply stating that there was no indication of the facilities involved in the production of chemical weapons (OPCW, 2018: 1.8).

A memorandum dated 14 March 2019 that protested this representation of facts written by a scientist in the FFM and addressed to the OPCW Director-General Fernando Arias was posted two weeks after the final report was published (Wikileaks OPCW Douma Docs, 27 December 2019). In the memo, the whistle-blower writes that about twenty inspectors 'expressed concerns over the final FFM report'. Furthermore, the memo's author wrote that the report did

> not reflect the views of the team members that deployed to Douma. Only one member of the fact finding team that went to Douma, a paramedic, is said to have contributed to the final version of the report. Apart from that one person, an entirely new team was gathered to assemble the final report, referred to as the 'FFM core team'. (Wikileaks OPCW Douma Docs., 27 December 2019)

The Wikileaks Douma site posted an email exchange from July 2018 in which it was determined that 'the eight OPCW inspectors deployed to Douma during the FFM (except one, a paramedic) should be excluded from discussions on the project' (Wikileaks OPCW Douma Docs., 27 December 2019).

Bustani was asked by Wikileaks to review the OPCW's Final Report released in March 2019 based on the work of the FFM whose role was to investigate the chemical attacks alleged to have occurred at Douma on 7 April 2018. The chemical attacks (or events) took place in CIA- and Saudi-backed (Jaysh Al-Islam) militia-controlled territory. The video 'evidence' depicting alleged victims was produced and released by the White Helmets.[11] The White Helmets' claims have been used as a primary source by leading media outlets, including the *Guardian* and the *New York Times*, which have also attacked the White Helmets' critics, as per Sterling (2018). Here, as observed elsewhere, a critical review of western claims-making regarding the vilified targets of the US-led military-industrial-intelligence complex is castigated as 'propaganda' or 'conspiracist'. Unlike Bellingcat, the journalists (including Robert Parry, Robert Fisk, Eva Bartlett, Vanessa Beeley, Max Blumenthal and Seymour Hirsh) who are brought into the frame of direct or indirect rebuke have in the main provided in-depth reporting from the field (see, for example, Fisk, 2018). Regarding an earlier (August 2013) chemical attack near Damascus, Seymour Hirsh published a report in the *London Review of Books* that found that the attack was carried out by an armed *opposition group* with active support from Turkey (Hirsh, 2014).[12]

In reviewing the OPCW's findings for Wikileaks, Bustani wrote:

> The convincing evidence of irregular behaviour in the OPCW investigation of the alleged Douma chemical attack confirms doubts and suspicions I already had. I could make no sense of what I was reading in the international press. Even official reports of investigations seemed incoherent at best. The picture is certainly clearer now, although very disturbing. (Wikileaks, 23 October 2019)

The OPCW responded to this public exposé by its whistle-blowers by holding an inquiry into the leaking by both 'Inspector A' (Ian Henderson), whose primary dissent concerned the lack of foundation for the Final Report's conclusion that the cylinders came from the air, and 'Inspector B', who remains anonymous, but was the chief author of the FFM's initial report, whose main findings were excluded from the Final Report. The OPCW sought to portray these inspectors as 'rogue' and 'low level', marginal or anterior to the main work of the Douma investigation. They were described as 'disgruntled ex-employees' and the OPCW even sought to deny them the status of whistle-blower: 'they are not whistleblowers'.

A third investigator, a former OPCW senior official who also remains anonymous, rebuked the OPCW for removing the members of the original FFM. In addition, this whistle-blower said in an interview in October 2019 that a delegation of three US officials from Washington visited the offices of the OPCW in The Hague on 8 July 2018, and 'implored the dissenting inspectors to accept the view that the Syrian government carried out a gas attack in Douma and chided them for failing to reach that conclusion' (Maté, 2020b). It is quite telling that the efforts of Inspector B to meet with the team that was set up after this meeting in The Hague was reframed as an effort to influence the findings (in Wintour and McKernan, 2020).

Henderson had attempted to meet with the drafters of the Final Report but was rebuffed, so then decided to address a special session of the UNSC where he submitted his account of the investigation. He said that he was told: "'this is too big;' 'it's too late now;' 'this would not be good for the [Technical Secretariat's] reputation;' 'don't make yourself a martyr;' and '*but this would play into the Russian narrative*'", and that he would never be permitted to meet with the Director-General (Henderson, 2020). Henderson responded to the inquiry's reporting by asking, 'why would a pair of the top Inspection Team Leaders, both with impeccable records … suddenly go rogue?' (Maté, 2020a). Inspector B said:

> 'You have our utmost reassurance sir, that neither of us has ever tried to cause harm to your, or should I say, our Organisation,' B wrote. 'We were there when it was created. We grew as it grew. We saw three Director Generals come and go, and we, as now, fervently believed in its mission – a shared goal that you are charged with carrying forward and to which we have contributed so much.' (in Maté, 2020a)

On 28 June 2019, the third anonymous investigator also wrote in an internal memo in private support of two other OPCW investigators:

> 'I fear those behind the crimes that have been perpetrated in the name of "humanity and democracy,"' the official confided, 'they will not hesitate to do harm to me and my family, they have done worse, many times, even in the UK. … I don't want to expose myself and my family to their violence and revenge, I don't want to live in fear of crossing the street!'. (in Maté, 2020b)

In a response to the OPCW's 6 February 2020 investigation into the leak of the engineering assessment to the Working Group, McKeigue et al. (2019) provided a summary of the errors, omissions and conflicts of interest that they believe makes the OPCW's work on the 2018 attack and also the previous reports on the 2017 and 2015 attacks unreliable. Of these, they observe that there is 'no comparison with epidemiology or toxicology of chlorine release incidents', that there were no quantitative results of the chemical analysis provided, that the evidence of the staging of the pictures of victims and of the witness testimony that the hospital dousing scene was staged was ignored or downgraded, and that a modified report was substituted for the original interim report, which stated that there was insufficient evidence to find that chlorine was released from the cylinders. Also suppressed were inconsistencies in eyewitness accounts and the engineering assessment (McKeigue et al., 2020: 3–13). McKeigue, Miller and Robinson allege political interference, and observe that there is a troubling history of intelligence insertions into OPCW investigations into the attack in Talmenes in 2014:

> We noted that information for the FFM's investigation of the alleged chlorine attacks in April to May 2014 was provided by the CBRN Task Force set up by Hamish de Bretton-Gordon,

> who revealed also that during 2013 he had been undertaking covert activities *for an agency that can only have been MI6*. Videos of an alleged impact site in Talmenes, provided by de Bretton-Gordon to the FFM, were later examined for the Joint Investigative Mechanism by a forensic expert, who identified 'inconsistencies' that were *unmistakable evidence of staging*. This calls into question all other evidence from the CBRN Task Force. (McKeigue et al., 2020:13, emphasis added)

Identities and Review

With respect to the absolute requirement that the media examine and question contradictory claims of far-reaching significance, the evidence in this case is that opinion-leading media outlets have demonstrated very little appetite for exploring the implications of the politicisation of the OPCW or the alleged 'doctoring' of initial findings by its inspectors. Even the Wikileaks exposé was only a blip against the tide; there was no significant coverage by the *New York Times* or the *Washington Post* to review and explore the documents and the implications, and *Newsweek* reporter Tareq Haddad resigned when his editors rejected his attempt to report on the leaks (Neimuth, 2019). For Neimuth, the lack of media coverage on the issue prompted the question of whether 'the equivalent of a British-style D-notice has been sent by the CIA and the State Department to editorial boards in the US, Europe and elsewhere' (Neimuth, 2019).

The *Guardian*, a centre-left newspaper, appeared to react joyously to the release of the findings of the OPCW's inquiry into the leaks, claiming that its findings 'strike a blow to Russian denials', thus ascribing to Russia what was in fact emanating from the evidentiary problem pointed out by the OPCW whistle-blowers (Wintour & McKernan, 2020). The *Guardian* article reported Director General Fernando Arias's claim that the investigators demonstrated 'egregious behaviour', that they had 'manifestly incomplete information on the investigation' and that 'their views were not backed by the evidence' (Wintour & McKernan, 2020). The *New York Times* published reports by Reuters and the Associated Press that also 'aired the inquiry's conclusions without a scintilla of critical scrutiny' (Maté, 2020b). Concerning the blip referenced above, as in other cases, it is independent investigative journalists such as Aaron Maté who offer the strongest evidence-based criticism of the official narrative. Maté's reporting *was* prominently displayed in the *Nation*, but the story is also primarily an observation that American media is 'ignoring' evidence of an OPCW 'whitewash' (Maté, 2020b).

With respect to academia and industry, as has been well-established, findings are linked to funding. With regard to the scrutiny of security actors, most academics find it fruitful to augment and refine nice distinctions in the legitimacy or effective capacity of the official line and stated objectives (e.g. Andrew et al., 2020). We have highlighted US politicisation of the OPCW in relation to two events of significance to US foreign policy and US hegemony (Mearsheimer & Alterman, 2001). We have also noted the remarks from Henderson in which it was suggested to him that the matter is 'too big,' and too political (involving a Russian narrative) and that the

OPCW reputation is at risk apparently, if it makes a finding inconsistent with the line already advanced by a consensus of US-allied intelligence-informed governments. Noteworthy is the following comment by Schneider, a research fellow at Berlin's Global Public Policy Institute:

> I thought the organisation was slow and reactive in their initial response to the leaks, ceding the field and allowing the narrative to spin out of control. This is not surprising. The OPCW secretariat is very careful to avoid anything that might be viewed as 'politicising' what they see as their 'technical' work. Obviously, not all signatory states see eye to eye on this issue. So they [the secretariat] fell back on the independent investigation as a procedural tool. (in Wintour & McKernan, 2020)

The publication of such a statement in the *Guardian* immediately following the release of the OPCW's inquiry report, especially in light of the efforts to 'school' the media in such initiatives as the IfS, may be reasonably interpreted as very timely indeed in dousing the embers of the alternative narrative. A reading of the documents available on the Wikileaks (2020) site does not support Schneider's conclusion that the conflict here is between a political view perpetrated by Russia and a technical view perpetrated by scientists at the OPCW. McKeigue et al. (2020: 2) reported that, 'in violation of Article VIII of the Chemical Weapons Convention, the Chief of Cabinet allowed US officials to attempt to influence the inspectors in July 2018'. This is to be expected; and it began, it might be argued, with Bolton's visit to The Hague in April 2002.

Its treatment by investigators, by managers in the OPCW and then by reporters, editors and publishers in leading media outlets suggests that currently it is almost an impossibility to represent two contradictory and opposed views of an event once it has reached the highest level of political significance. The original OPCW draft report (OPCW, 2018) and the view of at least one chief expert is that staging was more plausible than the interpretation that the chemicals emanated from the sky in the cylinders. Given the strategic value of such an act at that specific time for the Assad forces, it is difficult to find reporting that cites military authorities to link the action with a rational military objective or strategy. The alternative narrative is more likely true, and casts the event as an intelligence crime, an act involving intelligence support and facilitation, resources in its masking (including the pressure on the OPCW), and an official narrative that is reiterated by mainstream media and academic and industry authorities.

In an article by Gavan Patrick Gray (2019), the Skripal and Douma cases are reviewed against the threshold of initiating unilateral military aggression. Legal standards require a level of certainty with regard to evidence of culpability, and in cases of proposed aggression, media and government must undertake to make that case observant of provable facts and with regard to counter-arguments. Where governments and their spokespersons or established media 'fail to offer critical assessment' (Gray, 2019: 135) or smear counter-arguments as conspiracy theory, as has been done by Roul (2018: 11) and others (including the IfS), there is a disservice to the tenets of liberal democratic governance.

Recalling the case of the *Rainbow Warrior* bombing discussed in the previous chapter and in mind of the sceptical review of what appears on the face of it to be a highly politicised operation of forensic examination by the JIT and the OPCW, we may be in a position to capture the abutment of justice and intelligence where there is much at stake. In the OPCW, as an agency of recording and analysis, we can begin to see the outlines of the intelligence smear. The disparaging comments regarding OPCW whistle-blower Henderson (by the *Guardian* and the OPCW chair) are consistent with expectations—whistle-blowers are rogue, misinformed, and in bed with the enemy. The bonanza for intelligence is the relative supineness of media and academia, but that is also not taken for granted. That is to say, we can appreciate that what is discernible or captured as crime depends upon the relative politicisation of all of the mechanisms of discernment and capture. The reaction by the US and its supporters to the downing of MH17 and to the alleged poisonings and use of chemical weapons is consistent with US efforts to exploit its domination of the instruments of the 'rules-based order'.

Conclusion

The *intelligence smear* is an artefact of the interaction of security intelligence with sovereign necessity or decisionism and the requisites of a public prosecution of a crime. First, intelligence blurs *the principles of legality*; in redacting, it subtracts from the legal discourse, pushing out a factional but apparently consensual national security discourse in its stead. Second, it *pulls* the political into a security array or *dispositive* according to which 'the real' of the political is what passes for the public dissemination of security intelligence. In subtracting from legality and adding to the political, security intelligence produces a storyline, and does so largely alongside a security intelligence consensus, which is itself a product of the array of interests that maintain apparent solidarity behind discrete political differences. See Figs. 6.1 and 6.2.

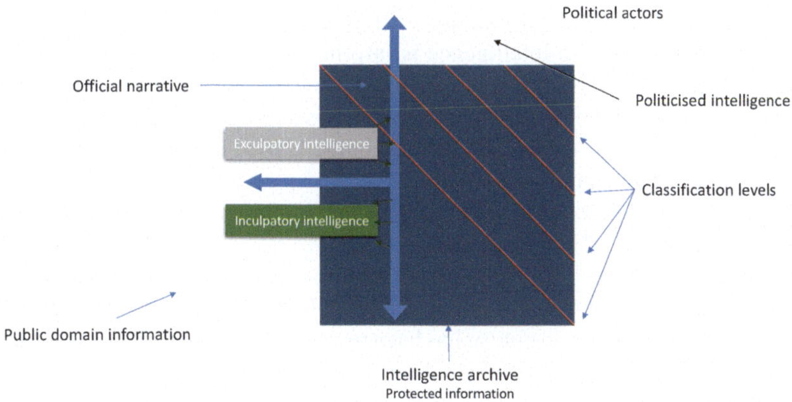

Fig. 6.1 Official narrative, intelligence archive, political influence and orientation of evidence - our crimes

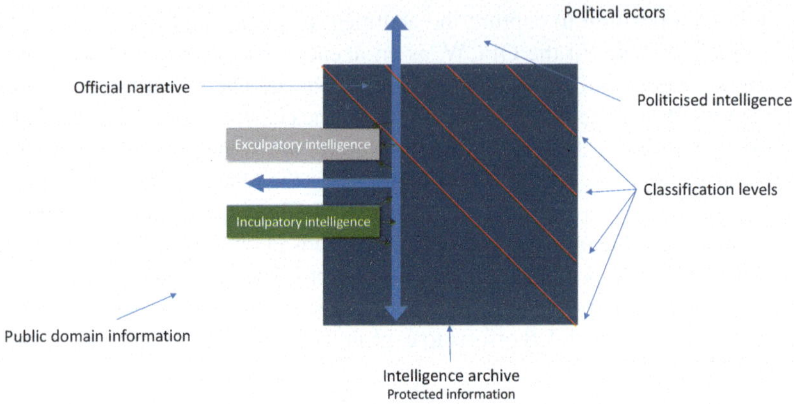

Fig. 6.2 Official narrative, intelligence archive, political influence and orientation of evidence - their crimes

In this regard, the *smear* is the exploitation of security politics by intelligence; in the fertilisation of various seemingly apolitical (or bipartisan) agendas or interest groups it capitalises on oblique reference to state auspices and exclusions.[13] Accordingly, if the control of actionable political information through intelligence is one well-articulated (if exceptional) practice, 'endarkened governance'—the condition in which institutions subvert the traditional legal and political accountabilities—is a consequence of the intelligence uptake. As the exploitation of protocols of non-disclosure and authorisation become ubiquitous and further categories for the production of state intelligence are set, traditional understandings of 'intelligence' and 'security' in relation to representative liberal politics become stretched and broken—or reviewed as the old normal.

It is incontestable that intelligence actors and actions, guided by a version of the strategic objective and supporting ideological 'truths', will be drawn upon to take pre-emptory or mopping up information operations (see, for instance, Berkowitz and Goodman, 2000: 139–42). Intelligence is informed by the meta-frame or ordering principle (Buzan, 1999: 8) as this is shaped by the state's strategic or policy considerations including public opinion. As we have observed previously, where there is consensus agreement on the righteous cause of the US-led hegemon we may expect it to overcome bipartisan disunity. During the Trump administration, deep ruptures impacted reviews of that righteousness, and this has expressed a consequent, public division in the depths of intelligence community.

The forensic record of the Douma and MH17 events will now be permanently compromised. Evidence that was required has not been collected, has been gathered by interested parties to the dispute or has been reviewed by tribunal bodies that cannot follow an equality of arms principle of discovery. In the meantime, the review of that investigation is also slanted, as predetermined by the terms of reference, in favour of one disputant. Even if one takes the position that these events are now the object if not the product of hybrid or asymmetric war, the argument by the protagonists within the western agencies making the claim that this is an emergent, preferred tactic of Russia, China and Iran is unreasonable on its face. If indeed not guilty of the alleged crimes, those actors are at a decided disadvantage in waging an information operations campaign; they do so reactively after the event, narrative and review has been played out, at least in part. They will be well aware that they are coming up as already vanquished in any public relations contest with the west.

In the meantime, what criminal intelligence actors and their supporters would like us to believe is that there is much more to the story that, if you could only know it, would bring you back into the fold of the official narrative. In this there is a continuity in interest and ideology between the transactional operations and the members of elite media, academic and government establishments. Sometimes those interests and ideologies are stretched too far and exposed to be threadbare. Sometimes the operations are exposed in their duplicity, or perhaps even insouciance with regard to that exposure (such as the behaviour of some of the DGSE agents in New Zealand). When we can plainly see straightforward interests being pursued by criminal means against people and institutions of liberal democracy we are spared having to dig deep to discover the contrasting work of Seymour Hirsh or Aaron Maté and Eliot Higgins.

If the bombing of the *Rainbow Warrior* was a failure from the point of view of intelligence both within and without New Zealand, the poisoning of the Skripals may be regarded, in contrast, as a success. This was an intelligence crime, no matter which version of the events are to be believed, but it was not a crime that saw criminal justice instruments and institutions asserting supremacy over the national security state. If Russia is not responsible, there was still a concerted effort inside British and allied intelligence to *smear* Russia with the crime. If Russia is responsible, reliable protocols for collecting and analysing evidence appear not to have been followed, nor was the operation explained sensibly as in the interests of the Kremlin. In the meantime, the apparent politicisation of the OPCW and its finding in support of Syrian responsibility for the Douma (and other) chemical attack(s), if proven, would be evidence that UN bodies are also prone to sustained pressure from the most powerful intelligence and security actors and that the procedures used by such organisations for evidence collection and examination may be selected or discarded without adequate explanation. Of course, and again, if proven, this would have implications for any effort to establish a reliable or legitimate set of instruments so that the present state of international criminal justice is not a mockery of itself.

Notes

1. 'We' may be variously limited. NATO is one means of distinguishing us and them. The Five Eyes is another. For signals intelligence the Five Eyes consists of the US, the UK, Australia, New Zealand and Canada. The 9 Eyes is these 5 plus France, Denmark, the Netherlands and Norway. The 14 Eyes is these 9 plus Belgium, Germany, Italy, Spain and Sweden.
2. For selection, we focus on the US and its presumptive security state interests. This is not because it is the worst actor, but because this account is authored by an Anglo-American, so it is my house.

3. SC Res 2166, UN SCOR, 69th sess, 7221st mtg, UN Doc S/RES/2166 (21 July 2014) ('Resolution 2166').
4. Convention on International Civil Aviation, opened for signature 7 December 1944, 15 UNTS 295 (entered into force 4 April 1947).
5. In addition, Ukraine was known to be violating the Minsk protocols, which was an agreement between Russia, the Donetsk People's Republic, the Luhansk People's Republic and the Organization for Security and Co-operation in Europe to implement a ceasefire in the Dombass. Both Russia and Ukraine had been failing to meet the terms of the agreement, no doubt contributing to the collapse of the ceasefire agreement Minsk 1 and Minsk 11.
6. On 23 November 2006, Alexander Litvinenco, also a former Russian intelligence agent, died from a three-week illness following exposure to the radioactive element polonium-210, which was apparently introduced to his teapot at the Millennium Mayfair Hotel. Evidence of that exposure was confirmed by the testing of dozens of persons, including a test of 38 Israelis who were staying at the hotel (Brosh-Nissimov et al., 2008: 101). This prior event appears to have primed expectations among the authorities, the media and the public.
7. In the meantime, Johnson had also stated that the UK chemical weapons research centre at Porton Down assured him that the chemical agent used had come from Russia, a claim explicitly contradicted when Porton Down said that it identified the substance as a Novichok class agent but had no way of determining its origin. The receiving hospital initially identified the substance as fentanyl.
8. In the meantime, the DSTL received unwanted media attention for its practice of deliberately exposing about 1000 animals per year (monkeys, pigs, guinea pigs, mice and rats) to 'compounds, simulated blasts and biological pathogens known to cause extreme suffering and death' (Dalton, 2019, citing Jessamy Karotog of Animal Aid).
9. Sir David is a visiting Professor in the War Studies Department of King's College London and was formerly Security and Intelligence Coordinator in the Cabinet Office, Permanent Secretary Home Office, and Director GCHQ and Deputy Undersecretary of State in the Ministry of Defence.
10. Other than a reference to the OPCW Report (2018), the references for the paper are mainly from the EU, NATO and UK Government sources and documents (such as the NATO Council Statement, EU Council Statement, the UK Government National Security Capability Review, and statements from Boris Johnson and Theresa May).
11. Like Bellingcat, the White Helmets have been funded by the National Endowment for Democracy. Even more interesting, they were created in Turkey by a former MI5 agent and have received at least US$55 million from the British Foreign Office and US$23 million from the Agency for International Development. The White Helmets also received millions of dollars of funding from the Kingdom of Qatar, which, as Parry observes, also backs extremist terrorist groups (Parry, 2018).

12. Lloyd and Postal (Hirsh, 2014—see Letters) rely on their own technical findings on the direction and distance of the rocket (not from Syrian government-controlled territory) to counter a claim against Hirsh's contention made by an advocate of the version of events put by Bellingcat's Eliot Higgins.
13. From the point of view of those who serve the sovereign (through the auspices of the doctrine of national security), the 1990s represented a dark period of conflicting and destructive tendencies. In an article in the *Defense Intelligence Journal*, John E. McClaughlin (1997), then Deputy Director for Intelligence of the CIA, wrote that declining intelligence budgets challenged the CIA to provide essential information to policymakers on problems on the horizon concerning 'nonproliferation, counterterrorism, narcotics, and international crime' as well as troublesome hotspots including China, Russia, Iran, Iraq and North Korea.

References

Aberbach, J. D., & Rockman, B. A. (1976). Clashing beliefs within the executive branch: The Nixon administration bureaucracy. *The American Political Science Review, 70*(2), 456–468.

Andrew, C., Aldrich, R. J., & Wark, W. (Eds.). (2020). *Secret intelligence: A reader*. New York: Routledge.

Arms Control Association. (2020, May). *Timeline of the Syrian chemical weapons activity, 2012–2020*. https://www.armscontrol.org/factsheets/Timeline-of-Syrian-Chemical-Weapons-Activity.

Asthana, A., Roth, A., Harding, L., & MacAskill, E. (2018, March 12). May issues ultimatum to Moscow over Salisbury poisoning. *The Guardian*. https://www.theguardian.com/uk-news/2018/mar/12/russia-highly-likely-to-be-behind-poisoning-of-spy-says-theresa-may.

Australian Federal Police. (2019, November). *MH17 investigation: New call for witnesses on who commanded deployment of the missile*. AFP.org.au. https://www.afp.gov.au/news-media/media-releases/mh17-investigation-new-call-witnesses-who-commanded-deployment-missile.

BBC News. (2018a, March 29). *Sergei Skripal: Who is the former Russian intelligence officer*. BBC News. https://www.bbc.com/news/world-europe-43291394.

BBC News. (2018b, April 12). *No-one speaks for me: Yulia Skripal*. BBC News. https://www.bbc.com/news/uk-43733765.

BBC News. (2018c, March 9). *Military deployed after spy poisoning*. BBC News. https://www.bbc.co.uk/news/uk-43344725.

BBC News. (2018d, March 11). *Salisbury diners told to wash possessions*. https://www.theguardian.com/uk-news/2019/mar/01/salisbury-officially-ruled-safe-12-months-after-skripal-poisoning.

BBC News. (2018e, March 12). *Russian spy: Highly likely Moscow behind attack, says Theresa May*. BBC News. https://www.bbc.co.uk/news/uk-43377856.

BBC News. (2018f, March 19). *BBC rejects complaints over Jeremy Corbyn's 'Russian' hat*. BBC News. https://www.bbc.com/news/entertainment-arts-43463496.

Beinkov, A. (2018, March 15). *Trump, May, Merkel, Macron statement blames Russia*. Business Insider. https://www.businessinsider.com/trump-may-merkel-and-macron-issue-joint-statement-blaming-russia-for-sergei-skripal-poisoning-2018-3.

Bellingcat. (2020, March 9). *The impossible conspiracy fuelling Russia's MH17 defence*. Bellingcat.com. https://www.bellingcat.com/news/uk-and-europe/2020/03/09/the-impossible-conspiracy-fuelling-russias-mh17-defence/.

Berkowitz, B. D., & Goodman, A. E. (2000). *Best truth: Intelligence in the information age*. New Haven: Yale University Press.

Blumenthal, M., & Ames, M. (2019, January 8). New documents reveal a covert British military-intelligence smear machine meddling in American politics. *The Gray Zone.*

Borrett, V., Timperley, C. M., Formanc, J. E., & Tang, C. (2018). Investigative science and technology supporting the Organization for the Prohibition of Chemical Weapons (OPCW). *Australian Journal of Forensic Sciences, 51*(6), 611–622.

Boyd-Barrett, O. (2016). *Western mainstream media and Ukraine Crisis: A study in conflict propaganda.* Routledge.

Boyd-Barrett, O. (2019). The great game for EurAsia and the Skripal affair. In O. Boyd-Barrett & T. Mirrlees (Eds.), *Media imperialism: continuity and change* (pp. 89–104). New York: Rowman and Littlefield.

Brosh-Nissimov, T., Havkin, O., Davidovitch, N., Poles, L., & Shapira, C. (2008). Suspected radioactive contamination: evaluation of 45 Israeli citizens potentially exposed to polonium-210 in London. *Israel Medical Association Journal, 10*(2), 99–103.

Buzan, B. (1999). Change and insecurity reconsidered. *Contemporary Security Policy, 20*(3), 1–17.

Carruthers, S. (2019). *Countering disinformation: A case study of government responses to Russian information warfare. Praha* (Master's thesis). Charles University, Faculty of Social Sciences, Institute of Political Science.

Clarke, R. (2004). *Against all enemies: inside America's war on terror*. New York: Basic.

Corbin, J. (2018, November 22). *Skripal poisoning: policeman's family 'lost everything' because of Novichok.* BBC News. https://www.bbc.com/news/uk-46290989.

Corera, G. (2018, March 23). *Russian spy: Inside UK lab that identified nerve agent.* BBC News. https://www.bbc.com/news/uk-43520534.

Costanzi, S., Machado, J. H., & Mitchell, M. (2018). Nerve agents: What they are, how they work, how to counter them. *ACS Chemical Neuroscience, 9*(5), 873–885.

Dalton, J. (2019, February 20). Deadly Porton Down nerve agent tests left animals gasping, writhing and shaking before dying. *The Independent.* https://www.independent.co.uk/news/uk/home-news/porton-down-animal-tests-guinea-pigs-chemical-weapons-experiments-a8788711.html.

Dutch Safety Board (Onderzoeksraad voor Veiligheid, OVV). (2015, October). *Dutch Safety Board, crash of Malaysia Airlines Flight MH17: Hrabove, Ukraine, 17 July 2014* (Final Report).

Entman, R. (2003). Cascading activation: contesting the White House's frame after 9/11. *Political Communication, 20,* 415–432.

Falk, R. A. (2015). *The Vietnam War and international law (Volume 3: The Widening Context).* Princeton: Princeton University Press.

Feaver, P. D. (1996). The civil-military problematique: Huntington, Janowitz, and the question of civilian control. *Armed Forces & Society, 23*(2), 149–178.

Fisk, R. (2018, April 17). The search for truth in the rubble of Douma: and one doctor's doubts over the chemical attack. *The Independent.* https://www.independent.co.uk/voices/syria-chemical-attack-gas-douma-robert-fisk-ghouta-damascus-a8307726.html.

Giddens, A. (1986). Action, subjectivity and the constitution of meaning. *Social Research, 53*(3), 529–545.

Glyn, J. (2018). Russian spy games: A Novichok fact check. *Eureka Street, 28*(5), 15.

Government of the Netherlands. (2020). *MH17 Incident: The Criminal Investigation.* https://www.government.nl/topics/mh17-incident/achieving-justice/the-criminal-investigation.

Gray, G. P. (2019). Evidentiary thresholds for unilateral aggression: Douma, Skripal and media analysis of chemical weapon attacks as a casus belli. *Central European Journal of International & Security Studies, 13*(3), 133–165.

Hassan, M. (2018, March 30). 'We know where your kids live': How John Bolton once threatened an international official. *The Intercept.*

Henderson, I. (2020). *Statement to a meeting during the OPCW Conference of States Parties or to an Arria-formula meeting of the UNSC.* The Gray Zone. https://thegrayzone.com/wp-content/uploads/2020/02/Henderson-Testimony-UN.pdf.

Hirsh, S. (2014, April). The red line and the rat line. *London Review of Books, 36*(8). https://www.lrb.co.uk/the-paper/v36/n08/seymour-m.-hersh/the-red-line-and-the-rat-line.

Irish, J. M., Pennetier, Reueters. (2018, March 15). France wants more prof that Russia was behind the Skripal Poisoining before it does anything. Business Insider.

Johnson, B. (2018, March 27). West takes a stand to halt reckless ambitions. *The Sunday Times*. https://www.thetimes.co.uk/article/west-takes-a-stand-to-halt-reckless-ambitions-jsxhv2878.

Kingsley, P., & Pérez-Peña, R. (2018, March 6). In poisoning of Sergei Skripal, Russian ex-spy, UK sees Cold War echoes. *The New York Times*.

Knott, M. (2014, July 18). Tony Abbott criticises Russia's response to MH17 tragedy as 'deeply unsatisfactory'. *Sydney Morning Herald*.

Kolman, B. (2019). Spreading of disinformation as part of hybrid security threats: Skripal case. In *Security Forum 2019 Conference Proceedings*. Matej Bel University. https://www.academia.edu/download/60460912/Security_forum_2019_120190902-82315-7ijg5o.pdf#page=51.

Lavery, M. J., & Wolf, R. (2019). The life-threatening rash of poisoning. *Clinics in Dermatology, 37*(2), 136–147.

Lerner, M. J. (1980). *The belief in a just world: A fundamental delusion*. Boston: Springer.

Maté, A. (2020a, March 5). *Exclusive: OPCW whistleblowers confront leadership's attacks, cover-up of Douma deception*. The Grayzone. https://thegrayzone.com/2020/03/05/opcw-whistleblowers-attacks-cover-up-douma-deception/.

Maté, A. (2020b, July). Did Trump bomb Syria on false grounds: The American media is ignoring leaks from the OPCW that suggest a whitewash. *The Nation*. https://www.thenation.com/article/world/opcw-leaks-syria/.

Mathews, R. (2002). The OPCW at five: Balancing verification in evolving circumstances. In T. Findlay & O. Meier (Eds.), *Verification yearbook 2002*. London: Verification Research, Training and Information Centre.

McGhee, S., Finnegan, A., Angus, N., & Clochesy, J. (2020). Nerve agents: A guide for emergency nurses—part 1. *Emergency Nurse, 28*(3).

McGovern, R. (2014, July 19). *Facts needed on Malaysian plane shoot-down*. Antiwar.com. https://www.antiwar.com/blog/2014/07/19/facts-needed-on-malaysian-plane-shoot-down/.

McKeigue, P., Miller, D., & Robinson, P. (2019). *Briefing note on the final report of the OPCW Fact-Finding Mission on the alleged chemical attack in Douma in April 2018*. Researchgate. https://www.researchgate.net/publication/332801562_Briefing_note_on_the_final_report_of_the_OPCW_Fact-Finding_Mission_on_the_alleged_chemical_attack_in_Douma_in_April_2018.

McKeigue, P., Miller, D., & Robinson, P. (2020). *Update on the OPCW's investigation of the Douma incident* (Technical Report). https://www.researchgate.net/publication/341930005_Update_on_the_OPCW%27s_investigation_of_the_Douma_incident.

McLaughlin, J. E. (1997). New challenges and priorities for analysis. *Defense Intelligence Journal, 6*(2), 16.

Mearsheimer, J. J., & Alterman, G. (2001). *The tragedy of great power politics*. WW Norton.

Mendick, R. (2018, March 9). Russian spy may have been poisoned at home, police believe, as military deployed to Salisbury. *The Daily Telegraph*.

Murphy, S. D. (2002). US initiative to oust OPCW Director-General. *The American Journal of International Law, 96*(3), 711.

Murray and Agencies. (2014, July 18). MH17: Hillary Clinton says Russian-backed rebels likely shot down plane. *The Guardian*. https://www.theguardian.com/world/2014/jul/18/mh17-hillary-clinton-says-russian-backed-rebels-likely-shot-down-plane.

Neimuth, N. (2019, December 28). *New WikiLeaks documents expose doctoring of chemical weapons report to justify 2018 US attack on Syria*. World Socialist Website. wsws.org. https://www.wsws.org/en/articles/2019/12/28/opcw-d28.html.

Nepovimova, E., & Kuca, K. (2018). Chemical warfare agent NOVICHOK: Mini-review of available data. *Food and Chemical Toxicology, 121*, 343–350.

Omand, S. D. (2018, April). *From nudge to Novichok: the response to the Skripal nerve agent attack holds lessons for countering hybrid threats* (Working Paper). Hybrid CoE.

Organisation for the Prevention of Chemical Weapons (OPCW). (2018). *Report of the Fact-Finding Mission regarding the incident of alleged use of chemicals as a weapon in Douma, Syrian Arab Republic, on April 7 2018*. First Draft Interim. Wikileaks. OPCW Douma Documents. https://wikileaks.org/opcw-douma/document/FirstdraftInterimReport/.
Organisation for the Prevention of Chemical Weapons (OPCW). (2019). *Report of the Fact-Finding Mission regarding the incident of alleged use of chemicals as a weapon in Douma, Syrian Arab Republic, on April 7 2018*. OPCW. https://www.opcw.org/sites/default/files/documents/2019/03/s-1731-2019%28e%29.pdf?utm_medium=email&utm_campaign=OPCW%20Issues%20Fact-Finding%20Mission%20Report%20on%20Chemical%20Weapons%20Use%20Allegation%20in%20Douma%20Syria%20in%202018&utm_content=OPCW%20Issues%20Fact-Finding%20Mission%20Report%20on%20Chemical%20Weapons%20Use%20Allegation%20in%20Douma%20Syria%20in%202018+CID_48bc58f8c18deb3191baba457f96ffd8&utm_source=Email%20marketing%20software&utm_term=final%20report.
Osborn, A. (2018, 20 March 20). *Soviet-era scientist says he helped create poison in UK spy attack row*. Reuters. https://gulfnews.com/world/europe/soviet-era-scientist-says-he-helped-create-poison-in-uk-spy-attack-row-1.2191597.
Parry, R. (2016a, March 16). *Mainstream media is lost in Ukraine*. Consortiumnews.com. https://consortiumnews.com/2014/03/16/mainstream-us-media-is-lost-in-ukraine/.
Parry, R. (2016b, September 21). *Troubling gaps in the new MH-17 report*. Consortiumnews. https://consortiumnews.com/2016/09/28/troubling-gaps-in-the-new-mh-17-report/.
Parry, R. (2016c, June 5). *MH-17 probe relies on Ukraine for evidence*. Consortiumnews. https://consortiumnews.com/2016/06/05/mh-17-probe-relies-on-ukraine-for-evidence/.
Parry, R. (2018, April 21). *Beware of the White Helmets*. ConsortiumNews. https://consortiumnews.com/2018/04/21/beware-of-white-helmets-bearing-news/.
Rawnsley, A. (2018, May 18). Corbyn's cross-eyed attitude towards the Kremlin doesn't inspire confidence. *The Guardian*. https://www.theguardian.com/commentisfree/2018/mar/18/jeremy-corbyn-sergei-skripal-attack-putin.
Reuters Staff. (2019, June 20). *Malaysian PM says Russia being made a scapegoat for downing of flight MH17*. Reuters. https://www.reuters.com/article/us-ukraine-crisis-mh17-malaysia-idUSKCN1TL0OW.
Rosenfeld, S. (2012). *Subversives: the FBI's war on student radicals and Reagan's rise to power*. New York: Farrar, Straus and Giroux.
Roul, A. (2018). Skripals', Novichoks and Russia: toxic mystery deepens amid denial. *Journal of Chemical and Biological Weapons (CBW Magazine)*, Summer, 10–12.
Salam, Y. (2018, June 29). Russia's Lavov: UK at fault in Skripal case. *Politico*.
Sanders-Zakre, A. (2018). Russia charged with OPCW hacking attempt. *Arms Control Today, 48*(9), 30–31.
Santos, R., & dos Santos, N. (2018, August 8). She thought it was perfume: It was actually a Soviet-era nerve agent. *CNN*. https://edition.cnn.com/2018/07/19/europe/novichok-poisoning-perfume-bottle/index.html.
Schreuer, M. (2018, September 14). Russians planned attack on lab testing Salisbury nerve agent, Swiss say. *New York Times*. https://www.nytimes.com/2018/09/14/world/europe/russians-salisbury-swiss-lab-sabotage.html.
Seeker, T. (2019, 4 January). *Was the Integrity Initiative behind the Salisbury poisoning?* https://stanvanhoucke.blogspot.com/2019/01/skripal.html.
Silk, M. (2020, June 23). Defence lawyer stuns court by arguing MH17 probe may not be fact-based. *New Daily*.
Sipalan, J. (2019, June 21). Russians made a 'scapegoat' after MH17 report released, says Malaysia PM. *The Sydney Morning Herald*. https://www.smh.com.au/world/europe/putin-claims-no-proof-russians-downed-mh17-20190621-p51ztv.html.
Sky News. (2019, January 8). *Poisoned spy's house to be dismantled by military*. https://news.sky.com/story/sergei-skripal-poisoned-spys-house-to-be-dismantled-by-military-11601741.

Sputnik News. (2018). *Novichuk formula was first published in a book: ex French intelligence officer*. Sputniknews.com. https://sputniknews.com/analysis/201803151062574601-novichok-formula-published-book/.

Sterling, R. (2018, November 9). *Western media attacks critics of the White Helmets*. Monthly Review Online. https://mronline.org/2018/11/09/western-media-attacks-critics-of-the-white-helmets/.

Stevens, R. (2019, January 7). *UK Integrity Initiative heavily involved in Skripal affair*. World Socialist Website. https://www.wsws.org/en/articles/2019/01/07/inte-j07.html.

Stewart, H. (2018a, April 19). Russia spread fake news via Twitter bots after Salisbury poisoning: Analysis. *The Guardian*. https://www.theguardian.com/world/2018/apr/19/russia-fake-newssalisbury-poisoning-twitter-bots-uk.

Stewart, H. (2018b, March 15). Corbyn under fire from own MPs over response to PM's Russia statement. *The Guardian*. https://www.theguardian.com/uk-news/2018/mar/14/jeremy-corbyn-under-fire-over-response-to-pms-russia-statement.

Stone, J. (2018, March 15). Emmanuel Macron to announce measures in response to nerve agent attack on former spy. *The Independent*. https://www.independent.co.uk/news/uk/politics/emmanuel-macron-france-russia-nerve-agent-attack-spy-uk-salisbury-a8256951.html.

US House of Representatives. (1979). *95th Congress Report of the Select Committee on Assassinations: Second Session Findings and Recommendations*. Washington: US Government Printing Office.

United Nations. (2018, March 14). *Moscow 'highly likely' behind Salisbury chemical attack, Prime Minister of United Kingdom says in letter to Security Council: Russian Federation calls statement irresponsible, threatening*. United Nations. SC/13247. https://www.un.org/press/en/2018/sc13247.doc.htm.

United States Congress. Senate. Select Committee to Study Governmental Operations with Respect to Intelligence Activities, & Church, F. (1976). *Final report of the Select Committee to Study Governmental Operations with Respect to Intelligence Activities, United States Senate: together with additional, supplemental and separate views*. US Government Printing Office.

Urban, M. (2018). *The Skripal files: the life and near death of a Russian spy*. Henry Holt and Company.

Van der Pijl, K. (2018a). *Flight MH17, Ukraine and the new Cold War: prism of disaster*. Manchester: Manchester University Press.

Van der Pijl, K. (2018b, July 9). *Why was Malaysian Airlines Flight MH17 shot down by Kees van der Pijl, Embassy of the Russian Federation in Australia*. https://australia.mid.ru/web/en.

Van der Pijl, K. (2020). *The coming trial of the MH17 suspects: the case against the prosecution—part 1*. The New Cold War. https://www.newcoldwar.org/the-coming-trial-of-the-mh17-suspects-the-case-against-the-prosecution/.

Whitman, J. (1998). The UN specialized agencies, peacekeeping and the enactment of values. *Journal of International Peacekeeping, 5*(4), 120–137.

Wikileaks. (2020). *OPCW Douma Documents*. https://wikileaks.org/opcw-douma/.

Williams, S. (2016). MH17 and the international criminal court: a suitable venue? *Melbourne Journal of International Law, 17*(1), 210–237.

Wintour, P., & McKernan, B. (2020, February 8). Inquiry strikes blow to Russian denials of Syria chemical attack UN watchdog's investigation rebuts claims it manipulated evidence of Douma incident. *The Guardian*.

Chapter 7
The Intelligence Crime Blur: Shaping Opinion, Smudging Records and Spiking Policy

> 'Ambiguity is part of our guidelines. … We've mapped and analysed the whole phenomenon globally. … Not just United States. Not just campuses, but campuses and intersectionality and labour unions and churches. … We started to establish a project called Israel cybershield. … A civil intelligence unit which … acts upon the activists in the BDS movement. … Using the most sophisticated intelligence system, data system in the Israeli market. … If you want to win a campaign your actions must be as vague as possible. Just as I worked on the military cases such as Hezbollah, terrorist funds or Syria or other countries as an intelligence officer, we didn't go to the other side and tell him what we do. *We left him in the dark*.'
>
> Sima Vaknin-Gill, D-G of Ministry of Strategic Affairs, in Al Jazeera, 2017, emphasis added

Introduction

In this chapter we will bring together some of the main threads and themes of the critical institutional evaluation of intelligence crime presented in this book. As has been explored in the previous chapters, crime emerges as an event categorised by authorities to more or less warrant the subjection of evidence to analysis and authoritative review. In this respect, justice must be seen to be done. Disclosure and equality of arms are two key terms in the adversarial criminal process and, as we have seen in Chap. 2, proper forensic discovery. This means that what is hidden from the defence must not be exculpatory (or where the defence is made aware of a crime, inculpatory). It is no accident, as well, that a 'jury of one's peers' is also incorporated into the architecture of liberal democratic justice: judgment is made in front of 'the people' as government policy is meant to derive from free and open debate.

In Chap. 4, with our analysis of 9/11, we began to explore the consequences where an event skips along quickly to confirmatory review. The need to see the event according to the most benign narrative compromises forensic and criminal justice independence. Where the state has nominated itself as the primary victim or complainant and that state is the world's hegemon, the institutional room for impartial

W. B. de Lint, *Blurring Intelligence Crime*,
https://doi.org/10.1007/978-981-16-0352-5_7

truth discovery or an unbiased tribunal maintaining the integrity of evidence (under an equality of arms) will be perceived as 'quaint'.[1]

In much political crime, justice will be 'miscarried' upon injunctions from the sovereign and its assertion of operational protocols and legal norms. For as long as there has been a modern state it has mobilised, whether effectively or not, a secret sovereign capacity that preserves the discretionary necessity or the power to act—even against bureaucratic and legal exigencies (Schmitt, 1988: 5; Holquist, 1997). In this regard, there has always been a contest between the public interest and the secret state in modern liberal democracies. The conflict concerns the question of how we may regard the inter-penetration of power and knowledge in the operation of the intelligence bureaucracy and government secrecy (Agamben, 1998). There are distinct, longstanding traditions that collide in the juncture between law's knowledge and the sovereign's knowledge (Horn, 2003; Smart, 2002). For the most significant of political crimes, 'justice' is framed by the necessity of the sovereign; a big event is in its attribution a test of sovereign vitality, and the executive does not wish to leave this to an *uncertain* resolution in other institutional dominions. The event is pre-emptively *defined* by the sovereign—or the unitary executive—as a test of its capacity to restore or advance its vitality.

An understanding of the problem—and of intelligence crime—requires a recasting of the home/away, friend/enemy distinction that informs assumptions about the government of disorder (Aradau & van Munster, 2009). As has been recently observed, in a condition of a claimed permanent emergency, freedom is a remainder—that is, it is what is left over after the sovereign with its scythe has sliced through the array of liberal democratic institutions to keep dangerous bads from precious goods (Rajah, 2011; Weaver, 1995). Accordingly, where the prosecution overwhelms the defence with an avalanche of information (that it cannot possibly interpret with the resources it has) or where public interest immunity is claimed (where information is not made available to protect sources and methods, for instance), justice may *not* be seen sufficiently to be done (de Lint & Kassa, 2017).

In Chap. 5, the relative power-knowledge of intelligence over criminal justice was reviewed across several diverse crimes/events. The *Rainbow Warrior* bombing provided an unusually clear window into an intelligence operation because it was so thoroughly dissected by unrestricted and independent criminal justice investigation and a locally supportive media whose fact-based observations were incontrovertible. In contrast to what is allegedly at play in the Epstein–Maxwell case, the political authorities in New Zealand were not obstructed from taking a clear path in that police investigation, although it was completed so quickly that they may not have finished morning tea. This brings into focus that there is much that is not visible in the networked relations of authorities within and across the justice–intelligence divide. Whatever remained hidden with the sinking of the *Rainbow Warrior*, one can say that not too much of it, as far as New Zealand was concerned, did not 'belong to justice'. Arguably, this is also because there was no strong division within New Zealand's political establishment. The New Zealand state was firm and unified in its approach and remedy to that terrorist act. Hopefully the reader may permit some speculative licence, with the question being raised of whether the Epstein–Maxwell case, in contrast, reveals a split within the 'deep politics' of the state or sovereign, one that permits a view into the machinations of influence, manoeuvrings beyond and extensive with its locus, even within the heart of the nation-state. This recalls a point to be made concerning Gill's (1994) useful metaphor of the 'Gore-Tex state' and his accompanying diagram (1994: 80) by which the 'secret state' is depicted as self-sustained or metaphorically isolated from the international system. However, it is evident that even the intelligence of the hegemon is *relatively compromised* by its networked relations. France is no hegemon, and as a member of the Nine Eyes is networked into intelligence sharing arrangements. Whether that community was sealed or leaked through to New Zealand authorities is not known. 'Intelligence community' solidarity, when it exists, is a two-edged sword: through its tentacles across nation-states and into other institutional dominions (defence, department of state, policing, cyberdefence) it can light sparks attracting a rush of attention. In what follows below, intelligence spiking of foreign policy is explored as one feature of the intelligence blur.

In Chap. 6, we focused on prominent intelligence crimes committed by and for 'them'. These draw on ad hoc or permanent multinational investigatory bodies that may be more or less compromised by the weight of political interest to confirm the allegation. Where convenient or helpful to strategy, such crimes are very quickly narrated via keen information operations. In this, which we will pick up below as a second element of the intelligence blur, is the work of intelligence in its maintenance of or influence on the archive or record of the event. As at least alleged by whistle-blowers, investigative journalists and perhaps one or two intrepid academics, the OPCW and the JIT were, like the 9/11 Commission, influenced to provide support to an official narrative. Where liberal democracies are justified in their politics of informed consent, the relative inconstancy between a national security archive and a public record of governing is a matter of tremendous importance, and this is not lost on any of democracy's true advocates. In this regard, the vicious prosecution of Julian Assange is telling.

The third feature of what we are referring to as the intelligence blur is information operations. Alongside the danger of the fudging of liberal democratic opinion is the production of national security stories or information operations. To properly make up a modern nation-state is to properly tell a tale about how government is keeping the nation secure and well-resourced. This involves preparing a sufficient cohort of hearts and minds for sacrifice, not only of blood but also of reason. One of the more recent iterations of this effort is the unfolding of securitisation. As we observed with respect to the interventions in support of the UK–EU–US narrative on Douma, there are some new kids on the block that have been funded to support information operations around hybrid threats.

Shaping Liberal Democratic Opinion

In his seminar on the birth of the reason of the state, Foucault (1988) argued that life or living was the object of the police, which was instrumentalised between the end of the sixteenth and end of the eighteenth centuries to maximise government for the vitality of the governed in support of the nation-state. Police practices and techniques were a concrete expression of political knowhow, connecting needy or threatening individuals to the state's knowledge about its security.[2] In his examination of the emergence of the modern liberal state, Holquist (1997) distinguishes policing from surveillance, where policing concerns the ordering of society and surveillance seeks to transform it. For Holquist (1997: 418), surveillance is a 'subfunction of the modern form of politics, of which totalitarianism is one expression'. The development of dossiers or analysis of whole cohorts of resistance became a specialised function within state bureaucracies or governments. For instance, knowledge about families, markets, religious views and political opinion is cultivated through census data and other polling and analysis (Rose, 1999; Dean, 2002).[3] Holquist (1997) provides a fascinating account (for an account on Britain see Monger, 2012) of the development of tools of the state, specifically the production of propaganda or public relations, to assure the commitment of all citizens, but especially of officials and troops. Policing and surveillance were the product of an emergent concern not merely to uncover opinion or mood but to develop the capacity to act on people or population. Surveillance was used to identify opinion and then to tease out where intervention into specific cases was needed, including selecting people for re-education or elimination as a contaminant to the body politic (459).

The modern state developed the means to elicit regular reports on the population's attitudes and to intercept correspondence, and then developed methods to quantify and analyse compliance or relative obedience to government.[4] In tsarist and White Russia, *zemstvos* were self-governing units established during the Great Reforms as 'society's antipode to the autocratic state' (Holquist, 1997: 427). The Cheka circulars of 1920–1921 and other documents, and the information apparatus of the 'reading hut' (*izba-chital' nia*), an out of the way shack containing state propaganda leaflets, were innovations in this regard. In the Ufa region, in 1915, *zemstvos* established an 'entire network of reading huts at the village level' (427) to 'transform benighted peasants into enlightened citizens' (427). As a whole, the tools were created to 'harness the country's 'vital forces' according to a standard set of questions that evaluated the mood of the 'zemstvo personnel and officials'. The huts were described as 'enlightenment' units and Holquist observes that the effort was not only socialist but was also of a piece with the changing nature of politics from territorial to governmental. Holquist quotes the propaganda of the time:

> Our work should concentrate on the information for only when the Cheka is sufficiently informed and has precise data elucidating organizations and their individual members will it be able … to take timely and necessary measures for liquidating groups as well as the individual who is harmful and dangerous. (Holquist, 1997: 415, citing Cheka circulars 1920–1921)

Holquist demonstrates how modern states developed the tools to impose themselves via the aspirations of people, an economy of human motivation quantified by surveillance.[5] A dedicated effort to shape hearts and minds was needed if the will of the sovereign was to be projected through the outposts of empire. Surveillance produced reflexive engagement and self-monitoring and was constructive in the elaboration of the modern project of politics.

If we jump ahead in time and across to the US, political opinion or ideology management is also the object of current surveillance programs of the intelligence agencies. This has been on a slow boil. In the post–World War II period up to the mid-1950s, there was an anti-communist counter-cultural initiative led by Senator McCarthy that blacklisted university lecturers, artists and performers, writers, directors and producers in the film industry, which came to a head in the Army–McCarthy hearings of 1954, after which McCarthy's star faded (Gibson, 1988). In the 1960s, civil rights and anti-war demand groups generated large-scale public protests that brought out riot police and the National Guard. Popular movement leaders foisted political demands that were countered by establishment politicians and covert domestic surveillance. In the FBI's COINTELPRO (1956–1971), the CIA's Operation CHAOS (1967–1974) and the NSA's Project MINARET (1967–1973) there was independent but high-level coordination around the effort to suppress and repress 'subversives' (Rosenfeld, 2012), such as through the use of watch lists on ex-Cubans, socialists, communists, Black Panthers and civil rights activists. As documented by Rosenfeld (2012: 5), academics and student activists were surveilled and harassed and the focus was 'not law enforcement but political', as was ruled by US District Court Judge Marilyn Hall Patel. Against these 'subversives', the FBI was the pointy end of the stick and undertook to carry out 'dirty tricks' including blackmail (Martin Luther King) and homicide (Black Panther Fred Hampton) (Churchill & Vander Wall, 1990: 103). Following the findings of the House Committee on Assassinations (United States Congress, 1976),[6] President Ford famously signed into law, on February 1976, Executive Order 11905, which prohibited any US government member from carrying out a political assassination, even abroad, during peacetime.

Regarding the information operations or analysis domain, in 1967, *Ramparts Magazine* exposed the intelligence community's infiltration of media outlets and citizen front groups that were in existence up until that date. In 1977, Carl Bernstein of the *Washington Post* calculated that at that time there were 400 US journalists who had worked for the CIA since 1952 (Bernstein, 1977). Wilford (2009) observes that it is the institutional collaboration between major news agencies and the CIA that is telling. One of these agencies was the *New York Times*, which under CIA Director Allen Dulles signed a secrecy agreement that gave the *Times* 10 'reporters' or staffers for its foreign bureaus. Similarly, CBS's news president had a private 'hot phone' to make direct contact with CIA headquarters (Hanover, 2015). As attested to by ex-intelligence agents (Goddard & Coleman, 1993; Goodman, 2017; McGehee, 2015), officers took up postings as journalists (from stringers to executives) and inserted information into mainstream news, to the extent that distinguishing white propaganda[7] from 'clean copy' has flummoxed intelligence agencies *themselves* (McGehee, 2015). *New York Times* reporter Tad Szule, appearing for hearings regarding the 'CIA and the Media' in front of the Permanent Select Committee on Intelligence (1978), observed that he was looking for Czechoslovakia troop concentrations and to touch base with the Defense Intelligence Agency to 'compare notes' and concluded that the area of intersection between intelligence and journalism 'became so blurred and so gray' (in Permanent Select Committee, 1978: 116–117).

Domestic surveillance activities apparently abated somewhat in the 1970s and early 1980s, arguably in consequence of the public outcry against the revelations of such. Following the various intelligence commissions of the late 1970s (Pike, 1977; United States Congress, 1976), intelligence agencies were banned from implementing disinformation campaigns (also known as psychological operations or psyops) around domestic targets. However, it is argued by Wilford (2009) that what was described in the *Ramparts* article and disclosed by Frank Wisner, former CIA head of Office of Policy Coordination (OPC), whose metaphor—the mighty Wurlitzer—Wilford used in the title of the book, has since then only become slicker and more sophisticated. Donald Rumsfeld's classified position document, the *Information Operations Roadmap*, advanced 'the goal of information operations as a core military competency' and sought a greater interoperability between the public affairs function and secret psychological operations (Shanker & Schmitt, 2004) and the shuttering of the Pentagon's Office of Strategic Influence, also tasked with planting propaganda, which apparently lived on under cover. The extent of media-embedded intelligence is not currently known, but there is some public information concerning the collaboration between intelligence and third parties on information operations, involving big public relations firms, political data firms and security related think tanks or research institutions. With regard to the role of public relations in the US, propaganda campaigns have been contracted out to private companies including the Lincoln Group and Rendon Group, the latter of which was paid to assist in the public relations campaign buttressing support for the US incursion against Iraq, and whose CEO was appointed to a secret committee to coordinate propaganda efforts, the Counter Terrorism Information Strategy Policy Coordinating Committee (see Miller & Rampton, 2001).

Regarding political data or data firms specialising in political opinion sorting or surveillance inserts, there has been an explosion of applications that have recently come to light, notably through Wikileaks and Anonymous. For example, Cambridge Analytica, an affiliate of British firm SCL, which has a background in military-style 'psychological operations' and is funded partly by New York fund manager Robert Mercer, was touted to be capable of 'predicting voter personalities and manipulat[ing] their behaviour using 5000 data points' (Westby et al., 2019).The firm has offered 'psychographic profiling on lawmakers who work on committees or sub-committees' who are 'dealing with legislation that the firm's clients require action on' (Wikileaks, 2016). Facebook developed an app—a quiz that ultimately captured data on up to 87 million people. This data was then sold to Cambridge Analytica to be used to psychologically profile US voters. Facebook was fined US$5 billion for privacy violations after the Wikileaks exposure (BBC News, 2019).

At a time of heightened policy anxiety around 'fake news', the European Centre of Excellence for Countering Hybrid Threats (Hybrid CoE) claims to counter alleged falsity through its strategic digital intelligence capacity (information and disinformation through social media). Established in Helsinki in 2017, the Centre's functions include: to be a platform for nations to come together to share best practices, build capability, test new ideas and exercise defence against hybrid threats; to be a neutral facilitator between the EU and NATO through strategic discussions and exercises; and to lead the conversation on countering hybrid threats through research and the sharing of best practice (www.hybridcoe.fi). The governments of member states are the main actors, funding organisations and beneficiaries for Hybrid CoE. Participation in Hybrid CoE is open to EU member states and NATO allies upon signing of the memorandum of understanding (finlex.fi). The EU and NATO actively participate in the activities of the Centre, which has 27 participants (as of October 2020).

Hybrid CoE operates under Finnish legislation and enjoys legal immunity and diplomatic status. From that standpoint it is keenly observant of European security, inside and outside NATO and close to Russia, particularly St Petersburg. The targets of this and similar agencies will be the familiar enemies of the US-led rules-based order (Russia, China, Iran, Syria and Venezuela). In Chap. 6, we referenced how the Hybrid CoE, under the writing of Omand, inserted itself into the debate about the poisoning of the Skripals.

Hybred CoE is one of several new agencies that are being established to order heightened information warfare anxieties and capacities.[8] The Israel Project, created to disseminate pro-Israeli disinformation through social and mainstream media, is another hybrid warfare vehicle. Linked to Israeli government bodies including the Ministry of Strategic Affairs, the Ministry of Foreign Affairs and the Director of Intelligence, Project members provide reports to their anonymous handlers in intelligence in Israel via a server that is off limits to US-based Americans, and receive instructions back. According to al Jazeera (2017), this organisation amasses intelligence to gain the upper hand on its 'opponents' and 'adversaries' and to 'swarm' organisations like the Associated Press to create an 'echo chamber' that will compel editors to change storylines or headlines in favour of Israeli views. The Israel Project peppers journalists from multiple directions at the same time with a preferred view to 'create a crisis' regarding the management of the issue, a crisis that bifurcates and manufactures the establishment position as anti-BDS and anti-Palestinian. This investigative reporting also alleges that the Israeli Ministry of Strategic Affairs uses cyberwarfare attacks, including Denial of Service against pro-BDS actors and agencies outside its sovereign borders, using such programs as Sensus, so that message boards and other social media formats can be examined with respect to their pro-BDS messaging and a strategy quickly put in place to take them down (Al Jazeera, 2017).

In early 2020, in what was touted as the 'intelligence coup of the century', Miller (2020) reported that since the early 1970s a Swiss company, Crypto AG, under the code name 'Rubicon', had been secretly controlled by the CIA in partnership with the NSA and the German intelligence agency, BND. Crypto AG devices that had been sold to over 120 countries since the early 1970s contained codes that the CIA had the key to break. These inserted intelligence Trojan horses into the heart of internal government correspondence inclusive of tactical and strategic planning, permitting government intentions to be swallowed up and counter-intelligence to be spat out. This permitted the collection of intercepted communications between actors involved in high-level terrorism, bombings, disappearances, torture and assassinations (Miller, 2020).

Wikileaks, under Vault 7 (Wikileaks, 2020), contains more than two dozen tranches of documents that feature information on illicit intelligence operations. This information includes: NSA bugging operations against UN Secretary-General Ban Ki-moon and private conversations between world leaders of 'friendly' governments; CIA projects to infect Apple Mac computer firmware; and, most importantly for this analysis, under the codename 'Marble', 676 source code files 'for the CIA's secret anti-forensic [program] used to hamper forensic investigators and anti-virus companies from attributing viruses, trojans and hacking attacks to the CIA' (Wikileaks, 2017). No one familiarising themselves with these Wikileaks documents will come away believing that they are protected from intelligence-led information operations, particularly if what they are doing may impact government in a direction that is not preferred by its vigilant guardians.

A century after the 'reading huts' were strategically positioned to be stumbled across so that 'enlightened citizens' could be made from peasants (Holquist, 1997: 427), information operations assume the same objective but also wish to, as per Vaknin-Gill above, erase the traces back to their origin. In hybrid threat operations, actors may use both private and government funds to set up organisations (assets) the role of which appears to be to shape public opinion from the margins of plural democracy. If so, in the Hybrid CoE and the Israel Project, information operations enlist social science and liberal democratic institutional forms in the 'dark arts' of tradecraft. The hybrid threat posture is consistent with the 'ice cold war', whereby something is out of order according to a *precautionary* cold war footing. To traditional cold war friend/enemy ontology is thus added an intelligence freeze, which denies the means to unpack the causal order of event and ramifications and denies the access to underpinning facts. Asymmetric attacks are presumed directed to an outpost that then makes sensible and responsible the fusion of civilian and domestic safety and military capacity and method. Mainstream media such as the *Guardian* and the *New York Times* regularly draw from propaganda sources and predictably ridicule calls for the reinvestigation of major events that dot the frontline. Thus, the object-lesson: a line of reading huts connected by a disciplining theme or ordering principle.

In light of recent developments and historical continuities, Robinson (2019) suggests the need to expand research into the field of political communication to seriously consider psyops in 'critical propaganda studies'. This may be only the beginning of what is needed. Such study needs to problematise how cases are closed based on purportedly definitive findings despite the many departures from robust standards in the investigative process, as sovereign political interests intrude upon examining and reviewing bodies (as discussed in Chaps. 5 and 6), and how incidents or events pop up in media with a ready narrative including a casus belli as part of the firming up of strategic and policy preferences.

Smudging the Record: Pre-Emptive Counter-Forensics

In investigating the Kennedy assassination, Chief Justice Earl Warren famously acceded to the newly created executive's wish to simplify the enemy and the narrative. Warren was called into discussions with newly confirmed President Lyndon B. Johnson after turning down the opportunity to chair what became the President's Commission on the Assassination of John F Kennedy and, based on Johnson's description of the matter, was ultimately convinced that he had a civic duty to prevent a public panic and World War III. In obediently defending society, Warren denied the commissioners access to autopsy photos and witnesses that would have confirmed that Oswald was well-known to intelligence and had met the CIA's Head of Assassinations for the Western Hemisphere in Mexico City six weeks prior to the assassination.[9] Warren also supported the redaction of 6 million pages of records pertaining to the assassination (only 40,000 were made available). According to former US Army Intelligence Officer John Newman (2008), after the *JFK Assassination Records Act of 1992*, most of those redacted documents were released and were found to support the view of rogue covert CIA complicity and involvement. As Newman concluded from his close reading of the released files, after unwrapping the legend that involved Oswald with the Cubans and the Soviets, it is evident that the FBI, the CIA and the Joint Chiefs of Staff were all implicated in the next layer, but only for incompetence: Oswald was transparently on the security index and had no business being anywhere near the presidential cavalcade in Dallas (Newman, 2008). In the event, compartmented secrecy meant that only a sliver of high-echelon agency complicity was required, and Newman believes that counter-intelligence chief James Jesus Angleton had the level of clearance to set up Oswald as a problem that sensible crisis management would want to bury.

The public record of 9/11 will for a long time be unlikely to yield enough of the archive to provide a definitive account of causes, including the presumption that it was made possible by a failure of intelligence, a position that has followed 'in the wake of nearly every war and terrorist bombing' since Pearl Harbour (Borer et al., 2014: 811). The interpretability of the archive has supported the shaping and obstruction of intelligence inquiries and to evade or direct blame and responsibility away from both Democratic and Republican actors. In April 2020, President Trump followed previous administrations in not yielding to pressure from victims' families and other groups to release more of the secret archive, especially concerning the Saudi and/or foreign state tie-ins. The documents are sought by families seeking to criminally prosecute those responsible for 9/11, including foreign actors. US Attorney General William Barr, supported by Director of National Intelligence Richard Grenell, 'invoked unprecedented claims that the documents' (Woodward, 2020)—possibly inculpatory regarding Saudi state involvement—must not be made available in order to 'protect national security interests' (in Woodward, 2020). Grenell wrote that the documents contain: 'highly sensitive and classified national security information concerning foreign government information, intelligence activities, sources and methods, and information concerning foreign relations and foreign activities of the United States, including confidential sources' (in Woodward, 2020). Barr added that 'even public discussion of and justification for the documents' secrecy must also be kept secret' (Woodward, 2020).

Assistant Director of the National Archives and Records Administration's Center for Legislative Archives, Matt Fulgham, said that of the 575 cubic feet of 9/11 Commission records, a third have been reviewed for possible release but many of these documents will remain withheld or heavily redacted indefinitely. About two-thirds of the material is still classified by agencies that provided documents to the Commission under ORCON or Originator Control (Paltrow, 2011). Excluded transcripts and video archives include those from: FBI language specialist Behrooz Shashar, who testified to the Commission about a plot called 'Kamikaze pilots'; Lieutenant Colonel Tony Shafer, who met with Philip Zelikow to inform him about 'Able Danger' and the identification of 9/11 terrorism suspect Mohammad Atta before the attacks; and Norman Mineta, whose testimony to the Commission suggested that Vice-President Dick Cheney gave an order not to shoot down a plane that was approaching restricted Washington airspace, which was not mentioned in the final Commission report; and a 30-page summary of the April 2004 interview conducted by all 10 commissioners with President George W. Bush and Vice-President Cheney (Fenton, 2011). Some unique and original National Security Archives documents that may have been responsive to Commission queries were stuffed into socks and underclothing and ferreted out of the building by Clinton's designated representative to the Graham-Ross Committee, Sandy Berger (US House of Representatives, 2007).[10]

Wherever actors carry out prima facie criminality in the name of the nation's security, individuals who expose those activities are viewed as directly threatening the information control regime that hard-line proponents of the national security state prefer (Gill, 1994). Former Australian Attorney-General of the Australian Capital Territory, Bernard Collery, and an unidentified former Australian Secret Intelligence Service (ASIS) officer (Witness K) were being prosecuted in 2020 regarding the communication of intelligence information. Collery was on trial for conspiring with his client, who was involved in the illegal bugging operation that ASIS carried out against the negotiating team of Timor-Leste in 2004 to learn its position during bilateral discussions over the division of lucrative mineral and other deposit rights under the sea between the two countries (Cunliffe, 2020). The case was exposed by an independent Member of Parliament, Andrew Wilkie, who maintained that the intelligence cover was concealing 'the real criminals – the people who ordered the illegal bugging' (Cunliffe, 2020). Cunliffe reports that the major beneficiary of the negotiations of Australia's initial deal was Woodside Petroleum, and that the Foreign Minister at the time, Alexander Downer, made a public comment that Australia was working in Woodside's interests during the negotiation, a firm for which he also became a paid consultant after leaving politics (Cunliffe, 2020). Foreign Affairs department head at the time of the bugging, Ashton Calvert, took a directorship from Woodside not even a year after the crime (Cunliffe, 2020). The Australian Government used Section 39 of the *National Security Information (Criminal and Civil Proceedings) Act 2004* (ACT) (NSIA) to prohibit the disclosure of information acquired or prepared by the Australian Secret Intelligence Service (ASIS). Originally passed with a suite of counter-terrorism laws in 2004, the legislation has since been used to muzzle and prosecute intelligence whistle-blowers. In a closed hearing under the NSIA, summary evidence was provided to a judge without the defendant (Witness K) present for cross-examination. The claimed information concerned the illegalities, but also kept the trial (in whole or in part) from public reporting or witnessing. The procedure permitted information to be used as evidence despite that it cannot live up to the rules of evidence that have been developed over centuries by the courts.

Founder Julian Assange used Wikileaks to reveal information brought to it by whistle-blowers to expose a selection of the hidden archive of the US state, defence and intelligence communities. The whistle-blowers include US Army intelligence analyst Chelsea Manning (Iraq War Logs), accused NSA analyst Edward Snowden, accused CIA officer Joshua Schulte (Vault 7) and possibly Democratic Party staffer Seth Rich (Democratic National Committee email hack, Wikileaks, 2020). For this, Assange has been the subject of highly irregular prosecutorial and intelligence procedures enacted across jurisdictions in Britain, Sweden and the US. In September 2020, Assange was in remand in harsh solitary confinement in Belmarsh Prison fighting extradition to the US on espionage charges. The Westminster Chief Magistrate ruling on Assange's extradition is Lady Emma Arbuthnot, about whom Curtis and Kennard (2019) claim there are too close ties to the British military establishment, particularly through her husband, Lord Arbuthnot, former defence minister and a paid chair and advisor to UK arms contractor the Thales Group.

> Thales also has major contracts with the MOD [Ministry of Defence] including a £700 m drone project and a £600 m deal to maintain the royal navy's warships. One of Thales' lucrative business lines is 'cybersecurity' and its website disparagingly refers to WikiLeaks and Assange personally as being able to 'steal' information. Thales produces 'watch-keeper' drones used by the British military in Afghanistan which have been exposed in WikiLeaks releases. Arbuthnot is a strong supporter of drones: he was the chair of the defence committee when it produced a report highly supportive of British operations in 2014 which recommended 'bringing watchkeeper to full operating capability'. (Curtis & Kennard, 2019)

Previously, the CIA is alleged to have supported and received information from UC Global, a security consulting firm that won the contract to provide security for the Ecuadorian Embassy in London in 2016, where Assange sought refuge between 2012 and 2019. In 2019, when the Ecuadorian leadership changed in favour of US interests, British police were permitted to forcibly remove him from sanctuary. UC Global head David Morales was charged in Spain's High Court in October 2019 with violating Assange's privacy and attorney–client privileges when it conducted an apparently illegal surveillance operation on Assange and his visitors and legal team (Blumenthal, 2020). According to Max Blumenthal, the ties between UC Global and the CIA operated through a middleman, Sheldon Adelson's Sands Corporation:

> This investigation will further establish the US government's role in guiding UC Global's espionage campaign, shedding new light on the apparent relationship between the CIA and Adelson's Sands, and expose how UC Global deceived the Ecuadorian government on behalf of the client Morales referred to as the 'American friends.' Thanks to new court

> disclosures, The Grayzone is also able to reveal the identity of Sands security staff who presumably liaised between Morales, Adelson's company, and US intelligence. According to court documents and testimony by a former business associate and employees of Morales, it was Adelson's top bodyguard, an Israeli-American named Zohar Lahav, who personally recruited Morales, then managed the relationship between the Spanish security contractor and Sands on a routine basis. After their first meeting in Vegas, the two security professionals became close friends, visiting each other overseas and speaking frequently. During the spying operation, Lahav worked directly under Brian Nagel, the director of global security for Las Vegas Sands. A former associate director of the US Secret Service and cyber-security expert, Nagel was officially commended by the CIA following successful collaborations with federal law enforcement and intelligence agencies. At Sands, he seemed to be an ideal middleman between the company and the US national security state, as well as a potential guide for the complex surveillance tasks assigned to Morales. (Blumenthal, 2020)

It was further reported that 'plans to poison or kidnap' Assange from the Ecuadorian embassy 'were discussed between sources in US intelligence' and UC Global (Quinn, 2020).

There are more instances of interference in Assange's human rights. The UN Special Rapporteur on Torture, Nils Metzer, reported that Assange was showing:

> 'all the symptoms typical for prolonged exposure to psychological torture' and demanded immediate measures for the protection of his health and dignity. However, what we have seen from the UK Government is outright contempt for Mr. Assange's rights and integrity. … Despite the medical urgency of my appeal, and the seriousness of the alleged violations, the UK has not undertaken any measures of investigation, prevention and redress required under international law. … While the US Government prosecutes Mr. Assange for publishing information about serious human rights violations, including torture and murder, the officials responsible for these crimes continue to enjoy impunity. (UNHR, 2019)

Noteworthy is the UK Government's response to Metzer's intervention. It did not provide the additional information requested, was confident to 'flatly reject' the findings and demonstrated no willingness to consider the recommendations (UNHR, 2019). As has been widely observed since at least the Ellsberg case,[11] those seeking to make the record of intelligence crimes public for review face extraordinary pressure on their resolve and are subject to unusually severe retaliatory treatment. As we noted previously in relation to this smudging of the record, there would appear to be little daylight between the judiciary charged with taking oversight of the prosecution and intelligence and security interests in the framing and disposition of the case.

Analysis

A criminal case and prosecution produce an archive that is more or less visible depending on the standpoint of persons seeking to view or review it. In the rhetoric of legality, disclosure is an absolute necessity in an adversarial system that seeks just outcomes. Potentially exculpatory or doubt-productive information possessed by police or the prosecution must be made available, otherwise the procedure places justice in disrepute. A courtroom and a forensics lab differ in the practices that maintain their respective institutional knowledges. Both are dependent or built up on principles of contestability or refutation and public access to their core 'texts' and 'propositions', where legal truth requires a balance of power between adversaries in front of a neutral arbiter. For cases involving political actors or national security, the view and review of that archive is contingent or dependent on the inscription of that information by intelligence actors deploying security communications law or operations permitting directives (see Figs. 3.2, 3.3 and 6.1). The intelligence product is information that is relatively exclusive to and transactional for the consumer and is valued for possessing both properties. Intelligence is a power-knowledge deriving from a reference to alleged facts not in evidence, and actions not fully or sometimes even partially acknowledged by the consumer-authoriser (as discussed in Chap. 3).

On the one side, rule of law or 'process' liberals and instrumental or 'outcome' conservatives alike are ill-equipped ideologically or bureaucratically to obtain adequate records and reports of clandestine intelligence agency activities. As per our discussion in Chap. 3, access to such information is restricted to individuals who have been cleared by security intelligence authorities. The restriction of information may be overturned at the highest authority and courts are provided with intelligence summaries that are derived from a narrative out of information that is not externally reviewable (de Lint & Kassa, 2017). On the other side, there is a movement or bending into the intelligence understanding of the requisite procedures as also discussed previously (see, for example, William Bar above), whereby it is accepted as per legislation and precedent that sensitive secrets must remain the dominion of the sovereign and judges must assume a good faith execution of the brief (Roach, 2010).

It may be fruitful to review the distinction between justice and intelligence with reference to 'systems of exclusion', as provided by Foucault in his essay 'The discourse on language' (1972). Foucault refers to the variety of practices that maintain a particular body of knowledge or govern the will to knowledge. Included in these are the mechanisms that protect the base assumptions or founding affirmations and the institutional and professional self-understandings that maintain institutional knowledge forms. Also included are internal rules that arrange principles of classification, ordering and distribution of texts and the distinction between primary and secondary authorities (Foucault, 1972: 221). In outlining the function of disciplines, Foucault notes the priority of building criteria, or an endless supply of fresh propositions that fit into and reinforce the hierarchical order of a given field over meaning or hermeneutics (225). Thus, 'disciplines constitute a system of control in the production of discourse, fixing its limits through the action of an identity taking the form of a permanent activation of the rules' (224). In addition, Foucault observes which conditions must be met for subjects to be qualified to speak, a phenomenon he refers to as 'rarefaction'. Finally, discourses require 'fellowship', or the preservation and reproduction of stipulations on circulation and the maintenance of their truth claims (225). How propositions are allowed to shape a field, who is qualified to speak and make claims, and how claims and claims makers are vouched for by others in a community of peers are significant to understanding the power relations of governmental rationalities.[12]

These exclusions inform how politics may be thought up and intelligence crimes known. For cases involving political actors or national security, the view and review of the archive is contingent or dependent on the inscription of that information by intelligence actors. The classification of key information as off limits to police and prosecution or the practice of providing a summary of information according to the values and principles of intelligence agencies provides for a default position in which the defendant may be unable to reasonably provide a defence and has no true equality of arms.[13] It also provides cover so that operations that are embarrassing or worse may be shielded from public discovery. The style or modality of government may be a reading up of the approved releases from the secret or hidden archive, a review that permits only privileged knowing by cleared authorities that cannot adequately inform the public.[14]

The strategic intelligence leak exploits the latent force of the hidden archive. The timed or calibrated disclosure maximises influence because it may overdetermine a preferred interpretation in the absence of the genus of facts from which it is chosen. While the chief executive is constrained in dealing with the 'invisible government' (Wise & Ross, 1967) because he or she will take a grave risk in going directly to the people on matters of (even contested) national security,[15] careerists within agencies charged with a national security mandate will selectively disclose national security information to promote a policy agenda (Marchetti et al., 1974). Politicians up to and including prime ministers and presidents operate knowing that disgruntled members of the 'invisible government' can undercut their purposes by leaking information (Wise & Ross, 1967). In the meantime, authorised but unsourced disclosures and leaks allow the security bureaucracy to augment its capacity and knowledge-edge as information is published on the basis that it promotes security and intelligence agendas and grows the security dispositive. Release decisions are made according to an interpretation of security interests at a high level of insulation from democratic politics. Since such information release often serves political authority as it is interpreted by intelligence agencies themselves, the timing of intelligence leaks will occur at key decision points. In this way the intelligence archive capitalises on the modal shift of information to knowledge or the fault-line between the retention of actionable information and its dissemination in the service of deniable interests.[16]

Bridging Across Partisan Divisions by Spiking (Foreign) Policy

As we have been observing, there is in principle a distinction between the judicial function to ensure a degree of compliance with legality and the executive function to support the security order. Likewise, there is also in principle a strong distinction between the military and civilian dominion. Huntington (1997) and Janowitz (1961) contend that in liberal democracies this military–civilian distinction must be negotiated when confronting political enemies with martial instruments. For example, our information operations or psyops alongside other defence-based covert means are meant for our enemies and should not by blowback (or intentionally) be used to persuade or compel the domestic electorate.

In practice political institutions are more or less normative, rule-bound and opportunistic (Weber, 1994). This observation captures the division presented in the political science and criminology literatures, with most accounts taking the 'consensus' view that liberal democratic 'gentlemen', as Henry Stimson describes, 'do not read each other's mail' (in Kruh, 1988: 65). In security and intelligence studies inclusive of the political economy of intelligence and security and political policing there has been interest in accounting for and explaining the blurring of this distinction between outward-facing and inward-facing security and order (see, for example, Garland, 2012; Aradau & van Munster, 2009). In these accounts, there is either oblique or direct reference to the presumptive liberal consensus that holds that the normative orientation of the rules-based international order is maintained *where it counts* over the action or covert operations of the exceptional executive. There is criticism of how liberal institutions have retreated from these power separations, encouraged by advocacy across the political establishment and the agencies and actors of national security (see, for example, Suskind, 2006).

For a minority of critical scholars there is a long history that discovers that modern liberal democracies have emerged from (Holquist, 1997) and into national security states (Neocleous, 2006) as liberal democracy works *through* liberal police (Donzelot, 2008) or the intelligence and the security dispositive (Dean, 2002). In practice, our own media and political institutions are at risk both as recipients and producers of malicious propaganda and of stoking a generalised fear in the mixing of opinion and facts (Altheide, 2019), although not necessarily as presented in hybrid threat agency documents. In recent experience, including in the condition of the presumptive permanent war, legislation and presidential directives have whittled away at the exception/norm distinction to provide the sovereign with the strategically necessary tools to fight the enemy abroad or at home with much the same alacrity and weaponry, in turn drawing down the restriction against blow-back or domestically faced information operations, as we have just observed.[17]

In support of this emergent 'new normal' is the resuscitation, revivified in US neoconservatism in the 1980s (Ehrman, 1995), of the criticisms of weak parliamentary democracy (Schmitt, 1988). Neoconservatives and interventionist liberals alike criticise the classic liberal position as too reluctant to accept the exception (from, for example, Locke's prerogative) and therefore too weak in the face of opponents against whom is needed a strong if not 'unitary' executive. The features of the neoconservative position include support for political elitism (bordering on authoritarianism), a glorification of intelligence and security operations, and encroachments on other institutional domains or power-division instruments of liberal democracy (the fourth estate, judiciary and legislative branch). In addition, there is already acceptance that defence is not just material or stemming from property dominion (such as US strategic and geopolitical interests and the fending off of the emerging China hegemon), but must be ideological ('they hate our freedoms'), so there must be a fluidity of the war-making and law-breaking capacity as expressed in the concept of hybrid threat awareness. In this regard, incidents or events, including 9/11, Douma and MH17, attract as if by gravitational force the baiting of the negative/positive or friend/enemy outpost. The events are seized upon as brute force provocations that disallow equivocation: institutions of check and balance and investigators and forensic scientists within the organisations empowered to recover and analyse the evidence are confronted with the hard choice; your findings will either support us or our enemies. Equivocation, as we saw with reference to the OPCW whistle-blower account, is considered tantamount to providing a gift of ammunition to the mullahs, communists or autocrats abroad, not to mention the conspiratorialists at home.

Analysis: New Normal Security and Deep Split Politics

The apparent contradiction between two of Mearsheimer's most famous contributions to political debate may help set the table for us. Mearsheimer and Walt (2007) supported the case that 'the Israel lobby' has been 'extraordinarily effective' in diverting US foreign policy in favour of Israel's regional interests. Operating mainly through the American Israel Public Affairs Committee (AIPAC), the lobby funds US politicians or their opponents, from presidential to municipal offices but with a focus on congressional races, depending on a scorecard that tabulates platform positions. Of particular interest is that Michael Scheuer, formerly of the CIA's Middle East desk, agreed with this assessment, also noting that the Saudi lobby was perhaps as dangerous to US interests.[18]

Mearsheimer is also well-known for the concept of offensive realism (Pashakhanlou, 2013). Following the main tenet of classical realism, it understands states as power-maximisers that will accede to a curbing of the necessary appetite for greater power and control only 'when they must'. The US, as a regional hegemon, will not accept the ascendancy of a competitor to its domination. With respect to China, Mearsheimer argues that there is an inevitable military conflict because China must support its own expanding interests and attendant sovereign position, while the US, in facing eclipse as the world's leading economy, must resort to its military superiority to avoid relegation to secondary status or interdependence in a multipolar system (Mearsheimer, 2010).

A common refrain in the criticism of Mearsheimer's arguments alerts us to the problem of designating and holding responsible a unified will when it comes to the exercise of sovereign state authority.[19] Critics maintain that the problem with offensive realism is that it arrests analysis at the door of the state as a coherent, self-serving actor in an international system of other such actors (Pashakhanlou, 2013). On this account, using the heuristic device of the system of state actors, analysts look at states at the wrong scalar, extrapolating from the psychology and situatedness of the human individual so that human psychology dimensions like fear and insecurity become paramount. But state action is the product of a confluence of interests, including lobbies and networks of power that all work to have their representations realised and their group, consortia, industrial and/or ideological interests advanced. Within security studies, other schools of thought have rightly taken the position that the relation between and the terms 'sovereign' and 'national interest' or 'national security' appear to have a solid integrity only from a standpoint that wishes to construct them and that there are many actors additional to the state that are pivotal to the operation of the 'international system' including NGOs, supranational organisations like the UN, and subnational organisations like AIPAC (Buzan, 1999; Bigo, 2006; Weaver, 1995).

In addition, security is a relation that is mediated, which is not to discount that it is also manifest in concrete violence. It takes the form of messaging that is directed to audiences concerning actions that might be taken. There is much discursive layering that circumscribes and reifies the essence of the national or sovereign capacity. The so-called nuclear football is the black leather satchel that the US president must have in reach wherever s/he goes. Its purpose is to confirm the president's identity and contains nuclear strike option response menus ranging from total to partial obliteration of the enemy (Dobbs, 2014). The hard facticity of the football cannot be dissolved or reduced to a mere abstraction, even where it only functions as a means of communication with military command as part of a chain of authority concerning existential defence. The messaging of security certainly does concern matters of consequence for the communicating parties, but in quantity and quality the vast majority involves a myriad of actors and interests proposing or reviewing security as communications for layer upon layer of discrete audiences (that is, in levels of classification).

That both security and intelligence are discursive 'products' is the take-away here. It is crucially important to actors in the security and intelligence array that politicians and other authorities stay 'on message' concerning pivotal matters or concerns that may result from a shift in the strategic gaze (say, from Russia to China, or from nuclear proliferation to radical extremism). Where the partisan split runs deep into the security array or dispositive, there is a danger that a revolutionary/counter-revolutionary sovereignty will be realised. Democratic presidential nominee Joe Biden stated on 11 June that '*the military* will intervene if Trump refuses to accept election loss' (Millman, 2020, emphasis added). Observers of 9/11 and the Kennedy assassination and their aftermath have asked the question, who was in a position to know what? Was this a coup against Kennedy from actors aligned with ex-CIA director Dulles and Vice-President Kennedy? Was 9/11 aided by insiders who ensured that America's defences were weak on the day? Is there a 'deep politics' (Scott, 1996), a network of actors or 'secret team' (Prouty, 2011) that is able to mobilise the compartmented national security bureaucracy to force anti-democratic policy choices (deHaven-Smith & Witt, 2009)? Where so-called rogue intelligence actors find a willing environment to mobilise or enable illicit networks in organised crime or political terrorism and are able to layer the activity under multiple national security covers and legends, there is a plausible basis for asking the question.

Russiagate exposes a deep rift between the elites of the two major political parties (Democrat and Republican) and their supporters and detractors within the Department of Justice, the FBI and the CIA, at least. Trump supporters have made the claim that the hack into the Democratic Party server occurred via a leak to Wikileaks from inside the party offices by a whistle-blower aiming to expose illegalities within the party, particularly to derail the nomination of Bernie Sanders, and an intelligence sting that failed to ensnare its target by connecting the transactions back to Putin or the Kremlin. This view takes support from the lack of confirmation in the Mueller Report: 'Ultimately, the investigation did not establish that the Campaign coordinated or conspired with the Russian government in its election-interference activities' (Mueller, 2019: 173).

On the other side, some Democratic Party supporters and much of the establishment media (including the *Washington Post*, the *New York Times* and the *Atlantic*) take heart from that part of the Mueller Report and from the Senate Select Committee on Intelligence (US Senate, 2020) finding revealing that Trump campaign chairman Paul Manafort's aide-de-camp, Konstantin Kilimnik, was a Russian agent, in constant or almost daily contact with Manafort, and that they communicated through encrypted and correspondence-erasing technologies and shared access to an email account. They also cite the 2017 'intelligence community' assessment of the Office of the Director of National Intelligence (ODNI, 2017) that claims that there is 'high confidence' of Russian interference, despite the equivocation in the term 'high confidence' (ODNI, 2017: 13) and the oddity that the ODNI's report dedicated so much space to *Russia Today*'s coverage of political divisions (Ford, 2019: 14). Intelligence will seek to support its own senior leadership for the victorious side where there is an ideological division that pulls apart the sovereign capacity and integrity (see Fig. 7.1)

There is the additional question of the separation of national and transnational intelligence interests. If, as suggested by Mearsheimer and Walt (2007), there has been a longstanding and successful campaign by the Israeli state and its supporters through AIPAC and other bodies to influence US foreign policy, is US national security sufficiently autonomous in the offensive realist view? If Epstein 'belongs to intelligence', how does his case reflect on a presumptive aggregation of US and

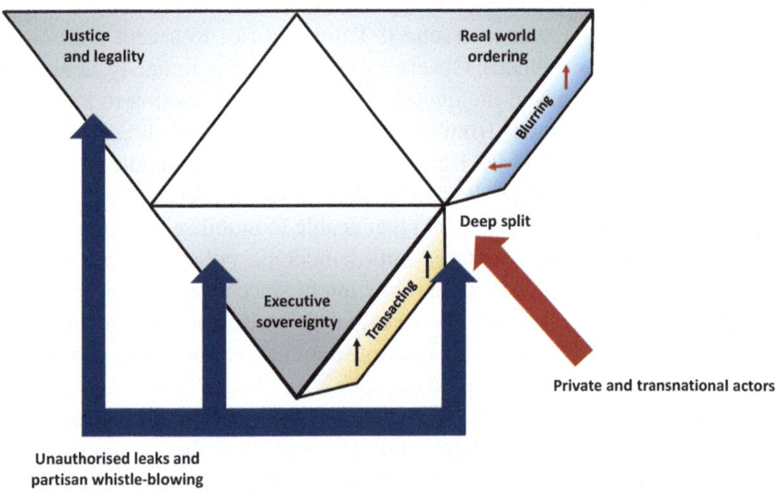

Fig. 7.1 The deep split partisan and external information operations and exploitations

Israeli interests? Where there is an ideological division that pulls apart the sovereign capacity and integrity or a threatened deep political split, intelligence will seek to assure that its own senior leadership will emerge hand in glove with the victorious side—on *that* analysis, it can ill afford to deliver a bad product.

Currently, the Western security and military gaze is shifting from terrorism to 'combatting peer competitors' or the 'great-power rivals' Russia and China (Klare, 2019). As per Secretary of Defense Jim Mattis, 'Long-term strategic competition – not terrorism – is now the primary focus of U.S. national security' (cited in Klare, 2019). US political leaders will now be averse to making overtures to take a less bellicose posture towards the Kremlin and Putin. The framing of 'foreign interference' is also being revivified to target the 'usual suspects' narrative (Russia, China and states resisting the US hegemon). This framing is supported by strategic leaks from the relatively dark archive or through the intelligence filter. Finally, criticism and calls for further investigation of the forensic evidence of the particular casus belli will continue to be ridiculed as conspiracist or worse. Even a straightforward review of the record is subjected to an intelligence 'cancel culture'—as per the hybrid threat protocol—in which any suspicion of 'our' intelligence activities is equated with conspiracist thinking.

In September 2020, the Kremlin was alleged to have followed up its dismal public relations or hybrid war failure that was the Skripal incident with a further poisoning, this time of Russian opposition leader Alexei Navalny. Navalny fell ill on a flight between Moscow and Siberia, where he was treated in hospital and tested for chemical agents—of which it did not find evidence. Russia then permitted Navalny to be transported to Germany, where Angela Merkel announced that a military laboratory had 'identified unequivocally' that he was poisoned with a Soviet-era nerve agent (Olterman & Walker, 2020). It was then determined that the agent was Novichok. In actions replicating the Skripal case, Germany made official statements that expressed concern over the 'astounding act' and appealed to Russia to conduct an investigation (Olterman & Walker, 2020). It was reported that 'two independent European labs and the OPCW identified the toxin as 'belonging to the Novichok group (Bellingcat Investigation Team, 2020). Meanwhile, Russia asked for the test results and for an answer from Berlin to the Russian prosecutor general on the Russian inquiry (Olterman & Walker, 2020). Bellingcat published an article alleging that Russia's military intelligence agency (GRU) 'was responsible' and its security agency (the FSB) 'was behind' the attacks on Navalny as well as Skripal (Bellingcat Investigation Team, 2020) but noted that 'no law enforcement agency in any country' was investigating the poisoning of Navalny. Filling the gap, Bellingcat published details of its own investigation (and its methodology, with *CNN* and *der Spiegel* as investigative partners), that provided the names and passport photos of three 'operatives' from a 'clandestine unit' of the FSB who 'followed Navalky to the city of Tomsk where he was ultimately poisoned' (Bellingcat Investigation Team, 2020). Meanwhile the incident precipitated a 'fresh warning from the Chancellor's office' that it 'would not rule out sanctions against Nord Stream 2' (Olterman & Ambrose, 2020), a pipeline 90% complete and long an object of US foreign policy objection for its cementing of energy interdependencies between Germany and Russia (Boyd-Barrett, 2019).

Giddens (1986) refers to the 'absent totality', or the taken for granted 'peripheral' knowledge or information; it consists, for our purposes, of all of the 'settled facts' about Skripal, Douma, 9/11, Epstein, MH17 and countless such events. Statements in passing, concerning these 'settled facts'—such as 'KSM, the *mastermind of 9/11*', or 'Epstein, who *committed suicide* while awaiting a court date'—sit unremarkable in the background, blurred out of immediate consciousness, while also assisting the unconscious cognitive connections and narrative construction. The work of these peripheral facts is not peripheral to establishment media editors. They will be acutely conscious of the difference between 'Epstein, who died in custody' and Epstein, 'who committed suicide in custody.' Likewise, the Russian and Syrian poisonings are layered into the background as incontestable facts (such that any scepticism about them is deemed to be conspiracy theorising), providing the 'solid' totality that is then a ready reference as more of the same is piled on top.

What is made available for noting, particularly in relation to spectacular political events via significant political or cultural figures, may be manipulated by the strategic release of information from the archive, and through all of the distortions and misdirections brought to bear through information operations. If, as according to critical realists in law (critical realist studies), what the judge is eating for breakfast forms part of the tableau of the court and jurisprudence (does he eat factory farmed pork? is she careful to purchase strawberries not picked from exploited migrant labour?), the selections and intrusions of information into the publicly available archive is likewise what becomes the absent totality, shaping the consideration of likely suspects or logical motives for higher order crimes. Security intelligence ordering is accomplished, in part, through sectioning the political terrain and exploiting oblique references to what may be said to be there by those who also help to choose what cannot be seen.

The point here is that US intelligence would have had some additional intelligence of criminal actions in significant events from which to select the 'knowing' or strategic release and the layering of cover on the record. 'Rubicon' enabled the lead agencies in the US and Germany to make reference to 'facts' protected from further public scrutiny, in part because it is deemed legitimate to argue for the protection of the secret operation and its actors. That is to say, it permitted highly placed actors to develop a dark archive that, given the importance of staying on top of the public and private record of both friend and enemy actor intentions and motivations, permitted the selective parsing of that record according to the preferred ordering narrative of the day. As NSA whistle-blowers Edward Snowden and William Binney have shown, the latter regarding his program Thin Thread, a proper understanding of the object of intelligence must attend to proven practices and not only the mandated rhetoric. These practices are proactive in that they intrude into private lives only where there is something that may shift the establishment or ordering of preferences against those in a position to decide. Intelligence agencies seek to gain a kind of proprietorial relation with information that may have significant transactional or ordering implications (yes, also in the text in this book). When they collect and process information as intelligence and then have it developed in rarefaction and fellowship, they capitalise on the craft authority of the actors and the exclusive circulation of truth-making.

Politicising the Review of Political Crime

In traditional 'street crime', it is the relative politicisation of the courts, police and corrections that distinguishes a country or society by which is measured the level of corruption of criminal justice (as non-observance of the principles of legality in the rule of law). Vital to the persistence of the modern liberal and also social democratic ideal is the capacity of the ideological apparatus inclusive of civil society institutions. Horizontally and constitutionally, the separation of government branches is among the necessary devices; and an independent or free press, and other institutions such as a research academy, a rights-protective NGO sector, are likewise instrumental, either to check or extend political power. To ensure the vertical reviewability of executive authority, it is the relative bureaucratic, police and security separation that will be observed.

At the level of the apex crime (inclusive of acts involving intelligence agencies), a willing lightening of this liberal democratic ballast is to be expected (Berlinski, 2009). Agencies that are mandated or authorised to carry out investigations of breaches of international law or states' obligations to treaties or UN conventions may be politicised on the assumption that there is any case the so-called lesser evil, and that findings are in any event 'weaponised' for or against the preferred order of either the state or the enemies of the state (Buzan, 1999).

Consequently, high-echelon review, auditing or evaluation is corrupted and avoids truly independent fact finding. The review is an object, as we have previously mentioned, consistent with the strong belief that sovereignty ought to be maintained by security through the protection of the so-called existential preferences and exceptions. The *place* of the enactment of these exceptions is also then the locus from which actors will prefer or insist on being reviewed. For many in government, if security sovereignty is taken seriously by its practitioner-protagonists it will not do, as it might be expressed, to permit reviewing or auditing by anyone extraneous to the inner circle. The point is that if a criminal responsibility finding is to be made that may implicate international military and political action; thus, it will not surprise us to see states' attempts to minimise gross violations and the subservience of evidentiary and prosecutorial standards and requirements to the requirements of the hegemon, whoever that may be. That this is so should be quite familiar to most observers of politics and law. After all, the modernisation of the state through the principles, more or less observed, of legality was to set it up with a new legitimacy, the credibility of liberal democratic superiority (Wikse, 1978). Its defence from internal collapse requires the finessing of its optics.

The realm of corporate or political crime is similar with respect to this understanding of necessity and sovereign capacity. Economic actors 'know' the economic levers and the agents and actions that stimulate or retard economic growth or development. There is a blurring (or conflict of interest) where the identification of delegitimising forces or criminal action requires intimate knowledge of industry. 'Agency capture' is a term used to describe the quandary encompassing the necessity of intimate industrial knowledge on the part of regulatory actors that then too strongly enculturates those regulators to the values of industry, political expedience and careerism. Political actors are similarly confronted with a further or deeper problem in the democracy and legitimacy gap that arises where sovereign government action presumed to be for national security permits 'all means defensible' in its protection. Those capable of interrogating the deepest permutations or deep politics of these so-called protections are also ensnared in the confidentiality and secrecy requirements according to which the official narrative is chosen and perpetuated. Intelligence capture, like securitisation and agency capture, is the normalisation of national security necessity through the preferences of the intelligence community.

Institutions of criminal justice and international law are also prone to capture and this is a feature of the intelligence blur. Distinct priorities of criminal justice and rule of law legality are smudged out to accommodate the preferences emanating from the centre of deep intelligence. The brief on the necessary adaptations are provided by actors at the apex of the 'permanent' security intelligence bureaucracy to relatively captured careerists in oversight agencies. The politicisation of instruments of verification and administration of global security protocols, conventions and agreements has been the subject of a host of academic papers and reports. Beginning with the UNSC, it is almost axiomatic to understand it as an agency operating in relative dependence on interest groups including those representing arms manufacturers and weapons procurement (Shorrock, 2008). The representation of international 'atrocity crimes' in vehicles including the International Criminal Court (ICC) has notably slanted away from the US-led proxy wars (Chomsky, 2015).

Conclusion

With hybrid threat and the normalisation of information operations in the everyday of political and cultural discourse, the whodunnit of significant transactional incidents is at one level a check-up on public credulity or a pulse-taking for war or other-than-war engagements. In the meantime, the intelligence *blur* acts to disappear the forensics and crime of intelligence from the public record. Inserted into foreign policy, it is masked inside the architecture of a compartmented labyrinth.

The intelligence *blur* is then the means to discredit or render preposterous any inquiry that may reveal the evidence of such crimes. For example, in recommending the use of the 'conspiracy theory' to discredit Mark Lane's (1966) book and calls for a subsequent re-examination of the Kennedy assassination, the CIA engages in techniques deployed against the grain of the transparency, equality of arms adversariness and cross-examination of evidence.

The *blur* depends on exceptionalism, most importantly the modulation of the visibility element of the dispositive. Here visibility builds and is built into the security assemblage. This has consequences for how politics and security may be conceived. This is to say that systems of exclusion are not prior to the construction of the 'facade' of discursive formation. On the contrary, the style or modality of government involves a reading up of the approved or super-ordinate archive, a reading that not only cannot be fully informed, but that also, at a deep level, incorporates the expectation that there is no place of truth or light outside the endarkened archive.[20]

We may now extend our consideration of the institutional conflict between intelligence and criminal justice. They are differentiated in terms of visibility, accountability and common basis, among other dimensions. But these distinctions are too much predicated on the old normal in which classical liberalism is the template and intelligence crime the deviation. Following the normalisation of intelligence, or the routine insertion of its rhetoric and means—and drawing on its otherwise unseen archive—into everyday news, there is now an intelligence filter that recasts the everyday experience of culture and politics. As observed by Horn (2003), this new normal is consistent with what Deleuze and Guattari (1987: 352) refer to as the 'furore' of the warrior. In this regard, it embodies the 'immeasurable' and irruptive event, in its 'multiplicity'. It is not fixed into permanent strata but nomadic and de-territorialising. The ethos of the warrior brings:

> a furor to bear against sovereignty, a celerity against gravity, secrecy against the public, a power [puissance] against sovereignty, a machine against the apparatus.

Horn (2003: 63) avers that state knowledge and war knowledge may be contrasted. The state is fixed and rooted to place and forced to represent the problem of order in the subservience of force to law. It is reliant on but contrasted to the 'war machine', of which speed, secrecy, violence and cunning are the necessary dimensions.[21] So, welcome the 'furore' of the war machine. Gape in awe at crime that is much too cold before it is much too hot.

Notes

1. Roberto Gonzales wrote a memo for the Bush adminstration in january 25, 2002: 'This new paradigm renders obsolete Geneva's strict limitations on questioning of enemy prisoners and *renders quaint* some of its provisions requiring that captured enemy be afforded such things as commissary privileges' (emphasis added, quoted in Cohen, 2012).
2. In Dean's (2002: 37) view, the development of the liberal or modern police is a paradoxical hybridisation of cameralist persuasion by the coercive sovereign. According to analysts including Dandeker (1990), Holquist (1997), Dean (2002), and Donzelot (2008) modern liberal democracies depend on the cultivation of institutions of civil society through the generation of informational resources.
3. In Giddens' view (1986), the development of a relatively autonomous civil society meant that the coercive exercise of control needed to be supplemented, and in some cases supplanted, by informational control. There are some distinctions, but overall an uncertain democracy is countered by authoritarian certainties and this is accepted in respected scholarship. As Arendt (1973) has indicated, the response of political communities to the irreconcilable necessities of capitalism and liberalism produces adaptations, including authoritarian liberalism (Bruff, 2014).

4. Holquist is interested in the meaning of the surveillance documents as they were published by authorities who needed to be able to count on hearts and souls of conscripted soldiers on the front line. The Russian archives provided reports of surveillance organs of popular moods; these were systems aggregating attitudes. They provided the fodder for sculpting and gardening (Bauman, 2000) human material according to politico-societal interests.
5. Holquist observes that the differences between the Tsarist regime and the Soviet regime shows the expression of politics in surveillance. Where the Tsarist regime exercised policing only and minimally through interceptions of dissidents through their Black Offices (only 49 people), the Soviet regime learned about the whole population; it established 'information networks' and produced detailed summaries of popular opinion (10,000 officials) or near 'total' information on political moods. This was not specific to Bolshevism. All political regimes viewed politics as deriving from representation and legitimacy out of popular sovereignty and thus politics as tool for sculpting society 'operating on populations to realise this blueprint' (Holquist, 1997: 434). He notes that the emerging interest in surveillance or gathering and acting on opinion was modelled on the Cabinet noirs of Napoleonic France (438). In Germany, the interception of mail was also enormous in scale and the French began to rely on interceptions extensively in early 1917 when the mood of the army and population was concerning for it (419–424).
6. Which also concluded the Kennedy assassination to involve more than one gunman.
7. Unofficial strategic releases include what is also called 'white propaganda' or the dissemination of information through unofficial channels including media outlets.
8. Other advocacy organisations, like the neoconservative Foundation for the Defense of Democracies, helped to set up (counter) 'disinformation' projects like IranDisInfo to push regime change or US destabilisation campaigns and also, in early 2019, target Human Rights Watch and Iranian-American activists and journalists for their de-escalation work. The Iran Disinformation Project, launched in late 2018, was funded by the US Department of State's Global Engagement Center (Davison, 2019).
9. Gerald Ford acted as an inside informant on the Warren Commission for J. Edgar Hoover and the FBI, providing them with the names of Commission members (possibly Richard Russell and Hale Boggs) who were unconvinced by the lone gunman theory (Andrews, 2018).
10. The above paragraph is quoted in large part from de Lint (2020).
11. This involved the Pentagon Papers and then the break-in to Ellsberg's psychiatrist's office by the group connected to the Watergate hotel break-in to spy on the Democratic Party in a thread of connections that would prove very troublesome for the Nixon White House (see Ellsberg, 2003).
12. Please note, this paragraph is largely reproduced from de Lint and Bahdi (2012).

13. Some prominent recent conceptualizations of the conduct of conduct more or less follows the double-bind of the Foucauldian diagram (Foucault 1990: 140) and includes risk (O'Malley, 2004), insurance (Ericson et al., 2003), information (Poster, 1990) and contingency (Dillon, 2006). In addition, crime (Simon, 1997), security (Zedner, 2010), control (Deleuze, 1992; Garland, 2012), surveillance (Lyon, 2001), waste (Bauman 2013), unease (Bigo, 2002) and exclusivity (Young, 1999) is an articulation of anatomo-politics and the unfolding/collapsing liberal ideological project.
14. At the top echelon of political crime there is a blurring of interests and processes that feature the good faith presumption (de Lint & Kassa 2017). However, highly placed agency officials and actors within the judiciary (Chief Justice Warren) and legislative branches (the Gang of Eight) may be intoxicated by proximity to the nation's most important secrets and schooled to be unified behind the public relations of a bipartisan team. The nature of intelligence oversight and control is such that the executive and legislative branches will often lack the will and the ability to fully explore how and where adaptations or innovations to practice (consistent with criminal illegality) have taken root and flourish. As illustrated in the cases above and in Fig. 7.1, as a dispositive security intelligence is a web of sticky attachments that may involve highly placed political actors in criminal actions that, where exposed, compromise 'national security.' The bipartisan filtering that pertains to congressional intelligence reporting conserves cover where intelligence agency actors may support an equal opportunity compromising of Republican and Democratic leadership. For those not completely trusted with respect to official reporting and recording, the domain of intelligence crime research and analysis will suffer from a lacuna of strong evidence leaving it somewhat speculative and provisional. Self-reports, inspector-general reports as well as accountability audits are unlikely to be very useful as strong sources into what might actually be the story or narrative, given the secrecy, confidentially and national security barriers. And on the other side of the ledger, where information is power, access to privileged information acts like a tonic in government and industry. Losing clearance is experienced as excommunication, signalling severance from the intelligence authority and leading to disenchantment with it. In the meantime, accounts that are reliant on unauthorized whistle blower exposes and on the work of investigative journalists or disenchanted or 'fallen' agents may be dismissed as a salve to conspiracists.
15. External knowledge of security intelligence is developed on the basis of three broad types of information: authorized and unauthorized 'security leaks', official disclosures, and security oversights. There are two kinds of back-channel leaks, but both may be seen as covert divulgences: the first is an externally oriented, strategic or tacitly authorised release of information, information that has been surrendered unofficially but serves the overall organisational or policy aims of the security intelligence service.
16. The obverse of secrecy, persuasion (Wilsnack, 1980) gains in power (to a point) where there is plausible reference to a stock of excluded knowledge from which

it is drawn. Unless there is a legitimacy gap, if all one knows about the war with Oceana is what is provided in the dramatisation from official (Big Brother) or quasi-official sources (the *New York Times*) then one's view of the war effort is likely to be shaped through the tone of those releases. If what one thinks one knows is drawn from sources that are viewed as independent of government interests (but are actually products of systems of exclusion) that persuasive power is all the greater.

17. In the United States the NDAA reversed the Posse Comitatus Act that restricts the militarisation of domestic security order (see Dougherty 2008).
18. Noam Chomsky (2015) is among those to point out that the military procurement or industrial complex and oil interests are at least as powerful in lobbying U.S. presidential and congressional views with respect to foreign policy.
19. It may be at least provisionally accurate to claim that NGOs in civil society act to constrain military-market and military-state relations along the contours of international legal rules and obligations (insisting on compliance with the Geneva conventions, Nuremburg principles, the UNCHR, and a host of other provisions). However, as noted above that constraint is understood to be ancillary, dependent on perceived existential necessity, from which emanates national security exceptions to rule of law norms. As Schmitt (1988) argued, from the point of view of managing national security a dictatorship of liberal parliamentarianism is inferior to a dictatorship of the head of state. There are countless attempts to resolve the dilemma of the necessity of the norm-creating but boundless head of state. Even under offensive realism, the 'international system' in international relations is understood at least to subordinate the sovereign head to its disciplining properties. However, making the utterance that 'nothing is off the table' is merely to reiterate the meme of sovereign independence and to claim the legitimacy of acting with some contempt toward those who would willingly be subservient to exogenous 'rules-based' authorities and their enforcement. On the contrary, if these are to have power, they must be dominated by 'us' and *our* rules-based order.
20. Please note, this paragraph is reproduced from de Lint (2008) courtesy of *Windsor Yearbook Access to Justice*.
21. 'The war machine is Deleuze and Guattari's name for an unleashed and unlimitable enmity, a dynamic of all that is warlike: its capacity for metamorphosis and camouflage, for speed and a strategic relationship to space. Secrecy and the betrayal of secrets, disinformation and the violation of treaties, propaganda and conspiracy are elements of this war machine, which cannot be subsumed under the principles of national sovereignty. It is the modern partisan, the clandestine "irregular fighter" that could be called the paradigmatic embodiment of the Deleuzian war machine' (Horn 2003: 63).

References

Agamben, G. (1998/1995). *Homo sacer: Sovereign power and bare life* (D. Heller-Roazen, Trans.). Stanford, CA: Stanford University Press.

Al Jazeera. (2017). *The lobby: USA. Electronic Intifada.* https://electronicintifada.net/content/watch-film-israel-lobby-didnt-want-you-see/25876.

Altheide, D. (2019). *Media worlds in the postjournalism era.* Routledge.

Andrews, E. (2018) *9 Things you may not know about the warren commission.* History Commons. October 28. https://www.history.com/news/9-things-you-may-not-know-about-the-warren-commission.

Aradau, C., & Van Munster, R. (2009). Exceptionalism and the 'war on terror': Criminology meets international relations. *British Journal of Criminology, 49,* 686–701.

Arendt, H. (1973). *The origins of totalitarianism.* Houghton Mifflin Harcourt.

Bauman, Z. (2000). *Modernity and the holocaust.* New York: Cornell University Press.

Bauman, Z. (2013). *Wasted lives: modernity and its outcasts.* Wiley.

BBC News. (2019, July 24). *Facebook to pay record $5 billion to settle privacy concerns.* https://www.bbc.com/news/business-49099364.

Belllingcat Investigation Team. (2020, September 14). FSB team of chemical weapon experts implicated in Alexey Navalny Novichok poisoning. Bellingcat. https://www.bellingcat.com/news/uk-and-europe/2020/12/14/fsb-team-of-chemical-weapon-experts-implicated-in-alexey-navalny-novichok-poisoning/.

Berlinski, C. (2009). The dark figure of corruption. *Policy Review, 155,* 71.

Bernsten, C. (1977, October 20). The CIA and the media. *Rolling Stone.*

Bigo, D. (2002). Security and immigration: Toward a critique of the governmentality of unease. *Alternatives, 27*(1), 63–92.

Bigo, D. (2006). Internal and external aspects of security. *European Security, 15*(4), 385–404.

Blumenthal, M. (2020, May 14). 'The American friends': New court files expose Sheldon Adelson's security team in US spy operation against Julian Assange. *The Grayzone.* https://thegrayzone.com/2020/05/14/american-sheldon-adelsons-us-spy-julian-assange/.

Borer, D. A., Twing, S., & Burkett, R. P. (2014). Problems in the intelligence-policy nexus: Rethinking Korea, Tet, and Afghanistan. *Intelligence and National Security, 29*(6), 811–836.

Boyd-Barrett, O. (2019). The great game for EurAsia and the Skripal affair. *Media Imperialism: Continuity and Change,* 89.

Bruff, I. (2014). The rise of authoritarian neoliberalism. *Rethinking Marxism, 26*(1), 113–129.

Buzan, B. (1999). Change and insecurity reconsidered. *Contemporary Security Policy, 20*(3), 1–17.

Chomsky, N. (2015). *Rogue states: The rule of force in world affairs.* Haymarket Books.

Churchill, W., & Vander Wall, J. (1990). *The COINTELPRO papers.* Boston: South End. http://chinhnghia.com/Cointelpro_Papers.pdf.

Cohen, A. (2012, February 6). The torture memos: Ten years later. *The Atlantic.* https://www.theatlantic.com/national/archive/2012/02/the-torture-memos-10-years-later/252439/.

Cunliffe, I. (2020, August 17). Witness K in in the dock but institutions vital to Australia's democracy are on trial. *The Guardian.* https://www.theguardian.com/commentisfree/2020/aug/17/witness-k-is-in-the-dock-but-institutions-vital-to-australias-democracy-are-on-trial?CMP=Share_iOSApp_Other.

Curtis, M., & Kennard, M. (2019, November 14). Julian Assange's judge and her husband's links to the British military establishment exposed by WikiLeaks. Declassified UK. https://www.dailymaverick.co.za/article/2019-11-14-julian-assanges-judge-and-her-husbands-links-to-the-british-military-establishment-exposed-by-wikileaks/.

Dandeker, C. (1990). *Surveillance, power and modernity: Bureaucracy and discipline from 1700 to the present day.* Polity.

Davison, D. (2019, May 31). *Is the state department funding attacks on activists?* LobeLog. https://lobelog.com/is-the-state-department-funding-attacks-on-activists/.

de Lint, W. (2008). Intelligent security. *The Windsor Yearbook of Access to Justice, 26*(2), 195–240.

de Lint, W. (2020). Criminology 9/11. *Globalizations, 17*(7), 1157–1177.
de Lint, W., & Bahdi, R. (2012). Access to information in an age of intelligencized governmentality. In M. Larsen & K. Walby (Eds.), *Brokering access in information* (pp. 115–141). Vancouver: University of British Columbia Press.
de Lint, W., & Kassa, W. (2017). On Being bent for security: Barristers in terrorism prosecutions in Australia. *Journal of Law and Society, 44*(2), 169–199.
Dean, M. (2002). Liberal government and authoritarianism. *Economy and Society, 31*(1), 37–61.
deHaven-Smith, L., & Witt, M. T. (2009). Preventing state crimes against democracy. *Administration & Society, 41*(5), 527–550.
Deleuze, G. (1992). Postscript on the societies of control. *October*, 59(Winter), 3–7.
Deleuze, G., & Guattari, F. (1987). *A thousand plateaus* (B. Massumi, Trans.). Minneapolis: Minnesota University Press.
Dillon, M. (2006). Governing through contingency: The security of biopolitical governance. *Political Geography*. https://doi.org/10.1016/j.polgeo.2006.08.003.
Dobbs, M. (2014, October). The real story of the 'football' that follows the president everywhere. *Smithsonian Magazine.*
Donzelot, J. (2008). Michel Foucault and liberal intelligence. *Economy and Society, 37*(11), 15–34.
Dougherty, C. (2008). Necessity hath no law: Executive power and the posse comitatus act. *Campbell Law Review, 31*(1), 1–50.
Ehrman, J. (1995). *The rise of neoconservatism: Intellectuals and foreign affairs, 1945–1994.* Yale University Press.
Ellsberg, D. (2003). *Secrets: A memoir of Vietnam and the Pentagon Papers.* Penguin.
Ericson, R. V., Doyle, A., Barry, D., & Ericson, D. (2003). *Insurance as governance.* University of Toronto Press.
Fenton, K. (2011). *Disconnecting the dots: How 9/11 was allowed to happen.* Trine Day.
Ford, Derek R. (2019). US sovereignty must not be defended: Critical education against Russiagate. *Educational Philosophy and Theory, 51*(1), 14–17.
Foucault, M. (1972). The discourse on language. In *The archaeology of knowledge.* New York: Pantheon.
Foucault, M. (1988). The political technology of individuals. In L. Martin, H. Gutman, & P. Hutton (Eds.), *Technologies of the self: A seminar with Michel Foucault* (pp. 145–162). Amherst: University of Massachusetts Press.
Foucault, M. (1990). *The history of sexuality: An introduction Volume I* (R. Hurley, Trans.). New York: Vintage.
Garland, D. (2012). *The culture of control: Crime and social order in contemporary society.* University of Chicago Press.
Gibson, J. L. (1988). Political intolerance and political repression during the McCarthy Red Scare. *American Political Science Review, 82*(2), 511–529.
Giddens, A. (1986). Action, subjectivity and the constitution of meaning. *Social Action, 53*(3), 529–545.
Gill, P. (1994). *Policing politics: Security intelligence and the liberal democratic state.* Routledge.
Goddard, D., & Coleman, L.K. (1993). *Trail of the octopus: From Beirut to Lockerbie—Inside the DIA.* Bloomsbury.
Goodman, M. A. (2017). *Whistleblower at the CIA: An insider's account of the politics of intelligence.* City Lights Books.
Hanover, N. (2015, August 17). *The mighty Wurlitzer: How the CIA played America.* World Socialists Web Site. Wsws.org.
Holquist, P. (1997). Information is the alpha and omega of our work: Bolshevik surveillance in its pan-European context. *Journal of Modern History, 69*(3), 415–450.
Horn, E. (2003). Knowing the enemy: The epistemology of secret intelligence. *Grey Room, 11,* 58–85.
Huntington, S. P. (1997). *The clash of civilizations and the remaking of world order.* Penguin Books India.

Janowitz, M. (1961). *The professional soldier: A social and political portrait*. New York: Free Press of Glencoe.

Klare, M. (2019, June 2). *Tomgram: Michael Klare, fighting the next war, not the last*. TomDispatch.com. http://www.tomdispatch.com/post/176570/tomgram%3A_michael_klare%2C_fighting_the_next_war%2C_not_the_last/.

Kruh, L. (1988). Stimson, the black chamber, and the 'gentleman's mail' quote. *Cryptologia, 12*(2), 65–89.

Lane, M. (1966). *Rush to judgement*. New York: Holt, Rinehart, & Winston.

Lyon, D. (2001). *Surveillance society: Monitoring everyday life*. McGraw-Hill Education (UK).

Marchetti, V., Marks, J. D., & Wulf, M. L. (1974). *The CIA and the cult of intelligence*. New York: Knopf.

McGehee, R. W. (2015). *Deadly deceits: My 25 years in the CIA*. Open Road Media.

Mearsheimer, J. (2010). The gathering storm: Chinese challenge to US power in Asia. *Chinese Journal of International Politics, 3*(4), 381–396.

Mearsheimer, J. J., & Walt, S. M. (2007). *The Israel lobby and US foreign policy*. Macmillan.

Miller, G. (2020, February 11). The intelligence coup of the century: for decades the CIA read the encrypted communications of allies and adversaries. *Washington Post*. https://www.washingtonpost.com/graphics/2020/world/national-security/cia-crypto-encryption-machines-espionage/.

Miller, L., & Rampton, S. (2001). The Pentagon's information warrior: Rendon to the rescue. *PR Watch, 4*(8), 11–12.

Millman, O. (2020, June 12). Biden predicts military will intervene if Trump refuses to accept election loss. *The Guardian*. https://www.theguardian.com/us-news/2020/jun/11/joe-biden-donald-trump-military-election-lose.

Monger, D. (2012). *Patriotism and propaganda in First World War Britain: the national war aims committee and civilian morale*. Liverpool University Press.

Mueller, R. S. (2019). *Report on the investigation into Russian interference in the 2016 presidential election Volume I*. Washington, DC: US Department of Justice. https://www.justice.gov/storage/report_volume1.pdf.

Neocleous, M. (2006). From social to national security: On the fabrication of economic order. *Security Dialogue, 37*(3), 363–384.

Newman, J. (2008). *Oswald and the CIA*. New York: Carroll & Graf.

O'Malley, P. (2004). *Risk, uncertainty and government*. Routledge-Cavendish.

Office of the Director of National Intelligence (ODNI), National Intelligence Council. (2017, January 6). *Assessing Russian activities and intentions in recent US elections, intelligence community assessment 2017-01D*. https://www.dni.gov/files/documents/ICA_2017_01.pdf.

Olterman, P., & Ambrose, J. (2020, September 7). Alexei Navalny out of induced coma and is responsive, says Berlin hospital. *The Guardian*. https://www.theguardian.com/world/2020/sep/07/alexei-navalny-taken-out-of-induced-coma-and-is-responsive-berlin-hospital?CMP=Share_iOSApp_Other.

Olterman, P., & Walker, S. (2020, September 3). Alexei Navalny Novichok finding prompts calls for answers from Moscow. *The Guardian*. https://www.theguardian.com/world/2020/sep/02/alexei-navalny-poisoned-with-novichok-says-german-government-russia.

Paltrow, S. (2011, September 8). *Exclusive: National Archives sits on 9/11 Commission records*. Reuters. https://www.reuters.com/article/us-sept11-archive/exclusive-national-archives-sits-on-9-11-commission-records-idUSTRE7872QI20110908.

Pashakhanlou, A. H. (2013). Back to the drawing board: A critique of offensive realism. *International Relations, 27*(2), 202–225.

Pike, O. (1977). *CIA: The Pike report*. Bertrand Russell Peace Foundation.

Poster, M. (1990). *The mode of information*. Oxford: Polity Press.

Prouty, L. F. (2011). *The secret team: The CIA and its allies in control of the United States and the world*. Skyhorse Publishing.

Quinn, B. (2020, October 1). US intelligence sources discussed poisoning Julian Assange, court told. *The Guardian.* https://www.theguardian.com/media/2020/sep/30/us-intelligence-sources-discussed-poisoning-julian-assange-court-told.
Rajah, J. (2011). Punishing bodies, securing the nation: How rule of law can legitimate the urbane authoritarian state. *Law & Social Inquiry, 36,* 945.
Roach, K. (2010). The eroding distinction between intelligence and evidence in terrorism investigation. In N. McGarrity, A. Lynch, & G. Williams (Eds.), *Counterterrorism and beyond* (pp. 48–68). Abington: Routledge.
Robinson, P. G. (2019). Expanding the field of political communication: Making the case for critical propaganda studies. *Frontiers in Communication, 4,* 26.
Rose, N. (1999). *Powers of freedom: Reframing political thought.* Cambridge: Cambridge University Press.
Rosenfeld, S. (2012). *Subversives: The FBI's war on student radicals and Reagan's rise to power.* New York: Farrar, Straus and Giroux.
Schmitt, C. (1988). *The crisis of parliamentary democracy.* Cambridge, MA: MIT Press.
Scott, P. D. (1996). *Deep politics and the death of JFK.* California: University of California Press.
Shanker, T., & Schmitt, E. (2004, December 13). Pentagon weighs use of deception in a broad arena. *New York Times.* https://www.nytimes.com/2004/12/13/politics/pentagon-weighs-use-of-deception-in-a-broad-arena.html.
Shorrock, T. (2008). *Spies for hire: The secret world of intelligence outsourcing.* New York: Simon & Schuster.
Simon, J. (1997). Governing through crime. In Lawrence M. Friedman & George Fisher (Eds.), *The crime conundrum: Essays on criminal justice* (pp. 171–189). New York: Westview Press.
Smart, C. (2002). *Feminism and the power of law.* London: Routledge.
Suskind, R. (2006). *One percent doctrine: Deep inside America's pursuit of its enemies since 9/11.* Simon & Schuster.
United Nations Human Rights, Office of the Commissioner. (2019, November 1). UN expert on torture sounds alarm again that Julian Assange's life may be at risk. UNHR. https://www.ohchr.org/en/NewsEvents/Pages/DisplayNews.aspx?NewsID=25249.
United States Senate, 116th Congress. (2020). *Report of the select committee on Intelligence United States Senate on Russian active measures campaigns and interference in the 2016 U.S. Election: Volume 5—Counterintelligence threats and vulnerabilities.* Washington: US Government Printing Office. https://www.intelligence.senate.gov/sites/default/files/documents/report_volume5.pdf.
United States. Congress. Senate. Select Committee to Study Governmental Operations with Respect to Intelligence Activities, & Church, F. (1976). *Final report of the select committee to study governmental operations with respect to intelligence activities, United States Senate: Together with additional, supplemental and separate views.* US Government Printing Office.
US House of Representatives, Committee of Oversight and Government Reform. (2007, January 9). *Sandy Berger's theft of classified documents: Unanswered questions.* https://www.google.com/url?sa=t&rct=j&q=&esrc=s&source=web&cd=&cad=rja&uact=8&ved=2ahUKEwjd-KuDrtjrAhXxyzgGHRQlBjYQFjAAegQIAxAB&url=https%3A%2F%2Ffas.org%2Firp%2Fcongress%2F2007_rpt%2Fberger.pdf&usg=AOvVaw0-vecGIc33OVZVS4xjWKwz.
US House of Representatives (1978, April 20). The CIA and the media. Hearings, Subcommittee on Oversight, Permanent Select Committee on Intelligence, US House of Representatives.
Weaver, O. (1995). Securitisation and desecuritisation. In R. D. Lipshutz (Ed.), *On security* (pp. 46–86). New York: Columbia University Press.
Weber, M. (1994). The profession and vocation of politics. *Weber: Political Writings,* 309, 313–315.
Westby, J., Amnesty International, Big Data Researcher, (2019). 'The great hack:' Cambridge Analytica is just the tip of the iceberg. Amnesty International. 24 July. https://www.amnesty.org/en/latest/news/2019/07/the-great-hack-facebook-cambridge-analytica/.
Wikileaks. (2016, April 26). *Cruz firm readies for psychological ops at GOP convention.* DNC Emails Archive. Wikileaks.org. https://search.wikileaks.org/?q=Cambridge+Analytica.

Wikileaks. (2017, March 31). *Marble framework*. Wikileaks.org. https://wikileaks.org/vault7/#Marble%20Framework.
Wikileaks. (2020). *Vault 7*. CIA hacking tools revealed. https://wikileaks.org/ciav7p1/.
Wikse, J. (1978). Marx on authenticity and the liberal view of man. In M. McGrath (Ed.), *Liberalism and modern polity* (pp. 21–33). New York: Decker.
Wilford, H. (2009). *The mighty Wurlitzer: How the CIA played America*. Boston: Harvard University Press.
Wilsnack, R. W. (1980). Information control: A conceptual framework for sociological analysis. *Urban Life, 8*(4), 467–499.
Wise, D., & Ross, T. B. (1967). *The espionage establishment*. New York: Random House.
Woodward, A. (2020, April 16). Trump administration won't release 9/11 secrets to victims' families. *The Independent*. https://www.independent.co.uk/news/world/americas/us-politics/11-attacks-trump-documents-victims-families-ag-barr-a9469251.html.
Young, J. (1999). From inclusive to exclusive society: nightmares in the European dream. In *The exclusive society*. London: Sage.
Zedner, L. (2010). Security, the state and the citizen: The changing architecture of crime control. *New Criminal Law Review, 13*(2), 379–403.

Chapter 8
Conclusion

Introduction

Intelligence crime is observed but not attributed as such in countless books, articles and reports by investigative reporters, amateur or lay investigators and industry whistle-blowers. The task here has been to draw attention to crimes that involve intelligence actors or assets in the pursuit of policy or government objectives. A secondary task has been to provide a reasoned basis for an analysis of this type of malfeasance.

In this analysis it may be objected that we have fudged the distinction in conduct norms that belong under domestic public law and a host of provisions that cobble together expected conduct in foreign affairs. On the contrary, we are merely applying the constant of crime to domestic and foreign affairs where, as we have been frequently reminded, the classic liberal binary (citizen/non-citizen, crime/war) and its protections are no longer apt under authoritarian liberalism (Bruff, 2014) and an apparently permanent asymmetric warfare footing. The latter has been ushered in and used to excuse the erosion of protections (Gee, 2015) so that even US citizens may denied habeas corpus and assassinated on an intelligence assessment (Gross, 2009).

Yes, under the idealised form of classic liberal democracy, justice is visible and our governments depend upon informed consent. Government authority, in the ideal, is constrained through a balance of powers between branches of government. It is periodically tested in democratic processes (like free elections) and government action is known by mandate and authority is reviewable in its decision-making. What we are experiencing currently has been there all along, according to many observers (such as Neocleous, 2006) but is now ironically more visible and also more provocatively justified by its famous advocates across establishment political parties.

That said, there is a distinction or binary that remains quite evident arising from the presumptive standpoint. Where the intelligence crime is committed by 'us' and in advance of security policy, there is a powerful counter-forensics on the side of

W. B. de Lint, *Blurring Intelligence Crime*,
https://doi.org/10.1007/978-981-16-0352-5_8

government. It is not everyday practice that a defence team will have the capability to close off and control access to the scene of the alleged criminal act, interview witnesses, collect exculpatory evidence under a robust chain of custody, place under seal from prosecution all information until it is proven to have evidentiary value, or pass all potentially exculpatory forensic evidence to its technicians and analysts for reporting to a court. The government can do all of this on the promise or oath of carrying out these activities to a high standard of citizen (or defendant) ethics.

This is because intelligence crime divides actors into patriots and insurgents. For other crimes, it may be permissible to celebrate justice for the opposing side to the victim, but where the victim of intelligence crime is also the protagonist in the ideological battle that is an ice cold war, investigators will face pressure to review an investigation in terms of how it will help the enemy. In the cases of 9/11, MH17 and Douma, the investigative bodies were compromised by political interest or the examination of the evidence was incomplete or unable to provide a reliable account of the fatal inconsistencies, or both.[1]

Therein lies the rub. Whereas it is efficient and necessary that in a liberal democracy there is a presumption that public officials will exercise their duty in good faith for the public good, that assumption does not hold on the common sense interpretation where an organisation or institution has a long record of deceptive practices for which it has infrequently been held responsible or accountable. Where the intelligence blur is in the frame, the performance of the authorities can be expected to deviate from the everyday; but that this is definitively the case is not easily provable given the efforts at concealment that are supported by all levels of government. This, then, is not a book about crime discovery as such, but about how crime is discovered and framed through power-knowledge, and specifically the intelligence dispositive.

We contrasted the quest for certainty in forensics and intelligence (in Chaps. 2 and 3). As we observed in Chap. 2, there are standards employed to minimise contextual bias and maximise the independence of the investigator and forensic examiner, on the prima facie experience that crime will be reviewed politically the more political the crime. Related to the power-knowledge concept, a criminal incident is brokered institutionally. In the ideal-type, criminal justice seeks a legal order, forensic science seeks a scientific order and intelligence seeks a sovereign order (to maintain the vitality of the sovereign). As we have observed in Chap. 3 and in other places in this book, an open investigation may be anathema to the requisites of certainty where government must nominate itself in the role of the complainant and in this way establish the parameters of the investigation. When it does this through a criminal justice dramatisation, it represents itself in a process usually against a more or less absent or hobbled adversary. To close the circle, this process does not occur in open or adversarial contestability, but through the prism of the information operations that mediate big crime.

In this regard, no-one has access to the full archive of intelligence crime and particularly the apex or big crime variant, and whoever possesses transactive intelligence is also unlikely to be in a position to share it without risk or permission. This is a conundrum, to be sure, and it has left the official narratives largely in place, reproduced as if unproblematic in academic discourse and available records review. Yes, and as has been explored here, there is a glimpse of what may be transpiring in the dark, which in rare circumstances sees daylight (as in the case of the *Rainbow Warrior* bombing). This, however, rarely sets us off track from the affirmation that the routine actions of our state actors are unremarkable and certainly not criminal. That the aberration is really in the exposure rather than the practice is lost in the everyday interpretation of the event, as supported by establishment media and academic review. For the most part, the minority position that such actions are not irregular is dismissed because it cannot replicate the means of access to evidence (and its smudging) enjoyed by vested government authorities.

What is presented here is that minority view. It will run counter to the consensus of official and scholarly opinion. It is partial, incomplete, and even partisan. As discussed previously, knowledge is dependent on institutional power relations; this is what is meant by power-knowledge; those who can, refer to by a nudge and a wink to an absent totality or to the public scatology of the intelligence archive. This is not to discount that some accounts will survive the scrutiny of multiple authorities, but others will fail in short order. We assert that the lack of institutional resolve to identify or discover, test and analyse evidence that inculpates the intelligence criminal should not be depended upon to claim the relative innocuousness of intelligence crime impact.

The concluding chapter is traditionally about remedy. However, reference to a positive resolution is merely hopeful rhetoric; in practice it will be a little too optimistic given what has been observed in this book and referencing the necessary imperviousness of transactional actors. Given the meta-rhetoric or double-speak of reforms (reliant on obdurate practices and offering plausible legality), it is at best naïve and at worst contradictory to present a wish list of remedies. Readers or actors individually do not possess the power-knowledge locus to take the measures that in any case have been frequently called for. That said, it is sensible to make the call for counter-intelligence and national security non-proliferation agreements or treaties. These are needed to arrest the troubling escalation of information operations (particularly in hybrid threat tools and services) that now threaten to produce deep scepticism and 'conspiracy theorising' about all 'facts' that concern political opinion and security, military or strategic matters. This is merely wishful, of course, as such reforms will not be accepted or adopted (or there will be great fun in lying about their adoption) by any nation-state actor or security-intelligence consortium that enjoys the capacity of resistance.

Here, we do not seek to propose a remedy for weaknesses in the presumptive frame. Instead, as suggested in previous chapters, the objective is somewhat more limited, provisional and perhaps nuanced. In this analysis, the assumption is that crimes that may be committed by actors who are supported by our intelligence agencies or national security interests will fall outside the defaults of crime scene investigation and forensic examination. It is necessary to specify some of those defaults in order to provide support for this argument, which is otherwise obvious from the objective of national security legislation. Again, while the point is plain to non-specialised observers, it fails to be registered in most scholarly review; even in most critical accounts of the crimes of the powerful there is inadequate regard for how big crimes may escape adequate scrutiny by scholars because of the reliance on representations of crime events that are produced by interested authorities and official summaries of the evidence archive. Departures from regular or routine practices may be indicative of the presence of criminal intelligence actors, and such aberrations of crime scene and forensic protocol may be 'trace evidence' or 'fingerprints' of an intelligence malfeasance. This is the preferred frame of critical forensics.

In what follows we will present a few summary observations. Below are listed the elements of intelligence crime in terms of objectives, means and actors:

- Objective
  - advance the sovereign's or sponsor's strategic position.
  - achieve sponsor's information operations objectives.
- Means
  - identify (distinguish)
    - make target distinctions based on an ordering principle or ideology (dimensions are consistent with key elements of bias or hate crime)
  - Compromise (dominion)
    - use tradecraft (covert transactions in discrete, compartmentalised actions)
    - draw target into (il)licit networks (maintain in place)
  - Action (harvest)
    - in its common variation, covert 'direct action' to neutralise the target
    - in its apex variation, direct action inclusive of terror or a 'shock and awe' spectacle
  - Redirect (account)
    - exploit information operations to secure preferred victim attribution in a pre-conceived narrative.
    - exploit national security exceptions to fend off criminal justice review
- Actors (either/or)
  - Covered (assets) - deniable, untraceable or compromised (covered by legends, confidentially, oaths, etc.).
  - Cloaked (agents)—deniable, sequestered, defended, decriminalised (eg. pardoned)

Security Intelligence and Intelligence Crime[2]

Much of the modern liberal understanding of law, security and crime depends on a bifurcation according to which the internal affairs of the state are guided by the pastoral order (care of each and all, maximisation of economy, cultivation of expectations through predictabilities of the rule of law, attention to quotidian needs), and external affairs are conditioned by the existential order (each against all, territorial imperatives, relations of unease) (Valverde, 2008; Bigo, 2002). Currently, we see a blending of the exceptional and the quotidian, evident especially in the internal operation of security and policing.[3] If sovereign law still requires subjects that are differentiated through a process of exclusion or, as per discipline, through a process of reform, managing the beast within has required regulatory and preventative governance or an articulation between sovereignty and biopolitics, or traffic regulation that distinguishes licit from illicit flows. Following Foucault, this is evident in the normalisation of the exception, and in the immobilisation of the political (Mouffe, 2006) by the power-knowledge of the security intelligence dispositive. It is also seen in the stretching or breaking of political rationality or the concrete expression of the connective tissue between the state's knowledge of its conditions and preconditions and intelligence practices and techniques.

The phenomenon is apparent in the reversal of the predicate as exclusions at the level of everyday life are made to satisfy the appetite for exception in the normalisation of necropolitics (Mbembe, 2019). Accordingly, a security dispositive emanates from the kernel of the sovereign contained by dominion to develop a networked power-knowledge capable of claiming the right to kill or expose to death through political violence any cohort or population, whether local of foreign.

Indeed, the study of intelligence in this way also explores how the politics of exception, the power to make sovereign decisions about life and death, is infiltrating to heterogenous organisations alongside or inside quotidian security strategies. In the broadest sense of the term, police surveillance and information operations do indeed contribute to how individuals may be visible and actionable in their political ontology to government authority and in the mobilisation of security, but the special relationship with visibility that characterises intelligence may suggest a further iteration of political rationality. If security is a discursive formation then it involves another instance of practices that articulate objects and subjects of rule for sovereign-intelligence modality and modulations. That is to say, if security as a discursive formation or dispositive is embedded in the practice of policing, it might be argued that sovereign-intelligence is a further unfolding of discursive practices that is attended by a distinctive set of ontological and epistemological preconditions.[4]

What we are calling the intelligence blur depends on exceptionalism, most importantly the modulation of the visibility element of the dispositive. The argument here is that exceptionalism also girds population and quotidian security. A naturalisation of the friend/enemy binary in the everyday administration of justice and of forensic agencies has consequences; it works to 'bend' institutions in support of the big fight. Thus, systems of exclusion are not prior to the 'faciality' of discursive formation (that is why the building of patterns by looking for effects or by inspecting the archives of subordinate narratives). On the contrary, the style or modality of government may involve a reading up of the approved or super-ordinate archive, a reading that not only cannot be fully informed, but at a deep level rests on the assumption that access to information depends on a careerism and elite position in the security establishment, and the standpoint for the rest is normally and rightfully one of blind trust and endarkenment. This element of the dispositive of liberal democratic states is what is highlighted here.[5]

Crimes Too Big to Prosecute and Political Retrenchment

Durkheim (1975) is familiar to sociologists and criminologists as the father of structural functionalism and for making the point that the nature of social reaction to crime is somewhat determinative or constructive of the social norm. Social solidarity depends on a consensus response; the social response is calibrated to the outrageousness of the crime stimulus. The alternative is a state of derangement, of anomie, a condition that has served as solidarity's antithesis in much thinking about crime.

Durkheim's focus was on the relation between crime and the social order. The maintenance of the political order is not frequently explained as a function of crime and through concepts of criminology, except by critical and radical criminologists, and by Black (1983), who referred to the functionality of crime control as a form of self-help. Black has had much to say that is instructive about the behaviour of criminal law and particularly how it operates to harness properties that possess social or cultural value, including established expectations of conduct. So, for instance, where someone is aggrieved because of a loss or harm perceived to have resulted from a discarding of a reasonable expectation there may be a resort to self-help, which is 'the expression of a grievance by unilateral expression such as personal violence or property destruction' (Black, 1983: 34). One take-away from this is that crime also emanates from the assertion of some form of order (or social control, for Black). As we shall see, there is a circularity here that recalls Tilly's (1985) point regarding the emergence of the political order from organised lawlessness. When Ericson (2007) uses the term 'counter-law' as inclusive of surveillance and laws that undermine rule of law legality, the concept is also a reflection on a nostalgic view of law's purity, or independence from sovereignty or raw power (see also Smart, 2002).

Perhaps this nostalgia is what some of us encounter with much radical criminology as it reviews crime from the standpoint of revolution or political alterity. For many if not most of us on the critical side of the ledger, the relation of crime to the political order is understood as a matter of the differential power of a ruling elite or class. Law and order are presumptively presented from the point of view of the political ideology of liberalism, neoliberalism and capitalism. For scholars including Quinney (1970), Box (2002) Wacquant (2009), Bruff (2014) and others, the expropriation of valued resources (including labour) for private profit depends on a system of official disenfranchisement and marginalisation that is secured by criminalisation, banishment and imprisonment.

The view that the response to crime may restore political order is part of quotidian, everyday or unconscious noting (Giddens, 1986). If crimes are useful to the social, why should they not be useful to the political? Concerning so-called street-level crimes of murder and assault, drug trafficking and sexual exploitation, many political campaigns have been successfully run on the back of a conjectured failure to harness the tools of the state to properly respond to the criminal threat. The 'tough on crime' campaigns have secured an authoritarian neoliberal political order (Wacquant, 2009; Bruff, 2014) and, in doing so, they invoke a culture of fear or unease (Bigo, 2002); indeed, they may go further still and game the conditions that push towards the more authoritarian remedy (de Lint & Kassa, 2015). In this effort, in the lead up to the November 2020 elections, President Trump attempted to launch a law and order campaign by sending federal agencies out to democratic cities and where, according to his second impeachment indictment, he was supporting a failed campaign by *causing* civil unrest.

This is where a reliance on crime for politics cosies up to a reliance on political actors for crime. The positive duty to protect may be implicitly or explicitly withheld. The political is the distribution of self-help according to certain interests and values (Black, 1983). The state may choose not to send resources for policing or security to certain places, and this may stem from the simple expedient that without an adequate tax base there are too many 'free riders' (Spitzer & Scull, 1977). On the other side, police may be sent to quell a public protest with maximum force to send a message on behalf of the political leadership (de Lint & Hall, 2009: 274–280). In counter-terrorism cases, police may be paying an informant to purchase bomb-making equipment or to encourage an adrift youth to take action amounting to a terrorism crime (Aaronson, 2011).

With apex crime we have been concerned with crimes that have a potential or manifest impact on the political order. By most common understanding, political homicide and terrorism involve an outrage against a political target. The conservative response is to use the event as a means to assert nationalistic sentiments and lament the decay of traditional mores. The liberal response is to review and *depoliticise* the matter as the relative deprivation of liberal freedoms and individual or civil rights. The radical response is to note the event as an indication more or less of the total failure of the political ideology. In short, the critique of political restoration is that it is too muted (conservative), too strong (liberal) or too contradictory (critical), and ultimately too doomed (radical). In the meantime, criminologists on the whole have not been interested in problematising this class of acts or have thought their classification to be overcome by subjectivity or arbitrariness. Qualitatively such acts may not merit candidacy for inquiry, and quantitatively they are infrequent and irregular and as such provide weak scaffolding for theory or policy. As per the postmodern review, these critiques or reviews 'understand' the political as by default inert or reactive.

In this regard, academics, politicians, journalists and cultural leaders are more likely to hedge on how and to what extent elite political interests become consensus values. Liberalism is popularly understood in the United States and elsewhere as a cushion between capitalism and democracy. Even where liberal analysts accept that elites may be organised and furtive, that furtive organisation is said to be exposed by means of liberal institutions that then are touted as essential if the reconciliation between democracy and capitalism is to continue on. In this accord, there is a reluctance to observe that in their operations liberal institutions may be working more in the preservation of values that are anathema not only to classic liberalism and democracy, but also to a free market. In the pivotal domain of intelligence and security, NGOs represent the front line of the 'rules-based order'. The US wishes to instrumentalise, discipline or dominate liberal institutions such as the OPCW, bringing it into the security-intelligence dispositive; refined liberal distinctions are encouraged to act as such, but to uphold these distinctions is not to violate the 'root' us/them binary of the international system. A democratic order is the visible means, but beneath that visibility is the internecine conflict between natural law and justice values and the raw necessity of realist might.

In the event, there is a reluctance to 'see' in this that there is a motive, plan and a furtiveness in its accomplishment. In other words, there is a reticience to attribute to significant political events the machinations of 'dark actors' or 'dark actor-networks', inclusive of their criminality. On the contrary, it is in their blundering ineptness or dismal pettiness that such actors and agencies are regularly depicted as motivated. Such is the reluctance that there is a lacuna of work that investigates the gap between popular accounts of covert elites and academic scholarship. The concept and discourse of 'conspiracy' has been used to fill in this gap.

A Conspiratorial Re-View: Radical Scepticism and Critical Forensics[6]

Hofstadter (2012) identifies belief in conspiracy as a 'paranoid style' of politics that is dangerous to liberal democracy. Scepticism of government accounts of events or phenomena and the suspicion that such events may have involved secret conniving or planning by well-placed actors is a view that entered sociology with the elite theorists, including Pareto (1966), Mosca (1961), and Michels (Nye, 1977), a theme taken up by C. Wright Mills (1956). According to Inglehart (1997: 79), especially in the more 'advanced societies' there is a 'diminishing confidence that science and technology will solve humanity's problems'. The decline of trust in mainstream media and other institutions has supported the search for answers in alternative authorities, and this has stimulated interest in and fear of conspiracy theories.

Belief in 'some kind of conspiratorial narrative' is endorsed by over half of the US population (Oliver & Wood, 2014: 953). At a time when the establishment news media is increasingly regarded as untrustworthy or deficient with respect to its selectivity of topics, accuracy of facts and journalistic assessment (Kohring & Matthes, 2007: 239), and thus as 'manufacturing consent' (Herman & Chomsky, 2010), there has been a shift to social and alternative media where expert discourse is doubted in a pushback against knowledge stratification.

Dentith and Keeley (2018) distinguish between *generalist* and *particularist* conspiracy. Generalists say that conspiracy thinking is already *irrational* and the belief in conspiracy in the thinking of the person unwarranted. Also, generalists tend to think that anyone smitten by one conspiracy belief is prone to believe in multiple conspiracy theories (Sunstein & Vermeule, 2009). Particularists will investigate each conspiracy theory to check its irrationality or basis against the available evidence. Dentith and Keeley (2018) reject the tautological view that conspiracy thinking is already irrational (Popper, 2006; Sunstein & Vermeule, 2009). Dentith and Keeley (2018) argue that dismissing sceptics as 'conspiracy theorists' on the view that believers in one conspiracy will be believers in others is to be indifferent to the fact that in social and political life specific conspiracies have been exposed by intrepid journalists and others. There is no clear road to debating irrational believers, they maintain, because people in 'attitude-consistent silos' (Miller et al., 2016: 824) will be immune to pluralism, logic and fact-based evidence. A cultural studies perspective similarly rejects the generalist position, maintaining that 'conspiracy theorizing' is 'supported by real historical events and embodies a radical form of reflexivity, criticism and scepticism about every truth claim' (Aupers, 2012: 24).[7]

Douglas et al. (2019: 4–5) define 'conspiracy belief' as belief in a specific conspiracy theory and also 'conspiracy thinking' or 'conspiracy mindset' as proneness or tendency or preference in choosing explanations of events in terms of conspiracist dimensions. Alongside generality the key dimension of conspiracy is the rationality of the explanation of a phenomenon (Dentith & Keeley, 2018). I would propose that the attribution of rationality is a function of power/knowledge or the explanation's location or embeddedness within and across established disciplinary formats (Foucault, 1972). An irrational argument is one which violates internal incongruence or relations of logic or being. Within a discipline, a poor argument is one which does not follow the conventions or format of discursive coherence. What often makes the attribution of conspiracy irrational is the nature of its connection or association with other, relatively precarious explanations in a meta-narrative.

On these dimensions an explanation may be offered within the frame of conventional or establishment discourse that lacks logical coherence, as represented by 'c.' On the other hand, an explanation can fall outside of the assumption basket of establishment or official discourse and still offer a logical coherence, as represented by 'b'. There are also many explanations of events that will be pro-establishment and nevertheless irrational (some claims regarding 'crimes by them' will fall into this quadrant). Lastly, there is the most frequently occupied space, where the anti-establishment explanation is irrational (see Fig. 8.1).

A-D, Establishment View of Anti-Establishment Conspiracy

What the establishment media most often offers is a simplification 'a-d.' Accordingly, there is a presumption that the anti-establishment explanation is by default irrational (and gathers up other irrational explanations—as per 'b-d' below) and the pro-establishment explanation is by default rational and supports and is supported by other rational disciplinary discourses.

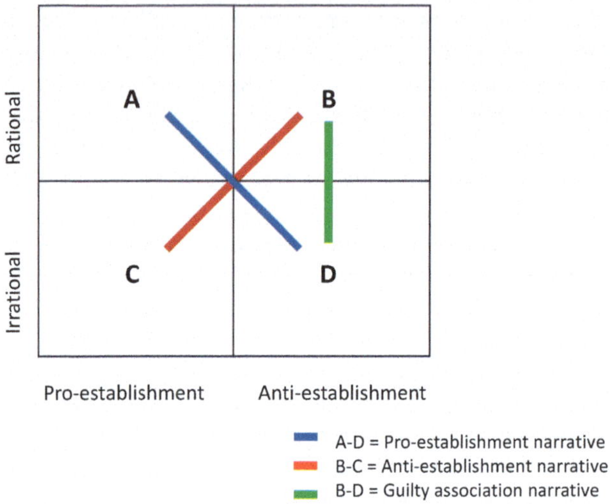

Fig. 8.1 Conspiracy Formats by Establishment and Rational Discourse

Within establishment news reporting media, there is an editorial convention to bundle alternative to official explanations of events including 9/11 and 7/7 together with generalist and irrational conspiratorial viewpoints and their protagonists.

For example, *The Guardian* ran a story under the headline 'Who really blew up the twin towers', a headline, by the way, that probably inadvertently states that the twin towers *were blown up*. The story features reference to 9/11 Scholars for Truth, a group of 75 university professors that the Guardian paraphrases as 'determined to prove that 9/11 was a hoax' (Asquith, 2006). *The Guardian* attempts to discredit the views of these scholars as irrational, or 'based on bad science,' citing a professor of fire protection engineering, Jonathan Barnett, before going on to claim that 'many of the 9/11 scholars have a history of defending conspiracy theories… and that "global secret societies" control the world (Asquith, 2006)

The result of this practice is demonstrated in Fig. 8.2, where 'David Ray Griffin' is used as the single search term in the Gale Onefile News database (12 November 2020). David Ray Griffin is best known for several books critical of the official 9/11 narrative. As can be seen from the figure below (Fig. 8.2), the main association is not 9/11, but conspiracy.

B-C, Anti-Establishment View of Establishment Conspiracy

On the flip side, what we see in the narrative of many critics of apex crimes and elite conspiracies is a 'b-c' dyad. In this, an anti-establishment view of the phenomenon is supported by means of rational discourse and the official or pro-establishment view is irrational.

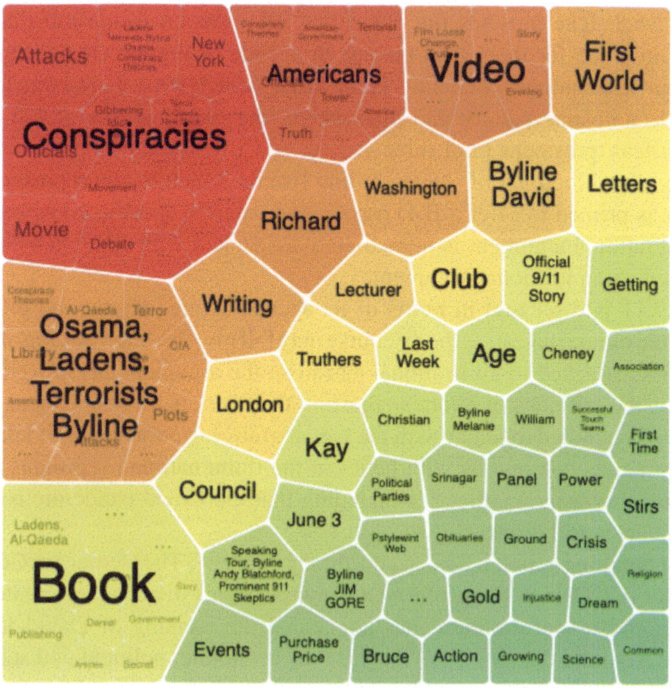

Fig. 8.2 Gale Onefile News Term Cluster: 'David Ray Griffin'

Taking 9/11 for illustration, there is reasoned argument in a vast quantity of literature and commentary, almost none of which is engaged in academic journals, that criticises the official narrative and/or offers an alternative conspiracy theory. The standpoint of groups like Architects and Engineers for Truth on 9/11 is that there is a lack of reason or logic in the official narrative. It is, as David Ray Griffin documents, full of distortions, lies and omissions. Some, like van der Pijl (2019), support the view that Israel-associated agents had a hand in 9/11. Van der Pijl, a political scientist who has authored dozens of refereed journal articles and books in prestigious venues, has made his arguments consistent with the rigour of mainstream academic discourse, but Van de Pijl is not invited as an exemplar of 9/11 criticism by mainstream media.

B-D, Guilt by Association: David Icke

One or two further possibilities are of interest. For instance, there may be a pattern, 'b-d', a 'guilty association narrative', where persons espousing anti-establishment theories of conspiracy seek to place a rational argument against the official narrative concerning an event within a generalist and irrational metanarrative involving multiple conspiracies.

At one level, Icke presents the claim that 9/11 was an inside job that put the conditions in place for the US to pursue an agenda of regime change. In this, he is consistent with authors including Peter Dale Scott (1996). However, Icke links this event to a cosmic pattern and plan where 'the illuminati' or global elite and every American president (and three British and two Canadian prime ministers) are of a reptilian bloodline of shape-shifting lizards. Much media representation of apex crime is primed to offer a B-D association where a specific conspiracy claim involving a rational argument is immediately associated with generalist conspiracy claims based on an irrational argument.

Where 9/11 is discussed in terms of its agents, actors, causes and effects in a critique of the official narrative the discourse may fall into 'b', but where an alternative explanation is attached to an irrational narrative, the argument has moved into 'd.' Importantly, the critiques of Scott, suggesting that there is a conspiring agency, are quite routinely bundled together with the metanarrative irrationalities of Icke, so that 9/11 conspiracy is continuous with belief in the illuminati and reptilians and with other irrational conspiracy theories including that the Covid pandemic is a plot to establish a new world order.

Another bundling is that between conspiracy and hate. The Center for Countering Digital Hate (CCDH), a nonprofit NGO 'that seeks to disrupt the architecture of online hate and misinformation' has applauded the banning of David Icke from Twitter and Youtube. Its aim is to 'increase the economic, political and social costs of all parts of the infrastructure - the actors, systems and culture - that support, and often profit from hate and misinformation' (Counterhate.co.uk). The site bundles identity-based hate, climate change denial and health misinformation with 'shoddy journalism' and misinformation' and works with 'practitioners in diverse fields, such as political science, behavioural psychology, neurology, the law, countering violent extremism (CVE), counterterrorism and child protection to develop strategies that strengthen tolerance and democracy and counterstrategies to new forms of hate and misinformation.'

CCDH founder and CEO, Imran Ahmed, who also sits on the steering committee of the UKs Commission for Countering Extremism, has involved itself in a campaign to de-platform David Icke. Icke is regularly censured by reference to hate speech, and there is a concerted effort to hoist Icke in support of the tie-in between hate speech and misinformation and general conspiracy, where a wildly irrational position and general conspiracy concerning a secretive elite is offered to support censorship for the protection of vulnerable groups (which is the hate speech assumption).

To illustrate, the irrational conspiracist and the person offering a rational critique of alleged government cover-up ends up with more or less equal associations of general conspiracy. In the Gale Onefile News database (November 12, 2020) (Fig. 8.3), the search term David Icke yields the same first order conspiracy association as does David Ray Griffin.

Ironically, by branding sceptics who question government accounts 'conspiracy theorists', various state-supported actors have been given relative discursive freedom to carry out what deHaven-Smith and Witt (2009) calls state crimes against democracy (SCAD). Even alternative political journals may be reticent to investigate this

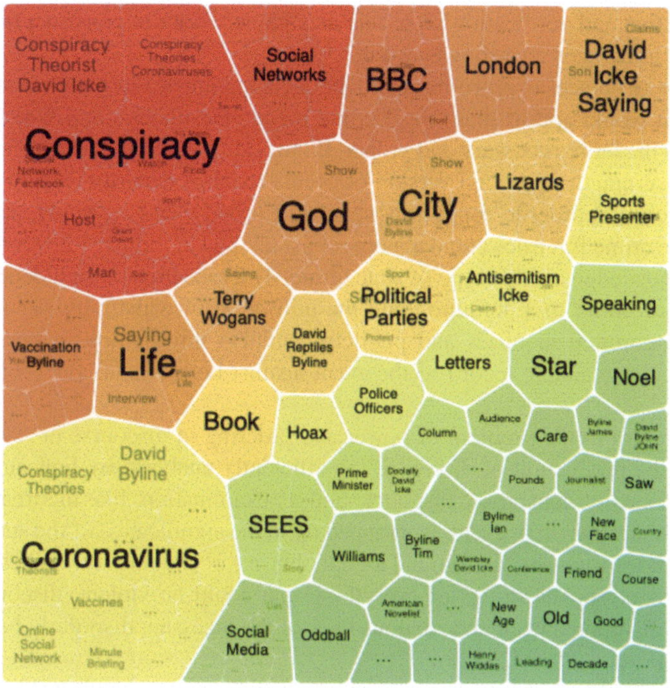

Fig. 8.3 Gale Onefile News Term Cluster: 'David Icke'

terrain; they may believe there is not much with regard to the alternative narratives to investigate; on the other hand, they may fear that if they do the label 'conspiracy theorist' will damage their integrity. So, while a portion of government action is committed to acting without public exposure, to suggest that furtive government actors plan to do things and keep them from us is to risk being brushed aside with the generalist conspiracy label. In the meantime, a significant segment of government *is* engaged in the 'paranoid style'.

Summary

The fraught epistemology of apex and intelligence crime has divided academic and popular discourse and accounts. There is very little scholarly work that has attempted to bridge the divide between the government and 'conspiracy' narratives, largely because there is a presumption that scholarship must depend on official records if it is to be robust. However, this reticence on the part of academics does not stand up where the researcher takes seriously the proposition that crimes may be organised by state actors, and may involve information control (such as cover-up or confidentiality agreements), and that therefore alternative-to-official sources of information and their collection and verification protocols may be necessary to construct rational or reasonable inferences regarding an event.

If governments seek to prevent or quell the development of alternative 'conspiracy' narratives it would appear that robust crime scene investigation and forensic practices are all the more necessary and proper. If the reality of intelligence crime is such that the government or official version of events requires departures from standard or best practice in order to support its version of order, then case study analyses of intelligence crime forensics entail a more robust method of inquiry into (and thereby building knowledge of) this type of state crime. The case method will depend upon selection according to a definition and the utilisation of whistle-blower accounts, public and coronial inquiries and publicly available information in the effort to crosscheck the available record of the event against both official and 'conspiracy' narratives.

Let us return to the problem of power and ordering in discourse or 'systems of control in the production of discourse' so efficiently analysed by Foucault (1972: 224). The locus of conspiracy discourse and its examination, like the treatment of the official narrative of an event, is wrapped up in the significance of the state (if not society). It is informed by 'a profound logophobia, a sort of dumb fear of these events, of this mass of spoken things of everything that could be violent, discontinuous, querulous, disordered even and perilous in it, of the incessant disorderly buzzing of discourse' (Foucault, 1972: 229).

This logophobia is driven by an aversion to discontinuity, and in this aversion may be the basis of the wish that a consensus view may be transposed with reference to a 'wider' (more accurately merely a more opaquely partisan!) ideological root. Foucault notes on the contrary that these discourses must be understood in their specificity and discontinuity, which is to say their incapacity to project a presumptive deeper and greater truth residing in the archive (Foucault, 1972: 229).

To now bring this back again to what is in play with the newfound interest in the attachment of 'conspiracy belief' or 'conspiracy mindset', our logophilia and phobia is now where Foucault saw them half a century ago. After the postmodern turn, there is an absorption of deep scepticism and a distrust of positive methodologies that appear too much to bring under the control of a final disposition the disorder or irruption of events. It is not necessary to accept this account in its entirety. Making a spectacle out of ordering is the cynical sidebar and may well be a strong legacy of 9/11. Such events also are not happily accounted for by reference to revolution, reversal or a successor ideology. Consequent to this observation, the charge of irrationality is now not quite sufficient to discredit the conspiracist, specific or general. However, absent a powerful ordering tonic, the future may be medieval in its disconnections. Especially where the event is made up for an ordering pivot, the position of the accuser must be unavoidably partisan and embedded. Social media silos in being somewhat cast adrift, are disconnected. As we have explored, they are relatively detached, floating hungrily among other discursive truth bubbles.[8]

Simulation, Meta-Rhetoric: It Is Control, Not Justice, Which 'Must Be Seen to Be Done'

If there is public scepticism of government claims and at the same time government scepticism of public opinion, an adaptation may be the normalisation of competence *through* ritual demonstration. As such, government is *demonstrated*, and security, as perhaps the strongest claim of government, is likewise judged in terms of its finesse in talking up its own performance. This is merely to express what is already well-understood about the management of crime (Garland, 2012) and the desire to demonstrate that management in the wake of the irruptive spectacle (de Lint et al., 2007; Gamson, 1995). It is not that security is accomplished, but rather that it is seen in the form of a perpetual performance (permanent war) and viewed and reviewed according to the line of targets (Afghanistan, Iraq, Libya, Syria, Russia, China and hybrid threat) and perhaps with respect to the finesse with which events are or are not apex crimes.

The well-known legal maxim 'justice must not only be done but be seen to be done' refers to the important point that appearances are not merely epiphenomenal. On the one hand, there is the 'making up' of the majesty of legal authority (Hay, 2004) or the constitution of a system hoisted on the petard of an idealised humanity. On the other hand, there is Kafka's (1988) parable of the man at the gates, waiting for 'justice' to finally appear, perhaps to fix interpretation or end interminable suspense. 'Justice' may be no more than the acceptance that something resembling an effort at resolution has taken place. In this reading, justice is never anywhere except in the perception that it is somewhere.

The security spectacle (nothing is ever really secure, but signal events are objects that light a pathway toward reordering) is not fraudulent because it resonates as effective even if the claim of threat is not as it appears. The ordering spectacle simplifies the problem (around a common subject, to be sure) and satisfies the normative (again, around a preferred subject or target) without needing to carry out a bloody battle involving the principals in a 'hot war' contest over resources. The in/security event is not a failure because it facilitates the norm-clarifying exercise on a grand scale. Seen from the vantage point of the need to point to progress down the pathway, the spectacular irruption feeds the dispositive, including institutional knowledge, from the scale of local communities up to the regional and global, and in this its measure is effective as policy. In this regard, General Wesley Clark (in Greenwald, 2011) saw 9/11 as a 'policy coup'.

The construction of solidarities or 'we-ness' has depended not only on an affirmation of justice or humanity in the countering of criminality in a social order.[9] It has also required the maintenance of sovereign vitality in a relatively porous international or geopolitical order. This has produced a situation where the effort to chase hybrid offender-enemies and defend victim-friends confounds public and private distinction. In the hunt for offender-enemies the dignity, inviolability or even humanity of the individual can no longer be permitted to act as a limiter. In the context of 'asymmetrical warfare' every disclosure may be exploited by the ubiquitous enemy, so must known in anticipation by a capable sovereign. Combined with the information paradigm, this means an endless hunt for code and code-breaking. This occurs, given the control paradigm, in a manner that is deliberately ambiguous: information control includes the requirement not to telegraph code-breaking efforts.

Political crime is politically interested; it refracts ideology, sometimes through a partisan lens. The 9/11 Commission captured the events of September 11 through a bipartisan lens, meaning that it permitted the glimpse of the crime through the red and blue filters of Democratic and Republican interests. In relation to MH17, the review or investigation has not only been through the intelligence filter but also through the selective capture and veto of nation-state objectives. There are two, three or sometimes even more interested parties who may seek to tease out of the archive or public view of the event information that is deemed to compromise a national security claim that each such party may make. What remains is the public 'photoshopped' version.

Disorder, Knowledge and Political Direction

Crime facts depend upon depoliticised or objective instruments, agencies and even the actors responsible for reporting, recording and analysing phenomena. Governmental authority depends on the official publications and pronouncements regarding observed facts or policy that it produces. Intelligence crimes emerge fully loaded as political products for a postmodern condition—infused with established power-knowledge, incredulous of those who would wish to insist on the modernist meta-narrative and its separation of 'fact' and 'opinion' (as per Lyotard, 1984). Security speech acts are already constitutive; they produce a narrative, an official narrative, or governmental position or standpoint regarding an event or big crime.[10] Horn (2003: 64) notes that intelligence knowledge is contrasted to academic research inasmuch as the former is not 'universally valid, verifiable, and openly accessible [and] durable'. With respect to this verifiability or discoverability, the habitat of dark disorder is the nexus between the permanent bureaucracy and the dark arts of tradecraft and statecraft.

Intelligence crime cuts deep into the political, the state and the domain of the sovereign. In that domain is the discretion to choose the exception to the rule. That decision-making to bend or break the rule is carried out according to a realist framing by those actors who *can* do so. That capacity does not necessarily rest with the political leader or leadership, although often sovereignty and political leadership are overlapping. In the decision to bomb the *Rainbow Warrior*, the authorisation in the first case came from the political leaders in the Mitterrand government. With regard to 9/11 or the Epstein–Maxwell case, the question of authorisation depended on the genesis of the event, or whether it is accounted for by the official narrative or the counter-narrative. If the latter, it is reasonable to posit that intelligence actors, who build their capacity and capabilities in tradecraft in a contest with an ideological other, deploy various illicit means in that effort.

In this respect, dark disorder is a further extension of the logic of precaution and pre-emption in a closed world. In criminology, disorder concerns the representation of conduct by individuals or other agents that are criminogenic, so that in social disorganisation theory *places* may support a crime contagion. Disorder is dark where it isn't visible or representable; its strength, vitality, scale and target are a matter of the explication of expert agents who draw on the secret archive.

Visible and dark disorder may be contrasted. In the former, there may be a site where sex, alcohol or gambling is transacted at bargain basement prices in an impoverished part of a city. The disorder is visible even to inexpert opinion, involves deviation from normative conduct, produces victims and victimisation in societies where there need be no corruption of officials, and separates crime and criminals from police and politics. In the latter, we have, for instance, 9/11, MH17 or Douma. For information on such events we rely on high-ranking government officials and international bodies who obtain their intelligence from experts in security and intelligence (Bellingcat, the Hybrid CoE or the Integrity Institute). These agencies, in turn, refer to open sources or highly placed sources in intelligence who are familiar with an archive of intelligence that is presumed to support the story being told. When it is time to complete the investigation, there is a fully formed context bias that enables the inculpatory evidence to be fast-tracked while exculpatory evidence is not collected, analysed or tested by forensic bodies (NIST, OPCW). In consequence, behind the police tape, but more importantly behind the identification of a crime site, is an event that is *selectively visible* or is only contentiously encountered 'in the raw'. It is visible only to specialised agencies and state actors who can then provide to the laity or civilians a redacted glimpse of its 'actuality'.

In this respect it is important to distinguish security along the lines of sovereignty and national and transnational cultural values. National and international interests are often conflated and confused, which actually enhances the capacity of the security intelligence actors to do the work of *countering* law and politics (we made reference to an adaptation of Gill's Gore-Tex state figure). Although not made explicit in national security mandates, the protection or defence of government institutions, national interests, and transnational interests and institutions requires that the *common threat ideology* be promulgated. Accordingly, what is dangerous to government institutions is dangerous to national interests is dangerous to transnational interests and institutions. The common threat ideology is not pronounced when we review incidents like MH17 from the vantage point of whodunnit as a lay member of the public. It does inform national security actors and their understanding of commitment to *national* security. For security actors the term 'national security' implies reference to a common front or plural interests across nations that wish to maintain good standing within a US-led alliance.

In this regard, *national* security agencies may obtrude both sovereign state and cultural politics in the ostensible service of the also quite indistinct *international order*. In doing so, they occlude the right of citizens to know their own government's planning and action, a move built into the very language of domestic national security mandates. Interoperability across the governmental, national and transnational domains is forced against the grain of self-government in liberal democracies and the view that government must stem from the maximum individual liberty. In this fashion, national security comprises a deep fissure between discrete sovereignties, joining them yet remaining somewhat disconnected from its own 'residency requirements'.

The arts of the state are more or less endarkened: they are distinguished on the crucible of access to knowledge and life. 'We' is already a projection of political identity: 'we' cringe at the role of intelligence in the control of conduct within liberal democracies 'like ours'. That cringing both accepts and rejects the totalising discourse. As an illustration, the al-Qaeda network was a 'convenient instrument', an 'unpredictable intelligence asset' of Western statecraft 'for the orchestration of illegal and corrupt covert operations' (Ahmed, 2005: 31). Whether that included 9/11 remains in doubt.

According to de Lint and Virta (2004: 475), the corequisite of security is the ordering and 'fixing' of knowledge according to predetermined boundaries and dogmas and a centralised power or 'ordering principle'. Far from a means of discovering the machinations of pro-state and counter-state ordering, the utilisation of agencies engaged with dark disorder is ideological. In presenting a partial and obviously distorted picture of threat to the public at large, these intelligence actors work to promote a fearful regard for a purported attack against valued resources or institutions, including the franchise and the vote. In this, ordering is construed as information control, enacted through protocols of intelligence compartmentalisation and access privileges and disinformation production in the layering of 'fake' on top of 'real' objectives and agendas. As an outpost, agencies like the IfS and the Hybrid CoE attract resources and gravitas in the elaboration of the dispositive.

It is understood that we live in postmodern times with respect to the intersection between governmental authority and scientific methodology or epistemologies, and within this postmodern condition there are many places to stand from which to discover existential threats, which is to say there are many ways to develop the assumptions on which to build a narrative of existence or threat. With representational events, acts are pointed at to purport a crime wave and finesse public opinion in favour of a preferred bifurcation of security. Moving from the precautionary or pre-crime event to what we call dark disorder, public policy is to be predicated on an understanding of both knowledge and authority that remains 'endarkened' or out of reach of transparency, visibility, replicability (see Bogard, 1996).

This brings us to our last point. Much criminology is concerned with responding to crime, including conceptualising the tools used to discover and investigate and then redress the most fractious problems of order on the pivot of criminality. On the other hand, security studies and policy related to intelligence and defence is concerned with deploying the tools of the state or the national security apparatus to redress social problems on the plinth of the security order. This is where we enter the world of hybrid threats. As we have seen, under the hybrid rubric, these are events or actions that are not investigated under the guise of criminal discovery and deterrence (the dominion of criminality). Rather, they are 'dressed up' or constituted as threats to the institutions of society as reviewed already by intelligence analysts or actors in their role of protecting societal security (the dominion of the security order). The reference to disorder and wrongdoing that is suggestive of criminality does not in this case permit so-called hybrid actions to be addressed as criminality according to the expectations of criminal justice norms. On the contrary, the preference is to link the problem to the military denotation (hybrid war), and its permissiveness (or sovereignty ambiguity). The logic and ethos of preparedness for external and internal threats, war and terrorism, hybrid interference and influencing elections bring the militaristic thinking around fighting both unknown and known enemies into everyday security, policing and criminal justice without the requirements of an identified crime. On the other hand, it appears that the assumptions upon which threats are perceived and selected for review signal the relative imperviousness of government to common security concerns. In this regard, the Hybrid CoE and its regimen may be reviewed according to what is out of the picture, including attacks by so-called friends who wish to shape other so-called friends' internal politics.

Conclusion

Do we really know big crime? Do we really know it when it belongs less to criminal justice and forensic examination than to intelligence and political imperative? The short answer is that big crimes are like looming icebergs, suggestive, but largely impenetrable to the public gaze. Since we know crime in the main through the preferred narrative of government authorities, the bigger the crime, the bigger will be the political interest and cover and the more compromised the crime scene and forensic examination.

In this book we have problematised several interrelated factors, to add to previous research on crime uptake or manufacture, that may be used to unpack intelligence crimes. Firstly, there is the matter of the behaviour of knowledge about crime. Since the criminal event in this case involves security and intelligence interests and agencies the phenomenon is subject to extra blurring or smudging, so it goes beyond knowing something in terms of errors, corruption or systematic failure. Here, the discovery is also a problem of how to know things when they are relatively obscure, remote, arcane and belong to a corpus that is subject to information control by well-placed actors. This ties into the property of sovereign discretion, an interest and principle that is defended oftentimes as a stand-in for the existential security of the nation-state; since the action deniable by state authority, it is also for many analysts not a crime. We have also been concerned to see this in terms of a critical institutional review. In part, this gets us from depending on a legalistic definition of criminality. To repeat the paraphrase, the crimes with which we are concerned are a claiming of politics by other means; it is necessary to observe some institutional separation—even if somewhat nostalgic—in the tripartite institutional array of justice, law enforcement and security intelligence.

Finally, it is interesting to observe the conspiracy discourse as an echo or pantomime of the intelligence operation. If, as we have simplified it, intelligence is essentially covert conspiratorial transactions supported by the state, then *generalist* 'conspiracy theorising' is a pastiche of the real thing: it is a *parody* of the 'paranoid style', a prepubescent son shuffling around in his father's oversized dress shoes showing off the daily routine of going to the office. If an echo and pantomime, it is everywhere heard and now ubiquitous. This pastiche is an almost daily occurrence. In this regard, the 'real thing' of intelligence has regularly been covered as mere comedy (as in *Get Smart* or *The Spy Who Shagged Me*—two favourite cultural treatments that see intelligence as basically noble but sometimes overrun by rogue and wicked actors or as a place of bizarre incompetence). It is unsurprising that the more deep the criticism the more visceral the reaction and the desire to cast it as the musing of a crazy ignoramus.

Notes

1. In the meantime, it is striking that in these incidents the alleged perpetrator is presumed to carry out the crime to vilify him or herself because there is otherwise an absence of benefit (Russia for Skripal, MH17, Assad government for Douma, bin Laden for 9/11). This, too, is how these crimes differ from other homicides, for instance. It would appear that these actors run afoul of offensive realist dogma as well, as defined by Mearsheimer (Pashakhanlou, 2013).
2. This section is reproduced from de Lint (2008).
3. In part Foucault wanted to make the argument that political rationality does not arise simply from political philosophy. The problem of rule is the reconciling of the integration of individuals into totalities with extant knowledge and disciplining tools in the service of a continuous vehicle, which at that time at least was the state. To put it another way there is the discovery of reason of state in terms of discursive preconditions. That knowledge of individuals and populations was necessary for the state's existence is reflected in the distinction between quotidian and existential security. If state criminality 'is the crime of all crime' (Rothe, 2009) this is because the state is like a big family whose original fortune must be made the object of cover-up and denial (Cohen, 2001).
4. Deleuze and followers (Walters, 2006; Hardt & Negri, 2000) argue that in societies of control, there is a movement to 'immanent social orders that understand themselves as 'consumer societies', 'information societies' or 'risk societies'.' The control society according to Deleuze can be characterised in terms of the spatiality of power: thus no longer institutional sites of confinement and their practices but 'open networks of power which operate through variable combinations and productions of desire, lifestyle, anxiety and fear which have the market as their paradigm' (Walters, 2006: 191). Secondly, there is transformation in the dominant mechanism and images of social order: now the figure of communication, in particular modulation and feedback instead of the well-ordered city as per discipline. The changing schema of individual and collectivities, with Deleuze seeing 'dividuals' with their context not the mass or society but proliferating databanks, samples, profiles, markets, a shift in the subjects of power. Power relations act through fragments and their novel integration or

sampling. Being a fragment of a whole person, the dividual is articulated by the password and its distributions of access and status in the constitution of privileged populations. The control society produces abject populations who cannot gain accesses and are 'rendered beyond the limits of the livable' and given 'a purely negative value' (Walters, 2006).

5. And now we are at a point where it is not the state, but the security apparatus or hybrid network that stands in for the necessary knowledge of individuals and groups and the methods of their incorporation into a totality. Knowledge and practices of the security network see past the state and contest dominion over who needs to be excluded and who must be sacrificed to maintain the practice of security. In addition, slippage of the individual and population across borders produces further dis-aggregations (of identities, groups, cohorts) that are mediated by political rationalities through practices that do not anymore 'see' the problem of contingent groups of people but rather contingent information bundles. At the heart of this is the intelligence operation, built bottom up from the requisite of existential rights and exclusionary practices but now capturing or arresting the flow of contraband data bundles.
6. A conspiratorial re-view locates power behind cultural or political screens and strongly determinative agencies that lie beyond the reach of the tools of empirical recovery (Aupers, 2012: 30). From a critical institutional and sociology of knowledge perspective, there is no pure vantage point from which to make an evaluation, as all actors are embedded in organisational, occupational-cultural and socio-political contexts across socioeconomic hierarchies. It is notable that social systems are produced by institutions that in a risk environment are evasive or opaque, perhaps increasingly so, and produce an experience of time-space disembedding (Giddens, 1990).
7. Doubt concerning epistemological foundations and methodological rules has been part of modern science since the sixteenth century. More recently, postmodernists have taken the position that underlying almost every human endeavour there is a set of conditions or assumptions that most institutional discourses render invisible. As we have discussed in this book, the foundation of the sovereign state is one such institutional discourse, where constituent illegalities and contradictions are swept into the margins or disappeared with the gravestones of displaced peoples (Tilly, 1985; Fanon, 1963). An additional consequence of the postmodern turn is that where it is more or less accepted that certainty is a discursive intervention, the good storyline or strong narrative is not unlike the subordinated storyline: not exactly true but perhaps presented with more finesse.

   In practice, procedures and rules permit room that is occupied by discretion and cross-cutting institutional or organisational objectives. These may be interpreted as fissures between the concrete blocks of objective administration. The means of rarefaction, permission to speak as an expert, fellowship, stipulations on the circulation of information and the maintenance of the truth claims (Foucault, 1972) are all building blocks through which and around which there is some discursive porosity. Wiggle room around rules and procedures may be understood as the outline of the clasp of sovereign exception; the space in which to project the periodic intrusion of exceptional practices that sets aside or exploits the give between or within the processes or procedures in regular operation. Crudely understood, the rules give way to or are interpreted to accommodate the pressure from strong political, cultural and administrative interests or forces. The postmodern condition of doubt and scepticism provides fertile ground for what is regularly referred to as the corruption of the 'noble cause' variety or on other bases, including the support of organisational-cultural or political-cultural interests. As discussed above, the rhetoric of forensics is largely in place to protect and maintain exclusive discursive dominion or the institutional and professional self-understandings that maintain institutional knowledge forms.

8. Doubt concerning epistemological foundations and methodological rules has been part of modern science since the sixteenth century. More recently, postmodernists have taken the position that underlying almost every human endeavour there is a set of conditions or assumptions that most institutional discourses render invisible. As we have discussed in this book, the foundation of the sovereign state is one such institutional discourse, where constituent illegalities and contradictions are swept into the margins or disappeared with the gravestones of displaced peoples (Tilly, 1985; Fanon, 1963). An additional consequence of the postmodern turn is that where it is more or less accepted that certainty is a discursive intervention, the good storyline or strong narrative is not unlike the subordinated storyline: not exactly true but perhaps presented with more finesse.

   In practice, procedures and rules permit room that is occupied by discretion and cross-cutting institutional or organisational objectives. These may be interpreted as fissures between the concrete blocks of objective administration. The means of rarefaction, permission to speak as an expert, fellowship, stipulations on the circulation of information and the maintenance of the truth claims (Foucault, 1972) are all building blocks through which and around which there is some discursive porosity. Wiggle room around rules and procedures may be understood as the outline of the clasp of sovereign exception; the space in which to project the periodic intrusion of exceptional practices that sets aside or exploits the give between or within the processes or procedures in regular operation. Crudely understood, the rules give way to or are interpreted to accommodate the pressure from strong political, cultural and administrative interests or forces. The postmodern condition of doubt and scepticism provides fertile ground for what is regularly referred to as the corruption of the 'noble cause' variety or on other bases, including the support of organisational-cultural or political-cultural interests. As discussed above, the rhetoric of forensics is largely in place to protect and maintain exclusive discursive dominion or the institutional and professional self-understandings that maintain institutional knowledge forms.

9. Today the lack of certainty between boundaries and the absence of clear designations between inside and outside exacerbates a condition of ambiguity

and destabilization. In part, this collapse is a result of the re-bordering of the political of the nation-state in the context of the push for unencumbered commerce and trade. In another part, it is the consequence of the dissolution of jurisdictional differences. Nancy Fraser (2003: 167) notes that

> social ordering is no longer nationally bounded, nor correlated with a national state, nor centred in any single locus of coordination. Rather, the locus of governmentality is being unbundled, broken up into several distinct functions, and assigned to several distinct agencies which operate at several distinct levels, some global, some regional, some local and subnational.

10. Edwards uses the term 'closed world' (Edwards, 1997) to contrast the epistemology of intelligence and security to scientific or academic knowledge discovery systems.

References

Aaronson, T. (2011, September-October). The best terrorists money can buy. *Mother Jones*. https://www.motherjones.com/politics/2011/07/fbi-terrorist-sting-targets/.

Ahmed, N. M. (Ed.). (2005). *The war on truth: 9/11, disinformation, and the anatomy of terrorism*. Arris.

Asquith, C. (2006, September 6). Who really blew up the twin towers. *The Guardian*. https://www.theguardian.com/education/2006/sep/05/internationaleducationnews.highereducation.

Aupers, S. (2012). 'Trust no one': Modernization, paranoia and conspiracy culture. *European Journal of Communication, 27*(1), 22–34.

Bigo, D. (2002). Security and immigration: Toward a critique of the governmentality of unease. *Alternatives*, Special Issue, 63–92.

Black, D. (1983, February). Crime as social control. *American Sociological Review*, 34–45.

Bogard, W. (1996). *The simulation of surveillance: Hyper-control in telematic societies*. Press Syndicate of the University of Cambridge.

Box, S. (2002). *Power, crime and mystification*. Routledge.

Bruff, I. (2014). The rise of authoritarian neoliberalism. *Rethinking Marxism, 26*(1), 113–129.

Cohen, S. (2001). *States of denial: Knowing about atrocities and suffering*. New York: Wiley.

deHaven-Smith, L., & Witt, M. T. (2009). Preventing state crimes against democracy. *Administration & Society, 41*(5), 527–550.

de Lint, W. (2008). Intelligent security. *The Windsor yearbook of access to justice, 26*(2), 195–240.

de Lint, W., & Hall, A. (2009). *Intelligent control: Developments in public order policing in Canada*. Toronto: University of Toronto Press.

de Lint, W., & Kassa, W. (2015). US counterterrorism security: Fraud, failure or fruitful spectacle. *Critical Criminology, 23*(3), 349–369.

de Lint, W., & Virta, S. (2004). Security in ambiguity: Towards a radical security politics. *Theoretical Criminology, 8*(4), 465–489.

de Lint, W., Virta, S., & Deukmedjian, J. (2007). The simulation of crime control. *American Behavioral Scientist, 12,* 1631–1647.

Dentith, M. R., & Keeley, B. L. (2018). *The applied epistemology of conspiracy theories: An overview*. https://philarchive.org/archive/DENTAE-2.

Douglas, K. M., Uscinski, J. E., Sutton, R. M., Cichocka, A., Nefies, T., Ang, C., et al. (2019). Understanding conspiracy theories. *Advances in Political Psychology., 40*(1), 3–35.

Edwards, P. (1997). *The closed world: Computers and the politics of discourse in the Cold World era*. Cambridge: MIT Press.
Ericson, R. V. (2007). *Crime in an insecure world*. Cambridgeand Malden: Polity Press.
Fanon, F. (1963). *Concerning violence in wretched of the earth*. http://www.openanthropology.org/fanonviolence.htm.
Foucault, M. (1972). The order of discourse. In *The archaeology of knowledge*. Vintage.
Fraser, N. (2003). From discipline to flexibilization: Rereading Foucault in the shadow of globalization. *Constellations, 10*(2), 160–171.
Gamson, W. A. (1995). Constructing social protest. *Social Movements and Culture, 4*, 85–106.
Garland, D. (2012). *The culture of control: Crime and social order in contemporary society*. University of Chicago Press.
Gee, H. (2015). National insecurity: The National Defense Authorization Act, the indefinite detention of American citizens, and a call for heightened judicial scrutiny. *The John Marshall Law Review, 49*(1), 69–100.
Giddens, A. (1986). Action, subjectivity and the constitution of meaning. *Social Action, 53*(3), 529–545.
Giddens, A. (1990). *The consequences of modernity*. Stanford: Stanford University Press.
Greenwald, G. (2011, November 25). Wesley Clark and the neocon dream. *Salon*. https://www.salon.com/2011/11/26/wes_clark_and_the_neocon_dream/.
Gross, M. L. (2009). Asymmetric war, symmetrical intentions: Killing civilians in modern armed conflict. *Global Crime, 10*(4), 320–336.
Hardt, M., & Negri, A. (2000). *Empire*. Harvard University Press.
Hay, D. (2004). Property, authority, and the criminal law. In A. Sarat (Ed.), *The social organization of law* (pp. 75–83). Los Angeles: Roxbury.
Herman, E. S., & Chomsky, N. (2010). *Manufacturing consent: The political economy of the mass media*. Random House.
Hofstadter, R. (2012). *The paranoid style in American politics*. Vintage.
Horn, E. (2003). Knowing the enemy: The epistemology of secret intelligence. *Grey Room, 11*, 58–85.
Inglehart, R. (1997). *Modernisation and postmodernisation: Cultural, economic and political change in 43 societies*. Princeton, NJ: Princeton University Press.
Kafka, F. (1988). Before the law. In Nahum N. Glatzer (Ed.), *The collected short stories*. London: Penguin.
Kohring, M., & Matthes, J. (2007). Trust in news media: Development and validation of a multidimensional scale. *Communication Research, 34*(2), 231–252. https://doi.org/10.1177/009365020629807.
Lyotard, J. F. (1984). *The postmodern condition: A report on knowledge* (Vol. 10). University of Minnesota Press.
Mbembe, A. (2019). *Necropolitics*. Duke University Press.
Miller, J. M., Saunders, K. L., & Farhart, C. E. (2016). Conspiracy endorsement as motivated reasoning: The moderating roles of political knowledge and trust. *American Journal of Political Science, 60*(4), 824–844.
Mills, C. W. (1956). *The power elite*. New York: Oxford University Press.
Mosca, G. (1961). On the ruling class. In T. Parson (Ed.), *Theories of society: Foundations of modern social theory*. New York: Free Press.
Mouffe, C. (2006). *On the political*. Verso.
Neocleous, M. (2006). From social to national security: On the fabrication of economic order. *Security Dialogue, 37*(3), 363–384.
Nye, R. A. (1977). *The anti-democratic sources of elite theory: Pareto, Mosca, Michels*. London: Sage.
Oliver, J. E., & Wood, T. J. (2014). Conspiracy theories and the paranoid style(s) of mass opinion. *American Journal of Political Science, 58*(4), 952–966.
Pareto, V. (1966). *Vilfredo Pareto: Sociological writings*. New York: Praeger.

Pashakhanlou, A. H. (2013). Back to the drawing board: A critique of offensive realism. *International Relations, 27*(2), 202–225.

Pope, W. (1975). Durkheim as a functionalist. *Sociological Quarterly, 16*(3), 361–379.

Popper, K. (2006). The conspiracy theory of society. In David Coady (Ed.), *Conspiracy theories: The philosophical debates*. London: Ashgate.

Quinney, R. (1970). *The social reality of crime*. Transaction Publishers.

Rothe, D. L. (2009). *State criminality: The crime of all crimes*. Lexington Books.

Scott, P. D. (1996). *Deep politics and the death of JFK*. Berkeley, CA: University of California Press.

Smart, C. (2002). *Feminism and the power of law*. London: Routledge.

Spitzer, S., & Scull, A. T. (1977). Privatization and capitalist development: The case of the private police. *Social Problems, 25*(1), 18–29.

Sunstein, C. R., & Vermeule, A. (2009). Conspiracy theories: Causes and cures. *Journal of Political Philosophy, 17*(2), 202–227.

Tilly, C. (1985). War making and state making as organized crime. In T. Skocpol, P. Evans, & D. Rueschemeyer (Eds.), *Bringing the state back in*. New York: Cambridge.

Valverde, M. (2008). Police, sovereignty and law: Foucauldian reflections. In M. Drubber & M. Valverde (Eds.), *Police and the liberal state*. Stanford: Stanford University Press.

Van der Pijl, K. (2019). *Academic corruption, the Israel lobby, and 9/11, or, why I have resigned from my emeritus status at the University of Sussex*. http://keesvanderpijl.nl/wp-content/uploads/2019/05/Academic_Corruption_the_Israel_Lobby_and.pdf.

Wacquant, L. (2009). *Punishing the poor: The neoliberal government of social insecurity*. Duke University Press.

Walters, W. (2006). Border/control. *European Journal of Social Theory, 9*(2), 187–203.

The manufacturer's authorised representative in the EU is Springer Nature Customer Service Centre GmbH, Europaplatz 3, 69115 Heidelberg, Germany. If you have any concerns regarding our products, please contact ProductSafety@springernature.com

Printed and bound by CPI Group (UK) Ltd, Croydon, CR0 4YY
30/09/2026
02225498-0008